CAPTIVE HISTORIES

ALSO BY EVAN HAEFELI AND KEVIN SWEENEY

Captors and Captives: The 1704 French and Indian Raid on Deerfield

Captive Histories

English, French, and Native Narratives of the 1704 Deerfield Raid

EDITED BY Evan Haefeli and Kevin Sweeney

University of Massachusetts Press AMHERST AND BOSTON

LC 2006004255
ISBN 1-55849-542-8 (library cloth ed.); 543-6 (paper)

Designed by Dennis Anderson
Set in Dante with Poetica display by dix!
Printed and bound by The Maple-Vail Book Manufacturing Group

Library of Congress Cataloging-in-Publication Data

Captive histories : English, French, and Native narratives of the 1704 Deerfield raid
/ edited by Evan Haefeli and Kevin Sweeney.
    p.   cm. — (Native Americans of the Northeast)
    Documentary supplement to: Captors and captives. c2003.
    Includes bibliographical references and index.
    ISBN 1-55849-543-6 (pbk. : alk. paper) —
    ISBN 1-55849-542-8 (library cloth : alk. paper)
  1. Abenaki Indians—Wars.   2. Abenaki Indians—History—Sources.
  3. Indian captivities—Massachusetts—Deerfield—History—Sources.
  4. Indians of North America—Wars—1600–1750.
  5. United States—History—Queen Anne's War, 1702–1713.
  6. Deerfield (Mass.)—History—Colonial period, ca. 1600–1775.
  I. Haefeli, Evan, 1969–   II. Sweeney, Kevin, 1950–
  III. Haefeli, Evan, 1969– Captors and captives.   IV. Series.
  E99.A13C364 2006
  974.4'02—dc22
                2006004255

British Library Cataloguing in Publication data are available.

For the members and staff of the Pocumtuck Valley Memorial Association

In recognition of 135 years of work devoted to preserving and interpreting the history of Pocumtuck and Deerfield, Massachusetts. Without their efforts, this book and others could not have been produced.

CONTENTS

ILLUSTRATIONS

MAPS

PREFACE

CAPTIVITY NARRATIVES have a special place in American culture, and Deerfield has a special place in the history of both, thanks to the Reverend John Williams's *The Redeemed Captive Returning to Zion*. There are clear historical reasons for Deerfield's prominence in the history of captivity narratives and the narrative of American history. Williams was the first New England minister to be captured by a French and Indian war party. He was one of over a hundred captives taken at Deerfield in the winter of 1704. Returning to Boston through a prisoner exchange, Williams composed the narrative that has been reprinted time and time again since it first appeared in 1707. It was not the first captivity narrative published in America, but it is one of the most famous. Only Mary Rowlandson's 1682 *The Sovereignty and Goodness of God* rivals it in the amount of attention Americans have lavished on it over the centuries.

New Englanders and later Americans came to see the 1704 raid on Deerfield and *The Redeemed Captive* as typical examples of the American frontier experience, an impression that has been enshrined in numerous historical accounts. It helped spark the strong local interest in history that ensured that Deerfield's story would be better preserved than that of most other New England towns. This attention inspired the foundation of a local historical society in 1870, the Pocumtuck Valley Memorial Association, and the establishment in 1952 of Historic Deerfield, Inc., making Deerfield an important site for the preservation and study of early American material culture and history. In the words of the historian Geoffrey Buerger, Deerfield has gained "national, and even international fame by its own insular, even parochial, interpretations" of the raid. But, as this collection demonstrates, there is more.

There was in fact little that was typical about either the 1704 Deerfield raid or the composition and dissemination of *The Redeemed Captive*. Compared with other Native and French raids on New England towns from 1689 to 1760, the raiding party that assaulted Deerfield in 1704 was unusually big and exceptionally diverse, including Native peoples from five distinct communities. The raid was also unusually destructive, resulting in the killing or capture of half of the village. Finally, the number of captives taken was remarkably large and they were taken to a wide variety of French and Native communities. An enduring interest in the event in several of these communities has generated other stories that provide rare comparative insights into the creation of historical memory and narratives of captivity.

Because captivity was an experience shared by captives and captors, captivity narratives, including those of Deerfield, have long been seen as valuable sources of information about the lives and cultures of Native captors as well as those of their captives. Those Deerfield narratives, in which captives spend significant amounts of time traveling with and living among Native peoples, show Native men and women as distinctive and even idiosyncratic individuals in a variety of settings, ranging from the heat of battle to the seasonal chore of maple sugaring. What distinguishes the experiences of Deerfield captives from those of many others is that traditions have emerged in several Native communities discussing and commenting on the very same captivity experiences. This situation creates an opportunity to read colonial captivity narratives in the light of not just one but several different Native narratives appearing over the past three hundred years.

The Deerfield raid is, therefore, an excellent starting point for re-examining early American captivity narratives and the colonial experience of captivity from new perspectives. Though the oft-reprinted *Redeemed Captive* stands at the core of this collection, it is juxtaposed to lesser-known stories of captivity composed by other Deerfield residents: Quentin Stockwell, Daniel Belding, Stephen Williams, Joseph Petty, and Joseph Kellogg. These stories challenge current assumptions about what are seen as classic Puritan captivity narratives because they present the raw material of captivity narratives without clerical editing and embellishment. Clerical editors, such as the Reverends Increase and Cotton Mather and their kinsman John Williams, usually "improved" stories of captivity by emphasizing religious trial and spiritual transformation, by sharpening the opposition between captors and captives, and by slighting the particular context in which captivity took place.

By including French and Native stories, this collection seeks to establish the broader context of colonial conflict that produced the English captivity narratives. Included are examples of two narrative genres from New France: the published *Jesuit Relations* and the memoirs of colonial military officers, recounting a career of service to the king. The Jesuit's narrative was based on reports by Huron/Wendat warriors who took part in the 1704 Deerfield raid; the memoir was written by Joseph-François Hertel, the father of Jean-Baptiste Hertel, who led the French raiders against Deerfield. In addition there are Native stories. Three little-known Abenaki and Mohawk stories of the 1704 raid are published here, one for the first time. They emerged out of their communities' oral traditions, passed on from one generation to the next until they were finally written down at various points during the nineteenth and twentieth centuries. The collection concludes with commentary by two present-day Native scholars: Taiaiake Alfred, a Mohawk political scientist and activist, and

Marge Bruchac, an Abenaki storyteller and anthropologist. They discuss their peoples' relationships to the phenomenon of captivity and the 1704 Deerfield raid.

Taken together, these French and Native stories and the previously unpublished English narratives suggest that the traditional focus on published Puritan authors has overlooked the richness and diversity of experiences out of which the Puritan captivity narratives emerged. This collection's focus on narratives about Deerfield is designed to provide an in-depth look at a particularly rich body of material that allows us to expand our understanding of captivity by seeing the ways in which peoples from all sides interpreted these experiences.

Evan Haefeli
Kevin Sweeney

ACKNOWLEDGMENTS

THIS VOLUME is an outgrowth of the research that produced *Captors and Captives: The 1704 French and Indian Raid on Deerfield,* which was published in 2003 by the University of Massachusetts Press. As with that volume, we owe a debt of gratitude to scholars, librarians, museum personnel, and other individuals who have studied the 1704 raid and participated in its commemoration in 2004. Like our earlier book, this volume builds on the work of Geoffrey E. Buerger, John Demos, and Rick Melvoin. In Deerfield, David Bosse, Sharmon Prouty, Penny Leveritt, Timothy Neumann, Martha Noblick, Joseph Peter Spang, and Phil Zea all made contributions to this project. In particular, the work of Angela Gobel Bain, Suzanne Flynt, Amanda Rivera Lopez, and Jessica Neuwirth, who were curators of the exhibition *Remembering 1704: Context and Commemoration of the Deerfield Raid* that was mounted in 2004 by Historic Deerfield, Inc., and the Pocumtuck Valley Memorial Association, helped shape this volume. At Kahnawake, Brian Deer provided invaluable assistance. Another member of the community at Kahnawake, Taiaiake Alfred, contributed directly to this volume by allowing us to reproduce part of a talk he gave in Deerfield in 1995. Marge Bruchac, an Abenaki scholar and storyteller, also provided an essay for this volume and helped us locate several sites mentioned in the texts.

A number of institutions and individuals provided us with materials and allowed us to reproduce these materials. Historic Deerfield, Inc., the Historical Society of Pennsylvania, the Neville Public Museum of Brown County, and Pocumtuck Valley Memorial Association granted permission to reproduce critical texts, several of them previously unpublished manuscripts that are included in this volume. Lynn Murphy provided us with a photograph of her grandmother Elizabeth Sadoques and a copy of the original version of the talk that her grandmother delivered in Deerfield in 1922 and gave us permission to use both of them in this volume. Members of the staffs at the Archives of the City of Montreal, the Bibliothèque Nationale de France in Paris, the Canadian National Archives in Ottawa, the Chateau Ramezay in Montreal, Historic Deerfield, Inc., the McCord Museum in Montreal, the National Portrait Gallery in Washington, the Newberry Library in Chicago, the Pocumtuck Valley Memorial Association, and the Wisconsin Historical Society assisted us in obtaining images for the volume. Le Conseil de Fabrique Notre-Dame-de-Liesse de Rivière-Ouelle provided us with a photograph of their recently restored ex-voto painting and permission to use it. Finally, René Chartrand went beyond the usual bounds of scholarly courtesy and very promptly provided an illustration.

Once again, we are fortunate to have maps produced by Kate Blackmer. She revised three maps that appeared in *Captors and Captives* and provided two new maps: one traces the routes of captives taken in 1677 and 1696 and the other plots the escape route taken by four captives in 1705.

We are grateful to several people who read the book at various stages and moved the project forward. The series editors, Colin Calloway and Barry O'Connell, gave this volume their blessing and support. The comments from outside readers for the press provided both encouragement and helpful suggestions. Suzanne Flynt, the Curator of the Pocumtuck Valley Memorial Association, read over the captions for the illustrations. Finally, Don Friary, the former Executive Director of Historic Deerfield, Inc., gave the book a close reading that sharpened our thinking in places and saved us from embarrassing errors.

It was again a pleasure to work with the staff at the University of Massachusetts Press, who provided a degree of personalized professional service that has undoubtedly spoiled us. Our editor, Clark Dougan, gave us the encouragement and freedom that we needed to shape this volume. Carol Betsch, who appears to understand better than we do what we are trying to do, shepherded the book through the production process. Deborah Smith's precise copyediting helped bring order to a disparate collection of texts and annotations. Our thanks to Nairn Chadwick for the excellent index.

Financially, this project benefited from the support of our home institutions. A grant from Amherst College's H. Axel Schupf '57 Fund for Intellectual Life paid for Kate Blackmer's maps and the other illustrations. Funds from Columbia University paid for the indexing.

Finally, we appreciate our families' willingness to put up with a couple more years of 1704.

EDITORIAL PROCEDURES

THIS COLLECTION brings together a variety of texts written down in three different languages, from four distinct cultures and spanning over three centuries from 1684 to the present. To ensure that they are all equally accessible to modern readers, we have modernized the spelling, punctuation, and grammar of all of the texts. In all cases we have indicated where the originals of these texts can be found so that interested readers can examine them and compare our edited versions with the originals.

Many of these texts have not been published before. In manuscript, these texts contain abbreviations, edits, and incomplete sentences. We have smoothed out the rough spots in these texts, filling in missing letters, correcting grammar, and inserting words where necessary to complete a sentence or clarify its meaning. Where we have inserted a word or phrase to clarify meaning we have placed it within brackets. Otherwise we have not indicated where letters had to be inserted to fill out words and to correct grammar.

The translations from the French are our own. In order to downplay the foreignness of these texts, we have anglicized the terms and phrases as much as possible without distorting the meaning of the original texts.

To keep the texts familiar for an English-speaking audience, we have employed the common English names for various Native peoples. Thus we use Mohawk, Huron, and Abenaki rather than Kanienkehaka, Wendat, and Wôbanakiak, the names by which these people refer to themselves in their own languages (see appendix A).

Because the generic term *Indian* was and remains widely used to describe the original inhabitants of the Americas and their descendants, we have allowed it to stand in many instances. Often we use *Native* (with a capital *N*) in place of the relatively modern term *Native American*.

The word *Sauvage* was employed by the French in the colonial period, with connotations closer to those of the English word *Indian* than of *savage*, though both colonial French and colonial English used *Sauvage* and *Indian* to describe peoples they recognized as different and often saw as inferior. While acknowledging the implications inherent in these terms, we intend no insult when we retain such terms in the original texts. Wherever possible, we have tried to refer to a specific group or individual in question by a specific name. As should be clear, these distinctions were very important, and a generic word of any sort, be it *Indian* or *Native American* often obscures significant differences among Native peoples.

Dating presents another challenge because of the difference in the calendars employed by the English and the French. The English still used the Julian calendar, which was eleven days behind the Gregorian used by most western European countries, including France (and is the one we use today). According to the Julian calendar the new year began on March 25 rather than January 1. English documents between January 1 and March 25 were often written with both years; thus, the English recorded the date of the Deerfield raid as February 29, 1703/04; for the French, the raid occurred on March 11, 1704. In all of the English documents reproduced in this volume and in the related head notes and footnotes, we have retained the Julian or Old Style dates, except where noted, though we give the year as beginning on January 1. The dates in the French documents and the related footnotes are Gregorian, or New Style.

Captive Histories

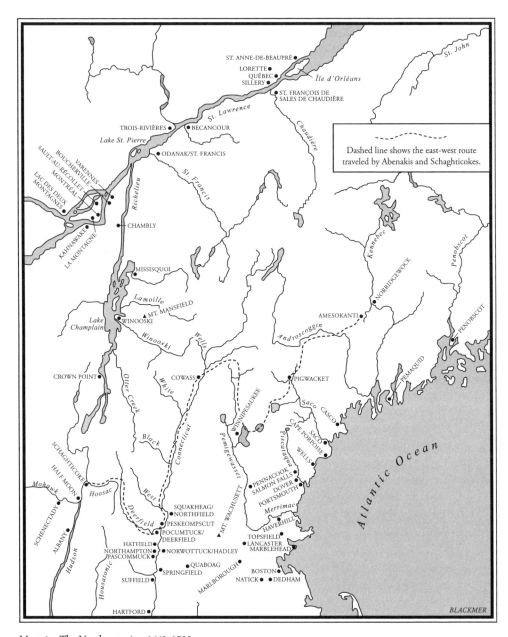

MAP 1. The Northeast, circa 1660–1725.

INTRODUCTION

O N THE morning of February 29, 1704, 250 to 300 Hurons, Mohawks, Abenakis, Frenchmen, Pennacooks, and Iroquois of the Mountain attacked Deerfield, the northwesternmost village in Massachusetts. By evening half of the village's population was gone, men, women, and children. The raiders killed 50 and captured 112, the largest number ever taken in a single raid on the New England frontier. The English death toll and the number of captives made it one of the most devastating assaults on a colonial village anywhere in the Northeast. At the same time, it was one of the costliest expeditions ever launched against New England by the French and their Native allies. Eleven of the raiders had been killed and at least 22 wounded, some mortally.[1]

Despite the devastation, the stories of the captives taken to Canada—those who returned as well as those who did not—have created the enduring legacy of the Deerfield raid. Since 1704, contemporaries and their descendants in many of the communities involved in the attack have struggled to make sense of the violent encounter by telling stories of the raid. These stories have played an important role in shaping historical memories of the colonial frontier. By affirming the communities' sense of who they were and therefore are, the stories do more than simply recount the past. They also preserve and defend homelands, erect and cross frontiers, and otherwise engage the dilemmas left by America's colonial past.

THE SETTING

For the English, the village of Deerfield in 1704 marked a frontier or boundary, the edge of New England. But for Native peoples it sat on an ancient crossroads. For centuries the site, marking an intersection between the Mohawk-Mahican trail that ran east and west and the route running north and south that followed the course of the Connecticut River (map 1), had been a home to Native peoples. Its most recent inhabitants were an Algonquian-speaking people called by the English the Pocumtucks. As Europeans entered the region in the 1630s, great changes followed the trade routes into Pocumtuck. First came deadly diseases that killed over 90 percent of the people in some villages along the Connecticut. Next came fur traders and with them growing indebtedness to English merchants who eventually sought to take Native land as repayment. Just to the south, Hadley and Northampton were built on the lands

1

of the Norwottucks. In the 1660s, war with members of the Five Nations of the Iroquois League destroyed the village at Pocumtuck and dispersed its people. They became prisoners of the Iroquois or sought refuge elsewhere in the Connecticut valley or in Canada.[2]

English colonists moved into Pocumtuck around 1670 and took possession of the rich meadowlands and Native fields. But its Native residents had not forgotten their homeland. Many joined in the attacks on English settlements during what came to be known as King Philip's War (1675–1677). Late in the summer of 1675 the beleaguered English settlement at Pocumtuck was abandoned. On September 18 many of its adult males died in a battle at Muddy Brook, which was subsequently renamed Bloody Brook. Serious fighting continued along the Connecticut River into the spring of 1676. On May 19 several hundred Natives from the region and refugees from elsewhere perished in an English attack on a Native village at Peskeompscut. A final offensive by English forces in the summer forced most of the remaining Native peoples to seek refuge elsewhere. But they did not abandon their ties to Pocumtuck.[3]

Some of the Natives driven from the Connecticut valley during King Philip's War returned in the late summer of 1677. On the morning of September 19, Natives under the leadership of Ashpelon, a Norwottuck or Pocumtuck, attacked Hatfield and Deerfield. Benoni Stebbins reported that the raiding party contained twenty-six people, two of them women, who were all "Norwooluck [i.e., Norwottuck] Indians save only one which was a Naraganset."[4] At Hatfield they killed twelve, wounded four, and captured seventeen. That evening they moved north to attack a small group of men attempting to re-establish the English settlement at Pocumtuck. Here the raiders killed one and captured four, including Stebbins and Quentin Stockwell. They then marched their prisoners north to Canada, making these captives the first of hundreds of New Englanders who would be carried north to Native and French villages along the Saint Lawrence River. Three of the captives were killed on the march north, but the others survived and were returned to New England in May 1678.

Benoni Stebbins and Quentin Stockwell survived their captivity and returned to establish another village at Pocumtuck, which the English renamed Deerfield. They were joined by other families drawn primarily from the neighboring towns of Hatfield, Hadley, and Northampton. The men in charge of these families were attracted to this frontier by the prospect of obtaining land and with it the opportunity to provide for their families. In 1688 Deerfield's inhabitants established a church and ordained as its minister John Williams, a recent graduate of Harvard College. At the time, the village contained about 250 residents.[5]

War soon returned to western Massachusetts. In 1688 Native peoples along

New England's northern frontier renewed their struggle to defend their home-lands from continuing incursions by English settlers. In 1689 war broke out be-tween England and France, plunging their colonies of New France and New England into conflict. Around 1690 the people of Deerfield erected a stockade to defend ten of the homes located in the center of the village. Because of its exposed location, Deerfield was targeted by several Native raiding parties. One of the more serious attacks occurred on September 16, 1696, when a party of Mohawks from Kahnawake killed four members of Daniel Belding's family and took him and four other residents prisoner. All told, Deerfield was attacked seven times during the Nine Years' War—also known as King William's War, which lasted from 1689 to 1697—suffering a total of twelve inhabitants killed, five wounded, and five captured.[6]

At the same time, Deerfield's location astride long-established routes of travel meant that Natives also came to trade and to visit. Contrary to the image created by later histories, the colonial frontier was not a strict line dividing French, Natives, and English from each other. Rather it was a wide zone of constant interaction where Natives spoke English and colonists such as Quen-tin Stockwell knew a Native language. For much of the 1690s a community of about 150 Natives, most of them former residents of the area, lived in a village about six miles south of Deerfield. Occasionally, Native allies of the English re-turning from raids against New France stopped by with their French prisoners. This seemingly isolated Puritan outpost remained a focal point for Native peo-ples moving north from Schaghticoke in New York to Odanak in New France to villages in what is today Maine. These connections can be traced in the movements of Chepasson, whose visit to Deerfield in 1690 ended in his impris-onment and death.[7]

After a brief interlude of peace from 1697 to 1702, war again broke out. But even as Deerfield repaired its defenses, it continued to receive visits from across the frontier. During 1702 or 1703 three Frenchman and at least one "Indian" seeking to establish peaceful trading relations settled in Deerfield. One of the Frenchmen, Jacques de Noyon, and "the Indian," Andrew Stevens, married Deerfield women. Then Native peoples warned the English of an impending attack. Most of the Abenakis and Pennacooks then living along the borders of Maine and New Hampshire wanted to remain "Neuters" in the growing con-flict between the English and French. Passing on news of French plans was one way to demonstrate their desire for peace with the English. These contacts re-minded Deerfield's residents that not everyone living beyond the frontiers of New England was hostile. But their efforts may have given the residents a false sense of security.[8]

THE CAPTORS

Then, on February 29, 1704, Deerfield was attacked. The raiding party was notable for both its size and its diversity. In addition to roughly 50 Frenchmen, there was a Native contingent of 200 to 250 men from five different communities: Abenakis from Odanak, Hurons from Lorette, Iroquois of the Mountain, Mohawks from Kahnawake, and Pennacooks from Cowass. It was a complex mix of men, bound together as much by ties of kinship and community as by politics and religion.

Lieutenant Jean-Baptiste Hertel de Rouville, an experienced partisan officer, commanded the French. The claim, cut in stone on one of Deerfield's many memorials, that "200 soldiers" took part in the raid was the invention of a nineteenth-century historian, Epaphras Hoyt. Though small, the French contingent included approximately ten Canadian-born nobles. These were all officers or cadets serving in the *troupes de la marine,* the colonial regulars stationed in New France. Many of them were related to each other. De Rouville was joined by three or four of his brothers, while Ensign René Boucher de la Perrière was accompanied by two of his nephews, Jacques-René and Pierre Gaultier, and another officer, Ensign François-Marie Margane de Batilly, related to him by marriage.[9]

Native-born Canadians drawn from the militia probably made up the bulk of the French contingent. Though their names are unknown today, it is possible to make some informed conjectures about their ages, residences, and experiences. They would have been young men, probably in their early twenties. It is likely that most of them came from Boucherville, Chambly, Montreal, Varennes, and Trois-Rivières, since those were the homes of their officers. This assumption is reinforced by the fact that some of the captives taken at Deerfield ended up in Boucherville, Chambly, Montreal, and Varennes (map 1). The young men of these particular communities were also more likely to have had experience with the fur trade than those from other parts of New France. They therefore knew how to shoot, snowshoe, and survive in the woods.[10]

The Natives who participated in the raid on Deerfield did so for different reasons. The Abenakis from Odanak probably saw the Deerfield raid as part of the third Anglo-Abenaki War, the latest (but not the last) in a series of wars against New England expansion dating to King Philip's War. Some of the people at Odanak were Pocumtucks or their descendants with claims to Deerfield's land. A close look at John Williams's narrative reveals a remarkable number of English-speaking Natives who were familiar with Puritan ways. This is not surprising: New England was, after all, their homeland.[11]

Pennacooks, who still lived in what is now northern New England, had joined the raiders as they traveled south. These Pennacooks had struggled to live in peace between the French and English empires. But neutrality became impossible as fighting broke out in the late summer and fall of 1703. Some Pennacooks participated in the August attacks on English settlements in Maine. The English retaliated by attacking Pennacook villages in September and October. Soon afterward, Pennacooks from Cowass called upon the French to join them in an attack on the English. Among those who joined the raiders was Wattanummon, a leader of his people and one of only two Native attackers known by name.[12]

The rest of the raiding party did not have direct ties to New England. The Iroquois of the Mountain and the Mohawks of Kahnawake, who lived near Montreal, and the Hurons of Lorette, who lived near Quebec, fought for other reasons. One was political—they were allies with each other and the French and had recently ratified this relationship in a great peace treaty at Montreal in 1701. The other was cultural. All of these communities were Iroquoian in culture and practiced the mourning war to capture prisoners to replace family members who had died. If a member of the community died unexpectedly and the established rites that channeled the grief of mourners failed to assuage the sense of loss resulting from the death of a relative, the women of the mourning household could demand a raid to obtain captives who, if worthy, could ease their pain by replacing the deceased through adoption or by suffering ritual execution. Such expeditions were directed at enemies who may or may not have been directly responsible for the death. Thus, taking captives as well as alliance with the French and other Natives encouraged these men, including a young Huron warrior named Thaovenhosen, to join the expedition against Deerfield.[13]

THE RAID

The 1704 attack on Deerfield had both trans-Atlantic and local origins. For the French and the English, the fighting began in 1702 as part of a major European war, the War of the Spanish Succession (1702–1713). In Europe, the war was ignited by the decision of the French king, Louis XIV, to support his grandson's claim to the Spanish throne. To prevent King Louis from gaining control of both Spain and its vast overseas empire, England and other European countries declared war on France. In North America, officials in New France concluded that the best defense was an aggressive offense as they sought to protect their underpopulated and vulnerable colonies by launching raids against the frontiers of New England. Once a decision had been made to launch an attack on New England, Deerfield was targeted. Its location was ideal: it was the most

exposed town in western Massachusetts, it was the closest New England settlement to the French base at Fort Chambly on the Richelieu River, and it was the
most accessible English town for Pennacooks living up the Connecticut River
at Cowass (map 1).

The people of Deerfield had at least five warnings between the spring of
1703 and February 1704 that they were about to be attacked. Most came from
New York, where colonists in Albany had access to information about what
was happening near Montreal. In early May 1703 they learned that a raiding
party of French and Indians had gathered at Fort Chambly and "may be expected every day at Derefd [Deerfield]." New warnings came in July and August, but French and Indian raiders did not. Early February 1704 brought fresh
warnings from New York "that some of our Indians have met with some french
Indians upon [Lake Champlain], who have told them that the french have a design either upon our northern frontiers or upon some place to the Eastward."
Twenty men from nearby towns were ordered to Deerfield to help defend the
village. The last ones arrived on February 25.[14]

The French and Native raiders entered Deerfield's stockade just before dawn
on February 29. Because the raiding party was made up of so many different
men who joined for such a variety of reasons, the attack was not well coordi-
nated. Competition for captives rather than cooperation and coordination
characterized the assault. Abenakis, Pennacooks, Mohawks, and possibly Iroquois of the Mountain took different members of the family of the Reverend
John Williams: three Abenakis from Odanak seized Williams; Wattanummon,
the Pennacook, took prisoner his ten-year-old son Stephen; and a Mohawk
from Kahnawake captured his seven-year-old daughter Eunice. In the chaos
and confusion some Deerfield residents managed to hide or escape, while a few
were able to mount a vigorous defense. Occupants of the Benoni Stebbins
house held out for over two hours, killing several of the attackers and wounding others. Still, the attackers killed 41 people inside the stockade—most of
them women and children—wounded an unknown number, and took 112
prisoners.[15]

The arrival of a mounted relief party from the neighboring towns drove the
attackers out of the stockade. Dismounting, the English pursued the raiders
into Deerfield's North Meadows. There they were ambushed and chased back
to the stockade. Two residents and seven men from neighboring towns died in
the Meadows Fight. But casualties among the raiders were heavy as well. Half
the French contingent had become a casualty of some sort. Twenty-two Frenchmen were wounded, among them De Rouville and one of his brothers, while
three were killed. Among the Natives, seven were killed, and an unknown

number were wounded, including the leader of the Hurons, who soon died from his wounds. For the raiders, it was one of the costliest assaults on the New England frontier.[16]

THE CAPTIVES

The size of the raiding party and the presence of Hurons, Iroquois, and Mohawks who were looking for people to capture and adopt, not kill, led to the taking of a record number of prisoners. The 112 Deerfield captives were a cross-section of New England society. Roughly half of the captives were male. They included prominent colonists, such as the Reverend John Williams, humble farmers, and young militiamen. There were also women and children of all ages. Sex and age played critical roles in shaping the captives' experiences. Two, both young men, quickly escaped. Ten adult women and six children are known to have been killed on the march. Two adult men starved to death. But because of their captors' interest in keeping them alive for either adoption or ransom, between eighty-six and eighty-nine of the Deerfield captives survived the almost three-hundred-mile trek through the snow to Canada.[17]

Clear patterns of experience emerge among the captives once they were in Canada. Here, the community of their captors also became a vital factor in determining their fates. Those taken prisoner by Pennacooks or Abenakis from Odanak passed fairly quickly into the hands of the French. For these people, taking captives had been a secondary consideration in joining the raid. By the end of the War of the Spanish Succession, no Deerfield captives remained permanently with either group, and apparently only three of all the English captives taken during the entire course of the war remained at Odanak. No captives remained at Lorette either, despite a clear desire among the Hurons to adopt. The village's small size and proximity to Quebec exposed the Hurons to the intrusions of French officials, making it nearly impossible to retain their English captives. Likewise, for the Iroquois of the Mountain, proximity to Montreal and intrusion by priests of the Sulpician order complicated efforts to hold on to their English prisoners. The Sulpicians were intent on turning the English into French Catholics, not Native American Catholics. To further this goal, they persuaded the Iroquois to marry two of the Deerfield captives—Josiah Rising and Abigail Nims—to each other. Eventually, the couple's ties to the Native village at Lac des Deux Montagnes diminished and their children became part of the neighboring French community at Oka. Only one Deerfield captive, eight-year-old Hannah Hurst, became an Iroquois of the Mountain and married into the community.[18]

At Kahnawake things were different. For several reasons, the Mohawks had more success at incorporating captives into their community. The mourning-war tradition was still strong. The population of the community was large. And politically, economically, and religiously it was relatively autonomous, having a strategic importance that prevented French priests and officials from interfering in their lives. In all, seven young Deerfield girls—Mercy Carter, Mary Field, Abigail French, Mary Harris, Joanna Kellogg, Rebecca Kellogg, and Eunice Williams—joined the community. Subsequently, four of these women and their Mohawk families would visit their English relatives. One, Rebecca Kellogg, chose to return permanently to New England, but only after she had lived for a quarter century at Kahnawake. She appears to have left behind a Mohawk husband and at least one child. The descendants of these and other English captives still live today in Mohawk communities.[19]

The French were actually the most successful group at incorporating English captives, a fact in which French-Canadians have taken great pride. English captives seem to have had an easier time crossing from one European culture to another than from a European culture to a Native American one. Furthermore, the French were the largest and strongest community in New France. As the narratives included in this collection reveal, French clergy and pious lay men and women made strenuous efforts to convert New Englanders to Catholicism. At the war's end, sixteen Deerfield residents remained in New France: ten females and six males. Most had been young when captured. When they came of age, they married into the lower orders of French society, living out their lives as farmers and craftsmen in Montreal and the nearby communities of Boucherville, Chambly, and La Prairie. In many ways their lives were not so different from what they would have experienced in New England.[20]

Most of the Deerfield captives returned to New England, sixty-two in all. But not all of them returned to Deerfield. About half moved to safer places, such as Connecticut or eastern Massachusetts. The former captives who did resettle in Deerfield, including John Williams, helped rebuild the shattered community. Williams remarried, rebuilt his home, and served his parishioners until his death in 1729. After the war's end, a few, like Joseph Petty, moved north to establish new frontier towns, such as Northfield.[21]

One aspect of the captivity experience that is often overlooked is that neither captives nor captors forgot the tie that had once bound them. Once peace was made, many veterans of the Deerfield raid went to visit their former captives, sometimes bringing their relatives. On other occasions, captives who had settled in Canada, or their children, went to visit New England. A few stayed, but most, like Eunice Williams, returned to die in Canada. For New Englanders, their absence was a wound that never healed.[22]

WILLIAMS FAMILY STORIES

If each of the eighty-six to eighty-nine persons who survived the march to Canada had written down his or her story, there would be a fairly wide variety of narratives to recount and to analyze. But there is not. Instead, Deerfield's captivity experience has been embodied in traditions centered on its two most famous captives—the Reverend John Williams and his daughter Eunice. The focus on these two individuals underscores the disproportionate role played by various Williams descendants—white and Native—in perpetuating historical traditions associated with this event. It is truly a family story or more precisely a series of stories shaped by the members of a remarkable family. Contributors to this volume include, along with the Reverend John Williams, his son, the Reverend Stephen Williams; his great-great-grandson, the Reverend Eleazer Williams; and even more distant descendants Elizabeth Sadoques and Taiaiake Alfred.

There are other reasons why stories about the 1704 raid have clustered around John and Eunice. At one level, each figure can be viewed as embodying a contrasting set of historical memories, demonstrating what has been one of the raid's enduring impacts: the articulation and perpetuation of distinct cultural identities out of many complex interactions and conflicts. The choices made by John and Eunice Williams have a clear appeal to the communities that chose to remember them. John Williams represents those who returned to New England. Stories about Eunice account for those who assimilated into their adopted homes. These personal choices contain morals about communal loyalty and identity that lack the complexity and ambiguity of someone like Rebecca Kellogg, who spent about half of her life in New England and the other half at Kahnawake.

At the same time, the stories by and about members of the Williams family have been used to make claims that transcend particular cultures and, more broadly, cultural boundaries. For Eleazer Williams, producing a biography of his great-grandmother Eunice was an effort to convince early nineteenth-century New Englanders that her life as a Mohawk and her faith as a Catholic were worth remembering and admiring. Elizabeth Sadoques used the story of Eunice to remind New Englanders of the Abenakis' enduring connections to their original homeland. The recent biography of Eunice by the historian John Demos, *The Unredeemed Captive: A Family Story from Early America,* also emphasizes cultural crossings.[23]

GENDER AND THE DEERFIELD RAID

Recent scholarly studies of New England captivity narratives emphasize the prominent roles of females such as Eunice as victims, subjects, and authors.[24] But in the case of Deerfield, all of the written accounts that survive from the period were composed or recounted by males, probably in part because most of the captives taken by French and Native raiders on the New England frontier between 1677 and 1760 were male.[25]

Disproportionately, those able to make it back to New England and write down their tales were also men. Most influential in this regard was the minister Stephen Williams, who in the 1720s began collecting Deerfield captivity accounts for a history of the frontier wars. For whatever reasons, all of the stories he compiled, in addition to his own captivity narrative, were recounted by men. The fact that none of the women who returned after the 1704 Deerfield raid wrote down or published her story undoubtedly reflects the dominant role men had in collecting and publishing captivity narratives. Rare was the woman who wrote her narrative herself. Generally women recounted their experiences to men, who transcribed them and saw them through publication. Mary Rowlandson's 1682 captivity narrative, *The Sovereignty and Goodness of God,* was an exception. But as the wife of a minister so was she. Most captive women, including those taken at Deerfield, were farmers of lower status and less educated than the members of ministerial families that dominated the production of New England captivity narratives. In the case of Rowlandson, who does seem to have written her account at her own initiative, it was only with the intervention of the Reverend Increase Mather that her account became New England's first published captivity narrative. Almost every other New England colonist, female or male, who published a captivity narrative did so at the behest of a man, usually a minister. Even John Williams's narrative was written at the behest of another minister, Cotton Mather. How, when, and why the accounts of New England captives came to be published often depended more on the political concerns of their male patrons than on the inherent qualities of their stories.[26]

Somewhat different considerations influenced the shaping and preservation of captivity stories in Native communities. The fact that the stories preserved in Native traditions often focus on a female, such as Eunice Williams, is due in part to the fact that a disproportionate number of young female captives were incorporated into Native communities. Iroquoian societies such as the Mohawks of Kahnawake, the Iroquois of the Mountain, and the Hurons of the Lorette were matrilineal and matrilocal and they appear to have had a prefer-

ence for female captives. In these societies making associations with female ancestors was particularly important for descendants in matters of family identity.
Where present, Catholic missionaries also appear to have targeted females for
conversion. For their own reasons Native women and female captives appear to
have responded to these efforts in numbers that increased their visibility in
records maintained at Native villages that had resident missionaries. Finally, for
the Abenaki at Odanak, New England captives—sometimes female, sometimes
male, but in the case of Deerfield, a young girl, Eunice Williams—helped preserve ties to homelands located within the expanding colonies in southern New
England. Here too, there is evidence of the role women played in shaping and
preserving historical memories.

ENGLISH NARRATIVES

Because of the generations of frontier warfare New Englanders engaged in
during the colonial period, the captivity experience had become quite familiar
by the eighteenth century. Ironically, this fact may have limited the number of
accounts that have come down to us. The presses of New England were not
interested in publishing every captivity experience. Only in certain circumstances and with the help of influential individuals could former captives such
as Quentin Stockwell and John Williams get their accounts into print. As a result, most captivity narratives were passed on orally, in stories and reminiscences told to family, friends, and neighbors. Occasionally they passed into
manuscript, as did that of Daniel Belding, who later in life recounted his capture in 1696 to Stephen Williams. But the intended audience for these manuscripts was always parochial—other New Englanders, not a trans-Atlantic
audience. They did not need to be formally published to become known to the
people that mattered.

John Williams's *The Redeemed Captive Returning to Zion* was published because several influential figures in Boston, notably the Reverend Cotton Mather,
felt that Williams's captivity had to be explained to the people of New England.
Since its publication in 1707, Williams's narrative has dominated the Anglo-
American story of the Deerfield raid (figure 1). It has been periodically republished in different parts of New England down to the present day. Scholars
consider it, along with Mary Rowlandson's *The Sovereignty and Goodness of God,*
as emblematic of the classic Puritan captivity narrative and thus one of the
cornerstones of early American literature.[27]

Captivity narratives are a literary genre that grew directly out of the colonial
American experience, though they had roots in English providence tales and

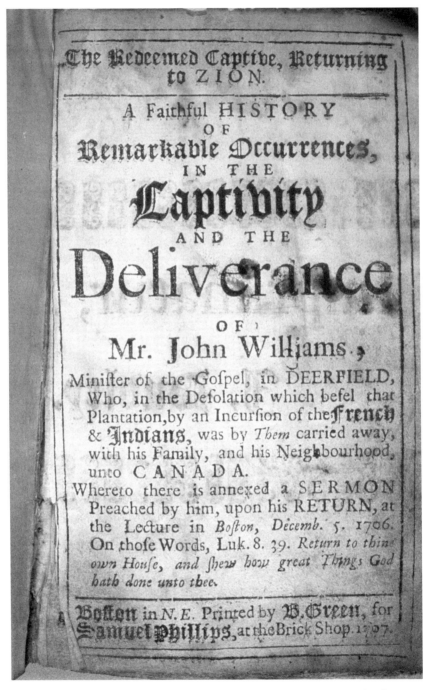

The Redeemed Captive, Returning to ZION.

A Faithful HISTORY

OF

Remarkable Occurrences,

IN THE

Captivity

AND THE

Deliverance

OF

Mr. John Williams,

Minister of the Gospel, in DEERFIELD, Who, in the Defolation which befel that Plantation, by an Incurfion of the French & Indians, was by *Them* carried away, with his Family, and his Neighbourhood, unto CANADA. Whereto there is annexed a SERMON Preached by him, upon his RETURN, at the Lecture in *Boſton*, *Decemb.* 5. 1706. On thoſe Words, Luk. 8. 39. *Return to thine own Houſe, and ſhew how great Things God hath done unto thee.*

Boſton in *N.E.* Printed by B.Green, for Samuel Phillips, at the Brick Shop. 1707.

FIGURE 1. Title page of the first edition of *The Redeemed Captive Returning to Zion*, by [the Reverend] John Williams, 1707. In the subtitle the words *Captivity* and *Deliverance* are printed in large, bold letters to emphasize the content and theme of the narrative. Only thirteen copies of the first edition survive; many of them were literally read to pieces. Photograph by Penny Leveritt, courtesy of Historic Deerfield, Inc.

stories of abduction by North African corsairs. From the earliest days of the encounter between Europeans and Native Americans, all sorts of people were taken captive. Europeans captured Natives and brought them back to Europe and sold them into slavery. Europeans also took Africans from Africa and forced them into slavery in America. But the first narratives of captivity were composed by Europeans who had been captured and held by Native Americans. The people of New England wrote and published more about this phenomenon than anyone else, because they had an active printing press and they believed the experience of captivity had a religious and political significance worth reading about. Thus was born what has come to be seen as the classic Puritan captivity narrative, considered by some to be America's first literary genre.[28]

Literary scholars have traced many of the genre's motifs, forms, and tropes down to the present in various aspects of American culture. Raiders appear suddenly and, without warning, violently fall upon an exposed village. Family members, particularly very young children, are often brutally killed. Stunned survivors of the assault are herded together and marched through the woods to Native villages or to French Canada. The narratives make much of the captives' sufferings and the possibility of death in the wilderness. Writers or their editors often present these trials as explicitly religious. The occasional mercies experienced along the way, such as assistance from a Native captor or the healing of an injury, are cited as evidence of God's providence. Those individuals who accept their fates and resign their fate to God's will pass successfully through the trial and are rewarded with redemption from their captivity and their enslavement to sin that is both physical and spiritual. Clerical introductions and codas sometimes urge readers to reform and mend their ways before they too are put to such a test.[29]

The belief of the influential Boston ministers Increase and Cotton Mather— father and son—that these stories illustrated God's continuing interest in New England led to their selective publication. In collecting and publishing the accounts, the Mathers were not thinking solely of their fellow colonists. They wanted the narratives to reach a wider, trans-Atlantic audience. In the 1680s, both men were engaged in religious, philosophical, and political debates with colleagues in England, and some of their captivity narratives, including those of Mary Rowlandson and the Deerfield resident Quentin Stockwell, were reprinted in England.[30]

By the time John Williams's narrative was published in 1707, the Mathers had begun putting captivity narratives to local political purposes. During the War of the Spanish Succession, Cotton Mather started collecting and publishing accounts of captivity in an effort to build a case for the removal of Joseph Dudley as the governor of Massachusetts. He hoped to use John Williams's story to further this agenda, but John Williams had other plans. He turned his narrative of the Deerfield raid and his subsequent captivity into an explicit defense of Dudley and his wartime policies.[31]

Like other captivity narratives, *The Redeemed Captive* was part spiritual autobiography, part sermon, and part jeremiad. Jeremiads were lamentations in the spirit of the Old Testament prophet Jeremiah that were intended to awaken and reform people by pointing out their sins and the likelihood of divine punishment. Jeremiads had become particularly prevalent as responses to tensions arising from cultural, economic, and political changes taking place in late seventeenth-century New England. As a rule, these changes were portrayed by ministers and other leaders as a falling away or a declension from the high standards of piety and righteousness that they associated with the first settlers of New England. A letter written by Colonel Samuel Partridge a month after the 1704 Deerfield raid documents this declension by providing a list of the failings of his contemporaries, especially those of the rising generation and the "middle sort." Because of their assumptions, the writers of jeremiads, such as Partridge, assumed that the real source of the problems afflicting New England lay within the hearts and souls of its inhabitants. If only they ceased to sin, God would soon set things aright. The problem was that the identity of the sins and the sinners was not always clear.

Cotton Mather, a leading practitioner of the jeremiad, undoubtedly found much to approve of in *The Redeemed Captive*. Williams makes clear his intention at the outset to prove "that days of fasting and prayer, without reformation, will not avail to turn away the anger of God from a professing people." He tells of the failure of his own congregation's day of prayer to stay God's wrath. Later, when he recounts his preaching from the Lamentations of Jeremiah, he reminds the reader again of the wrath that would befall a people who rebelled against God. And throughout, by skillful use of anecdotes, he urges readers to make use of the time and means that God grants them to reform.

Williams's narrative is also a spiritual journey in the vein of *Pilgrim's Progress* and Mary Rowlandson's 1682 captivity narrative. The Deerfield minister's captivity becomes a metaphor for a conversion. The things of this world most dear to him—his wife, his children, and eventually his congregation—are successively taken from him. His spirit is plunged to the depths of despair, raised up again, and again plunged downward. Only after he humbles his pride and submits to God's will is he supported through his trials by God's mercies. Passages from scripture and meditation on God's design comfort him in his grief. The journey through a rather vaguely rendered wilderness on the march to Canada becomes providential. The kindness of Indians, the healing of a swollen ankle, the snow sent to cover rough ice, the quieting of ill winds, and the discovery of unknown reserves of physical strength all have special meaning as signs of God's providence.

Despite these features, *The Redeemed Captive* diverges in its emphasis and possibly in its intended audience from the captivity narratives promoted by the Mathers. Rather than trying to prove to readers in England the existence of divine providence as the Mathers strove to do, John Williams addressed a New England audience that accepted it. His is not a world of declension where Puritan identity is in doubt and the role of providence in question. It is a world of frontier conflict where battle lines are clearly drawn. It is a world structured around an imminent foe: the Catholic French and their Native allies. The question is not whether God exists but whose side he is on.

In several other ways, Williams's story is unlike many other captivity narratives. Although it begins with his capture by Abenakis, most of the narrative deals with his captivity among the French, not Native peoples. And while most analyses of captivity narratives see them as commenting on the conflict between Native and European cultures, a close reading of Williams's text reveals that his real enemy is Catholicism and the French, not Native peoples or their cultures. The Natives he is hostile to are Catholic. He actually gets along fairly well with those who have not converted to Christianity. This distinction between religion and culture is very important in any consideration of *The Redeemed Captive* and its legacy.

Unlike Mary Rowlandson's 1682 narrative of her captivity, which was reprinted time and again for its vicious denunciations of Natives and their culture, *The Redeemed Captive* drew its lasting appeal from its power as an anti-Catholic tract. In fact, Williams's emphasis on the French Catholic threat would affect how Deerfield's conservative Protestant descendants would remember the raid. By the early nineteenth century, they would magnify the role of the French in the attack and downplay that of the Natives. Only in the later nineteenth century, when neither France nor Catholicism seemed so threatening, would the focus of interpretations of the raid and *The Redeemed Captive* switch to the colonial encounter with Native peoples.[32]

Whether by word of mouth or in print, Deerfield's stories about captivity provided a powerful framework for interpreting the frontier experience. They influenced the writing of colonial history into the twentieth century. Those writing about the 1704 raid in particular preserved the structure of John Williams's narrative in their accounts, though they usually replaced the Puritan minister's religious rhetoric with contemporary concerns with race and culture.[33] The lessons were no longer explicitly religious and narrowly Protestant but remained moral: courage and perseverance in the face of the enemy, and a determined defense of New England civilization against its foes. These more secular-minded historians focused on the Indian assaults, which one nineteenth-century author viewed as "the natural outgrowth of [their] taste for a state of warfare . . . a relish *not yet extinct*—and an insatiate desire for scalps."[34] The contrast between civilization and savagery became, if anything, stronger.

These later histories also dipped into a well of New England oral traditions that preserved unpublished stories of captivity. Lively local interest in memories and stories of the raid and in Deerfield's frontier history had begun even before the colonial wars ended. Some tales passed down within families, while others appear to have circulated freely throughout the town. The tales Deerfield residents told to a young girl who passed through town in 1763 impressed her so much that she recounted them in her autobiography written over sixty years later.[35] Nineteenth-century local historians Epaphras Hoyt, Stephen West Williams, and George Sheldon used family traditions as well as additional documentation to flesh out John Williams's tale of the raid.[36] Sheldon acknowledged residents' "tendency to exaggeration in tradition," and he did not hesitate to call an oral tradition "doubtful" if it did not accord with the facts as he understood them. All the same, he wrote them down.[37]

As with published accounts, these oral traditions usually conveyed messages that did more than preserve interesting anecdotes. One emphasized the French and Indians' ability to blend into the natural environment in order to surprise the village.[38] Other tales of mistreating captives or threats to kill them all in retaliation for the counterattack in the Meadows highlighted the raiders' treachery.[39] Another story about a fatal musket ball fired through a hole chopped in a door emphasized the colonists' vulnerability (figure 2).[40] Stories also moralized about the conduct of the English, criticizing, for example, a watchman who fell asleep at his post, while holding up the Christian example of a Deerfield woman who aided a wounded French officer.[41] Some traditions even recounted visits by former Mohawk and Huron captors and unredeemed captives, though these stories were usually recorded with genealogical information and did not become part of standard nineteenth-century histories of the destruction of the town.[42]

There are also several unpublished manuscript accounts by 1704 Deerfield captives, whose existence demonstrates that John Williams's account was not the only narrative framework available for understanding the experience. His narrative was merely the only one to be published and widely disseminated. Three other Deerfield residents wrote down their captivity experiences, providing an excellent opportunity to see how common men related to an experience that has long been defined by *The Redeemed Captive*. While they share some of John Williams's concerns, they also reveal that his response was only part of the way Puritans reacted to captivity.

FIGURE 2. Door, Ensign John Sheldon House, circa 1698, and nineteenth-century frame. The Ensign John Sheldon House, which survived the 1704 attack, came to be known as the "Old Indian House." An unsuccessful effort to save the house from demolition in 1848 was one of the first efforts at historic preservation in the United States. When the house was torn down, the door and some other architectural fragments were saved. Eventually the door with "jagged cuts, and bruises, now as then" was exhibited in the Memorial Hall Museum in Deerfield, which opened in 1880. The door is still on display in Memorial Hall, where it remains a focal point. The hole chopped in the door on February 29, 1704, is clearly visible in this old photograph. Photograph courtesy of the Pocumtuck Valley Memorial Association, Memorial Hall Museum, Deerfield, Massachusetts.

In Joseph Kellogg's account, which has never before been published, the religious encounter with the French is the overriding concern. His story is rare in that it provides a detailed description of the process of conversion to Catholicism in French Canada—exactly the fate John Williams feared most. Kellogg not only converted to Catholicism. He lived for years among the Natives and French in Canada, traveled widely as a fur trader, became one of the first Anglo-Americans to see the Mississippi River, and even joined a French military expedition against the English colony of New York in 1709. Though a convert who evidently enjoyed the life New France offered him, he eventually returned home to Massachusetts. There, Joseph converted back to Protestantism and worked as a translator and frontier diplomat, putting to use the linguistic and cultural knowledge he had gained in New France. Had he not been taken captive, he would undoubtedly have been indistinguishable from thousands of other men working farms across New England. For him, captivity was a truly transforming experience, but not a strictly spiritual one as *The Redeemed Captive* would have us believe.[43]

Just as dramatic in a different way were the experiences of four other Deerfield men, Thomas Baker, John Nims, Martin Kellogg (Joseph's older brother), and Joseph Petty. They ended their captivity by escaping from New France in the spring of 1705. Petty recounted their story in a letter he wrote to Stephen Williams in 1729. Williams, who was then a minister serving a parish in what is today Longmeadow, Massachusetts, intended to use Petty's story as source material for an account of the Indian wars that would demonstrate the workings of God's providence in New England. Such a project would have continued the work of the Mathers, who had written of the wars and captivity experiences of New England colonists for similar reasons. But for reasons not known, Stephen never finished his history. Joseph Petty's account remained as he wrote it, unpublished and lacking clerical "improvements." As a result, the focus in this narrative is on physical survival, not spiritual transformation.

Stephen Williams also composed an account of his experiences while a captive. The resulting narrative was not published until the nineteenth-century and still has not yet received the attention it deserves. Like many classic captivity narratives, but unlike his father's account, Stephen's narrative focuses on his interactions with Native peoples, not surprising since he spent most of his time as a prisoner of Abenakis, not the French. Nonetheless, his account lacks the religious preoccupations with the Bible and providence that scholars have thought to be characteristic of classic Puritan captivity narratives. Nor is its depiction of Native peoples and their culture as harsh as Mary Rowlandson's narrative. It certainly is not an admiring portrait, but it presents the point of view of a young boy rather than that of a combative adult. Native peoples appear as independent actors in the story, not just conduits of God's rebukes or mercies. These qualities make Stephen's story a refreshingly personal account of the experience of captivity.

FRENCH NARRATIVES

Alongside the versions of English captives, Puritan ministers, and New England antiquarians, alternative stories of the 1704 raid and distinct historical traditions relating to Deerfield have existed among French, Mohawk, and Abenaki communities descended from Deerfield's one-time attackers. Not surprisingly, the earliest of these accounts were written down by French officials and priests. In 1704, Philippe de Rigaud de Vaudreuil, the governor-general of New France, and Claude de Ramezay, the governor of the district of Montreal, both wrote reports of the raid as official communications to their superior the Comte de Pontchartrain, who was the Minister of the Marine and oversaw the administration of France's colonies. Their reports lay out the strategic calculations behind the raid and reveal unexpected disagreements over strategy and tactics involved in such raids. Often such reports were the basis for reports published in the *Mercure galant,* a semi-official newspaper published in Paris. Accounts of raids such as the attack on Deerfield also found their way into two other genres produced in New France: letters written by Jesuit missionaries that have come to be known as *The Jesuit Relations* and memoirs of service written by colonial military officers seeking promotion or ennoblement. Examples of both contain stories of the 1704 raid.

Since the first days of their missionary activity in Canada, members of the Society of Jesus, popularly known as the Jesuits, wrote and published accounts of their efforts to convert Natives to the Catholic faith. Their published letters were intended to reach educated Catholics throughout Europe to increase financial and political support for the Society's missionary activity. The Jesuits were highly educated men, able to learn the languages of the peoples they lived and worked with. They were also excellent writers and observers. Because of these traits their descriptions of Native societies and systems of belief have an almost ethnographic quality to them. Still, their purpose was to convert Natives to the Catholic faith and, while much can be learned from these writings about Native societies and cultures, the context in which these letters were produced must always be kept in mind.[44]

The earliest known Native account of the 1704 raid actually survives in one of the *Jesuit Relations.* It is found in Father Louis d'Avaugour's 1710 report to his superior on life in the Huron community of Lorette, whose warriors took part in the attack on Deerfield. Ironically, this community, the only Native community for which there exists a comprehensive documentary account of its role in the raid, has no oral tradition relating to the Deerfield captives. In fact, the 1704 Deerfield raid played such a small role in this community's history (none of the captives taken to this community remained after the war ended in 1713) that it had to be rediscovered from written sources.

D'Avaugour's letter served several functions. Ostensibly, it was a report of conditions at Lorette and its mission during the War of the Spanish Succession. But d'Avaugour's main goal in recounting life at the mission was to stress the importance of Jesuit missions to New France's military survival and spiritual well-being. To dramatize and humanize these points he singled out the actions of a pious young Huron warrior he calls Thaovenhosen.

While returning from the Deerfield raid, the Hurons' leader died of the wounds he had received during the attack. The Hurons then argued over the need to avenge their loss. A nephew of the fallen leader spoke for the traditional way of ritually torturing and killing one of their prisoners. Thaovenhosen, however, argued against this return to mourning-war culture by appealing to his fellow warriors' identity as Christian Hurons. Seeing that his audience was not moved by this call to Christian civility, he then put forth his own traditional right to decide the captive's fate based on his kinship to the dead leader. This argument carried the day, sparing one Deerfield captive, probably Jonathan Hoyt, an agonizing death. Here, though imperfectly, are preserved French and Huron perspectives on the religious dynamics of the Deerfield raid.

In contrast to the Jesuit and New England accounts, most of the other French sources are quite secular in orientation. The memoir of service written by Joseph-François Hertel in 1712 contains a second-hand account of events that took place during the Deerfield raid, undoubtedly communicated to him by his sons who participated in the attack. Such detailed retellings of a military officer's career played important roles in shaping New France's military and social hierarchies. Members of the local nobility along with officials from France and wealthy merchants stood at the apex of the colony's social hierarchy. Approximately three-quarters of the nobles in New France were military officers and virtually all of the military officers were nobles. Military officers, and thus most nobles, earned very little from their landholdings. They depended on government favor for commissions, promotions, and income. Officers from families who had not legally secured noble status, including both the Bouchers and the Hertels, also depended on the recommendation of the governor-general and the support of officials in France to obtain this coveted status.

Joseph-François Hertel's effort to see his family ennobled had begun in the early 1690s. He came close to obtaining letters of nobility but was rejected because he did not have enough wealth. His 1712 memoir marks another attempt.

This time he relied not only on his own deeds—deeds that had earned him the sobriquet "the Hero"—but also those of his many sons to prove the Hertels' worthiness of nobility. Since the 1690s his sons had served, suffered, and, in two instances died in the colonial regulars. In the end Hertel prevailed, and in 1716 his family became the eleventh—and last—Canadian family to be ennobled.

Most of the Canadian-born French participants on the Deerfield raid did not leave records of their experiences. Aspirations to nobility, reflections on grand strategy, and the conversion of Native peoples were probably not matters of primary concern to them. These men were also less likely to be literate than the clergy and nobles in New France and their New England counterparts. The stories that they undoubtedly recounted passed into oral traditions that regrettably do not survive for the 1704 raid. These men and their families also would have come to grips with the spiritual meaning of such a raid in ways different from those of the New Englanders. True, they were assailants rather than captives, but some did die and others lost companions in the attack. For them the beliefs of the Catholic Church played a more central role than calling to mind and reflecting upon biblical passages. In this context, the most evocative religious remembrance of frontier warfare is an early eighteenth-century votive painting in the church of Notre-Dame-de-Liesse that pictures a man praying next to two Canadian militiamen lying dead in a snow-covered landscape (figure 3).

NATIVE NARRATIVES

Native stories draw on the legacy of John Williams's daughter Eunice. Eunice never wrote down her story, though she must have talked about it. But when she did, it was probably in Mohawk, for in the years after her capture she forgot how to speak English. In the absence of her direct testimony, her story has been shaped by her literal, fictive, and spiritual descendants. Where John's legacy preserved a preoccupation with defense and the preservation of tradition and boundaries, Eunice's legacy confronts the tremendous changes brought by the arrival of European colonists in America. Persistence through the adoption of outsiders, the assimilation of new influences, and adaptation to situations not of one's own choosing are the themes of the Native narratives of captivity. Here Deerfield's captors become the heroes and sometimes even the victims.

When Native peoples brought their stories to the attention of American audiences, they were generally dismissed as factually unreliable. And, as Geoffrey Buerger has pointed out, there is good reason to doubt at least some of the factual assertions in at least one of the traditions, the Mohawks' "Story of the Bell." For their part, Natives recognized that their traditions did not always

FIGURE 3. Votive painting, showing Canadian militiamen and the Blessed Mary Virgin, who is holding the Christ child. Oil painting, first half of the eighteenth century, artist unknown. Notre-Dame-de-Liesse de Rivière-Ouelle de Québec. Votive paintings acknowledged and memorialized a vow made to the Virgin Mary or another saint during a time of danger or suffering. The exact circumstances that led to the commissioning of this particular painting are not known. However, René Chartrand has identified the individuals as militiamen (Chartrand, *Canadian Military Heritage*, vol. 1, *1000–1754* [Montreal, 1993], 119). The kneeling man prays to the Virgin Mary, who acts as an intercessor with the Christ child, and in answer to his prayers, he is spared the fate that befell the two other men. This painting, which is one of the most important examples of this genre, has recently been conserved by the Centre de Conservation du Québec. Photograph courtesy of Le Conseil de Fabrique Notre-Dame-de-Liesse de Rivière-Ouelle.

stand up to European historical standards of documentary accuracy. When asked, "And how much of this legend is historically true?" Alexandre, the resident of Kahnawake who retold the "Story of the Bell" in 1882, answered, "But very little I fear."[45] However, it should be noted that many New England histories also contain oral traditions and facts that are not borne out in historical records.[46]

But just as New England historians have long accepted that local oral histories can provide insight not available in written records, scholars are beginning to realize that Native traditions can do much the same. The true significance of these narratives usually does not lie in specific facts. The Native accounts provide rare testimony of the captors' perspective on events, conveying certain cultural truths about what Natives did and why. Moreover, as narratives not only by Natives but also by captors, they offer an invaluable perspective on the captivity experience.[47]

Mohawk Stories

Curiously enough, the earliest known Mohawk account of their raid on Deerfield is in the form of a captivity narrative, the oldest written version of which dates to the 1820s. In its earliest telling, however, the story does not mention Eunice, the Mohawks' most famous captive, or any of the other Deerfield captives. Instead the story is about a bell. It was said that a bell had been made in Europe for the church at Kahnawake. When it was being transported to Canada, a New England privateer captured it. Soon thereafter the bell was purchased by the Reverend John Williams and taken to Deerfield. Eventually the Mohawks learned of its fate and joined the Deerfield raid to liberate their bell, which they carried in triumph back to its rightful home in Kahnawake.[48] The complete version of the story published in this collection dates to the 1880s (figure 4).

Because the "Story of the Bell" is an oral tradition, it has varied in emphasis over the centuries, reflecting contemporary concerns. A version published in a Kahnawake elementary school text produced in the late 1970s sets the story within the context of Kahnawake's contemporary struggle for greater autonomy. Coming at a time when many Native American activists denounced portrayals of their ancestors that showed them as dependent on and submissive to Europeans, it explicitly counters the lurid images of "savage" Indians that have long dominated films, television, other popular media and even much historical writing.[49] By the 1970s Kahnawake's Mohawks also had become aware of the symbolic importance of Eunice Williams and this recent version of the story notes that "one family captured by the Kanienkehaka was the family of the Reverend John Williams who purchased the stolen bell." Eunice "was ad-

opted into a Kahnawake family. She learned to live as a Kanienkehaka and refused to leave Kahnawake and join her family in Deerfield." For a small
community that has confronted dramatic and difficult changes, Eunice's choice
to remain at Kahnawake are grounds for a positive sense of identity and soli-
darity with Mohawks past and present.[50]

Another Mohawk tradition deals at greater length with the story of Eunice
Williams's capture and adoption. Like the story of the bell, it first appears in
the mid-nineteenth century. Also like the bell story, it is about a loss that is replaced. The source of the loss in this story is a Mohawk child. The replacement
is Eunice Williams. Shortly before the raid, a Mohawk mother had been rendered inconsolable by the death of an infant daughter. She was "so much borne
down with" the loss, "some of her relations predicted that she could not survive
long. It was visible in her countenance that she was on the decline; she had lost
the vivacity which was a peculiar trait in her character before she was bereft of
her child." After the raid, Eunice filled the void: "the relations of her adopted
mother took much notice of her, and the children were instructed to treat
her as one of the family." The themes of both stories fit the patterns of the
mourning war. What mattered was not the fate of the individual captive but
the restoration of the community's well-being. Such was the role of Eunice
and, symbolically, the bell.[51]

The story of the bell and the narrative of Eunice probably shared the same
source: Eunice Williams's great-grandson, the Reverend Eleazer Williams.[52]

FIGURE 4. Carrying the Bell to Kahnawake. Drawing, 1976, Rita Phillips. This drawing shows
the triumphant Mohawks carrying their bell from Deerfield to Kahnawake. It was used to illustrate
a version of the story recounted in Mohawk and printed as "IEHWISTA' EKSTHA' " (The bell), in
KANIEN'KEHA' OKARA'SHON: A Mohawk Stories New York State Museum *Bulletin* 427 (November 1976): 132. Reprinted with permission of the New York State Museum, Albany.

Born a Mohawk and raised at Kahnawake, Williams spent most of his life attempting to shake off his Mohawk identity and gain acceptance as a white man, a search that led him to fashion and discard a series of public personae and made him a controversial figure. A sympathetically disposed biographer summarizes Eleazer's life thus: "Williams embraced three religions and as many sets of ancestors, assumed several fictional titles, authored a variety of historical fabrications, and left behind him a trail of debts and an astonishing reputation for mendacity."[53] In the early 1800s—around the time the story of the bell first appears in New England accounts—he visited and studied near his Deerfield relatives, with whom he seems to have identified closely. At this early stage of his career, Williams began distancing himself from his Mohawk antecedents and placing himself firmly on "the side of Civilization against Savagery"[54] and, one should add, on the side of Protestantism against Catholicism. In this context the story of the bell can been viewed as an effort to mute the "savagery" associated with his Mohawk heritage by providing a justification of the Mohawks' actions that emphasized their piety and de-emphasized the actual violence of the raid.

Eleazer Williams also appears to have crafted the story of Eunice's assimilation into Kahnawake in a way that might make it more acceptable to her New England relatives. He stressed her personal piety, denounced Jesuits, and downplayed the significance of religious differences among true Christians. He reported that the life of Catherine Tekakwitha, one of the early Mohawk settlers of Kahnawake famous for her saint-like piety and herself the daughter of an adopted Algonkian captive, "was held up to her [Eunice's] view," encouraging her conversion.[55] In this story it was not the connection to the Mohawks, or even precisely to the Catholic Church, but rather the chance to live a spiritually rich life in the example of Catherine that Williams's great-grandmother had defected from her English relatives and started a Mohawk family. Since New Englanders lamented Eunice's conversion to Catholicism and adoption of Mohawk culture, Eleazer seems to have been trying to present these choices in as acceptable a light as possible. Sadly, he underestimated the power of their racism. Though educated and ordained, Eleazer was sent west to minister to the Iroquois. He never gained a white congregation or the acceptance into New England society that he desired.[56]

In the final selection of Mohawk stories, Taiaiake Alfred brings together the various strands of Eunice, the bell, and the Williams family. A man who turns out to be a descendant of Eunice himself, Taiaiake came from Kahnawake to tell Deerfield the story of the bell in 1995. A professor and educator, he also offers some commentary on colonial history and Mohawk traditions, suggesting ways we can understand that history, and explains the ways in which contemporary Mohawks relate to their past. One of his most striking observations concerns the general lack of interest or knowledge at Kahnawake about the individual identities of the many English captives assimilated into the community in centuries past. This provides a strong contrast with the traditions of the Abenaki.

Abenaki Stories

Eunice Williams occupies a central place in the historical memory of some Abenaki families. Unlike the Mohawk stories, which are primarily concerned with connections of community, the Abenaki stories emphasize connections with place. This fact was evident as long ago as 1837, when a group of approximately two dozen Abenakis from Odanak arrived in Deerfield. They claimed to be descendants of Eunice Williams and referred to Deerfield as Williamsecook, the place of the Williamses. Deerfield residents were aware that Eunice had lived out her life as a Mohawk at Kahnawake, not an Abenaki at Odanak, but they accepted the Abenakis' claims to be Williams descendants. The Abenakis remained for a week, visiting sites associated with the attack and the Williams family and selling baskets that they had made.[57] During their visit, the Unitarian minister of Deerfield's First Church, the Reverend John Fessenden, preached a sermon in which he stressed "the workings of that mysterious providence, which has mingled your blood with ours, and which . . . admonishes us that God . . . hath made of one blood all nations of men."[58]

The next year a group of Abenakis returned to the area and stayed in nearby Northampton. Here the town's Democratic newspaper, the *Northampton Courier,* which had supported President Andrew Jackson and his policy of Indian removal, gave them a very different welcome. The paper sarcastically described their visit and proclaimed them the *"Miserable Remnants"* of "a slothful, ragged, dirty, squalid race."[59]

Nearly a hundred years later, in 1922, a descendant of one of the visitors by the name of Elizabeth Sadoques recounted the 1837 visit to Deerfield's local historical society. She too emphasized her personal descent from Eunice Williams. Her talk, which is included in the collection, provides us with the first Abenaki narrative of the 1704 raid on Deerfield and makes clear the differences between Mohawk and Abenaki priorities. For Sadoques, to be related to a prominent Deerfield family was important, because it symbolized her people's attachment to the area. As she pointed out, "a very beautiful portion of this country which is now the New England states and including the St. Lawrence River valley was the territory of the Algonquian Indians of which there are many divisions, the Abenaki being one division or tribe." Sadoques reminded her Deerfield audience, "these were the people who greeted the Pilgrims in 1620" only to be driven to Canada by the Pilgrims' ungrateful descendants. In Canada, the French "seeing the opportunity to use them for their Indian allies in New France ordered their soldiers to lead the unbroken spirits of the savages against the English settlers who had their lands. The result was many cruel massacres and the taking of many captives to Canada." [60]

Elizabeth Sadoques's story is less about the actual attack on Deerfield or Eunice's captivity experience than her ancestors' long-standing and continuing associations with the place. She tells of how the women of the family kept alive and acted upon the memory of their people's connection to New England. Elizabeth's mother, Mary, and her aunt Eunice "in response to the voice of their ancestors, have traversed the same course down the Quanitagook and have settled not far from its shores [Keene, N.H.], here rearing their children, near the great river of their forefathers." [61] This emphasis on place reflects a difference between the experiences of Algonquian peoples, who had lived in smaller, more mobile communities, and Iroquoian peoples, who lived in larger villages bound by a greater political allegiance to the Five (and later Six) Nations of the Iroquois League. Studies of contemporary Natives' sense of nationhood have contrasted an Algonquian emphasis on place and land with an Iroquoian focus on nation and community. Thus, these differing stories of the Deerfield raid reflect both historically rooted cultural distinctions and the two groups' different relationships to the actual raid. [62]

In the final piece in this collection, Marge Bruchac, an Abenaki storyteller and anthropologist, expands on the Sadoques story. She brings her story up to the present, indicating how Sadoques's descendants remain involved in the history and culture of the region. She also deepens our understanding of the visit and what it meant. Bruchac draws on a variety of materials—baskets, herbal lore, family tradition, and more traditional sorts of historical documents—to make a strong case for the deep attachment Abenakis have to their New England homeland and for the usefulness of oral traditions.

Bruchac's essay is a fitting conclusion to the collection. Her work reminds us that physical objects can provide access to the past in ways that texts cannot. Interpreting artifacts may be more of a challenge, but if examined closely, artifacts too have their stories to tell. In this way, people who otherwise have no written voice can speak to history. Now, a history that for so long has been dominated by a single text, John Williams's *Redeemed Captive returning to Zion*, can be understood through a range of them. None alone is authoritative or definitive. A more inclusive history lies in the combination and juxtaposition of these different avenues to the past.

NOTES

1. Evan Haefeli and Kevin Sweeney, *Captors and Captives: The 1704 French and Indian Raid on Deerfield* (Amherst: University of Massachusetts Press, 2003), 112–124.

2. Haefeli and Sweeney, *Captors and Captives,* 11–15.

3. Haefeli and Sweeney, *Captors and Captives,* 16–22.

4. "Narrative of Benoni Stebbins," in *Papers Concerning the Attack on Hatfield and Deerfield by a Party of Indians from Canada, September Nineteenth 1677* (New York: Bradford Series, 1859), 53. While the Norwottucks had lived in villages about fifteen miles south of Deerfield, the Narragansett's home had been in Rhode Island.

5. Haefeli and Sweeney, *Captors and Captives,* 22–27.

6. Haefeli and Sweeney, *Captors and Captives,* 27–31.

7. Evan Haefeli and Kevin Sweeney, "Wattanummon's World: Personal and Tribal Identity in the Algonquian Diaspora, c. 1660–1712," in *Actes du Vingt-Cinquième Congrès des Algonquinistes,* ed. William Cowan (Ottawa: Carleton University, 1994), 212–224, and James Spady, "As if in a Great Darkness: Native American Refugees of the Middle Connecticut Valley in the Aftermath of King Philip's War," *Historical Journal of Massachusetts* 23, no. 2 (1995): 183–197.

8. Haefeli and Sweeney, *Captors and Captives,* 88, 106–109.

9. Haefeli and Sweeney, *Captors and Captives,* 34–49.

10. Haefeli and Sweeney, *Captors and Captives,* 49–54.

11. Haefeli and Sweeney, *Captors and Captives,* 73–77.

12. Haefeli and Sweeney, *Captors and Captives,* 78–92.

13. Haefeli and Sweeney, *Captors and Captives,* 55–73.

14. Haefeli and Sweeney, *Captors and Captives,* 95–99, 109–111.

15. Haefeli and Sweeney, *Captors and Captives,* 112–119.

16. Haefeli and Sweeney, *Captors and Captives,* 119–124.

17. Haefeli and Sweeney, *Captors and Captives,* 125–142.

18. Haefeli and Sweeney, *Captors and Captives,* 211–221, 225. For a study of white captives among Native peoples, see June Namias, *White Captives: Gender and Ethnicity on the American Frontier* (Chapel Hill: University of North Carolina Press, 1993).

19. Haefeli and Sweeney, *Captors and Captives,* 221–225.

20. Haefeli and Sweeney, *Captors and Captives,* 238–249. See also William Henry Foster, *The Captors' Narrative: Catholic Women and Their Puritan Men on the Early American Frontier* (Ithaca, N.Y.: Cornell University Press, 2003).

21. Haefeli and Sweeney, *Captors and Captives,* 250–264.

22. Haefeli and Sweeney, *Captors and Captives,* 264–271.

23. John Demos, *The Unredeemed Captive: A Family Story from Early America* (New York: Knopf, 1994).

24. Noteworthy studies include Namias, *White Captives;* Kathryn Zabelle Derounian-Stodola and James Arthur Levernier, *The Indian Captivity Narrative, 1550–1900* (New York: Twayne, 1993); Christopher Castiglia, *Bound and Determined: Captivity, Culture-Crossing, and White Womanhood from Mary Rowlandson to Patty Hearst* (Chicago: University of Chicago Press, 1996); Michelle Burnham, *Captivity and Sentiment: Cultural Exchange in American Literature, 1682–1861* (Hanover, N.H.: University Press of New England, 1997); Pauline Turner Strong, *Captive Selves, Captivating Others: The Politics and Poetics of Colonial American Captivity Narratives* (Boulder, Colo.: Westview Press, 1999).

25. See Alden T. Vaughan and Daniel K. Richter, "Crossing the Cultural Divide: Indians and New Englanders, 1605–1763," *American Antiquarian Society Proceedings* 90 (1980): 53–57. For some insights into reasons why males were more likely to return, see Foster, *Captors' Narrative.*

26. Another possible exception is Susanna Johnson's narrative, published in 1796. For the more usual state of affairs, see the narratives of Hannah Dustan, Hannah Swarton, Elizabeth Hanson, Mary Kinnan, Rachel Plummer, Mary Fowler, Isabella McCoy, Jemima Howe, and others collected in Alden T. Vaughan and Edward W. Clark, eds., *Puritans among the Indians: Accounts of Captivity and Redemption, 1676–1724* (Cambridge: Harvard University Press, 1981). See also Richard VanDerBeets, ed., *Held Captive by Indians: Selected Narratives, 1642–1836* (1973; repr., Knoxville: University of Tennessee Press, 1994), and Colin G. Calloway, ed., *North Country Captives: Selected Narratives of Indian Captivity from Vermont and New Hampshire* (Hanover, N.H.: University Press of New England, 1992). Neal Salisbury argues that Rowlandson probably composed her account, published in 1682, between June 1677 and October 1678. Mary Rowlandson, *The Sovereignty and Goodness of God,* ed. Neal Salisbury (Boston: Bedford Books, 1997), 40.

27. The classic collection of Puritan captivity narratives, containing both Williams and Rowlandson, is Vaughan and Clark, *Puritans among the Indians.* For another influential collection see VanDerBeets, *Held Captive by Indians.*

28. On the origins of captivity narratives, see Vaughan and Clark, *Puritans among the Indians,* 1–28; James D. Hartman, *Providence Tales and the Birth of American Literature* (Baltimore: Johns Hopkins University Press, 1999); Linda Colley, *Captives: The Story of Britain's Pursuit of Empire and How Its Soldiers and Sailors Were Held Captive by the Dream of Global Supremacy, 1600–1850* (New York: Pantheon Books, 2002).

29. For the most important recent scholarship on captivity narratives see n. 24, and Gary L. Ebersole, *Captured by Texts: Puritan to Post-Modern Images of Indian Captivity* (Charlottesville: University of Virginia Press, 1995).

30. On trans-Atlantic debates about providence that engaged the Mathers, see Michael Winship, *Seers of God: Puritan Providentialism in the Restoration and Early Enlightenment* (Baltimore: Johns Hopkins University Press, 1996).

31. On the publication of *The Redeemed Captive,* see Haefeli and Sweeney, *Captors and Captives,* 175–182.

32. Evan Haefeli and Kevin Sweeney, "The Redeemed Captive as Recurrent Seller: Politics and Publication, 1707–1853," *New England Quarterly* 77, no. 3 (September 2004): 341–367.

33. This change actually began with Samuel Penhallow's *The History of the Wars of New-England with the Eastern Indians* (Boston: T. Fleet, 1726). For the change from a divine to a secular-heroic interpretation of New England's settler-soldiers that mirrored this historiographical shift, see John Ferling, "The New England Soldier: A Study in Changing Perceptions," *American Quarterly* 33, no. 1 (1981): 26–45.

34. George Sheldon, *A History of Deerfield, Massachusetts,* 2 vols. (Deerfield: privately printed, 1895–1896), 1:672.

35. Stephen Williams Diary, January 6, 1728, typescript transcription, microfilm edition, Historic Deerfield Library; [Stephen Williams], *Narrative of the Captivity of Stephen Williams,* ed. George Sheldon (Deerfield, Mass.: Pocumtuck Valley Memorial Association, 1889), app., 13–27; [Lucy Watson], "Mrs. Lucy Watson's memory & account of

New Settlers in the American Woods 1762, Chiefly Walpole, N[ew] H[ampshire]," 2–3,
Watson Family Papers, Box 2, Winterthur Library, Winterthur, Del.

36. Epaphras Hoyt, *Antiquarian Researches* (Greenfield, Mass.: A. Phelps, 1824),
186–195; Stephen West Williams, "Ancient History of Pocomptuck or Deerfield," app.,
19–21, Williams Papers, Pocumtuck Valley Memorial Association, Deerfield, Mass.

37. Sheldon, *History of Deerfield*, 1:301, 314.

38. [Watson], "Mrs. Lucy Watson's memory & account," 2–3; Hoyt, *Antiquarian Researches*, 186.

39. Sheldon, *History of Deerfield*, 1:314.

40. Sheldon, *History of Deerfield*, 1:311–312.

41. Sheldon, *History of Deerfield*, 1:307, 309–310.

42. Sheldon, *History of Deerfield*, 1:355–56; 2:139, 295; Emma Lewis Coleman, *New England Carried Captives to Canada between 1677 and 1760 during the French and Indian Wars*, 2 vols. (Portland: Me.: Southworth Press, 1925), 2:91, 117–118, 123; John Williams, *The Redeemed Captive Returning to Zion* (1707), ed. Stephen W. Williams (1853; repr., Bedford, Mass., [1987]), 175.

43. Haefeli and Sweeney, *Captors and Captives*, 261.

44. See Allan Green, *Mohawk Saint: Catherine Tekakwitha and the Jesuits* (New York: Oxford University Press, 2005).

45. See E. A. Smith, "The Story of the Bell," 219–220.

46. This is especially true for the nineteenth-century historians. But even in Demos's recent *Unredeemed Captive* some facts are disputable; see Evan Haefeli and Kevin Sweeney, "Revisiting *The Redeemed Captive*: New Perspectives on the 1704 Attack on Deerfield," *William and Mary Quarterly*, 3rd. ser. 52, no. 1 (1995): 8, 44.

47. Geoffrey Buerger, " 'Pavillion'd Upon Chaos': The History and Historiography of the Deerfield Massacre" (master's thesis, Dartmouth College, 1985), addresses the factual problems with the Mohawk "story of the bell of Saint Regis." Gordon Day, "Oral Tradition as Complement," *Ethnohistory* 19, no. 2 (1972): 99–108 argues these traditions can fill out the documentary record.

48. For a discussion and critique of the story of the bell, see Geoffrey Buerger, "Out of Whole Cloth: The Tradition of the St. Regis Bell" (paper presented at the Mid-Atlantic Conference for Canadian Studies, Bucknell University, 1986; copy in the Pocumtuck Valley Memorial Association Library, Deerfield, Mass.).

49. David Blanchard, *Seven Generations: A History of the Kanienkehaka* (Kahnawake, 1980), 208–209.

50. Blanchard, *Seven Generations*, 209.

51. De Saileville, "The Life and Captivity of Miss Eunice Williams," 235. This unpublished biography of Eunice Williams is a combination of facts, family and Kahnawake folklore, and romantic fiction. It must be used with care. For a similar assessment, see Demos, *Unredeemed Captive*, 299–300 n. 20.

52. Parkman, *A Half Century of Conflict*, vol. 2 of *France and England in North America* (New York: Library of America, 1983), 396–397; and Buerger, "Out of Whole Cloth," 2.

53. Geoffrey E. Buerger, "Eleazer Williams: Elitism and Multiple Identity on Two Frontiers," in *Being and Becoming Indian: Biographical Studies of North American Indians*, ed. James A. Clifton (Chicago: Dorsey Press, 1989), 115.

54. Buerger, "Eleazer Williams," 120.

55. De Saileville, "The Life and Captivity of Miss Eunice Williams," 243. See also Greer, *Mohawk Saint*.

56. Buerger, "Eleazer Williams."

57. *Greenfield Gazette & Mercury*, August 29, 1837; John Fessenden, *A Sermon, Preached to the First Congregational Society in Deerfield, Mass., and in the Hearing of Several Indians of Both Sexes, Supposed to be Descendants of Eunice Williams Daughter of Rev. John Williams, First Minister of Deerfield, August 27, 1837* (Greenfield, Mass.: Phelps and Ingersoll, 1837), 3–4.

58. Fessenden, *Sermon*, 14–15.

59. *Northampton Courier*, May 30, 1838, June 6, 1838. We are indebted to Paul Gaffney for these references.

60. Sadoques, "History and Traditions of Eunice Williams," 257, 258.

61. Sadoques, "History and Traditions of Eunice Williams, 261.

62. Lisa Philips Valentine, "Performing Native Identities," in Cowan, *Actes du Vingt-Cinquième Congrès des Algonquinistes*, 482–92.

THE SETTING

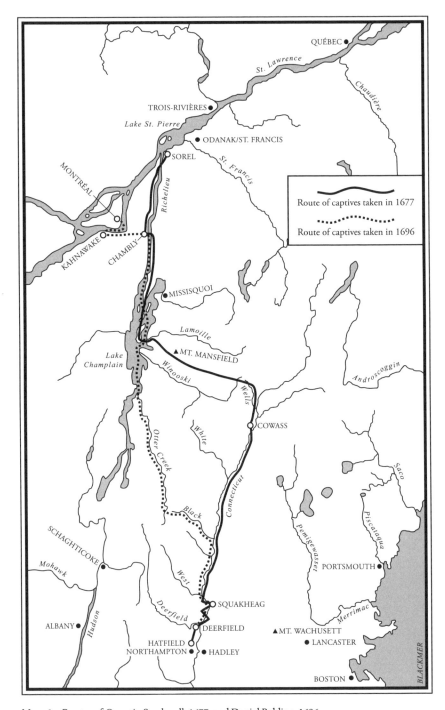

MAP 2. Routes of Quentin Stockwell, 1677, and Daniel Belding, 1696.

QUENTIN STOCKWELL'S RELATION OF HIS 1677 CAPTIVITY AND REDEMPTION, 1684

QUENTIN STOCKWELL

Q UENTIN STOCKWELL (c. 1640–1714) came to Deerfield in 1673, when it was still known as Pocumtuck. He and his wife, Abigail, were from Dedham, Massachusetts, the town that had been granted the Native lands at Pocumtuck by the government of Massachusetts. He boarded the village's first preacher, the young Samuel Mather,[1] a nephew of Increase Mather.[2] This connection with one of the most influential families of ministers in New England eventually helped get his captivity story into print. Stockwell and Samuel Mather both left when the village was evacuated in the fall of 1675. Samuel Mather went to Branford, on the coast of Connecticut, about as far away from the frontier as one could get in New England. Stockwell went to nearby Hatfield, Massachusetts. He and Abigail's first child, John, was born in October 1676. Stockwell returned to Deerfield with several other men in the spring of 1677 to begin resettling the village. Their families stayed behind and thus were not captured in the September 19, 1677, raid that took Stockwell to Canada.

Stockwell's captors were among the first New England Natives to seek refuge with the French in Canada. Until then, they had preferred to remain in their homeland. But by 1677 that was no longer possible. The lines of conflict that would shape the rest of the colonial period had been drawn. In the future, New England captivity experiences would involve French Catholics as much as Natives. Stockwell's experience thus came at a transition point in both the history of the New England frontier and the evolution of captivity narratives.

The narrative follows the version originally printed in Increase Mather, *An Essay for the Recording of Illustrious Providences: wherin, an account is given of many remarkable and very memorable events, which have happened in this last age; especially in New England* (Boston: Samuel Green for Joseph Browning, 1684), 39–58. The location of the original manuscript, if it survives, is not known.

1. Samuel Mather (1651–1728) preached at Deerfield but was never ordained there, so technically he was not the first minister. He did become the minister of Windsor, Connecticut, in 1684 and married the daughter of the colony's governor, Robert Treat.

2. Increase Mather (1639–1723) was a prominent minister in Boston and father of the Reverend Cotton Mather (1663–1728). Both played important roles in publishing captivity narratives.

After Stockwell's return from Canada in 1678, he and his family joined Samuel Mather in Branford. Mather probably persuaded Stockwell to write up his experiences and then passed the resulting narrative on to his uncle Increase, who he knew was collecting stories of extraordinary experiences. Like many former captives, Quentin Stockwell clearly did not want to risk being taken again. He did not take his family back to Deerfield. Instead, he moved in 1683 to Suffield, along the Connecticut-Massachusetts border. There he led the unadventurous life of a New England farmer until his death in 1714.[3]

Stockwell's story first appeared in 1684 as part of the Reverend Increase Mather's *An Essay for the Recording of Illustrious Providences.* This book was a collection of stories intended to prove that New Englanders enjoyed God's special favor.[4] The captivity narrative appeared in chapter two, which was dedicated to "remarkable preservations" of people who under normal circumstances should have died but did not. Other chapters discuss noteworthy thunderstorms, apparitions, demonic possession, and sudden inexplicable deaths.

This account is the second captivity narrative published in New England, after Mary Rowlandson's 1682 *Sovereignty and Goodness of God,* which was also published with the help of Increase Mather. Unlike Rowlandson's narrative or John Williams's 1707 *The Redeemed Captive Returning to Zion,* however, Stockwell's relation does not emphasize the religious significance of his "captivity" and "redemption" by quoting passages from the Bible and looking for evidence of God's providence in every twist of fate. The only explicit references made to the role of divine providence are in the opening paragraph and the addendum written by Increase Mather, as the Boston minister attempts to "improve" Stockwell's relation by placing it in a more religiously edifying interpretive framework.

However, Stockwell did see the hand of providence in the treatment that he received during his captivity and in his eventual return to New England. Upon his arrival in Albany he wrote the following letter to his wife Abigail:

> Albany May 22, 1678
>
> Loving wife,
>
> Having now opportunity to remember my kind love to thee and our child; and the rest of our friends, though we met with great afflictions and trouble since I see thee last. Yet here is now opportunity of joy and thanksgiving to God that we are now pretty well, and in a hopeful way to see the faces of one another before we take our final farewell of this present world.

3. George Sheldon, *A History of Deerfield, Massachusetts,* 2 vols. (Deerfield: privately printed, 1895–1896), 2:328–329.

4. Increase Mather, *An Essay for the Recording of Illustrious Providences* (Boston: Samuel Green for Joseph Browning, 1684), 39–58.

Likewise God hath raised up friends amongst our enemies and there is but 3 of us dead of all those that were taken away—Sergeant Plympton, Samuel Russell, Samuel Foot's daughter.

So I conclude being in haste, and

> Rest your most affectionate husband
> till death makes a separation
> Quintin Stockwell[5]

Despite his providential understanding of his deliverance, Stockwell's published story spends more time engaging with the religious beliefs of his Algonquian captors than quoting scripture. This may help explain why his narrative was never published again in colonial New England. Though his Protestantism is not in doubt, he comes off more as a trickster figure from a folk tale than as a zealous Puritan. His struggle for physical survival and the skill, kindness, and actions of captives and captors, not the power of God, take center stage in his story. Stockwell was more understanding and less hostile toward his Native masters than Rowlandson was in her account. Though little is known about Stockwell's early years, he had evidently had some contact with the Native peoples of Massachusetts. He was familiar with their language and some of the Natives he met during his captivity knew him. Native culture thus was not as strange to him as it was to other New England captives. Nor does he share John Williams's anti-Catholic agenda. Instead he is downright grateful to the French Catholics who eventually secured his release.

Perhaps the most distinguishing feature of Stockwell's narrative is how far he traveled. He and his fellow captives were the first New England colonists to make the three-hundred-mile journey overland to Canada. This fact combined with his semi-ethnographic description of aspects of Native American culture and the outright adventure of his journey rendered his account of great appeal to people who cared little about God's design for New England. Richard Blome, a publisher based in London with an interest in the topography of England's growing (and rather un-Puritan) empire, reprinted Mather's edition of Stockwell's narrative in his 1687 book *The Present State of His Majesties Isles and Territories in America*.[6] To make the narrative more accessible to a metropolitan English audience, he made slight variations in wording and phrasing.

Few other editors and printers brought out versions of Stockwell's narra-

---

5. *Selected Papers from the Sylvester Judd Manuscript*, ed. Gregory H. Nobles and Herbert L. Zarov (Northampton, Mass.: Forbes Library, 1976), 538.

6. Richard Blome, *The Present State of His Majesties Isles and Territories in America* (London: H. Clark, 1687); Linda Colley, *Captives: The Story of Britain's pursuit of Empire and How Its Soldiers and Civilians Were Held Captive by the Dream of Global Supremacy, 1600–1850* (New York: Pantheon Books, 2002), 403 n. 32.

tive, which has not received the same level of attention as other New England captivity narratives. Around 1940, Clark S. Yowell reprinted Blome's version of the narrative, renaming the author (for reasons unknown) and entitling it *The Account of John Stockwell of Deerfield, Massachusetts.*[7] Alden T. Vaughan and Edward W. Clark included it in their collection *Puritans among the Indians: Accounts of Captivity and Redemption 1676–1724.*[8]

§

[Stockwell's account is preceded by the story of Jabez Musgrove, who was shot through the head by an Indian and yet survived.]

A worthy person[9] has sent me the account which one lately belonging to Deerfield, (his name is Quentin Stockwell) has drawn up respecting his own captivity and redemption, with the more notable occurrences of divine providence attending him in his distress, which I shall therefore here insert in the words by himself expressed: He relates as follows:

In the year 1677, September 19, between sunset and dark, the Indians came upon us; I and another man being together, we ran away at the outcry the Indians made, shouting and shooting at some other of the English that were hard by.[10] We took a swamp that was at hand for our refuge; the enemy, espying us so near them, ran after us and shot many guns at us. Three guns were discharged upon me, the enemy being within three rod of me, besides many others before that. Being in this swamp that was miry, I slumped in and fell down; whereupon one of the enemy stepped to me with his hatchet lifted up to knock me on the head, supposing that I had been wounded and so unfit for any other travel. I (as it happened) had a pistol by me which, though uncharged, I presented to the Indian who presently stepped back and told me if I would yield I should have no hurt. He said (which was not true) that they had destroyed all

---

7. *The Account of John Stockwell of Deerfield, Massachusetts, Being a Faithful Narrative of His Experiences in the Hands of the Wachusett Indians . . . 1677–1678,* ed. Clark S. Yowell (Somerville, N. J.: privately printed, 1940?).

8. Alden T. Vaughan and Edward W. Clark, eds., *Puritans among the Indians: Accounts of Captivity and Redemption, 1676–1724* (Cambridge: Harvard University Press, 1981), 79–89.

9. The "worthy person" was probably Samuel Mather.

10. The raiding party of twenty-six Natives killed one and captured four in Deerfield. With the exception of one Narragansett from Rhode Island, all of the raiders were Natives of western Massachusetts.

Hatfield and that the woods were full of Indians.[11] Whereupon I yielded myself and so fell into the enemies' hands and by three of them was led away unto the place whence first I began to make my flight; where two other Indians came running to us, and the one lifting up the butt end of his gun to knock me on the head, the other with his hand put by the blow and said I was his friend.

I was now by my own house which the Indians burned last year and I was about to build up again, and there I had some hopes to escape from them. There was a horse just by which they bid me take. I did so but made no attempt to escape thereby, because the enemy was near and the beast was slow and dull. Then was I in hopes they would send me to take my own horses, which they did, but they were so frightened that I could not come near to them. And so [I] fell still into the enemies' hands, who now took me and bound me and led me away. And soon was I brought into the company of captives that were that day brought away from Hatfield which were about a mile off, and here methoughts was matter of joy and sorrow both, to see the company—some company in this condition being some[what] refreshing though little help anyways. Then were we pinioned and led away in the night over the mountains in dark and hideous ways about four miles further before we took up our place for rest, which was in a dismal place of wood on the east side of that mountain.[12] We were kept bound all that night. The Indians kept waking, and we had little mind to sleep in this night's travel. The Indians dispersed and, as they went, made strange noises as of wolves and owls and other wild beasts to the end that they might not lose one another, and if followed they might not be discovered by the English.

About the break of day we marched again and got over the great river at Pecomptuck River['s] mouth,[13] and there rested about two hours. There the Indians marked out upon trays [i.e., trees][14] the number of their captives and slain as their manner is [map 2]. Here was I again in great danger. A quarrel arose about me, whose captive I was, for three took me. I thought I must be killed to end the controversy; so when they put it to me whose I was, I said

---

11. The neighboring town of Hatfield, Massachusetts, was attacked earlier the same day by the same Native raiding party. The attackers killed twelve, wounded four, and took seventeen prisoners: three adults and fourteen children.

12. The mountain they crossed is Pocumtuck Ridge or East Mountain, which separates the valley of the Deerfield River from the valley of the Connecticut River.

13. The Pecomptuck or Pocumtuck River is the Deerfield River. They stopped at the point where the Deerfield River flows into the "great river" or Connecticut River.

14. There are period references to Natives marking such information on trees. We suspect that Stockwell phonetically spelled "trees" as "trays," and Increase Mather, who was probably unfamiliar with this Native practice, did not correct Stockwell's spelling.

three Indians took me. So they agreed to have all a share in me, and I had now three masters, and he was my chief master who laid hands on me first. And thus was I fallen into the hands of the very worst of all the company, as Ashpelon,[15] the Indian captain, told me, which captain was all along very kind to me and a great comfort to the English.

In this place they gave us some victuals which they had brought from the English. This morning also they sent ten men forth to town to bring away what they could find; some provision, some corn out of the meadow, they brought to us upon horses which they had there taken. From hence we went up about the falls[16] where we crossed that river again, and, while I was going, I fell right down lame of my old wounds that I had in the war,[17] and, while I was thinking I should therefore be killed by the Indians and what death I should die, my pain was suddenly gone and I was much encouraged again. We had about eleven horses in that company which the Indians made to carry burdens and to carry women.

It was afternoon when we now crossed that river. We traveled up that river till night and then took up our lodging in a dismal place and were staked down and spread out on our backs. And so we lay all night, yea so we lay many nights. They told me their law was that we should lie so nine nights, and by that time it was thought we should be out of our knowledge. The manner of staking down was thus: our arms and legs stretched out were staked fast down and a cord about our necks so that we could stir no ways. The first night of staking down, being much tired, I slept as comfortably as ever.

The next day we went up the river and crossed it and at night lay in Squakheag Meadows.[18] Our provision was soon spent, and while we lay in those meadows, the Indians went a-hunting, and the English army came out after us.[19] Then the Indians moved again, dividing themselves and the captives into many companies that the English might not follow their track. At night, having crossed the river we met again at the place appointed. The next day we crossed the river again on [the] Squakheag side, and there we took up our quarters for a long time. I supposed this might be about thirty miles above

---

15. Ashpelon (active 1670s–1690s) was apparently a Pocumtuck who had fled to Canada in the aftermath of King Philip's War. By the 1690s, he was living at the Native village at Schaghticoke in New York, the home of Native refugees from western Massachusetts.

16. The falls at Peskeompscut; today Turner's Falls, Massachusetts.

17. King Philip's War (1675–1677). It is unclear exactly where or when Stockwell was wounded.

18. The site of a former Sokoki village and of the English settlement of Northfield established in 1673 and abandoned in 1675 as a result of King Philip's War.

19. This was a party of militiamen sent up from Hartford, Connecticut. They went forty miles north of Hadley, Massachusetts, but failed to find the raiding party.

Squakheag,[20] and here were the Indians quite out of all fear of the English but in great fear of the Mohawks.[21] Here they built a long wigwam.

Here they had a great dance (as they call it) and concluded to burn three of us and had got bark to do it with, and (as I understood afterwards) I was one that was to be burned, Sergeant Plimpton another, and Benjamin Wait['s] wife the third.[22] Though I knew not which was to be burned, yet I perceived some were designed thereunto, so much I understood of their language. That night I could not sleep for fear of the next day's work. The Indians, being weary with that dance, lay down to sleep and slept soundly. The English were all loose; then I went out and brought in wood and mended the fire and made a noise on purpose, but none awakened. I thought if any of the English would wake we might kill them all sleeping. I removed out of the way all the guns and hatchets, but my heart failing me, I put all things where they were again. The next day when we were to be burned, our master and some others spoke for us, and the evil was prevented in this place. And hereabouts we lay three weeks together.

Here I had a shirt brought to me to make, and one Indian said it should be made this way, a second said another way, a third his way. I told them I would make it that way that my chief master said whereupon one Indian struck me on the face with his fist. I suddenly rose up in anger ready to strike again. Upon this happened a great hubbub, and the Indians and English came about me; I was fain to humble myself to my master, so that matter was put up.

Before I came to this place, my three masters were gone a-hunting. I was left with another Indian, all the company being upon a march. I was left with this Indian who fell sick so that I was fain to carry his gun and hatchet and had opportunity and had thought to have dispatched him and run away, but did not for that the English captives had promised the contrary to one another, because if one should run away that would provoke the Indians and endanger the rest that could not run away. While we were here, Benjamin [i.e., Benoni] Stebbins,[23] going with some Indians to Wachusett Hills,[24] made his escape from them. And when the news of his escape came, we were all presently called in

---

20. Thirty miles north of Squakheag/Northfield would place them near what is today Walpole, New Hampshire, not far from Bellows Falls.

21. Mohawks and other members of the Five Nations of Iroquois had joined with the English against King Philip and his allies and proved instrumental in their defeat.

22. John Plimpton (1620–1677) of Deerfield and Martha Leonard Waite (1649–?) of Hatfield. Benjamin Waite (1640–1704) died in the Meadows Fight during the 1704 raid on Deerfield. Plimpton was eventually burned to death, but Martha Waite returned with Stockwell.

23. Benoni Stebbins (1655–1704) of Northampton was taken at Deerfield with Stockwell. He returned to settle in Deerfield around 1682 and was killed during the February 29, 1704 attack.

24. Wachusett Hills are in north-central Massachusetts, in what is now northern Worcester County.

and bound. One of the Indians, a captain among them and always our great friend [i.e., Ashpelon], met me coming in and told me Stebbins was run away, and the Indians spoke of burning us, some of only burning and biting off our fingers by and by. He said there would be a court, and all would speak their minds, but he would speak last and would say that the Indian that let Stebbins run away was only in fault and so no hurt should be done us; fear not. So it proved accordingly.

While we lingered hereabout, provision grew scarce; one bear's foot must serve five of us a whole day. We began to eat horseflesh and ate up seven in all. Three were left alive and were not killed. While we had been here, some of the Indians had been down and fallen upon Hadley [Massachusetts] and were taken by the English, agreed with and let go again, and were to meet the English upon such a plain, there to make further terms.[25] Ashpelon was much for it, but [the] Wachusett sachems, when they came, were much against it and were for this: that we [the Indians] should meet the English, indeed, but there fall upon them and fight them and take them.[26] Then Ashpelon spoke to us English not to speak a word more to further that matter, for mischief would come of it. When those Indians came from Wachusett, there came with them squaws and children, about four score, who reported that the English had taken Uncas, and all his men and sent them beyond [the] seas.[27] They were much enraged at this and asked us if it were true. We said no; then was Ashpelon angry and said he would no more believe Englishmen. They examined us everyone apart; then they dealt worse by us for a season than before.

Still provision was scarce. We came at length to a place called Squawmaug River;[28] there we hoped for salmon, but we came too late. This place I account

---

25. These Natives apparently made an attempt to take the mill at Hadley in early October, but for some reason their efforts were frustrated and they instead parleyed with the English. They agreed to return on October 14 and make an agreement to release the prisoners. This scheduled meeting in Hadley never took place.

26. These Wachusett sachems were probably Nipmucks who had left Canada with Ashpelon's party but had parted company and headed east to rendezvous—somewhere in the area of Mount Wachusett—with a party of Pennacooks led by Wanalancet. This group of Pennacooks probably included Wattanummon (c. 1660–1712), who would capture Stephen Williams in 1704.

27. Uncas (1606?–1683 or 1684) was a leader of the Mohegan Indians in Connecticut and an ally of the English during King Philip's War. This report of his capture and sale into slavery overseas was false. However, in June 1677 Mohawks allied with the English had captured Uncas's son, Owaneco, and this incident was probably the source of the rumor that Uncas had been captured. It is also true that a number of Natives who fought with King Philip were sold into slavery after their surrender to the English.

28. Squawmaug is probably a corruption of M'skwamagok, which means salmon fishing place in Abenaki. Today this river is called the Wells River and it is located about 150 miles north of Deerfield in present-day Vermont. We want to thank Marge Bruchac for helping us identify this river.

to be above 200 miles above Deerfield; then we parted into two companies, some went one way and some went another way. And we went over a mighty mountain.[29] We were eight days a-going over it and traveled very hard, and everyday we had either snow or rain.

We noted that on this mountain all the water run[s] northward. Here also we wanted provision but at length met again on the other side of the mountain, *viz* on the north side of this mountain at a river that runs into the lake; and we were then half a day's journey off the lake.[30]

We stayed here a great while to make canoes to go over the lake. Here I was frozen, and here again we were like to starve. All the Indians went a-hunting but could get nothing. Diverse [i.e., several] days they powwowed but got nothing; then they desired the English to pray and confessed they could do nothing. They would have us pray and see what the Englishman's God could do. I prayed; so did Sergeant Plimpton in another place. The Indians reverently attended morning and night; next day they got bears. Then they would needs have us desire a blessing [and] return thanks at meals. After awhile they grew weary of it and the sachem did forbid us.

When I was frozen they were very cruel towards me because I could not do as at other times. When we came to the lake we were again sadly put to it for provision; we were fain to eat touchwood[31] fried in bear's grease. At last we found a company of raccoons, and then we made a feast, and the manner was that we must eat all. I perceived there would be too much for one time so one Indian that sat next to me bid me slip away some to him under his coat, and he would hide it for me till another time. This Indian, as soon as he had got my meat, stood up and made a speech to the rest and discovered [i.e., exposed] me so that the Indians were very angry and cut me another piece and gave me raccoon grease to drink, which made me sick and vomit. I told them I had enough so that ever after that they would give me none but still tell me I had raccoon enough. So I suffered much and, being frozen, was full of pain and could sleep but a little yet must do my work.

When they went upon the lake [i.e., Lake Champlain], and as they came to the lake, they light of [i.e., came upon] a moose and killed it and stayed there till they had eaten it all up. And entering upon the lake, there arose a great storm; we thought we should all be cast away, but at last we got to an island and there went to powwowing. The powwow said that Benjamin Wait and another man were coming and that storm was raised to cast them away. This

---

29. Part of the Green Mountain Range in Vermont. They probably passed very close to Mount Hunger and Mount Mansfield, the highest peak in Vermont.

30. The river is the Lamoille River and the lake, Lake Champlain.

31. Decayed wood with fungus.

afterward appeared to be true, though then I believed them not.[32] Upon this island we lay still several days and then set out again, but a storm took us so that we lay to and fro upon certain islands about three weeks. We had no provision but raccoons, so that the Indians themselves thought they should be starved. They gave me nothing so that I was sundry days without any provision.

We went on upon the lake, upon that isle, about a day's journey. We had a little sled upon which we drew our load. Before noon I tired, and just then the Indians met with some Frenchmen. Then one of the Indians that took me came to me and called me all manner of bad names and threw me down upon my back. I told him I could not do any more; then he said he must kill me. I thought he was about [to do] it, for he pulled out his knife and cut out my pockets and wrapped them about my face, helped me up, took my sled and went away. And [he] gave me a bit of biscuit as big as a walnut which he had of the Frenchman and told me he would give me a pipe of tobacco. When my sled was gone, I could run after him, but at last I could not run but went a foot-pace; then the Indians were soon out of sight. I followed as well as I could; I had many falls upon the ice. At last I was so spent I had not strength enough to rise again, but I crept to a tree that lay along and got upon it, and there I lay.

It was now night and very sharp weather. I counted no other but that I must die there. While I was thinking of death, an Indian hallooed, and I answered him; he came to me and called me bad names and told me if I could not go he must knock me on the head. I told him he must then so do; he saw how I had wallowed in that snow but could not rise. Then he took his coat and wrapped me in it and went back and sent two Indians with a sled. One said he must knock me on the head; the other said no, they would carry me away and burn me. Then they bid me stir my instep to see if it were frozen, I did so; when they saw that, they said [that] was *wurrengen* [i.e., *wunnegen,* "a good thing"]. There was a surgeon at the French that could cure me. Then they took me upon the sled and carried me to the fire, and they then made much of me, pulled off my wet [clothes] and wrapped me in dry clothes, made me a good bed. They had killed an otter and gave me some of the broth and a bit of the flesh. Here I slept till towards day and then was able to get up and put on my clothes; one of the Indians awakened and, seeing me go, shouted as [if] rejoicing at it.

As soon as it was light, I and Samuel Russell[33] went before on the ice upon a river.[34] They said I must go where I could on foot else I should freeze. Samuel

32. At this point, Benjamin Waite and Stephen Jennings (c. 1666–1701), whose wife, Hannah Stanhope Jennings (c. 1660– ?), and her two children by a previous marriage had been taken captive, were in fact heading north to Canada to negotiate for the captives' release.
33. Samuel Russell (c. 1669–1677) had been taken prisoner at Deerfield. He died in captivity.
34. The Richelieu River.

Russell slipped into the river with one foot. The Indians called him back and dried his stockings and then sent us away and an Indian with us to pilot us. And we went four or five miles before they overtook us. I was then pretty well spent; Samuel Russell was (he said) faint and wondered how I could live, for he had (he said) ten meals to my one. Then I was laid on the sled, and they ran away with me on the ice; the rest and Samuel Russell came softly after. Samuel Russell I never saw more nor know what became of him. They got but halfway, and we got through to Chambly about midnight.

Six miles from Chambly (a French town)[35] the river was open, and when I came to travel in that part of the ice I soon tired, and two Indians ran away to town, and only one was left. He would carry me a few rods, and then I would go as many, and that trade we drove and so were long going six miles. This Indian now was kind and told me that if he did not carry me I would die, and so I should have done sure enough. And he said I must tell the English how he helped me.

When we came to the first house there was no inhabitant. The Indian [was] spent; [we were] both discouraged; he said we must now both die. At last he left me alone and got to another house, and thence came some French and Indians and brought me in. The French were kind and put my hands and feet in cold water and gave me a dram of brandy and a little hasty pudding and milk. When I tasted victuals, I was hungry and could not have forborne it but that I could not get it. I lay by the fire with the Indians that night but could not sleep for pain. Next morning the Indians and French fell out about me because the French, as the Indians said, loved the English better than the Indians.

The French presently turned the Indians out of doors and kept me. They were very kind and careful and gave me a little something now and then. While I was here, all the men in the town came to see me. At this house I was three or four days and then invited to another and after that to another. At this place I was about thirteen days and received much civility from a young man, a bachelor, who invited me to his house, with whom I was for the most part. He was so kind as to lodge me in the bed with himself; he gave me a shirt and would have bought me but could not for the Indians asked a hundred pounds for me. We were then to go to a place called Sorel,[36] and that young man would go with me because the Indians should not hurt me. This man carried me on the ice one day's journey, for I could not now go at all. Then there was so much

---

35. Chambly was a seigneury established in 1672 by Jacques de Chambly (?–1687), a captain of the Carignan-Salières Regiment, next to a fort built in 1665. Eventually the fort took the name of Chambly as well.

36. Sorel began as a fort built in 1665 by Pierre de Saurel (1628–1682), a captain of the Carignan-Salières Regiment, and became Saurel's seigneury in 1672.

water on the ice we could go no further. So the Frenchman left me and provisions for me; here we stayed two nights and then traveled again, for then the ice was strong. And in two days more I came to Sorel.

The first house we came to was late in the night; here again the people were kind. Next day, being in much pain, I asked the Indians to carry me to the surgeon's as they had promised, at which they were wroth. And one of them took up his gun to knock me, but the Frenchmen would not suffer it but set upon him and kicked him out of doors. Then we went away from thence to a place two or three miles off where the Indians had wigwams. When I came to these wigwams some of the Indians knew me and seemed to pity me. While I was here, which was three or four days, the French came to see me, and it being Christmastime, they brought cakes and other provisions with them and gave to me so that I had no want. The Indians tried to cure me but could not; then I asked for the surgeon, at which one of the Indians in anger struck me on the face with his fist. A Frenchman being by, the Frenchman spoke to him. I knew not what he said and [he] went his way. By and by came the captain[37] of the place into the wigwam with about twelve armed men and asked where the Indian was that struck the Englishman, and took him and told him he should go to the bilboes and then be hanged.[38] The Indians were much terrified at this, as appeared by their countenances and trembling. I would have gone too, but the Frenchman bid me not fear; the Indians durst not hurt me.

When that Indian was gone, I had two masters still. I asked them to carry me to that captain that I might speak for the Indian. They answered [that] I was a fool. Did I think the Frenchmen were like to the English to say one thing and do another? They were men of their words, but I prevailed with them to help me thither, and I spoke to the captain by an interpreter and told him I desired him to set the Indian free and told him what he had done for me. He told me he was a rogue and should be hanged. Then I spoke more privately, alleging this reason: because all the English captives were not come in, if he were hanged, it might fare the worse with them. Then the captain said that was to be considered. Then he set him at liberty upon this condition, that he should never strike me more and every day bring me to his house to eat victuals. I perceived that

<hr>

37. The captain was in all likelihood Pierre de Saurel, who was actively engaged in the fur trade.

38. The French captain was threatening the Native with confinement and hanging. A bilboe consisted of a long iron bar with sliding shackles that attached to a prisoner's ankles and a lock that attached the bar to either the floor or the ground. Such punishments were rarely inflicted on Natives by the French in Canada. The captain's actions may have been prompted by the fact that France and England were at peace and had recently been allies during the Third Anglo-Dutch War from 1672 to 1674.

the common people did not like what the Indians had done and did to the English.[39]

When the Indian was set free, he came to me and took me about the middle and said I was his brother. I had saved his life once, and he had saved mine (he said) thrice. Then he called for brandy and made me drink and had me away to the wigwams again. When I came there, the Indians came to me one by one to shake hands with me, saying *wurregen netop* [i.e., *wunnegen netop*, "good," or "welcome friend"], and were very kind, thinking no other but that I saved the Indian's life. The next day he carried me to that captain's house and set me down; they gave me my victuals and wine, and, being left there awhile by the Indians, I showed the captain my fingers which, when he and his wife saw, he and his wife ran away from the sight and bid me lap [i.e., wrap] it up again and sent for the surgeon who, when he came, said he could cure me and took it in hand and dressed it. The Indians towards night came for me; I told them I could not go with them. They were displeased, called me rogue, and went away.

That night I was full of pain; the French did fear that I would die. Five men did watch with me and strove to keep me cheery, for I was sometimes ready to faint. Oftentimes they gave me a little brandy. The next day the surgeon came again and dressed me, and so he did all the while I was among the French.

I came in at Christmas and went thence May second. Being thus in the captain's house, I was kept there till Ben Waite came, and my Indian master, being in want of money, pawned me to the captain for fourteen beavers or the worth of them at such a day. If he did not pay, he must lose his pawn or else sell me for twenty-one beavers, but he could not get beaver and so I was sold.

[Addendum by the Reverend Increase Mather]

But by being thus sold he was in God's good time set at liberty and returned to his friends in New England again.[40] Thus far is this poor captive's relation concerning the changes of providence which passed over him.

There is one remarkable passage more affirmed by him. For he said that in their travels they came to a place where was a great wigwam (i.e., Indian house) at both ends was an image; here the Indians in the wartime were wont to pow-

---

39. For similar observations see Williams, "The Redeemed Captive," 107, 127. See also Letter of Claude de Ramezay, 83–86.

40. All of the captives, except John Plimpton, Samuel Russell, and Mary Foote (1674–1677), returned to New England. Returning with the captives were also two girls born in Canada: Canada Wait and Captivity Jennings.

wow (i.e., invoke the devil) and so did they come down to Hatfield, one of the images told them they should destroy a town; the other said no, half a town. This god (said that Indian) speaks true, the other was not good, he told them lies. No doubt but others are capable of declaring many passages of divine providence no less worthy to be recorded than these last recited, but inasmuch as they have not been brought to my hands, I proceed to another relation.

[Stockwell's relation is followed by the story of Ephraim How, who was shipwrecked for a year on an island off Cape Sable, Nova Scotia.]

THE CAPTURE AND DEATH OF CHEPASSON, 1690

COMMITTEE OF MILITIA AT NORTHAMPTON

I N JUNE 1690 two Native men, Chepasson and John Humphry, arrived in Deerfield. Chepasson, who had had prior dealings with Deerfield residents, came from Schaghticoke, a Native village on the east bank of the Hudson River not far from Albany, New York. This village was populated largely by Native peoples who had fled New England after King Philip's War (1675–1677) and placed themselves under the government or jurisdiction of the Mohawks of the Iroquois League. Residents of the village maintained close ties with the Eastern Abenakis in Maine and with other Native refugees from southern New England who lived at the Abenaki village of Odanak. In 1690, both of these groups of Abenakis were at war with the English and allied with the French, who were also at war with the English. Because of the Schaghticokes' continuing relations with the Abenakis, New Englanders regarded them with suspicion, even though the Schaghticokes were allies of the English. These suspicions, combined with Chepasson's actions and words, led to his imprisonment and death.

This account of Chepasson's captivity and death is not the kind of story usually classified as a captivity narrative, but it is included here because it is a reminder that Native peoples were also taken captive in seventeenth—and eighteenth-century New England. Chepasson's companion, John Humphry or Umphry, was an "Eastern Indian," a Pennacook or an Eastern Abenaki, who had been taken prisoner at some point during King Philip's War and had subsequently lived, probably as a servant, with John Gould of Topsfield, Massachusetts. Perhaps as many as a thousand Natives were taken prisoner during King Philip's War and were sold into slavery or servitude.[1] This letter also provides insight into the diverse and varied relations that existed between Deerfield's residents and Native peoples in the area. The village was a vital point in a zone of interaction involving the English, the French, and various Native peoples

---

The Committee of Militia at Northampton to Robert Treat, Esq., Northampton, June 19, 1690, Judd Manuscripts, Miscellaneous, 8:219–224, Forbes Library, Northampton, Mass. We want to thank James Spady for bringing this letter to our attention.

1. James D. Drake, *King Philip's War: Civil War in New England, 1675–1676* (Amherst: University of Massachusetts Press, 1999), 182.

that ran north to the Saint Lawrence River valley and stretched from the Hudson River valley to the coast of Maine. Schaghticokes and Native peoples in Canada came to Deerfield to trade. Mohawks of the Iroquois League stopped in the village as they returned with captives from raids on Canada. French prisoners, French traders, and French deserters found their way, willingly or unwillingly, to Deerfield. Some Native peoples who had fled the region after King Philip's War returned to settle about six miles south of the village in the mid-1690s. Finally, this letter provides a rare example of the place that enslaved blacks occupied between Native and English peoples on the New England frontier.

The letter was written by the leaders of the militia in Northampton, a town about fifteen miles south of Deerfield, to Governor Robert Treat of Connecticut. Ultimately, Deerfield's residents wanted this explanation of their actions conveyed to the Mohawks of the Iroquois League who considered the Schaghticokes and other Natives, such as Chepasson, as "belonging to their government." In this and several other incidents involving the Schaghticokes, the people of Deerfield had to obtain Iroquois approval of their actions or risk imperiling the Anglo-Iroquois alliance. A transcription of the letter has remained unpublished in the papers collected in the early nineteenth century by the Northampton antiquarian and historian Sylvester Judd.

§

These for the Honorable Robert Treat, Esq.[2]
Governor of His Majesty's Colony of Connecticut
Much Honored,

We understand from Colonel Pynchon[3] that the Maquas[4] are grieved that our men at Deerfield have seized two Indians[5] that belong to their government, and we are the more ready to give account, because we are satisfied in the cordial friendship of the Maquas, and that they will not countenance any

---

2. Colonel Robert Treat (c. 1622–1710) served as deputy governor of Connecticut from 1676 to 1683 and governor from 1683 to 1687 and from 1689 to 1698. From 1698 to 1708 he again served as deputy governor. During the late 1600s and early 1700s, officials in Hartford bore a special responsibility for the defense of the towns in neighboring western Massachusetts.

3. John Pynchon (1621–1703) of Springfield was a merchant and Indian trader who served as a magistrate and militia commander in western Massachusetts.

4. Maqua was an Algonquian name for Mohawks that was used by the English. In this instance the Mohawks referred to were members of the Iroquois League and allies of the English.

5. In contemporary English usage in New England "Indian" usually referred to Algonquian peoples and only occasionally to all Native peoples regardless of ethnicity.

treacherous or insolent carriage in such Indians as are under their jurisdiction,[6] nor desire us to suffer ourselves to be abused by any of their subjects.

The occasion of the seizing of Chepasson was not any groundless jealousy or light cause of suspicion, but such carriages as would be looked upon by any commonwealth to be intolerable. As the Indians expect friendship from us so they must carry friendly towards us and not take liberty to insult and threaten our people. If we bear such things, we shall not only lay ourselves open to contempt but betray our own lives.

The things that made the men at Deerfield [to] lay hold upon Chepasson were such as these: he acknowledged that the last year he fought for the French against the English, as is testified by Benoni Stebbins and Benjamin Barrett.[7] He having been a long time in Simon Beamon's debt,[8] and being required to pay it, he drew his knife and told him he would fight with him. He reproached the English, said they were all [only] boys and would not fight when the Frenchmen came but would cry as the Dutchmen did, and he said further that he saw the Dutchmen cry; this is testified to by Ebenezer Brooks.[9] He [i.e., Chepasson] acknowledged that the last year he was at the Eastward [i.e., Maine] as is attested by Mary Evans.[10] He threatened Benjamin Brooks to cut off his head the next day when he was weeding his corn.[11] Upon these occasions it was thought necessary to secure him. When he was in custody, he desired [that] a Negro[12] that watched him to let him have his gun that he might kill Goodman [Godfrey] Nims,[13] and on his refusal he desired his [i.e., the Negro's] knife for the same

---

6. Chepasson was living at the Native village at Schaghticoke, whose residents were under the protection of the Mohawks of the Iroquois League. These Natives were also allies of the English.

7. Benoni Stebbins (1655–1704) and Benjamin Barrett (1653–1690) were Deerfield residents. Stebbins died during the February 29, 1704, attack on Deerfield. They are suggesting that Chepasson took part in attacks on English settlements in New Hampshire and Maine during 1689.

8. Simon Beamon (1666–1712) was a Deerfield resident who was subsequently captured during the February 29, 1704, attack on Deerfield.

9. Chepasson appears to be claiming that he was present at the February 18, 1690, French and Indian raid on Schenectady, New York. Ebenezer Brooks (1662–after 1720) and his family lost their home during the February 29, 1704, raid but otherwise survived the assault unscathed.

10. Mary Evans (1652–?) was a Deerfield resident. She was also suggesting that Chepasson was involved in attacks on English settlements in Maine and New Hampshire during 1689.

11. Benjamin Brooks (1671–1755) was a younger brother of Ebenezer. He later removed to Springfield, Massachusetts.

12. The only Negro known to be living in Deerfield at this time was Robert Tigo (?–1695), a slave of the Reverend John Williams. The name Robert Tigo may be an anglicized version of Roberto Santiago, suggesting that he came to New England as a slave from a Portuguese or Spanish colony.

13. Godfrey Nims (?–1705). His home was destroyed and the members of his family killed or captured during the February 29, 1704, raid.

purpose. He [i.e., Chepasson] attempted to pull away his gun, [and] told him [that] he would not hurt him, but only Englishmen. When the watch came to the constable to take their charge, he derided them and told them the Englishmen were like boys and would not fight when the Frenchmen came, they would cry as the Dutch did.

The next day Chepasson offered the man that had the charge of him some money to let him go, which he refusing, Chepasson attempted to break away from him and being stronger than the young man got out of his hands. The man told him that if he offered to run, he would shoot him down, and as he [i.e., Chepasson] ran out of the gate he shot at him and slew him. Since the death of Chepasson, we have further evidence against him by the other Indian whom we have in custody, who confesses that [he] and Chepasson and Sossomon were at the taking of Cachecy [i.e., Cochecho, New Hampshire] at the time Major Waldron was killed.[14]

Having thus in a few words vindicated ourselves, we judge it necessary to add a few words, that we be upon some better terms with Indians that come down the river.[15] We labor under a double grievance—one is that some Indians come among us under a pretence of being friends and Albany Indians,[16] whom we have great reason to suspect for foes; the other is that some Indians who are employed against the French and make spoil upon them, do seem notwithstanding to hold some correspondence with our enemy Indians, and conceal from us such things as are of consequence to us. We understand by the Indians that we have in custody that there [is] a party of the enemy up the river who have some English captives with them. The same seems to be confirmed by the news from Albany. Yet the Indians that came in about a fortnight since with a French captive and had speech with them, told us nothing of them, nor Chepasson's company who lodged with them. And the Indians that came into Deerfield the last Sabbath will not own any such thing, and when several of our

---

14. The other Indian, John Humphry or Umphry, was an "Eastern Indian," a Pennacook or an Eastern Abenaki, taken prisoner at some point during King Philip's War. Major Richard Waldron was a prominent magistrate, military leader, and Indian trader who lived in a part of Dover, New Hampshire, known as Cochecho. In September 1676, during the waning days of King Philip's War, Waldron had used trickery to disarm and capture a group of 350 to 400 Natives that he had called to a meeting in Dover. Some of these captives were sold into slavery or servitude. On June 27, 1689, Pennacooks and Eastern Abenakis attacked Dover, killing 23 colonists and capturing 29. Among the dead was Waldron. Humphry and Chepasson were apparently among the attackers of Dover. Despite this act of revenge, memories of the 1676 Dover incident continued to fester and would be recalled by some to justify the 1704 attack on Deerfield. See Williams, "The Redeemed Captive," 109–111.

15. The Connecticut River.

16. Mahican, Schaghticoke, and Mohawk Indians who lived near Albany were often referred to as Albany Indians. See Williams, "Daniel Belding's 1696 Captivity," 57.

principal men in Northampton, Hadley and Hatfield desired to speak with the French captive that they might be informed in that matter and some other things of moment, the Indians utterly refused and went away in distaste.[17] While they carry thus we can have no dependence upon their friendship. The laws of friendship are mutual and if we must admit them into our towns, while they manifest so much good will to our enemies and contempt of us, we do not only debase but endanger ourselves. Having thus given this brief representation, we presume that you will plainly see that not the Indians but we have the greatest cause to complain. Thus with many thanks for your great readiness to do us all offices of love, and particularly for your late kindness in sending to our relief,

> We remain your humble servants,
> Aaron Cooke, Senior
> William Clark, Senior
> Joseph Hawley
> John Taylor, Senior
> Timothy Baker
> The Committee of Militia at Northampton[18]

Northampton, June 19, 1690
[Mr. Stoddard's writing][19]

---

17. This French captive was part of an original group of sixteen captives taken near the Rivière Puante [the Stinking River] opposite Trois-Rivières in New France by a raiding party of two Mohawks and thirteen Schaghticokes. They stopped at Deerfield as they returned from Canada but refused to allow their English allies to question their prisoners. Deerfield was frequently used as a stopping point by Native allies of the English as they returned from raids against New France.

18. Aaron Cooke, Senior (1613–1690), William Clark, Senior (c. 1609–1690), Joseph Hawley (1655–1711), John Taylor, Senior (c. 1641–1704), and Timothy Baker (c. 1650–1729).

19. The Reverend Solomon Stoddard (1643–1729) was the minister in Northampton from 1669 to 1729.

DANIEL BELDING'S 1696 CAPTIVITY, C. 1729

STEPHEN WILLIAMS

T HIS ACCOUNT of the captivity of John Gillett, Daniel Belding, and members of Belding's family, including his daughter Hester and his son Nathaniel, was recorded by the Reverend Stephen Williams (1693–1782) sometime around 1729. During this period Williams made several trips to Deerfield to gather stories of "the remarkable providences of God towards the people in that place in the wars with the Indians."[1] His account of Belding's captivity is an early example of the oral histories from which captivity narratives were fashioned. Unlike the captivity narratives published by the Reverends Mather, this captivity narrative has not been reworked or embellished by its clerical author. It lacks the frequent references to evidences of God's providence, citations to passages in the Bible, and the explicitly religious subplot of testing and redemption that are found in Mary Rowlandson's 1682 narrative and in John Williams's 1707 *The Redeemed Captive*. Instead, it resembles the more secular relation of Quentin Stockwell and other unpublished stories of captivity.

Daniel Belding arrived in Deerfield with his family around 1682. On September 16, 1696, a party of Mohawks from Kahnawake assaulted the village, killed four members of Daniel Belding's family, and captured him, two of his children, and two other residents of Deerfield. While returning to Canada, the Mohawks encountered a party of Natives allied with the English. In the ensuing fight, they killed two and captured two of these Indians.

The experiences of the prisoners—English and Native—provide unusual insight into the process of taking captives as it developed in the later 1600s. The Schaghticoke man who was taken captive anticipated a likely death by ritual torture, while the other Native captive, a Mohawk youth, was adopted into the

---

[Stephen Williams], *Narrative of the Captivity of Stephen Williams*, ed. George Sheldon (Deerfield, Mass.: Pocumtuck Valley Memorial Association, 1889), 14–17; and [Stephen Williams], Daniel Belding's captivity, Williams Papers, box 1, folder 10, Pocumtuck Valley Memorial Association, Deerfield, Mass. Reproduced with permission of the P.V.M.A.

1. Stephen Williams Diary, January 6, 1729, typescript transcription, microfilm edition, Historic Deerfield Library.

Mohawk village of Kahnawake. All of the English captives eventually found their way into the hands of the French, where the men worked as servants. They filled a pressing need for laborers that grew particularly acute in New France during wartime when the annual supply of indentured servants from France tended to dry up.

After the conclusion of peace with the Treaty of Ryswick in 1697, the English captives were returned to New England. John Gillett returned to New England by way of France in 1698. The Beldings returned to Deerfield in the spring of 1698. Daniel remarried within a year's time. In 1703 Hester married Ephraim Clark and settled in Stratford, Connecticut, far from the New England frontier. The elder Belding and Nathaniel escaped capture when Deerfield was attacked on February 29, 1704, but Daniel's second wife was captured and killed en route to Canada. Daniel married a third time, taking as his wife Sarah Mattoon, who had been widowed by the 1704 attack. Nathaniel died apparently unmarried in 1714.[2]

Stephen Williams's narrative of Belding's captivity was first published in 1837 as an appendix to a biographical memoir of John Williams written by Stephen West Williams, a collateral descendant of Reverend Stephen.[3] Stephen West Williams republished it in 1853 as an appendix to a new edition of *The Redeemed Captive*.[4] Deerfield's nineteenth-century historian George Sheldon published a more accurate transcription in 1889 as an appendix to Stephen Williams's narrative of his own captivity.[5] Two incomplete manuscript versions of the narrative can be found in the Williams Papers, in the collections of the Pocumtuck Valley Memorial Association. We have followed Sheldon's edition while checking it against the manuscript versions and making corrections.

§

2. George Sheldon, *A History of Deerfield, Massachusetts*, 2 vols. (Deerfield: privately printed, 1895–1896), 2:80–81, 173.

3. Stephen West Williams, *A Biographical Memoir of the Rev. John Williams, first minister of Deerfield, Massachusetts with a slight sketch of ancient Deerfield, and an account of the Indian wars in that place and vicinity; with an appendix containing the journal of the Rev. Doctor Stephen Williams, of Longmeadow, during his captivity, and other papers relating to the early Indian wars in Deerfield* (Greenfield, Mass.: C. J. J. Ingersoll, 1837).

4. John Williams, *The Redeemed Captive Returning to Zion*, ed. Stephen W. Williams (Northampton, Mass.: Hopkins, Bridgman and Company, 1853), 153–156.

5. [Stephen Williams], *Narrative of the Captivity of Stephen Williams*, ed. George Sheldon (Deerfield, Mass.: Pocumtuck Valley Memorial Association, 1889), 14–17.

September 16, 1696 John Smead[6] and John Gillett,[7] being in the woods looking [for] or tracking bees, were beset by a company of French Mohawks.[8] John Gillett was taken prisoner, and John Smead escaped. The Indians fearing a discovery by Smead, sixteen of them hastened away towards the town, and three were left with John Gillett.

It being lecture-day,[9] the people were got out of the meadows so they might attend the lecture, so that the enemy came as far as Mr. Daniel Belding's house, that was within gunshot of the fort.[10] Mr. Belding, being belated about his work, had but just got home from the fields, and left his cart that was loaded with corn, and went into the house and left his children with the cart. The Indians rushed upon them, and took him prisoner and his son Nathaniel, aged twenty-two years of age and his daughter Esther [Hester], aged thirteen years, and killed his wife and his sons Daniel and John, and his daughter Thankful. One of them took his son Samuel from the cart, but he kicked and scratched and bit so, that the Indian set him down and stuck the edge of his hatchet into the side of his head.[11] He twitched twice or thrice. [The Indian] pulled it [his hatchet] out and so left him for dead. As he came to himself he looked up and saw them running from him. [Samuel] bled considerably and brains came out at the wound and [he] went in [an] amazed condition toward the fort, til he came to the little bridge where he fell off and was carried to Mr. Williams[12] and was so bad as left for dead, but it pleased God his life was spared and his wound healed,

---

6. John Smead (1673–1720) lived out his life in Deerfield. He earned fame in the Meadows Fight in 1704, where he shot two Natives and received a wound.

7. John Gillett (1671–1755). On October 23, 1696, the Hampshire County Probate court granted administration of Gillett's estate, "he being killed or captured by the Indians, therefore as to his personal residence in Deerfield is dead." But he was not dead and he returned to New England in 1698.

8. A group of Mohawks from Kahnawake who were allies of the French.

9. A lecture was a sermon delivered during the week (in this case on a Wednesday) that addressed points of theology too technical or too abstract for a regular Sunday sermon. Lectures were often attended by neighboring ministers and one such sermon may have been given by one of the other ministers in western Massachusetts, with his clerical colleagues as well as residents of Deerfield in attendance. Attendance at such a lecture, unlike attendance at Sunday services, was not mandated by law.

10. The fort, or "great fort" as it was sometimes called, was not a military post but a stockade that had been built in 1690 by Deerfield's residents to protect ten houses situated in the center of the village.

11. Daniel Belding (1648–1731) and Elizabeth Belding (1654–1696) had the following children still living at home: Nathaniel (1675–1714), Daniel (1680–1696), Sarah (1682–?), Hester (1683–?), Samuel (1687–1750), Abigail (1690–1732), John (1693–1696), and Thankful (1693–1696).

12. The Reverend John Williams (1664–1729) was the town's minister and the author of *The Redeemed Captive*. It was not unusual for a minister to provide medical care in a town lacking a doctor.

and he is yet living.[13] He was once or twice accounted to be dying, and once accounted as dead a day or two after his being wounded. Abigail Belding, another daughter, was shot in the arm as she was running to the fort, but it was generally thought the bullet that struck her came from the fort. Sarah Belding, another of the daughters, hid herself amongst some tobacco in the chamber and escaped.

The people in the fort, being then at the public worship, were alarmed and shot from the fort, and wounded one of the enemy in the fleshy part of the thigh. The Indians fired at the fort, and wounded one Mr. [Zebediah] Williams[14] as he opened the gate.

The enemy presently withdrew,—[they] were not one quarter of an hour in doing the exploit—and were followed by some brisk young men into the meadow, who came within thirty rods of them and fired at them, and the Indians at them again, without damage on either side. The Indians killed some cattle that were feeding in the meadows. A boy that had the care of the cattle hid himself in the weeds and escaped. The enemy went up [the] Green River and came to their companions they had left with Gillett. John Smead came into the town soon after Mr. Belding's family were well off.

The first night the enemy lodged in a round hole near the river[15] above the rock[16] at Northfield,[17] where the fires were fresh [and from] thence went away for Canada by the way of Otter Creek, leaving Connecticut River (map 2). When they came near Otter Creek, they came upon some tracks of Albany Indians[18] that were going to Canada;—for in those times the Indians from Albany were wont to go scalping, as they call it, to Canada. They sent out their scouts and were upon the look-out, and at length discovered their smoke. And then they flung down their packs and painted themselves, and tied their English captives to trees and left two men to guard them, and then proceeded to their business. Having divided themselves into two companies, they set upon the secure company, which consisted of six men, and killed two of them, took two and two escaped. Among the slain was one Uroen, an Indian known among the

---

13. Samuel Belding (1687–1750) stayed in Deerfield, married in 1724, and had four or five children.

14. Zebediah Williams (1675–1706), no relation to the Reverend John Williams, was taken prisoner in October of 1703 and died in Canada in 1706. See Williams, "The Redeemed Captive," 152–153.

15. The Connecticut River.

16. Probably the rock now known as French King Rock and still visible at low water.

17. The English village of Northfield had been settled in 1673 on the site of the Sokoki village of Squakheag. It was abandoned by the English in 1675, resettled in 1685, and abandoned again in 1690.

18. Albany Indians refers to Mahicans, Schaghticokes, and Mohawks living in villages near Albany, New York. These Natives were allies of the English fighting the French and their Native allies living along the Saint Lawrence River.

English, and suspected to be a bloody fellow and sometimes mischievous to the English.[19] Of their own men, one was wounded in the fleshy part of the thigh, as one had before been at Deerfield. The prisoners were one a Schaghti-coke Indian,[20] and the other a young Albany Mohawk.[21]

When the skirmish was over, the English were brought up, and so they proceeded on their journey. Mr. Belding asked the Schaghticoke Indian (now his fellow-prisoner) what he thought the enemy would do with them. [He] replied, that they would not kill the English prisoners, but give some of them to the French, and keep some of them themselves; but he expected to be burned himself. But when they came to the lake,[22] one rainy night, they made no fires, and some of them lodged under the canoes, from which this Schaghticoke made his escape, having loosed himself by some means from his cords. And although he was pursued, the enemy could not recover him. As for the young Albany Mohawk, he was kept alive, being [one] of their own nation—the French Mohawks went from their nation over to Canada for the sake of the Romish religion.[23] When Mr. Belding and company came to the fort called Oso,[24] the males were obliged to run the gantlet. Mr. Belding, being a very nimble or light-footed man, received but few blows, save at first setting out, but the other two [men] were much abused by clubs, firebrands, and so forth.

They arrived in Canada October 9. Now they found what the Schaghticoke Indian had said to be true, for the Indians kept Mr. Belding himself and his daughter with them, and gave John Gillett and Nathaniel Belding to the French. John Gillett worked as a servant to the nuns at their farm, [and] Nathaniel Belding worked for the Holy Sisters.[25]

---

19. The Native village at Schaghticoke was populated largely by Native refugees who had fled there from New England after King Philip's War (1675–1677). Allies of the Five Nations of the Iroquois League and of the colony of New York, the Schaghticokes also maintained close ties with the Abenakis who lived at Odanak and Eastern Abenakis of Maine who were enemies of the New Englanders and allies of the French. Because of these continuing ties, New Englanders often distrusted the Schaghticokes. For a revealing example of this, see Committee of Militia, "The Capture and Death of Chepasson," 49–53.

20. A resident of the Native village of Schaghticoke.

21. A Mohawk of the Iroquois League.

22. Lake Champlain.

23. The Mohawk village of Kahnawake on the Saint Lawrence had its beginnings in a migration from the Mohawk valley of Mohawks and other members of the Iroquois League who moved north to find security and to practice the Roman Catholic faith.

24. "Oso," an English rendering of the French phrase, *au sault*, meaning "at the rapids," refers to the Jesuit mission at Sault Saint Louis, located at the Mohawk village of Kahnawake on the south shore of the Saint Lawrence River.

25. John Gillett apparently worked for the nuns of the Congregation of Notre Dame at their farm southwest of the village of Montreal at Pointe-Saint-Charles, and Nathaniel Belding worked at the hospital, the Hôtel-Dieu de Montréal, for the Hospital Sisters of Saint Joseph.

On the 9th of July following [1697], Mr. Belding was sold to the French, and lived as a servant with the priests at the Seminary.[26] His business was to wait upon them, and cut wood, make fires, and tend the garden. And [he] accounted himself favorably dealt with. In the winter following, Colonel Abraham Schuyler,[27] with some others, came to Canada, and brought with them a copy of the articles of peace between England and France,[28] and returned home with some Dutch captives.[29]

In April following [1698], Colonel Peter Schuyler,[30] and Colonel Abraham Schuyler, and the Dutch Domine,[31] with some others, came to Canada, and the French Governor[32] gave liberty to all captives, English and Dutch, to return home:—yea, allowed them to oblige all under sixteen years of age to return with them; those above that age were to be at their liberty [to leave or stay.] These Dutch gentlemen gathered up what captives, both English and Dutch, they could, and returned June 8. [They] took Mr. Belding and his children, and Martin Smith,[33] with about 20 more English, with them, and arrived at Albany in about 15 days, where the Dutch people showed to him a great deal of kindness, [and] offered to send him home directly to Deerfield. Colonel Schuyler clothed him and his children at the desire of his brother, Mr. John Belding[34] of Norwalk, [Connecticut], who paid him for the clothes, and so forth.

After about three weeks' stay at Albany, Mr. Belding and his children went

---

26. Daniel Belding worked at the Montreal seminary of the priests of the Congregation of Saint Sulpice, who were often referred to as the Sulpicians. In the published versions by Stephen W. Williams and George Sheldon, the location has been erroneously transcribed as "with the Jesuits in the Seminary."

27. Abraham Schuyler (1663–1726) was a fur trader and diplomat from a prominent Albany family.

28. The 1697 Treaty of Ryswick ended the Nine Years' War, sometimes called King William's War.

29. These Dutch captives were ethnically Dutch residents of the English colony of New York who had been taken in the 1690 raid on Schenectady. They or their ancestors had settled in the colony of New Netherland, which the English had conquered in 1664 and renamed New York.

30. Peter Schuyler (1657–1724) was Abraham's older brother. A merchant and fur trader, he served on the governor's council and was the first mayor of Albany.

31. Domine is the Dutch term for minister. Godfrey Dellius (1652–c.1714) served as the minister to the Dutch church at Albany from 1683 to 1699, where he made some efforts to convert the Mohawks to Protestantism.

32. Louis de Buade de Frontenac et de Palluau (1622–1698) was governor of New France twice from 1672 to 1682 and from 1689 until his death late in November of 1698.

33. Martin Smith (?–1704) had been captured on October 13, 1693. He returned to Deerfield in 1698 to discover that in his absence his wife, Sarah, had given birth to a child fathered by another man, had killed the child, and in turn had been executed for murder. Martin was killed during the February 29, 1704, attack on Deerfield.

34. John Belding (1650–1705?).

down the river to New York, where his brother had provided a place for his entertainment. From [New] York he went in a vessel to Stamford, and from there went to Norwalk to his friends, and after some stay there, returned to Deerfield. John Gillett got home a little before him by the way of France, and so to England, having received great kindness in England.

THE RAID

An Account of the
Destruction of Deerfield, 1704

Samuel Partridge

C OLONEL SAMUEL PARTRIDGE (1645–1740) of Hatfield was a county
judge, a member of the Governor's Council, and the most important
political leader in Hampshire County, the westernmost county of Massachusetts, when he assumed command of the county's militia regiment in
1703 following the death of Colonel John Pynchon of Springfield. He was not a
military professional by training, but he had fought in King Philip's War from
1675 to 1677 and as a lieutenant colonel in the militia had overseen the county's
northern defenses during the Nine Years' War from 1689 to 1697. To defend
western Massachusetts, Colonel Partridge depended primarily on the local
militia, the citizen soldiers of New England.

The defense of western Massachusetts was seen by authorities in Boston to be
in part the responsibility of the colony of Connecticut, since the Massachusetts
towns provided cover for the northern frontier of the neighboring colony. Colonel Partridge, however, had no authority over the governor and military officers
of the neighboring colony. In the aftermath of the February 29 Deerfield raid,
Partridge drew up a detailed report and table of losses inflicted by the French and
Indian raiders and forwarded it to Governor Fitz-John Winthrop of Connecticut
in the hope that it could secure Winthrop's assistance. Though the tone is urgent
and businesslike, concerned with the immediate military situation, elements of
Partridge's providential religious worldview are evident. His religious understanding of this military event is given fuller expression in a private letter he
wrote several weeks later that is reprinted elsewhere in this section.

It is a rare thing to have such an immediate and detailed account of a raid on
a New England village. The report itself and the table that accompanied it appear to have been composed on the spot. They undoubtedly incorporate the
first-hand accounts of survivors, as well as Partridge's own observations. It is
the most detailed English account of the assault on Deerfield and its immediate
aftermath as reinforcements poured in from neighboring Massachusetts towns
and eventually Connecticut.

The original of this report is in the Winthrop Papers at the Massachusetts Historical Society.
Reproduced from version published in George Sheldon, *A History of Deerfield, Massachusetts*, 2
vols. (Deerfield, privately printed, 1895–96),1:302–303.

§

An Account of the Destruction at Deerfield, February 29, 1703/4[1]

Upon the day of the date above said about 2 hours before day[break], the French and Indian enemy made an attack upon Deerfield, entering the fort[2] with little discovery, though it is said the watch shot off a gun and cried "arm," which very few heard. [The raiders] immediately set upon breaking open doors and windows, took the watch and others captive and had their men appointed to lead them away. Others improved in rifling houses of provisions, money, clothing, drink, and packing up and sending away. The greatest part standing to their arms, firing houses, and killing all they could that made any resistance, [and] also killing cattle, hogs, sheep and sacking and wasting all that came before them, except some persons that escaped in the crowds, some by leaping out [of] windows and some over the fortifications. Some ran to Captain Wells's garrison[3] and some to Hatfield[4] with little or no clothing on and barefooted which with the bitterness of the season caused them to come off with frozen feet and lie lame of them.

One house, *viz:* Benoni Stebbins's,[5] they attacked later than some others. That those in it were well awakened, being 7 men, besides women and children, who stood stoutly to their arms, firing upon the enemy, and the enemy [coming] upon them, causing several of the enemy to fall, of which was one Frenchman, a gentleman to [all] appearance.[6] The enemy gave back, [and] they strove to fire the house, [but] our men killed 3 or 4 Indians in their attempt. The enemy being numerous about the house, poured much shot upon the house; [but] the walls being filled up with brick, the force of the shot was repelled.[7] Yet they killed said Stebbins, and wounded one man and one woman, of which the survivors made no discovery to the assailants, but with more than ordinary courage kept firing, having powder and ball sufficient in said house. The enemy

---

1. The English still used the Julian calendar, which began the new year on March 25 rather than January 1; thus, dates in English documents between January 1 and March 25 were often written with both years.

2. "Fort" refers to the stockade built around the houses in the center of Deerfield.

3. The garrison house of Captain Jonathan Wells (1659–1739) was located south of the main stockade.

4. Hatfield was the closest town, twelve miles south of Deerfield.

5. The house of Benoni Stebbins (1655–1704) was located inside of the main stockade.

6. The French "gentleman" was undoubtedly Ensign François-Marie Margane de Batilly (1672–1704), who was mortally wounded during the attack.

7. New England builders sometimes used unfired brick to fill in the spaces between the studs in walls. This brickwork, known as nogging, was intended to insulate, not fortify, the house.

betook themselves to the next house[8] and the meeting house, both of which but about 8 rods [i.e., 44 yards][9] distant.

Our men yet plied their business and accepting of no quarter, though offered by the enemy, nor [did] capitulate, but by guns, giving little or no respite from the time they began—[they] say some of the men in the house shot 40 times and had fair shots at the enemy all the while—about an hour before day till the Sun about one hour and a half [hours] high at which time they were almost spent. Yet at the very pinch [i.e., critical moment] [and] ready to yield, our men from Hadley[10] and Hatfield—about 30 men, rushed in upon the enemy and made a shot upon them, at which they quitted their assailing the house and the fort also. The house at liberty, women and children ran to Captain Wells's fort.

The men with ours still pursued the enemy, all of them vigorously, causing many of the enemy to fall, yet being but about 40 men pursued too far, imprudently, [though] not altogether for want of conduct, for Captain Wells, who had led them called for a retreat, which they little minded. The enemy discovering their number, [and] having [laid] ambushes of men, caused our men to give back, though too late, being a mile from the fort. In their drawing off and at the fort [we] lost 11 of our men, *viz:* Sergeant Benjamin Waite,[11] Sergeant Samuel Boltwood and his son Robert Boltwood, Samuel Foot, Samuel Allis, Nathaniel Warner, Jonathan Ingram, Thomas Selden, David Hoyt, Joseph Ingersoll, and Joseph Catlin.[12] And after our men recovered the fort again, the enemy drew off, having at said house and in the engagements (as is judged by the best calculation we can come at) [they] lost about 50 men and 12 or 15 wounded (as our captive says)[13] which they carried off. And [it] is thought they

---

8. The house of Ensign John Sheldon stood just northeast of the Benoni Stebbins's house. Known as the "Indian House," it survived the attack and was not torn down until the mid-nineteenth century. The door, which was damaged in the assault, was preserved and ever since has been the centerpiece of local history exhibits.

9. There are 5.5 yards in a rod.

10. Hadley is fourteen miles south of Deerfield.

11. Benjamin Waite (1640–1704) was the husband of Martha, who had been a captive with Quentin Stockwell in 1677.

12. Robert Boltwood (1683–1704) of Hadley, Samuel Foot (c. 1676–1704) of Hatfield, Samuel Allis (1679–1704) of Hatfield, Nathaniel Warner (1681–1704) of Hadley, Jonathan Ingram (1676–1704) of Hadley, David Hoyt (1675–1704) of Deerfield, and Joseph Catlin (?–1704) of Deerfield all died in the Meadows Fight. Joseph Ingersoll (1675–1704) of Northampton and Thomas Selden (1677–1704) of Hadley were garrison soldiers who died in the fighting inside the main stockade.

13. Joseph Alexander (1681–1761) of Deerfield escaped and returned to Deerfield during the night of February 29–March 1.

will not see Canada again (and said captive [who] escaped says) they, *viz:* the enemy, went 6 miles that night.

About midnight the same night were gathered of our upper and lower towns near about 80 men which had thoughts with that number to have assaulted the enemy that night, but the snow being at least 3 foot deep and impassible without snowshoes (which we had no supply of)[14] and doubtful whether we could attack them before day, being in a capacity to follow them but in their path, [and] they in a capacity to flank us on both sides, being fitted with snowshoes and with treble our number, if not more. And some were much concerned for the captives, Mr. Williams's family especially, whom the enemy would kill, if we come on, and it was concluded we should too much expose our men.

The next day by 2 o'clock, Connecticut men began to come in and came by parties till within night at which time we were raised to 250 men in Deerfield, but the aforesaid objections and the weather very warm, and like to be so (and so it was with rain) we judged it impossible to travel, but as aforesaid to uttermost disadvantage, especially when we came up to them to an attack. (Providence put a bar in our way.) We judged we should expose ourselves to the loss of men and not be able, as the case was circumstanced, to offend the enemy or rescue our captives, which was the end we aimed at in all. Therefore desisting and having buried the dead, saved what we could of cattle, hogs and sheep, and other estate, [and] out of the spoils of the remaining inhabitants and some of our Northampton, Hadley and Hatfield men settled a garrison of 30 men or upwards under Captain Wells and drew off to our places.

---

14. While English colonists were familiar with snowshoes and their use, the men in Deerfield on February 29, 1704, were simply unprepared. On March 13, the Massachusetts legislature ordered that five hundred pairs of snowshoes and as many moccasins be sent to the frontiers, one quarter of them to the towns in western Massachusetts.

LETTER FROM WILLIAM WHITING TO GOVERNOR FITZ-JOHN WINTHROP, 1704

MAJOR WILLIAM WHITING (1659–1724) wrote this letter to Governor Fitz-John Winthrop (1638–1707) of Connecticut Colony to accompany the report and request for aid from Colonel Samuel Partridge that Whiting forwarded to Winthrop. Whiting was a member of the colony's Council of War, which was located in Hartford, and "Commander-in-Chief" of four hundred Connecticut soldiers raised to defend the colony and neighboring Hampshire County, Massachusetts. Fitz-John Winthrop had served as governor of the colony of Connecticut since 1698. At the time, Winthrop was at his home in New London, Connecticut. Despite the urgency of the situation, it is clear that the Council of War did not want to act without the governor's support.

The description of the attack contained in Whiting's letter was apparently drawn from the second-hand accounts of Connecticut militiamen who had rushed to the relief of Deerfield and possibly from Colonel Partridge's report. Though composed at some remove from the actual event, the letter does contain some crucial details. Like Partridge's report, the letter also explains in detail the reasons for not pursuing the retreating raiders.

William Whiting to Governor Fitz-John Winthrop, 1704, Winthrop Papers, Massachusetts Historical Society, Boston. This letter has been published in the *Collections of the Massachusetts Historical Society*, 6th ser. (Boston, 1889), 3:1176–177.

§

For her Majesty's Service, For the Honorable John Winthrop, Esq., Governor and Commander in Chief of her Majesty's Colony of Connecticut, these, in New London

Hartford, March the 4th 1703/04[1]

Sir:

This afternoon our forces returned from the county of Hampshire,[2] who give this sorrowful account of that action.[3] About two hours before day[break] on Tuesday morning last, some of the enemy got over the garrison [i.e., palisade] by the help of a drift of snow blown up against it, who immediately opened the gates by which means the rest entered without any opposition with horrid shouting and yelling alarmed the sleeping inhabitants and with fire and sword made lamentable desolation. It's judged the enemy consisted of between 3 or 4 hundred, the one half or more being French. By the best account [it] is supposed they killed about 49 persons and captivated near 100. The enemy it's judged have lost near forty besides wounded.

They quitted the town between 9 and 10, being pursued by a small party of about 30 men who came first to the relief of the distressed, whose courage was more worthy [of] applause than their conduct. Although they killed five, yet venturing too far lost nine [men] in the retreat ere they could recover [i.e., return to] the garrison.

When the other forces that marched up came upon the ground, a council of war was held, and by the majority concluded [it was] impractical to follow the enemy, the snow being near three foot deep. There was no traveling but in their path; therefore to venture would but expose themselves without any hopes of success. Whereupon [after] that [the Hampshire] county men returned, leaving only our men[4] in the garrison that night, who drew off the next morning. Captain Wells's house[5] with the persons therein safe, as also another[6] that was not forted, where were seven men [who] did bravely defend themselves, notwith-

---

1. The English still used the Julian calendar, which began the new year on March 25 rather than January 1; thus, dates in English documents between January 1 and March 25 were often written with both years.

2. The county then consisted of the towns along the Connecticut River that lay within the jurisdiction of Massachusetts. They formed the western frontier of Massachusetts.

3. The February 29, 1704, attack on Deerfield.

4. The militiamen from Connecticut.

5. The fortified garrison house of Captain Jonathan Wells (1659–1739), which stood south of the main stockade in the center of the village.

6. The house of Benoni Stebbins (1655–1704) stood inside the stockade and its defenders successfully beat off repeated attacks by the raiders.

standing many threatenings, promises and vigorous assaults made by the enemy.

They marched 5 or 6 miles that day as we are informed by a captive[7] that made an escape from them the first night [and] who gives this further account that his master informed him there came 600 in all over the lake,[8] whereof 200 were upon some other enterprise and not yet returned. The Council of War have signified this matter to the towns of Simsbury, Farmington, Waterbury, and Woodbury with advice to be upon their guard.[9]

Sir, this covers a letter from Colonel Partridge[10] directed to your Honor, wherein he refreshes [i.e., repeats] his desire of 60 or 70 men to be posted in those towns. Yesterday, pursuant to your Honor's letter to the gentlemen of the Council,[11] an express was sent to the Deputy Governor[12] respecting the men to be raised in the counties of New Haven and Fairfield [Connecticut], that they might be in a readiness to march as need should require, but it's possible nothing will be effected unless your Honor's pleasure be fully known in that matter. We are likewise informed some men are sent to Albany to advise them of this party of Indians, that if possible they may be intercepted in their return.

We are, Sir, you Honor's most humble and obedient servants,

By order of the Council of War,

William Whiting

[P.S.] Mr. Williams's wife and seven children [were] carried away.[13]

---

7. Joseph Alexander (1681–1761) of Deerfield escaped and returned to Deerfield on the night of February 29–March 1.

8. Lake Champlain.

9. These frontier towns in central and western Connecticut were all susceptible to attack by French and Native raiding parties.

10. Colonel Samuel Partridge (1645–1740) of Hatfield commanded the militia in western Massachusetts.

11. The Council of War.

12. Colonel Robert Treat (c. 1622–1710) served as deputy governor of Connecticut from 1676 to 1683 and governor from 1683 to 1687 and from 1689 to 1698. From 1698 to 1708 he again served as deputy governor.

13. In reality, two of the Williams children were killed outright during the attack and five taken prisoner.

LETTER FROM ISAAC ADDINGTON TO GOVERNOR FITZ-JOHN WINTHROP, 1704

I SAAC ADDINGTON (1645–1715), secretary of the colony of Massachusetts and a member of the Governor's Council, wrote this letter to Governor Fitz-John Winthrop (1638–1707) of Connecticut undoubtedly under instructions from Governor Joseph Dudley of Massachusetts, who was also the wartime commander-in-chief of the military forces of all of the New England colonies. Massachusetts looked to the colony of Connecticut to provide garrison soldiers—impressed militiamen—to help defend the towns in western Massachusetts. The need for such assistance became critical after the Deerfield raid. There were, however, limits to Dudley's ability to command his fellow governor. Rather than ordering Governor Winthrop to act, Addington writes to impress upon the Connecticut governor the critical need to act.

Addington's description of the actual attack was probably drawn from the reports of Colonel Samuel Partridge and others who conveyed to Boston first-hand accounts of Deerfield residents. So this letter is at best a second- or third-hand report of the actual attack. The letter's account of the response by local militia commanders would have been based more closely on Partridge's account of his actions.

§

Boston March 5 1703/04[1]

Honorable Sir:

It is presumed your Honor will receive an account from Colonel Partridge[2] of the tragedy acted by a party of the French & Indians, to the number of 150 or thereabout, upon the inhabitants of Deerfield on the last of February past,

---

Isaac Addington to Governor Fitz-John Winthrop, Winthrop Papers, Massachusetts Historical Society, Boston. This letter has been published in the *Collections of the Massachusetts Historical Society*, 6th ser. (Boston, 1889), 3:180–181.

1. The English still used the Julian calendar, which began the new year on March 25 rather than January 1; thus, dates in English documents between January 1 and March 25 were often written with both years.

2. Colonel Samuel Partridge (1645–1740) of Hatfield was commander of the militia in western Massachusetts.

when they entered that town some little time before the break of day, the watches being negligent of their duty, and were surprised. The enemy setting fire to the houses and killing and seizing upon the inhabitants as they came affrighted out of their houses. They have killed in all fifty seven, taken ninety captives, of which number is the minister and his family.

The fires being descried [i.e., caught sight of] at Hatfield,[3] Colonel Partridge posted away a company of sixty soldiers, who came to the place about sunrise, beat the enemy out of town, and thirty of them were left dead on the spot. And although a further reinforcement from Springfield[4] came in a short time to them, as also your forces,[5] yet no pursuit was made after the enemy; the pretense is the depth of the snow and fear least the enemy should kill the captives. About one half of the town is yet standing and a large house with good fort about it, where is Captain Wells with a sufficient number of men to defend it.[6]

And his Excellency[7] will not have it slighted; he had reinforced the place with twenty soldiers but four days before this mischief and has intimation by a captive that is escaped[8] that another party of the enemy to the number of 200 are abroad with [the] intent to fall upon some town on the river,[9] or on some of our northern frontiers. Wherefore his Excellency desires that your men may be continued sometime for the strengthening of Deerfield and Queboag[10] while ours are employed for the defense of the other parts where the enemy may be probable to make an impression [i.e., an attack]. Wherein his Excellency has given the necessary orders and has commanded me to give your Honor this brief account.

Who am, Sir your Honor's most humble servant

Isaac Addington

---

3. Hatfield is in Massachusetts, twelve miles south of Deerfield.

4. Springfield is in Massachusetts, about thirty miles south of Deerfield.

5. Militiamen from the towns around Hartford, Connecticut.

6. The home of Captain Jonathan Wells (1659–1739), the commander of Deerfield's militia, had been fortified by erecting a palisade around it. His house was south of the main stockade.

7. Governor Joseph Dudley (1647–1720) of Massachusetts was also governor-general of New England and overall commander of the military forces of New England during the War of the Spanish Succession (1702–1713).

8. Joseph Alexander (1681–1761) of Deerfield escaped and returned to Deerfield during the night of February 29–March 1.

9. The Connecticut River.

10. Brookfield, Massachusetts.

PARTRIDGE'S LAMENT, 1704

SAMUEL PARTRIDGE

T HE FOLLOWING letter by Colonel Samuel Partridge (1645–1740), the militia commander in western Massachusetts during the early 1700s, came to light only very recently, after the publication of *Captors and Captives: The 1704 French and Indian Raid on Deerfield.*[1] It survives as a typescript transcription in the correspondence of the Deerfield historian George Sheldon. The location of the original manuscript is currently unknown. This text replicates the transcription of the original made by Daniel White Wells of Hatfield and attached to a February 24, 1912, letter addressed to Sheldon. Wells, who coauthored a 1910 history of Hatfield with Reuben Field Wells and was familiar with Partridge's handwriting and signature, attested to the letter's authenticity.[2]

This letter provides some new information about the attack. Even more important, it shows how colonists in the immediate area attempted to come to terms with the raid. An abundance of writings by New England ministers document their use of such incidents to denounce the sins of their flocks, but Partridge's lament reveals the degree to which laymen shared their concerns and their understanding of such events.

Partridge was apparently writing to someone in Connecticut, but it is not clear to whom. Wells in his cover letter says that the original had been sent to him from Farmington, Connecticut. Evidently Partridge addressed his letter to a personal friend who was a public official, possibly the Connecticut governor Fitz-John Winthrop, who was in a position to send soldiers to help protect Deerfield. The letter is a prolonged jeremiad of the sort that New England clergymen were delivering in those years. Notice how even Partridge, the military commander of the region, sees the ultimate meaning of the assault not in relations between New England's residents and the French and Native peoples but in the spiritual state of New England. He did not see New England's foes as

---

Samuel Partridge to ?, Hatfield, March 31, 1704, Wars, box 1a, folder 8, Pocumtuck Valley Memorial Association, Deerfield, Mass. Reproduced with permission of the P.V.M.A.

1. Evan Haefeli and Kevin Sweeney, *Captors and Captives: The 1704 Deerfield Raid* (Amherst: University of Massachusetts Press, 2003).

2. Daniel W. Wells to George Sheldon, Northampton, February 24, 1912, Wars, box 1a folder 8, Pocumtuck Valley Memorial Association, Deerfield, Mass.

independent actors but simply tools of God's will, allowed to triumph at Deerfield in order to teach the backsliding New Englanders a lesson.

Hatfield, March 31, 1704

Kind and Loving friend,

Yours of the 23rd instant I received. I thank you for your Christian affection
therein expressed. It is not a small or little thing that has befallen us in the late
sore destruction of Deerfield but a vehement surprise to (especially the neighboring towns) all and calls for deep meditation. And as you well hint our hearts
ought to be concerned and much up in prayer and faith, that so we may the
better consider the works of the Lord and the operation of his hand, that when
his hand is lifted up we might see and be ashamed, [and] fall down in the dust
before God begging of him to show us wherefore he does contend with us in so
terrible a manner.

Indeed God has been wonderfully waiting to be gracious and striving to
show himself merciful to us, but have we not had a deaf ear to all his calls? May
we not look back with reflections upon ourselves and see how we have degen-
erated into the plant of a straying vine unto Him, declining in all orders and
stations? Have we that subjection in the rising generation, that spirit of truth,
justice, and righteous dealing, yeah, spirit for religion, love to the ways of God,
meekness, humility, fear, self-denial in the middle sort?[3] [Have we] that spirit
for godliness, plying the throne of grace, heavenly mindedness, an unspotted
conversation, hatred of sin, and the garments spotted with the flesh, terrible-
ness against it, indifferent about worldly interest, contentedness with what in
an honest way they could obtain—be it little or much—with charity and love in
the improvement of the same? [Have we] that spirit of government in families
(where the seeds of grace should be infused)? Did not both in rule there cause
submission and obedience in children and servants, else they smarted for it
with a serious admonition and instruction from the rule, as they sat down, rose
up, and walked by the way?

[We once had] towns ordering their affairs as might best promote the interest of their governments both civil and sacred [and] so fitted with men of fidelity and courage for the interest of religion and godliness, and themselves men
of truth, fearing God, hating covetousness, that under them we might have led

---

3. The "middle sort" or the "middling sort" was how contemporaries in England and its colonies described those members of society who were neither poor nor, like Partridge, members of
the elite. It is roughly comparable to the term "middle class" in its use and vague precision.

a quiet and peaceable life in godliness and honesty; the generality endeavoring to promote and uphold, yeah, strengthening the hands of authority by due testimony given in at all times against that which was sinful. Firstly, using all means in a brotherly way to recover any out of the gall of bitterness and bond of iniquity according to that rule 18 Matthew 15, 16, 17.[4] Not being afraid of ill will, but rather accounting it the only way to love in the issue, and that which is much more the favor of God.

Is it so now, or rather is it not far otherwise? Children and youth bold, impudent, refractory, foolish, wanton, ill-bred must have their own ways and wills ungoverned, yeah, if not hating government. And too much bringing them up in pride, idleness, and fullness of bread, fashioning themselves according to the world, yeah, French fashions. Mr. Boulton[5] near 100 years since [i.e., before] said in one of his books, that God would punish the English with or by the French because of their following their foolish fashions.

But will not these [things] be charged upon parents and leaders for, as it were, laying by the sword of government, only making a flourish of government, not duly executing the laws of God and man against these enormities? Hence comes in not attendance to family religious order: night walkings, company keeping, base lascivious carriages of young men and maids, drinking, [and] sporting. And then, being left of God, [they] fall into greater sins and by such means we have such number of robbers, idle companions, whore masters and whores. And when [they have] thus abused themselves and polluted the land, [only] a slender testimony given against it—a small fine—if not connived at [i.e., overlooked] and smothered [i.e., covered up] for want of due testimony.

[But] when the most pious and godly ones of the age past declared and so practiced that [for] fleshly sins, the flesh should be punished for them, [why] do we wonder now that God comes with such terrible strokes upon us? Have we not His word for it, that it shall be so? 11 Psalm throughout; the 50th Psalm from the 16th verse to the end,[6] and many other places in scripture.

---

4. Matthew 18:15 "Moreover if thy brother shall trespass against thee, go and tell him his fault between thee and him alone: if he shall hear thee, thou has gained thy brother." Matthew 18:16 "But if he will not hear thee, then take with thee one or two more, that in the mouth of two or three witnesses every word may be established." Matthew 18:17 "And if he shall neglect to hear them, tell it unto the church: but if he neglect to hear the church, let him be unto thee as an heathen man and a publican."

5. Robert Bolton (1572–1631), a Puritan minister in Northamptonshire, England, who published several books on issues involving materialism and spirituality, such as usury. Among the titles is *Helps to Humiliation*.

6. Psalm 11 "In the Lord put I my trust: how say ye to my soul, flee as a bird to your mountain? For, lo, the wicked bend their bow, they make ready their arrow upon the string, that they may privily shoot at the upright in heart. If the foundations be destroyed, what can the righteous

And in the middle sort [there is] a worldly spirit, might and main, striving to set up themselves in the world. Right or wrong [they are] endeavoring for it. Thence men have so many cheating ways and tricks to overreach one another, the effects [being] bartering and trading cannot endure. [They] do not inure themselves to labor, [but] spend abundance of their times in smoking and drinking and some to drunkenness besot themselves, so they are not fit to do service for God nor themselves and families. Multitudes of them turn their backs upon attending on God in all the ways and ordinances of His own appointment, under pretence of not being fit. And when will they be fit, think you, in such a way?[7]

Instead of a humble, penitent, mourning, repentant spirit, [there is] a spirit of murmuring and complaining, contentious backbiting hypocrisy, yet pretending for and desiring pre—[a line is missing here because of a tear in the original letter] the life and power of godliness. It is not serving God in word and in tongue that God requires, but in deed and in truth, denying ungodliness and fleshly lusts which war against the spirit.

We have need to pray for judges as at the first, and councilors, as at the beginning, for want of which the whole head is sick and the heart is faint.[8] For these things' sake the wrath of God comes on the children of disobedience. If we become a people of no understanding, He that made them will not save

---

do? The Lord is in his holy temple, the Lord's throne is in heaven: his eyes behold, his eyelids try, the children of men. The Lord trieth the righteous: but the wicked and him that loveth violence his soul hateth. Upon the wicked he shall rain snares, fire and brimstone, and an horrible tempest: this shall be the portion of their cup. For the righteous Lord loveth righteousness; his countenance doth behold the upright." Psalm 50:16–23 "But unto the wicked God saith, What hast thou to do to declare my statutes, or that thou shouldest take my covenant in thy mouth? Seeing thou hatest instruction, and castest my words behind thee. When thou sawest a thief, then thou consentedst with him, and hast been partaker with adulterers. Thou givest thy mouth to evil, and thy tongue frameth deceit. Thou sittest and speakest against thy brother; thou slanderst thine own mother's son. These things hast thou done, and I kept silence; thou thoughtest that I was altogether such an one as thyself: but I will reprove thee, and set them in order before thine eyes. Now consider this, ye that forget God, lest I tear you in pieces, and there be none to deliver. Whoso offereth praise glorifieth me: and to him that ordereth his conversation aright will I shew the salvation of God."

7. Partridge is criticizing those men and women who felt themselves unworthy and refused to become full church members and take communion, i.e., "attending on God in all the ways and ordinances of His own appointment." The minister in the neighboring town of Northampton, the Reverend Solomon Stoddard (1643–1729), was arguing that all morally upright adults had a duty to take communion and become full members of the church. The minister in Hatfield, the Reverend William Williams (1665–1741), a first cousin of the Reverend John Williams's, echoed Stoddard's calls.

8. Partridge is here referring to the time in early Biblical history known as the time of the Judges when the Israelites were ruled by political chiefs and religious prophets, the judges and councilors he mentions. The head and heart he is talking about here are those of the nation, often literally conceptualized as a human body at this time.

them. How much cause have we to cry mightily to God for the pouring forth of a spirit of grace and supplication on the generations coming, that they might not be a generation for wrath brought forth for the murderer and destroyer!

But to return to the awful token of God's displeasure in the sad and lamentable breaking waves of anger upon Deerfield. That so holy and good a man as the Reverend Mr. John Williams was, should, with 26 members of his church, be killed and carried into captivity! How amazing is this! The like has not been paralleled in New England.

What shall we say? As our Savior Christ said, were they greater sinners? No, surely, but rather, according to the best observation, more exact walkers than others in as much as they in a special manner had the rod of the enemy almost always over them, and it is well known [they] had more religious exercises than others, both by private meetings and public.

But what shall we say? If this be done to the green tree, what will become of the dry? The days may be coming, if not begun, that shall burn as an oven, and the proud shall be as stubble to that fire. It is a great frown that the Holy God sees meet to punish us with a false religion for our falseness in the true religion. We need your prayers and [those] of all good friends to cry mightily in [i.e., on] the behalf of us and of this poor land.

The surprise and advantage of the enemy was great, taking them mostly if not all asleep. Yet the providence of God is to be observed that the enemy could not destroy the whole, spiriting [i.e., inspiring] those seven in Benoni Stebbins' house to hold it against such a multitude. Yeah, after said Benoni[9] was killed, one man wounded and a woman [too], yet the other five holding it still notwithstanding the great proffers of good quarter if they [would] yield, the woman pleading hard for it and the house set on fire.

Yet at a window they killed the Indian that did it [i.e., set it on fire] at one end, who fell in his own fire and partly burned. Another attempted to burn it at the other end; one of the men slipped out at the door and shot him down, though they poured in shot on the house in great measure all the while.

Our discovery also of the light to Hatfield, upon which our men were almost ready to go before we had any post. Their resolution came to bear on the enemy before this little remainder [i.e., in those in the Stebbins house] had yielded, though [they were] upon the point of doing it. Upon which with about 40 of our men they made the enemy quit the fort, though [the enemy was] treble in number it is thought. Which, if it had not thus happened [and] the enemy

---

9. Benoni Stebbins (1655–1704) had been taken prisoner with Quentin Stockwell in 1677, but he returned to settle in Deerfield in the early 1680s.

had liberty but one hour more, doubtless they would have utterly destroyed the place. Thus in the mount God was seen, etc.

As the good martyr Anne Askew [10] said, pray, pray, pray, that God would be pleased to look down from heaven and see the innocents that the enemy hath spoiled and bereaved of house, home, relations, children, near and dear ones. Led into captivity or burned, 97; slain and stifled [i.e., smothered] in cellars and others [killed] in the [meadows] fight, 62; destroyed 30 houses and barns and in them and otherwise destroyed near £4000 worth of estate. We may say with the church in the lamentations, fear and snare is come on us, waste and destruction for which our eyes trickle down with tears without intermission. [11]

Your encouraging words as to men for our help is some encouragement to us. I pray promote it. Our lives hang in doubt and [as for our] estates we may look for destruction upon destruction until the Lord look down upon us. There is our greatest hope: they can go no further than God permits them. And were we fitted for deliverance, God could soon bring it about. But I shall trouble you too much with my broken discourse and therefore bid you farewell. Remember us at all times.

Your afflicted friend and servant,
Samuel Partridge

---

10. Anne Askew (1521–1546) was a Protestant gentlewoman burned at the stake as a heretic at the end of King Henry VIII's reign. John Foxe (1516–1587) included her story in his famous book *Acts and Monuments,* otherwise known as Foxe's book of martyrs, and thus immortalized her memory among English Protestants.

11. Lamentations of Jeremiah 3:47, 49: "Fear and a snare is come upon us, desolation and destruction"; "Mine eye trickleth down, and ceaseth not, without any intermission."

Philippe de Rigaud
M^{ts} de Vaudreuil
gouverneur du Canada
1650 + 1725

FIGURE 5. Philippe de Rigaud de Vaudreuil (c.1643–1725). Oil portrait, copied from the original, Henri Beau, 1923. A younger son of an old noble family of the province of Languedoc, Vaudreuil moved to New France in 1687 as an officer in the *troupes de la marine*. He married a Canadian woman and spent the remainder of his career in the colony, serving as governor from 1703 to 1725. Photograph courtesy of the National Archives of Canada, C010614.

LETTER FROM PHILIPPE DE RIGAUD DE VAUDREUIL TO THE MINISTER OF THE MARINE, 1704

T HE FOLLOWING document was the first French report of the raid against Deerfield, written within days of the French raiders' return to Canada. It was sent by the governor-general of New France, Philippe de Rigaud de Vaudreuil (c.1643–1725), to Jérôme Phélypeaux, Comte de Pontchartrain et de Maurepas (1674–1747), the minister of the marine who was in charge of the colonies from 1699 to 1715. Vaudreuil came from a noble family from the south of France that was not wealthy. He, like his father and two brothers, took up a career in the army. After fighting in Europe, he came to New France in 1687 as a captain in the colonial troops and immediately joined in the war against the Iroquois. His service and lineage convinced his superiors to promote him to governor of Montreal, commander of the troops, and finally in 1703, governor-general of New France. He well appreciated the importance of military service and patronage in the making and sustaining of a noble reputation (figure 5).

The minister stored this letter with all the other correspondence from the colonies in the official colonial archives, where it can still be found. This particular letter is exceptional, however. Usually the governor would compose a full report of all the important events in the colony in which a military expedition, such as that directed against Deerfield, would be only one of many incidents discussed. In fact, this is the case when the Deerfield raid is mentioned elsewhere in French sources. But, as our translation indicates, this letter is devoted entirely to the Deerfield raid and the consequences it held for the French.

The governor saw the Deerfield raid as part of a group of strategic concerns stretching from the western post of Detroit to Newfoundland and Acadia in the east. Most of his concerns focused on maintaining critical relationships with Native peoples who were allies or potential enemies. Of overriding importance to the governor was maintaining the peaceful disposition of the Iroquois League, whose member nations had, until the Great Peace of 1701, waged a destructive war against New France. Because he feared angering the Iroquois, he refrained from attacking the English in the colony of New York

---

Vaudreuil to Minister, 3 April 1704, C11A, 22:32–33, Archives Nationales de France, Paris.

and instead directed raids against the frontier towns of New England, such as Deerfield. Even the Abenakis' place in his calculations, though important, depended on their ability to counterbalance both the English and the Iroquois. Launching the raid on Deerfield in retaliation for English attacks on Abenaki villages helped demonstrate to the Abenakis the value of remaining allied to the French.

Preserving the avid support of nobles who served as officers in the colonial regulars stationed in Canada also played an important role in maintaining the security of New France. When a raid went well, as it arguably did at Deerfield, it gave New France's governor-general a chance to distribute patronage, an important part of his political power. Those officers who distinguished themselves by their service and loyalty could expect to be rewarded. The governor did not have the power to grant promotions in rank, but the minister of the marine, who did, relied on his recommendations. Military rank was a prized emblem of noble status, particularly for those who did not come from a wealthy, well-established noble family. Service as a military officer was also a valuable source of income, especially in a place like New France, where the traditional sources of noble revenue, from rents to seigneurial dues, produced little income. Thus Vaudreuil's request for favors was a matter of great consequence to the Canadian-born French officers who went on the Deerfield raid.

§

Monsieur de Vaudreuil
3 April, 1704
My Lord,

Sir De Subercase[1] having informed us by a ship that came here from Plaisance[2] last autumn of his need for us send him provisions, Monsieur the Intendant[3] and I judged it appropriate to allow several small ships to go there, and I am taking advantage of this occasion, My Lord, to inform you of what has happened in this country since the departure of *La Seine*.[4]

Neutrality continues to last with the Iroquois, My Lord, and I will not be the

---

1. Daniel D'Auger de Subercase (1661–1732) commanded a company of the colonial regulars stationed in New France from 1687 until he was appointed governor of Plaisance (or Placentia), the French colony in Newfoundland, in 1702. In 1706 he became governor of Acadia, where he fought off two English attacks before having to surrender to a third in 1710, making him Acadia's last governor.

2. Plaisance was the center of the French colony in Newfoundland.

3. The intendant, François de Beauharnois de la Chaussaye, Baron de Beauville (1665–1746), was in charge of the legal and financial affairs of the colony.

4. *La Seine* was the annual supply ship that sailed between France and New France.

one to break it. Following my intentions which I had the honor of informing you of in my last letter I am making no war that could turn them against us, sparing on their behalf the inhabitants of the lands of Albany. The lands of Boston are a different story, My Lord, as I have already had the honor of informing you.[5] The Abenakis having informed me that the English had killed some of their people the last fall and asking for my help, I sent this winter a party of 250 men, French as well and Indians, commanded by Sir De Rouville, *lieutenant reformé*[6] who acquitted himself very worthily. They took 150 prisoners and did not know the number of dead.[7] My Lord, he is an officer who deserves that you have the kindness to think of his advancement. He has not missed a war party since the war against the English has begun in this country. He commanded the one of last fall with Sir De Beaubasin.[8] He was wounded in this last one[9] and had with him four of his brothers.

Sir De Maricourt has died.[10] It is a great loss. He had a great deal of credit and authority among the Iroquois and I was counting on sending him there this spring. I know of no one other than his brother, Sir De Longueuil,[11] who can take his place and continue the deceased's work effectively. The Iroquois regard this family, My Lord, as being entirely in their interest, and it is of the greatest consequence for us to always have someone who has credit and authority with them to counterbalance the English who are ceaselessly within their villages.

My Lord, I continue to apply all my efforts to draw the Abenakis of Acadia[12] to our settlements, and if I can succeed as I hope to, I believe I will have ren-

---

5. The lands of Albany and Boston are the English colonies of New York and New England, which the French tended to refer to by their principal cities.

6. Jean-Baptiste Hertel de Rouville (1668–1722). A *lieutenant reformé* was a lieutenant on half-pay.

7. Fifty men, women, and children died in the attack. One hundred and twelve were taken prisoner. Two of these prisoners escaped. Nineteen were killed on the march to Canada and two starved to death.

8. Alexandre Leneuf de la Vallière de Beaubassin (1666–1712) was the son of a governor of Acadia. He and De Rouville commanded the French expedition that attacked Maine in August 1703.

9. The February 29, 1704, Deerfield raid; see Hertel Memoire, 210.

10. Paul Le Moyne de Maricourt (1663–1704) was the fourth of twelve brothers, several of whom became famous and influential military officers. Maricourt fought in the Nine Years' War (1689–1697) but made his mark in Iroquois diplomacy. He had been adopted into the Onondagas and used his position to help negotiate the Great Peace of 1701.

11. Charles Le Moyne de Longueuil (1656–1729) had been made a baron in 1700 with the support of the French governor-general-the only native-born Canadian to reach such a high rank of nobility. He had also been adopted by the Onondagas and took over his brother's role as diplomat to the Onondagas.

12. For the French at this time, Acadia generally referred to all the lands that now constitute the state and provinces of Maine, New Brunswick, and Nova Scotia.

dered a great service to his majesty and to the country, all the more so as this will allow us to no longer fear the Iroquois, having as many Indians as they.

The prisoners taken from the last place [i.e., Deerfield] claim, My Lord, that there is a real threat that we will be attacked this summer, and I do not tell you this as something absolutely certain but I promise you that I will neglect nothing to receive them well.

In this last raid, My Lord, we only lost three Frenchmen and several Indians. One of the three Frenchman was Sir De Batilly, ensign,[13] a very brave man and the second of his family[14] who has been killed in the service of the King. He has a brother named Sir Desforest,[15] a petit officer who very much deserves, My Lord, that you have the goodness to award him the rank his brother held.

As you desire, My Lord, I request the continuation of the happiness of your protection and I flatter myself with the honor of your remembrance of the favors that I asked of you this autumn.

I am, with deepest respect, My Lord,

Your very humble and obedient servant,
Vaudreuil
At Montreal this 3rd of April 1704.

---

13. François-Marie Margane de Batilly (1672–1704) was born in Montreal, the son of a French officer. Though noble, his father was not rich, undoubtedly inspiring François-Marie to make his mark as a brave soldier.

14. Charles Séraphin Margane de Lavaltrie (1669–1693) was killed during the Nine Years' War.

15. François Margane de Lavaltrie (1685–1750), like his brother, was an officer in the troops. He served in Labrador from 1701 until 1737. After his wife died in 1739 he became a priest, serving in and around Quebec until his death.

LETTER FROM CLAUDE DE RAMEZAY TO THE MINISTER OF THE MARINE, 1704

C LAUDE DE RAMEZAY (1659–1724) came from a Burgundian noble family whose prominence and wealth allowed him to enter with ease the highest levels of society in New France. Only five years after arriving as a lieutenant in the colonial troops in 1685, he purchased the post of governor of Trois-Rivières and married into one of the colony's leading families. Unlike poorer nobles such as Vaudreuil, who had to attain their status through hard fighting, Ramezay proved his nobility through his hospitality and building projects. Immediately after becoming governor of Trois-Rivières in 1690, he built two large stone houses. When he became governor of Montreal in 1704 he built another large stone house. These buildings remain architectural landmarks of Quebec's colonial past, enduring testaments to Ramezay's vision of his own status (figure 6).

Ramezay's aspirations brought him into conflict with Philippe de Rigaud de Vaudreuil (c. 1643–1725), New France's governor-general. He had the wealth, power, status, and connections to question Vaudreuil's judgment. And that is what he would do on several occasions during his tenure as governor of Montreal (1704–1724). Their rivalry manifested itself in disputes over the fur trade, colonial politics, and, as seen here, wartime strategy. Unfortunately for Ramezay, Vaudreuil was better at trans-Atlantic French politics. For most of his term as governor (1703–1725), Vaudreuil, with the help of his wife, Louise-Élizabeth de Joybert de Soulanges et de Marson (1673–1740), stayed on good terms with enough people in France and New France that he largely had his way and did not suffer any serious criticisms. As a result, his version of events on everything from disputes over the fur trade to the Deerfield raid predominated.

Ramezay's version of the Deerfield raid did not make it into the official French record. The minister in Paris soon rebuked him for his criticisms of Vaudreuil. But Ramezay's account is notable for two reasons. First, it is more

Ramezay to Minister, 14 November 1704, C11A, 22:71–81, Archives Nationales de France, Paris. The extracts are from verso 76 and 77 recto. A more legible version of this text can be found on pages 20–22 in a transcription of the letter contained in the Parkman Papers, vol. 62, Archives de la Marine, 1704–1709, Massachusetts Historical Society, Boston.

FIGURE 6. Claude de Ramezay (1659–1724). Miniature watercolor, copied from a portrait in the possession of descendants, date unknown, artist unknown. Ramezay, who came from a noble Burgundian family descended from Scottish immigrants, arrived in Canada in 1685 as a lieutenant in the *troupes de la marine* and was soon promoted to captain. In 1690 he obtained the post of governor of Trois-Rivères and married into one of New France's leading families. In 1704 he became governor of Montreal, a post he held until his death. Chateau Ramezay Museum collection, Montreal, 1998.1024.

factually accurate, downplaying the strength of Deerfield and the success of the raid. Second, it is critical of both the strategy of raiding New England that Vaudreuil and the Hertels thrived on and the use of Native allies. Although Cotton Mather once called the French and Indians "half one half the other, half Indianized French and half Frenchified Indians," his characterization clearly was not always appropriate.[1] The logic that had led to the Deerfield raid was not emblematic of an intrinsic compatibility between French and Indians but the result of a specific series of accommodations made by certain men. In short, it was a political choice, and a contested one at that. Notice Ramezay's concerns, his attitude toward Native peoples and the English captives and how they differ from Vaudreuil's priorities.

Vaudreuil had rushed to send news of the Deerfield raid in a special letter in early April.[2] Ramezay did not write about it until November in his end-of-the-year report to Jérôme Phélypeaux, Comte de Pontchartrain et de Maurepas (1674–1747), the minister of the marine. The Deerfield raid is only one of several events and problems reported on in a long letter of ten double-sided pages. Only the passages directly related to the Deerfield raid have been translated and reprinted here. Ramezay's criticisms went nowhere, but the attitudes that they reflected became increasingly influential in New France until these concerns came to a head during the Seven Years' War (1754–1763).[3] At stake was nothing less than the alliances between the French and Native peoples.

§

14 November, 1704
At Quebec
My Lord,
[**The letter begins with a lengthy discussion of local issues in New France, the fur trade, and Indian policy in the west before turning to the war against the English.**]
. . . Monsieur De Vaudreuil, instead of carrying out the plan of attack that I had put together, and that I had the honor to inform you of last year of going

---

1. Cotton Mather, "New Assaults from the Indians," in *Puritans among the Indians: Accounts of Captivity and Redemption, 1676–1724*, ed. Alden T. Vaughan and Edward W. Clark (Cambridge: Harvard University Press, 1981), 137. Mather's observation refers to the French and Native raiders who attacked Salmon Falls, New Hampshire, in 1690. The raid was led by Joseph-François Hertel de la Fresnière (1642–1722). He was accompanied by three of his sons, including Jean-Baptiste Hertel, the French leader of the 1704 raid on Deerfield.

2 See Letter from Philippe de Rigaud de Vaudreuil, 79–82.

3 See, for example, Ian K. Steele, *Betrayals: Fort William Henry and the "Massacre"* (New York: Oxford University Press, 1990).

this spring with seven or eight hundred Frenchmen and whatever Indians we could find to ravage the settlements above Boston from Salem to Piscataway,[4] where there is reason to believe that being masters of the countryside, we would have done much damage to the enemies of the King and we would have much glory for the nation, [and] the confidence of our mission Indians as well as the others, instead the actions he has taken which have produced exactly the opposite effect, as you will soon learn, My Lord.

Last winter Monsieur de Vaudreuil sent a detachment of forty-eight Frenchmen and about two hundred Indians who captured a small village of around forty houses, where they defeated or took prisoner about one hundred and fifty persons of all ages and of all sexes. They killed eleven men and about twenty-five women or children.[5] We lost in this expedition eleven French and Indians who were killed. It is impossible to imagine the cruelties carried out by the Indians on the return journey, killing about fifty-six women and children in cold blood,[6] which discredits the French nation, seeing that it was a man named Rouville, a *lieutenant reformé* in our troupes,[7] who commanded this party, to whom one can impute this cruel deed against the rights of man. They have, as we have learned, taken reprisal against Acadia,[8] which they have practically desolated and reduced to beggary without us having made any sort of effort to help that poor fledgling colony, even though we knew about it since the month of July, and it would have been easy to do so since there is an abundance of boats and wheat here. It is very much to be feared that the habitants, being unable to subsist except with the help of the English, will surrender to them.[9]

[**Ramezay moves on to a critical discussion of other expeditions against the English in Newfoundland and New England and problems with diplomacy and the fur trade in the Great Lakes region before closing.**]

My Lord,

> Your very humble, very grateful
> and very obedient servant,
> De Ramezay

---

4 The Piscataqua River in New Hampshire.

5 Fifty men, women, and children died in the attack.

6 Nineteen prisoners were killed on the march to Canada and two starved to death.

7 Jean-Baptiste Hertel de Rouville (1668–1722). A *lieutenant reformé* was a lieutenant on half-pay.

8 To avenge the assault on Deerfield, an expedition of roughly six hundred English and Native allies spent May and June 1704 ravaging the coasts of Acadia, killing a number of Abenakis and French, burning the French village of Grand Pré, and taking one hundred prisoners back to Boston.

9 Part of French Acadia was conquered by the English in 1710. Ever since then it has been known as Nova Scotia.

ENGLISH NARRATIVES

FIGURE 7. The Reverend John Williams (1664–1729). Oil portrait, c. 1707 (detail), artist un-known. It is believed that this portrait was painted around the time of Williams's return from New France. The painting of this portrait is one indication of the celebrity Williams experienced after his return from captivity. Photograph by Amanda Merullo, courtesy of Historic Deerfield, Inc.

THE REDEEMED CAPTIVE
RETURNING TO ZION, 1707

JOHN WILLIAMS

I N HIS lifetime the Reverend John Williams was often compared to Job because of his sufferings and those of his family.[1] Born in 1664 into the family
of a well-to-do Roxbury, Massachusetts, tanner and farmer, he graduated
from Harvard in 1683. He began preaching in Deerfield in 1686 and was
ordained in 1688. He married Eunice Mather, who was the daughter of the
late Reverend Eleazer Mather of Northampton—Increase Mather's brother
and Cotton Mather's uncle—and the stepdaughter of the Reverend Solomon
Stoddard of Northampton. This marriage allied Williams to three of the most
powerful and influential ministers in New England. Despite these connections,
he probably would have remained a relatively obscure rural parson if not for
the 1704 raid and the price that he and the members of his family paid. His
wife, Eunice, two of their children, and their two slaves were killed, while John
and five other of his children were taken captive. All but his daughter Eunice
returned. John remarried, resettled in Deerfield, and served his parishioners
until his death in June 1729 (figure 7).

Although in retrospect the publication of *The Redeemed Captive* appears to
have been inevitable, its writing and printing was an unusual, even remarkable
event. Publication of a compelling and instructive story, literary skill notwithstanding, was unlikely for most captives. Frontier residents, including "most
pastors in war-torn areas," had little time to write.[2] For those individuals who
did write, writing did not automatically translate into publication. There are at
least three other narratives by Deerfield captives taken in 1704 and none of them

---

This modernized text of *The Redeemed Captive* is based on the first printings of 1707 and draws
on three modern editions: *The Redeemed Captive Returning to Zion*, ed. Stephen West Williams
(Northampton, Mass.: Hopkins, Bridgman and Company, 1853); *The Redeemed Captive*, ed. Edward
W. Clark (Amherst: University of Massachusetts Press, 1976); and "The Redeemed Captive Re-
turning to Zion," in *Puritans among the Indians: Accounts of Captivity and Redemption, 1676–1724*, ed.
Alden T. Vaughan and Edward W. Clark (Cambridge: Harvard University Press, 1981), 167–226.

1. Job, the central figure of the Bible's Book of Job, is a pious, upright man whose faith is
tested by a series of misfortunes that God allows Satan to inflict. Through his trials Job learns to
accept God's judgment of him even if he cannot understand it.

2. George Selement, "Publication and the Puritan Minister," *William and Mary Quarterly*, 3rd
ser. 37, no. 2 (April 1980): 62.

was published during the author's lifetime. Oral traditions of the raid also existed in Deerfield. But only John Williams's story made it into print during the 1700s.

Publishing anything in colonial New England was an expensive proposition. Colonial authors or their sponsors had to pay if they wanted to be seen in print. Because of their long-standing ties to printers, the Reverends Increase and Cotton Mather usually played critical roles in bringing the first captivity narratives, including that of John Williams, into print. Cotton Mather felt strongly that Williams, the first New England minister to be taken prisoner by the French and Indians, had a particular responsibility to address concerns raised by his captivity. Immediately after Williams's return, Mather "sat with him and united counsels with him, how the Lord might have Revenues of Glory from his Experiences." Mather "particularly employed him, to preach my Lecture, unto a great Auditory (the General Assembly then also sitting) and, directed him, to show how great things God had done unto him." [3] This meeting produced Williams's 1706 sermon, "Reports of Divine Kindness" and inspired the writing and publication of *The Redeemed Captive* in 1707.

Despite the encouragement from Mather, the resulting narrative was the work of John Williams and incorporated attitudes that Mather did not share. Like Mather, Williams "improved" his experiences while a captive by putting his captivity within a framework of providential history. The captives' physical trials and spiritual afflictions at the hands of the French and the Indians provided religious lessons for Williams and the readers of his narrative. The loss of relatives, neighbors, and worldly goods taught them to depend solely on their faith in God, not their own efforts. Evidence of kindnesses and mercy by their captors were also due to God's providence. The Deerfield pastor hoped that these stories would provide inspiration for individual reformation and redemption and by this means produce a general reformation throughout all of New England. Williams's interpretations or "improvements" of his flock's captivity placed his text within the established traditions of both the public jeremiad and personal religious devotions that Cotton Mather and his father Increase had been promoting with captivity narratives during the preceding quarter century.

In other respects Williams's narrative broke with previous captivity narratives and the immediate political interests of the Mathers. The text's effusive dedication to Joseph Dudley at a time when the Mathers were working to secure his removal as governor of Massachusetts was a clear political signal of

---

3. [Cotton Mather], *Diary of Cotton Mather*, 2 vols. (Boston: Massachusetts Historical Society, 1911–1912), 1:567–568.

where Williams stood in the growing political controversy. Williams also emphasized that his return had depended on the release of the French privateer known as Captain Baptiste, an exchange opposed by the Mathers and commercial interests in Boston. In addition to shoring up support for an embattled royal governor, Williams's narrative sought to unite the people of New England by rallying them against the Catholic menace in New France. He devoted three-quarters of his text to debates with priests in Canada rather than to trials at the hands of Native captors and turned his book into more of an anti-Catholic tract than an Indian captivity narrative, though it clearly retained classic elements and concerns of this genre. Employing the rhetoric of antipopery against New England's Catholic foes, Williams deflected outward the internal animosities generated by the struggle between Dudley and his opponents and thus began *The Redeemed Captive's* dual career as captivity narrative and political pamphlet.[4]

After its publication in 1707, *The Redeemed Captive* was republished in 1720, 1758, 1773, 1774, 1776, 1793, 1795, 1800, 1802, 1811, and 1853. While continuing battles with French and Native American peoples undoubtedly played a role in promoting the subsequent publication of this captivity narrative, its reprinting usually owed more to internal battles: conflicts involving royal governors, agitation preceding the American Revolution, ideological divisions marking the early national period, and Protestant fears of Catholicism and Catholic immigrants. Conflict, not consensus, kept this particular captivity narrative in print—intermittently, given the ebb and flow of New England politics—for over a century, insuring that *The Redeemed Captive* reached the numbers of readers that it did and eventually joined the canon of early American literature.[5]

---

4. For the political context in which *The Redeemed Captive* was published, see Evan Haefeli and Kevin Sweeney, *Captors and Captives: The 1704 French and Indian Raid on Deerfield* (Amherst: University of Massachusetts Press, 2003), 164–184.

5. For a discussion and interpretation of the subsequent publication history of *The Redeemed Captive,* see Evan Haefeli and Kevin Sweeney, "*The Redeemed Captive* as Recurrent Seller: Politics and Publication, 1707–1853," *New England Quarterly* (September 2004): 341–367.

§

The DEDICATION

TO HIS EXCELLENCY,
JOSEPH DUDLEY, ESQ,
Captain-General and Governor-in-Chief,
in and Over Her Majesty's Province of the
Massachusetts Bay, in New England, etc.[6]

Sir.—It was a satirical answer, and deeply reproachful to mankind, which the philosopher [i.e., Aristotle] gave to that question, "What soonest grows old?" [He] replied, "Thanks." The reproach of it would not be so sensible, were there not sensible demonstrations of the truth of it in those that wear the character of the ingenious. Such as are at first surprised at and seem to have no common relish of divine goodness, yet too soon lose the impression: "They sang God's praise, but soon forgot His works." That it should be thus with respect to our benefactors on earth is contrary to the ingenuity of human nature; but that our grateful remembrance of the signal favors of heaven should soon be worn off by time is to the last degree criminal and unpardonable.

It would be unaccountable stupidity in me, not to maintain the most lively and awful sense of divine rebukes which the holy God has seen meet in spotless sovereignty to dispense to me, my family, and people, in delivering us into the hands of them that hated us, who led us into a strange land: "My soul has these still in remembrance and is humbled in me." However, God has given us plentiful occasion to sing of mercy, as well as judgment. The wonders of divine mercy, which we have seen in the land of our captivity, and deliverance therefrom, cannot be forgotten without incurring the guilt of the blackest ingratitude.

To preserve the memory of these, it has been thought advisable to publish a short account of some of those signal appearances of divine power and goodness for us, hoping it may serve to excite the praise, faith, and hope of all that love God, and may peculiarly serve to cherish a grateful spirit, and to render the impressions of God's mighty works indelible on my heart, and on those

---

6. Joseph Dudley (1647–1720) was the governor of Massachusetts from 1702 to 1715. A native of Massachusetts and a graduate of Harvard, he was distrusted by many in the colony because of his earlier service as royal official under the Dominion of New England from 1684 to 1689. John Williams, however, supported Governor Dudley, and his narrative's introduction was an explicit statement of his support at a time when Dudley's opponents were campaigning for his removal as governor.

who with me have seen the wonders of the Lord, and tasted of His salvation [so] that we may not fall under that heavy charge made against Israel of old, Psalm 78:11, 42 "They forgot his works, and the wonders he showed them. They remembered not His hand, nor the day that He delivered them from the enemy."

And I cannot, Sir, but think it most agreeable to my duty to God, our supreme redeemer, to mention your Excellency's name with honor, since heaven has honored you as the prime instrument in returning our captivity. Sure I am, the laws of justice and gratitude, which are the laws of God, do challenge from us the most public acknowledgments of your uncommon sympathy with us, your children, in our bonds expressed in all endearing methods of parental care and tenderness. All your people are cherished under your wings, happy in your government, and are obliged to bless God for you. And among your people those who are immediately exposed to the outrages of the enemy have peculiarly felt refreshment from the benign influences of your wise and tender conduct and are under the most sensible engagements to acknowledge your Excellency, under God, as the breath of their nostrils.

Your uncommon sagacity and prudence in contriving to loose the bonds of your captivated children [and] your unwearied vigor and application in pursuing them to work our deliverance, can never be enough praised. It is most notorious that nothing was thought too difficult by you to effect this design in that you readily sent your own son, Mr. William Dudley,[7] to undergo the hazards and hardships of a tedious voyage that this affair might be transacted with success, which must not be forgotten, as an expression of your great solicitude and zeal to recover us from the tyranny and oppression of our captivity.

I doubt not but that the God, whom herein you have served, will remember and gloriously reward you, and may heaven long preserve you at our helm, a blessing so necessary for the tranquility of this province in this dark and tempestuous season; may the best of blessings from the Father of Lights be showered down upon your person, family, and government; which shall be the prayer of,

> Your Excellency's
> most humble, obedient,
> and dutiful servant,
> John Williams

---

7. William Dudley (1686–1749), the youngest son of Governor Joseph Dudley, was sent to Quebec in 1705 as part of a delegation to negotiate the return of English captives held in New France. While in Canada he also gathered military intelligence.

March 3d, 1706–7[8]

The Redeemed Captive Returning to Zion

The history I am going to write proves that days of fasting and prayer, without reformation, will not avail to turn away the anger of God from a professing people. And yet witness how very advantageous gracious supplications are to prepare particular Christians patiently to suffer the will of God in very trying public calamities! For some of us, moved with fear, set apart a day of prayer to ask of God, either to spare and save us from the hands of our enemies or to prepare us to sanctify and honor Him in what way soever He should come forth towards us. The places of Scripture from whence we were entertained [in the forenoon], were Genesis 32:10–11: "I am not worthy of the least of all the mercies and of all the truth which thou hast showed unto thy servant. Deliver me, I pray thee, from the hand of my brother, from the hand of Esau, for I fear him, lest he will come and smite me, and the mother with the children." And [in the afternoon], Genesis 32:26: "And he said, 'Let me go, for the day breaketh.' And he said, 'I will not let thee go, except thou bless me.' " From which we were called upon to spread the causes of fear relating to our own selves or families before God; as also how it becomes us with an undeniable importunity to be following God with earnest prayers for His blessing in every condition. And it is very observable how God ordered our prayers in a peculiar manner to be going up to Him to prepare us with a right Christian spirit, to undergo and endure suffering trials.

Not long after, the holy and righteous God brought us under great trials as to our persons and families which put us under a necessity of spreading before Him in a wilderness the distressing dangers and calamities of our relations; yea, that called on us notwithstanding seeming present frowns, to resolve by His grace not to be sent away without a blessing. Jacob in wrestling has the hollow of his thigh put out of joint, and it is said to him, "Let me go"; yet he is rather animated to a heroic Christian resolution to continue [in] earnest for the blessing than discouraged from asking.[9]

On the twenty-ninth of February, 1703/4, not long before the break of day, the enemy came in like a flood upon us, our watch being unfaithful: an evil, whose awful effects in the surprise of our fort,[10] should bespeak all watchmen to avoid,

---

8. The English still used the Julian calendar, which dated the beginning of the year on March 25, and because of this practice they recorded the date of the raid as 1703/4, acknowledging the fact that much of western Europe began the year on January 1.

9. This is a reference to Genesis 32:24–28.

10. A reference to the stockade built around the houses in the center of Deerfield.

as they would not bring the charge of blood upon themselves. They came to my house in the beginning of the onset, and, by their violent endeavors to break open doors and windows with axes and hatchets, awakened me out of sleep; on which I leaped out of bed, and, running towards the door, perceived the enemy making their entrance into the house. I called to awaken two soldiers[11] in the chamber and returned towards my bedside for my arms. The enemy immediately broke into the room, I judge to the number of twenty, with painted faces and hideous acclamations. I reached up my hands to the bed tester[12] for my pistol, uttering a short petition to God for everlasting mercies for me and mine on account of the merits of our Glorified Redeemer, expecting a present passage through the Valley of the Shadow of Death, saying in myself, as Isaiah 38:10–11, "I said in the cutting off of my days, 'I shall go to the gates of the grave. I am deprived of the residue of my years.' I said, 'I shall not see the Lord, even the Lord, in the land of living. I shall behold man no more with the inhabitants of the world.'" Taking down my pistol, I cocked it and put it to the breast of the first Indian that came up, but my pistol missing fire, I was seized by three Indians who disarmed me and bound me naked, as I was in my shirt, and so I stood for near the space of an hour. Binding me, they told me they would carry me to Quebec. My pistol missing fire was an occasion of my life's being preserved, since which I have also found it profitable to be crossed in my own will. The judgment of God did not long slumber against one of the three which took me, who was a captain, for by sunrising he received a mortal shot from my next neighbor's house,[13] who opposed so great a number of French and Indians as three hundred[14] and yet were no more than seven men in an ungarrisoned house.[15]

I cannot relate the distressing care I had for my dear wife,[16] who had lain-in but a few weeks before;[17] and for my poor children, family, and Christian neigh-

---

11. There were at the time of the attack twenty "garrison soldiers" in Deerfield. These soldiers were not trained professionals but militiamen from the neighboring towns who had been ordered to Deerfield.

12. The testor is the canopy over a bed.

13. The neighboring house was the home of Benoni Stebbins (1655–1704), and it held out for about two-and-a half hours before a relief party arrived from the neighboring towns of Hadley, Hatfield, and Northampton. Stebbins was killed defending his home and two others were wounded.

14. Williams's estimate of 300 is fairly accurate, since the total number of attackers was between 250 and 300.

15. An "ungarrisoned" house is one that had not been fortified by the erection of a palisade around it.

16. Eunice Mather Williams (1665–1704) was the daughter of the Reverend Eleazer Mather (1637–1669) and the step-daughter of the Reverend Solomon Stoddard (1643–1729). She married John Williams in 1687 and they had eleven children.

17. Jerusha Williams had been born on January 15.

bors. The enemy fell to rifling the house and entered in great numbers into every room of the house. I begged of God to remember mercy in the midst of judgment, that He would so far restrain their wrath as to prevent their murdering of us, that we might have grace to glorify His name, whether in life or death, and, as I was able, committed our state to God. The enemies who entered the house, were all of them Indians[18] and Maquas,[19] insulted over me awhile, holding up hatchets over my head, threatening to burn all I had. But yet God beyond expectation made us in a great measure to be pitied, for though some were so cruel and barbarous as to take and carry to the door two of my children[20] and murder them, and also a Negro woman,[21] yet they gave me liberty to put on my clothes, keeping me bound with a cord on one arm, till I put on my clothes to the other, and then changing my chord, they let me dress myself and then pinioned me again. [They] gave liberty to my dear wife to dress herself and our children.

About sun an hour high, we were all carried out of the house for a march and saw many of the houses of my neighbors in flames, perceiving the whole fort, one house excepted, to be taken. Who can tell what sorrows pierced our souls when we saw ourselves carried away from God's sanctuary to go into a strange land exposed to so many trials: the journey being at least three hundred miles we were to travel; the snow up to the knees; we never inured to such hardships and fatigues; [and] the place we were to be carried to, a Popish country.

Upon my parting from the town, they fired my house and barn. We were carried over the [Deerfield] river to the foot of the mountain, about a mile from my house, where we found a great number of our Christian neighbors, men, woman, and children, to the number of a hundred,[22] nineteen of which were afterward murdered by the way, and two starved to death near Cowass[23] in a time of great scarcity or famine [that] the savages underwent there. When we came to the foot of our mountain, they took away our shoes and gave us in the

---

18. Williams referred to the Abenakis from Odanak and the Pennacooks as "Indians."

19. Williams used the word *Maqua* to refer indiscriminately to Iroquoain peoples: the Mohawks from Kahnawake, the Iroquois of the Mountain from the Island of Montreal, and the Hurons from Lorette. *Maqua* derives from an Eastern Algonquian word meaning "man eater" and was used by the Native peoples of New England to refer to the Kaniekehaka, the easternmost nation of the Iroquois League of the Five Nations. The English adopted this Algonquian word and later transformed it into Mohawk.

20. The raiders killed six-year-old John Williams Jr. and six-week-old Jerusha Williams.

21. Parthena, a slave of John Williams.

22. The actual number of captives was 112.

23. Cowass is today Newbury, Vermont.

room of them Indian shoes[24] to prepare us for our travel. While we were there, the English beat out a company that remained in the town and pursued them to the river, killing and wounding many of them, but the body of the army, being alarmed, they repulsed those few English that pursued them.

I am not able to give you an account of the number of the enemy slain, but I observed after this fight no great, insulting mirth as I expected and saw many wounded persons, and for several days together they buried [members] of their party and one of chief note among the Maquas.[25] The governor of Canada[26] told me, his army had that success with the loss of but eleven men: three Frenchmen, one of which was the lieutenant of the army,[27] five Maquas, and three Indians. But after my arrival at Quebec, I spoke with an Englishman who was taken in the last war and married there, and of their religion, who told me they lost above forty and that many were wounded. I replied, "The governor of Canada said they lost but eleven men." He answered, " 'Tis true that there were but eleven killed outright at the taking of fort, but that many others were wounded, among whom was the ensign of the French." "But," said he, "they had a fight in the meadow, and in both engagements they lost more than forty. Some of the soldiers, both French and Indians, then present, told me so," said he, adding that "The French always endeavor to conceal the number of their slain."[28]

[From Deerfield to the Connecticut River]

After this, we went up the mountain and saw the smoke of the fires in the town and beheld the awful desolations of our town. And before we marched any farther, they killed a sucking child[29] [belonging to one] of the English. There

---

24. The "Indian shoes" were winter moccasins, often called Indian stockings by the English. Winter moccasins covered the foot, ankle, and lower calf and kept the wearer warmer and drier than did low-cut leather shoes.

25. A leader of the Hurons was mortally wounded in the attack. See Louis d'Avaugour, "A Letter Concerning the Mission of Lorette in New France," 201.

26. Philippe de Rigaud de Vaudreuil (c. 1643–1725) was born in France, went to New France in 1687 as commander of the troops in Canada, and served as governor of the Montreal district from 1689 to 1703 and governor-general of New France from 1703 to his death.

27. Ensign François-Marie Margane de Batilly (1672–1704) was a noble and a Canadian-born officer in the colonial regulars stationed in New France.

28. French reports confirm that three French were killed and twenty or twenty-one wounded, including the French commander, Jean-Baptiste Hertel de Rouville. Eight Native warriors were killed, but there is no record of the number of Natives wounded. In all, these losses are among the highest, if not the highest, number of casualties suffered by a French and Indian raiding party in an attack on the frontiers of New England.

29. The child was probably Marah Carter (1701–1704).

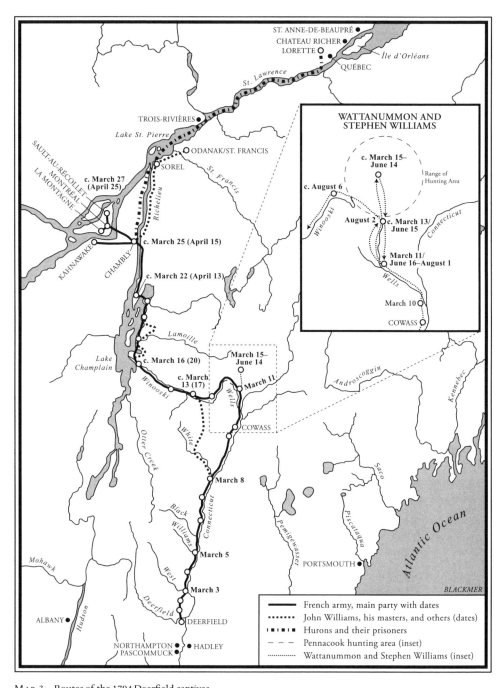

MAP 3. Routes of the 1704 Deerfield captives.

were slain by the enemy of the inhabitants of our town to the number of thirty-eight besides nine of the neighboring towns.[30] We traveled not far the first day; God made the heathen so to pity our children that, though they had several wounded persons of their own to carry upon their shoulders for thirty miles, before they came to the river, yet they carried our children, incapable of traveling, upon their shoulders and in their arms (map 3).

When we came to our lodging-place,[31] the first night, they dug away the snow and made some wigwams, cut down some of the small branches of spruce trees to lie down on, and gave the prisoners somewhat to eat, but we had but little appetite. I was pinioned and bound down that night, and so I was every night while I was with the army. Some of the enemy who brought drink with them from the town fell to drinking, and in their drunken fit they killed my Negro man,[32] the only dead person I either saw at the town or on the way. In the night an Englishman made his escape;[33] in the morning [March 1],[34] I was called for, and ordered by the general[35] to tell the English that, if any more made their escape, they would burn the rest of the prisoners.

He that took me was unwilling to let me speak with any of the prisoners as we marched; but on the morning of the second day [March 1], he being appointed to guard the rear, I was put into the hands of my other master who permitted me to speak to my wife when I overtook her and to walk with her to help her in her journey. On the way we discoursed of the happiness of them who had a right to an house not made with hands, eternal in the heavens and God for a father and friend; as also, that it was our reasonable duty quietly to submit to the will of God and to say, "The will of the Lord be done." My wife told me her strength of body began to fail and that I must expect to part with her, saying she hoped God would preserve my life and the lives of some, if not of all our children with us, and commended to me, under God, the care of them. She never spoke any discontented word as to what had befallen us, but with suitable expressions justified God in what had befallen us.

We soon made a halt in which time my chief surviving master came up, upon which I was put upon marching with the foremost, and so made to take my last farewell of my dear wife, the desire of my eyes and companion in many mercies and afflictions. Upon our separation from each other, we asked, for

---

30. Williams's count omits two residents and one garrison soldier from another town, making a total of fifty killed.

31. They stopped somewhere in the present-day town of Greenfield, Massachusetts.

32. This man was John Williams's slave Frank, the husband of Parthena.

33. Joseph Alexander (1681–1761) escaped and returned to Deerfield.

34. All of the dates in parentheses are in Old Style. Add 11 days to convert to New Style.

35. Lieutenant Jean-Baptiste Hertel de Rouville (1668–1722).

each other, grace sufficient for what God should call us to. After our being parted from one another, she spent the few remaining minutes of her stay in reading the holy Scriptures, which she was wont personally every day to delight her soul in reading, praying, meditating of and over, by herself in her closet, over and above what she heard out of them in our family worship.

I was made to wade over a small river[36] and so were all the English, the water above knee-deep, the stream very swift; and after that to travel up a small mountain; my strength was almost spent before I came to the top of it. No sooner had I overcome the difficulty of that ascent, but I was permitted to sit down and be unburdened of my pack. I sat pitying those who where behind and entreated my master to let me go down and help my wife, but he refused and would not let me stir from him. I asked each of the prisoners as they passed by me after her, and heard that in passing through the abovesaid river, she fell down and was plunged over head and ears in the water; after which she traveled not far, for at the foot of this mountain the cruel and bloodthirsty savage who took her, slew her with his hatchet at one stroke, the tidings of which were very awful. And yet such was the hardheartedness of the adversary that my tears were reckoned to me as a reproach.

My loss and the loss of my children was great; our hearts were so filled with sorrow, that nothing but the comfortable hopes of her being taken away in mercy, to herself, from the evils we were to see, feel, and suffer under (and joined to the assembly of the spirits of just men made perfect, to rest in peace and joy unspeakable, and full of glory, and the good pleasure of God thus to exercise us) could have kept us from sinking under at that time. That Scripture, Job 1:21, "Naked came I out of my mother's womb, and naked shall I return thither. The Lord gave, and the Lord hath taken away; blessed be the name of the Lord," was brought to my mind and from it that an afflicting God was to be glorified, with some other places of Scripture, to persuade to a patient bearing [of] my afflictions.

We were again called upon to march with a far heavier burden on my spirits than on my back. I begged of God to overrule in His providence that the corpse of one so dear to me, and of one whose spirit He had taken to dwell with Him in glory, might meet with a Christian burial and not be left for meat to the fowls of the air and beasts of the earth, a mercy that God graciously vouchsafed to grant. For God put it into the hearts of my neighbors to come out as far as she lay to take up her corpse, carry it to the town, and decently to bury it soon after. In our march they killed another sucking infant of one of my neighbors

---

36. The Green River in Greenfield, Massachusetts.

and before night a girl of about eleven years of age.[37] I was made to mourn at the consideration of my flock's being so far a flock of slaughter, many being slain in the town and so many murdered in so few miles from the town, and from fears what we must yet expect from such who delightfully imbued their hands in the blood of so many of His people.

When we came to our lodging place, an Indian captain from the Eastward[38] spoke to my master about killing me, and taking off my scalp. I lifted up my heart to God to implore His grace and mercy in such a time of need. And afterwards I told my master if he intended to kill me, I desired he would let me know of it, assuring him that my death after a promise of quarter would bring the guilt of blood upon him. He told me he would not kill me. We laid down and slept, for God sustained and kept us.

In the morning [March 2], we were all called before the chief sachems of the Maquas and Indians that a more equal distribution might be made of the prisoners among them. At my going from the wigwam, my best clothing was taken away from me. As I came nigh the place appointed, some of the captives met me and told me they thought the enemies were going to burn some of us for they had peeled off the bark from several trees and acted very strangely. To whom I replied, they could act nothing against us but as they were permitted of God, and I was persuaded He would prevent such severities. When we came to the wigwam appointed, several of the captives were taken from their former masters and put into the hands of others, but I was sent again to my two masters who brought me from my house.[39]

[Along the Connecticut River]

In our fourth day's march [March 3], the enemy killed another of my neighbors, who being nigh the time of travail,[40] was wearied with her journey. When we came to the great river,[41] the enemy took sleighs to draw their wounded, several of our children, and their packs, and marched a great pace. I traveled many

---

37. The infant was probably Hannah Carter, who was seven-months-old, and the girl, Jemima Richards.

38. The English referred to the Abenakis of Maine and the Pennacooks as Eastern Indians. This particular captain was most likely a Pennacook.

39. As Williams notes above, his third master, a leader among the Abenakis, had been killed assaulting Benoni Stebbins's house. On this council see D'Avaugour, "A Letter Concerning the Mission of Lorette in New France," 201–202.

40. This woman was possibly Waitstill Warner (1679–1704).

41. The English referred to the Connecticut River as the Great River. The party came to the Connecticut somewhere near what is today Brattleboro, Vermont.

hours in water up to the ankles. Near night I was very lame, having before my travel wronged [i.e., wrenched] my ankle bone and sinews; I thought, and so did others, that I should not be able to hold out to travel far. I lifted up my heart to God (my only refuge) to remove my lameness and carry me through with my children and neighbors if He judged it best; however, I desired God would be with me in my great change if He called me by such a death to glorify Him, and that He would take care of my children and neighbors and bless them. And within a little space of time I was well of my lameness, to the joy of my children and neighbors who saw so great an alteration in my traveling.

On Saturday [March 4] the journey was long and tedious; we traveled with such speed that four women were tired and then slain by them who led them captive.[42]

On the Sabbath day [March 5] we rested, and I was permitted to pray, and preach to the captives.[43] The place of Scripture spoken from was Lamentations 1:18: "The Lord is righteous, for I have rebelled against his commandment. Hear, I pray you, all people, and behold my sorrow. My virgins and young men are gone into captivity." The enemy, who said to us, "Sing us one of Zion's songs," were ready some of them to upbraid us because our singing was not so loud as theirs. When the Maquas and Indians were chief in power, we had this revival in our bondage to join together in the worship of God, and encourage one another to a patient bearing the indignation of the Lord till He should plead our cause. When we arrived to [i.e., in] New France, we were forbidden praying one with another or joining together in the service of God.

The next day [March 6], soon after we marched, we had an alarm on which many of the English were bound; I was then near the front and my masters not with me so I was not bound. This alarm was occasioned by some Indians shooting at geese that flew over them that put them into a considerable consternation and fright. But after they came to understand [that] they were not pursued by the English, they boasted that the English would not come out after them as they had boasted before we began our journey in the morning. They killed this day two women who were so faint they could not travel.[44]

The next day [March 7] in the morning before we traveled, one Mary Brooks,[45] a pious young woman, came to the wigwam where I was and told me

42. These women were possibly Hepzibah Belding (c. 1650–1704), Hannah Carter (1674–1704), Mary Frary (c. 1640–1704), and Mehitable Nims (1668–1704).

43. They stopped at a place about twenty-five miles north of Brattleboro, Vermont, along what is today known as the Williams River.

44. Possibly Elizabeth Corse (c. 1672–1704) and Esther Pomeroy (c. 1677–1704).

45. Mary Williams Brooks (1673–1704)—no relation to the Reverend John Williams—was taken prisoner with her husband, Nathaniel, and their two children, Mary and William. Only Nathaniel would return to New England.

she desired to bless God who had inclined the heart of her master to let her come and take her farewell of me. Said she, "By my falls on the ice yesterday, I wronged [i.e., injured] myself, causing an abortion [i.e., a miscarriage] this night so that I am not able to travel far. I know they will kill me today, but," says she, "God has (praised be His name) by His spirit with His word strengthened me to my last encounter with death." And [she] mentioned me some places of Scripture so seasonably sent in for her support. "And," said she, "I am not afraid of death; I can, through the grace of God, cheerfully submit to the will of God. Pray for me," said she, at parting, "that God would take me to Himself." Accordingly, she was killed that day. I mention it to the end I may stir up all in their young days to improve the death of Christ by faith to give them a holy boldness in the day of death.

[From the Connecticut River to the Winooski River]

The next day [March 8] we were made to scatter one from another into smaller companies, and one of my children was carried away with Indians belonging to the eastern parts.[46] At night my master came to me with my pistol in his hand, and put it to my breast, and said, "Now I will kill you, for," said he, "at your house you would have killed me with it if you could."[47] But by the grace of God I was not much daunted, and whatever his intention might be, God prevented my death.

The next day [March 9] I was again permitted to pray with that company of captives with me, and we [were] allowed to sing a psalm together. After which I was taken from all the company of the English, excepting two children of my neighbors, one of which, a girl of four years of age,[48] was killed by her Maqua master the next morning [March 10], the snow being so deep when we left the river that he could not carry the child and his pack too.

When the Sabbath came [March 12], one Indian stayed with me and a little boy[49] nine years old while the rest went a-hunting. And when I was here, I thought with myself that God had now separated me from the congregation of His people who were now in His sanctuary where He commanded the blessing, even life forever; and made me to bewail my unfruitfulness under and un-

46. The parties separated at what is today White River Junction, Vermont. His son Stephen (1693–1782) was taken by Wattanummon (c. 1660–1712), a Pennacook leader.

47. Notice that this man is speaking English. Unlike Stockwell, Williams had no familiarity with Native languages, but several of the Abenakis he encounters speak English.

48. The only girl who approximates this age and is known to have been killed on the march to Canada is Elizabeth Hawks (1697–1704), who was six years old at the time.

49. This boy is either Josiah Rising or Ebenezer Stebbins. Neither of them returned to New England.

thankfulness for such a mercy. When my spirit was almost overwhelmed within me at the consideration of what had passed over me and what was to be expected, I was ready almost to sink in my spirit. But God spoke those words with a greater efficacy than man could speak them for my strengthening and support: Psalms 118:17: "I shall not die but live and declare the works of the Lord." Psalms 42:11: "Why art thou cast down, oh my soul? And why art thou disquieted within me? Hope thou in God; for I shall yet praise Him, who is the health of my countenance and my God." Nehemiah 1:8–9: "Remember, I beseech thee, the word that thou commandedest thy servant Moses, saying, 'If ye transgress, I will scatter you abroad among the nations; but if ye turn unto me, and keep my commandments and do them, though there were of you cast out unto the uttermost part of the heavens, yet will I gather them from thence and will bring them unto the place that I have chosen, to set my name there.' " Those three places of Scripture, one after another by the grace of God, strengthened my hopes that God would so far restrain the wrath of the adversary that the greatest number of us left alive should be carried through so tedious a journey. That though my children had no father to take care of them, that word quieted me to a patient waiting to see the end the Lord would make. Jeremiah 49:11: "Leave thy fatherless children, I will preserve them alive, and let thy widows trust in me." Accordingly God carried them wonderfully through great difficulties and dangers.

My youngest daughter,[50] aged seven years, was carried all the journey and looked after with a great deal of tenderness. My youngest son, aged four years,[51] was wonderfully preserved from death, for though they that carried him or drew him on sleighs were tired with their journeys, yet their savage, cruel tempers were so overruled by God that they did not kill him, but in their pity he was spared and others would take care of him; so that four times on the journey he was spared, till at last he arrived at Montreal where a French gentlewoman,[52] pitying the child, redeemed it out of the hands of the heathen. My son Samuel[53] and my eldest daughter[54] were pitied so as to be drawn on sleighs when unable

---

50. Eunice Williams (1696–1785) remained with the Mohawks at Kahnawake, converted to Catholicism, married a Native man, and had a family.

51. Warham Williams (1699–1751) returned to New England, attended Harvard College, and became the minister in Waltham, Massachusetts in 1723.

52. Warham was ransomed by Agathe de Saint-Père (1657–1747 or 1748). She was the wife of Pierre Legardeur de Repentigny (1657–1736) and the sister-in-law of Charles Legardeur de Croisille (1677–1749), who took part in the 1704 Deerfield raid.

53. Samuel Williams (1690–1713), despite his conversion to Catholicism, returned to New England.

54. Esther Williams (1681–1751) returned to New England and later married the Reverend Joseph Meacham and settled in Coventry, Connecticut.

to travel. And though they suffered very much through scarcity of food and tedious journeys, they were carried through to Montreal. And my son Stephen, about eleven years of age, [was] wonderfully preserved from death in the famine where of three English persons[55] died and after eight months brought into Chambly.[56]

My master returned on the evening of the Sabbath [March 12] and told me he had killed five moose. The next day [March 13] we were removed to the place where he killed them. We tarried there three days till we had roasted and dried the meat. My master made me a pair of snowshoes, "For," said he," you cannot possibly travel without, the snow being knee-deep." We parted from thence heavy laden. I traveled with a burden on my back, with snowshoes, twenty-five miles the first day of wearing them and again the next day [March 17] till afternoon, and then we came to the French River.[57]

[From the Winooski River to Lake Champlain]

My master at this place took away my pack and drew the whole load on the ice, but my bones seemed to be misplaced and I [was] unable to travel with any speed. My feet were very sore, and each night I wrung blood out of my stockings when I pulled them off. My shins also were very sore, being cut with crusty snow in the time of my traveling without snowshoes. But finding some dry oak leaves by the river banks, I put them to my shins and in once applying them were healed. And here my master was very kind to me, would always give me the best he had to eat, and, by the goodness of God, I never wanted a meal's meat during my captivity though some of my children and neighbors were greatly wounded (as I may say) with the arrows of famine and pinching want, having for many days nothing but roots to live upon and not much of them neither.

My master gave me a piece of Bible, never disturbed me in reading the Scriptures, or in praying to God. Many of my neighbors also found that mercy in their journey to have Bibles, psalm books, catechisms, and good books put into their hands with liberty to use them; and yet, after their arrival at Canada all possible endeavors were used to deprive them of them. Some of them say their Bibles were demanded by the French priests and never redelivered to them, to their great grief and sorrow.

---

55. Two men taken at Deerfield starved to death near Cowass: Deacon David Hoyt (1651–1704), one of Deerfield's leading residents, and Jacob Hickson (1683–1704), a garrison soldier from Hadley, Massachusetts. See Williams, "What Befell Stephen Williams," 164–165.

56. Fort Chambly had been a French post since 1665. A new fort had been built in 1702. The expedition that attacked Deerfield had gathered at Chambly.

57. The French or Onion River is today known as the Winooski River.

My march on the French River was very sore, for, fearing a thaw, we traveled [at] a very great pace; my feet were so bruised and my joints so distorted by my traveling in snowshoes that I thought it impossible to hold out. One morning a little before break of day my master came and awakened me out of sleep, saying, "Arise, pray to God, and eat your breakfast, for we must go a great way today." After prayer I arose from my knees, but my feet were so tender, swollen, bruised, and full of pain, that I could scarce stand upon them without holding on the wigwam. And when the Indians said, "You must run today."

I answered I could not run.

My master, pointing out his hatchet, said [to] me, "Then I must dash out your brains and take off your scalp."

I said, "I suppose, then you will do so, for I am not able to travel with speed." He sent me away alone on the ice.

About sun half an hour high he overtook me for I had gone very slowly, not thinking it possible to travel five miles. When he came up, he called me to run; I told him I could go no faster. He passed by without saying one word more, so that sometimes I scarce saw anything of him for an hour together. I traveled from about break of day till dark, never so much as set down at noon to eat warm victuals, eating frozen meat which I had in my coat pocket as I traveled. We went that day two of their day's journey as they came down. I judge we went forty or forty-five miles that day. God wonderfully supported me and so far renewed my strength that in the afternoon I was stronger to travel than in the forenoon. My strength was restored and renewed to admiration. We should never distrust the care and compassion of God who can give strength to them who have no might and power to them who are ready to faint.

When we entered on the lake [i.e., Lake Champlain], the ice was very rough and uneven, which was very grievous to my feet that could scarce endure to be set down on the smooth ice on the river. I lifted up my cry to God in ejaculatory requests that He would take notice of my state and some way or other relieve me. I had not marched above half a mile before there fell a moist snow about an inch and a half deep that made it very soft for my feet to pass over the lake to the place where my master's family was—wonderful favors in the midst of trying afflictions!

We went a day's journey from the lake to a small company of Indians who were a-hunting. They were after their manner kind to me and gave me the best they had, which was moose flesh, groundnuts, and cranberries but no bread; for three weeks together I ate no bread. After our stay there and undergoing difficulties in cutting wood, [I] suffered from lousiness, having lousy old clothes of soldiers put upon me when they stripped me of mine to sell to the French soldiers in the army. We again began a march for Chambly. We stayed at a branch of the lake,[58] and feasted two or three days on geese we killed there. After another day's travel, we came to a river[59] where the ice was thawed. We made a canoe of elm-bark in one day; and arrived on a Saturday [April 15][60] near noon at Chambly, a small village where [there] is a garrison and fort of French soldiers (figure 8).

[At Chambly]

This village is about fifteen miles from Montreal. The French were very kind to me. A gentleman[61] of the place took me into his house and to his table and lodged me at night on a good feather-bed. The inhabitants and officers were very obliging to me the little time I stayed with them and promised to write a letter to the governor-in-chief[62] to inform him of my passing down the river. Here I saw a girl taken from our town and a young man[63] who informed me that the greatest part of the captives were come in and that two of my children were at Montreal, and that many of the captives had been in three weeks before my arrival. Mercy in the midst of judgment!

As we passed along the river towards Sorel,[64] we went into a house where was an Englishwoman of our town who had been left among the French in order to [arrange] her conveyance to the Indian fort. The French were very kind to her and to myself and gave us the best provision they had, and she embarked with us to go down to Saint Francis Fort.[65] When we came down to the first inhabited house at Sorel, a Frenchwoman came to the riverside and desired us to go into her house, and, when we were entered, she compassioned our state and told us she had in the last war been a captive among the Indians[66] and

---

58. Possibly Missisquoi Bay.

59. The Richelieu River, which flows north from Lake Champlain to the Saint Lawrence River.

60. We estimate the date as April 15, 1704 Old Style, which means the others had arrived around March 25.

61. This man was probably Joseph-François Hertel de la Fresnière (1642–1722), the seigneur of Chambly and the father of Jean-Baptiste Hertel, who had led the French raiders against Deerfield.

62. Governor-General Philippe de Rigaud de Vaudreuil (1643–1725).

63. Probably Thankful Stebbins (1691–1729) and her older brother John Stebbins Jr. (c. 1685–1760). Unlike most of the Deerfield captives, who had been taken prisoner by Natives, the members of the Stebbins family were probably in French custody during the march to Canada. The fact that their sister Abigail had married the French fur trader Jacques de Noyon ensured that the Hertels kept an eye on them. Thankful married into the local community and lived there for the remainder of her life. John returned to Deerfield.

64. Sorel, like Chambly, began as a French fort in 1665 but by 1704 was a settlement as well.

65. Located at the Abenaki village of Odanak.

66. This Frenchwoman would have been referring to the Second French-Iroquois War, which had begun around 1684 and lasted until peace was made in 1701. The French in Canada sometimes

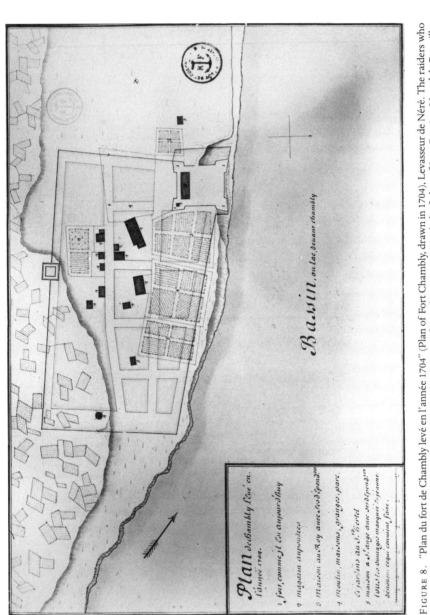

therefore was not a little sensible of our difficulties. She gave the Indians something to eat in the chimney-corner and spread a cloth on the table for us with napkins, which gave such offense to the Indians that they hastened away and would not call in at the fort. But wherever we entered into houses, the French were very courteous.

When we came to Saint Francis River, we found some difficulty by reason of the ice, and, entering into a Frenchman's house, he gave us a loaf of bread and some fish to carry away with us; but we passed down the river till night, and there seven of us supped on a fish called a bullhead or pout[67] and did not eat it up, the fish was so very large. The next morning we met with such a great quantity of ice that we were forced to leave our canoe and travel on land. We went to a French officer's house, who took us into a private room out of the sight of the Indians, and treated us very courteously.

[At Saint Francis]

That night we arrived at the fort called Saint Francis, where we found several poor children who had been taken from the Eastward the summer before,[68] a sight very affecting, they being in habit very much like Indians and in manners very much symbolizing with [i.e., resembling] them.[69] At this fort lived two Jesuits, one of which was made superior of the Jesuits at Quebec.[70] One of these Jesuits met me at the fort gate and asked me to go into the church and give God thanks for preserving my life. I told him I would do that in some other place. When the bell rang for evening prayers, he that took me bid me go, but I refused (figure 9).

The Jesuit came to our wigwam and prayed a short prayer and invited me to sup with them, and justified the Indians in what they did against us, rehearsing some things done by Major Waldron above thirty years ago, and how justly God retaliated them in the last war,[71] and inveighed against us for beginning

---

referred to it as the Twenty Years' War. This conflict overlapped with the European and colonial contest known as the Nine Years' War, or King William's War as the English called it, which lasted from 1689 to 1697. Most likely she had been a prisoner of the Iroquois League.

67. Probably a species of catfish, though today the name bullhead designates a relatively small species.

68. In August 1703, French and Indian raiding parties attacked several English villages along the coast of Maine.

69. See Stephen Williams's comments on this in "What Befell Stephen Williams," 167.

70. The Jesuit priests who met Williams were Jacques Bigot (1651–1711) and Vincent Bigot (1649–1720), both of whom had worked in the missions to the Abenakis in Maine. Vincent was superior general of the Jesuit missions in New France from 1704 to 1710.

71. Major Richard Waldron (c. 1616–1689) of Dover, New Hampshire, was a prominent fur trader and a member of the governor's council of New Hampshire. In 1676, he had treacherously

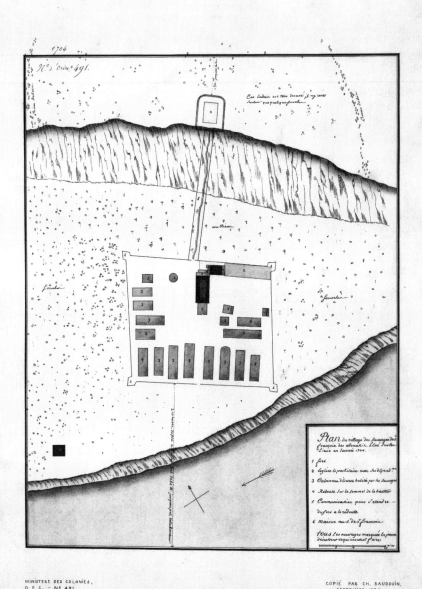

FIGURE 9. "Plan du village des Abenakis levé en l'année 1704" (Plan of the Abenakis' village, drawn in 1704), Levasseur de Néré. This plan shows the palisaded fort that surrounded the Abenaki village at Odanak. Its shape replicated that of European-style forts with bastions at its four corners. The plan shows (2) the Jesuit mission and (6) the home of Joseph Hertel de Saint François, the brother of Jean-Baptiste Hertel de Rouville. The plan underscores the role played by Native villages in the defense of New France and the close ties between the Hertels and the Abenakis. The Reverend John Williams stopped at the home of Joseph Hertel when he was a prisoner. FR.CAOM. Aix-en-Provence (France) Amérique septenrionale 491 (p.f. 5b) All rights reserved. Photograph courtesy of the National Archives of Canada, NMC000-4901.

this war with the Indians, and said [that] we had before the last winter, and in the winter, been very barbarous and cruel in burning and killing Indians.[72] I told them that the Indians in a very perfidious manner had committed murders on many of our inhabitants after the signing [of] articles of peace,[73] and, as to what they spoke of cruelties, they were undoubtedly falsehoods, for I well knew the English were not approvers of any inhumanity or barbarity towards enemies.

They said an Englishman had killed one of Saint Casteen's relations,[74] which occasioned this war; for, say they, the nations, in a general council, had concluded not to engage in the war, on any side, till they themselves were first molested, and then all of them as one would engage against them,[75] and that began a war with them; and that upon the killing of Casteen's kinsman, a post was dispatched to Canada to advertise [i.e., notify] the Maquas and Indians that the English had begun a war. On which they gathered their forces, and the French joined with them to come down on the Eastern parts; and that when they came near New England, several of the Eastern Indians told them of the peace made with the English and the satisfaction given them from the English for that murder. But the Maquas told them it was now too late, for they were sent for and were now come, and would fall on them if without their consent they made a peace with the English. [They] said also that a letter was shown to them from the governor of Port Royal,[76] which, he said, was taken in an English ship, being a letter from the queen of England to our governor writing how she approved his designs to ensnare and deceitfully seize on the Indians; so that being enraged from that letter and being forced, as it were, they began the present war. I told them the letter was a lie forged by the French.

The next morning the bell rang for Mass. My master bid me go to church. I refused. He threatened me and went away in a rage. At noon the Jesuits sent for

---

captured about 400 Natives. In retaliation, Abenakis had attacked Dover on June 17, 1689, and tortured Waldron to death.

72. The English had raided Abenaki settlements in the months between August 1703 and February 1704.

73. In June 1703 Governor Dudley had met with Abenaki leaders in Casco, Maine, in an effort to maintain the Anglo-Abenaki peace.

74. Jean-Vincent d'Abbadie de Saint-Castin (1652–1707) married a Penobscot woman and settled in the region. An English man had in fact killed an Abenaki related to Saint-Castin. This murder prompted Dudley's peace conference.

75. This refers to the 1701 Great Peace of Montreal between the French and various Native nations, ending the decades-long war with the Five Nations of the Iroquois League.

76. Jacques-François Monbeton de Brouillan (1651–1705) had served as governor of Placentia, Newfoundland, from 1691 to 1701 and governor of Acadia from 1702 until his death. Port Royal was the capital of Acadia. He did in fact attempt to embroil the Eastern Abenakis and Pennacooks in a war with the English by various subterfuges, including the forged letter described in the text.

me to dine with them, for I ate at their table all the time I was at the fort. And after dinner they told me the Indians would not allow of any of their captives staying in their wigwams while they were at church and were resolved by force and violence to bring us all to church if we would not go without. I told them it was highly unreasonable so to impose upon those who were of contrary religion, and to force us to be present at such a service as we abhorred was nothing becoming Christianity. They replied they were savages and would not hearken to reason but would have their wills. [They] said also, if they were in New England themselves, they would go into [the] churches and see their ways of worship.

I answered, the case was far different, for there was nothing (themselves being judges) as to [the] matter or manner of worship but what was according to the word of God in our churches; and therefore it could not be an offense to any man's conscience. But among them there were idolatrous superstitions in worship. They said, "Come and see, and offer us conviction of what is superstitious in [our] worship." To which I answered, that I was not to do evil that good might come of it, and that forcing in matters of religion was hateful. They answered the Indians were resolved to have it so, and they could not pacify them without my coming; and they would engage they should offer no force or violence to cause any compliance with their ceremonies.

The next Mass, my master bid me go to church. I objected; he arose and forcibly pulled me out by my head and shoulders out of the wigwam to the church that was nigh the door. So I went in and sat down behind the door, and there saw a great confusion instead of any Gospel order, for one of the Jesuits was at the altar saying Mass in a tongue unknown to the savages [i.e., Latin], and the other between the altar and the door, saying and singing prayers among the Indians at the same time and many others were at the same time saying over their Pater Nosters and Ave Mary [Marias] by tale from their chaplets, or beads on a string.[77] At our going out, we smiled at their devotion so managed, which was offensive to them, for they said we made a derision of their worship. When I was here, a certain savagess died. One of the Jesuits told me she was a very holy woman, who had not committed one sin in twelve years.

After a day or two the Jesuits asked me what I thought of their way now [that] I saw it? I told them I thought Christ said of it, as Mark 7:7–9: "Howbeit in vain do they worship me, teaching for doctrines the commandments of men. For laying aside the commandment of God, ye hold the tradition of men, as the washing of pots and cups and many other such like things ye do. And He

---

77. A chaplet is one-third the length of a rosary and, like a rosary, is used for counting prayers.

said unto them, 'Full well ye reject the commandment of God that ye may keep your own tradition.' " They told me they were not the commandments of men, but apostolic traditions of equal authority with the holy Scriptures. And that after my death I would bewail my not praying to the Virgin Mary, and that I should find the want of her intercession for me with her Son, judging me to hell for asserting the Scriptures to be a perfect rule of faith, and said I abounded in my own sense, entertaining explications contrary to the sense of the pope regularly sitting with a general council explaining Scripture and making articles of faith. I told them it was my comfort that Christ was to be my judge and not they at the Great Day, and, as for their censuring and judging of me, I was not moved with it.

One day a certain savagess taken prisoner in [King] Philip's War, who had lived at Mr. Bulkley's at Wethersfield,[78] called Ruth, who could speak English very well, and who had been often at my house, but now proselyted to the Romish[79] faith, came into the wigwam. And with her [came] an English maid who was taken [in] the last war,[80] who was dressed up in Indian apparel, could not speak one word of English, who said she could neither tell her own name or the name of the place from whence she was taken. These two talked in the Indian dialect with my master a long time after which my master bade me cross myself. I told him I would not; he commanded me several times, and I as often refused.

Ruth said, "Mr. Williams, you know the Scripture, and therefore act against your own light, for you know the Scripture saith, 'Servants, obey your masters.' He is your master and you his servant."

I told her she was ignorant and knew not the meaning of the Scripture, telling her [that] I was not to disobey the great God to obey any master, and that I was ready to suffer for God if called thereto. On which she talked to my master; I suppose she interpreted what I said.

My master took hold of my hand to force me to cross myself, but I struggled with him and would not suffer him to guide my hand. Upon this he pulled off a crucifix from his own neck and bade me kiss it, but I refused once again. He told me he would dash out my brains with his hatchet if I refused. I told him I should sooner choose death than to sin against God. Then he ran and caught up his hatchet and acted as though he would have dashed out my brains.

Seeing I was not moved, he threw down his hatchet, saying he would first

---

78. Gershom Bulkeley (1636–1713), a minister and doctor, had been the pastor in Wethersfield, Connecticut, from 1666 to 1677. King Phillip's War lasted from 1675 to 1677.

79. English Protestants referred to Roman Catholicism as the Romish faith or popery and called the pope the Bishop of Rome.

80. The Nine Years' War, 1689–1697.

bite off all my nails if I still refused. I gave him my hand and told him I was ready to suffer. He set his teeth in my thumbnails and gave a grip with his teeth, and then said, "No good minister, no love God, as bad as the devil," and so left off.

I have reason to bless God, who strengthened me to withstand [my master]. By this he was so discouraged as nevermore to meddle with me about my religion. I asked leave of the Jesuits to pray with those English of our town that were with me, but they absolutely refused to give us any permission to pray one with another and did what they could to prevent our having any discourse together.

After a few days the Governor de Vaudreuil, governor-in-chief, sent down two men with letters to the Jesuits desiring them to order my being sent up to him to Montreal, upon which one of the Jesuits went with my two masters and took me along with them, as also two more of Deerfield, a man and his daughter about seven years of age.[81] When we came to the lake,[82] the wind was tempestuous and contrary to us so that they were afraid to go over; they landed and kindled a fire and said they would wait awhile to see whether the wind would fall or change (map 4).

I went aside from the company among the trees and spread our case with the temptations of it before God and pleaded that he would order the season so that we might not go back again but be furthered on our voyage that I might have opportunity to see my children and neighbors and converse with them and know their state. When I returned, the wind was more boisterous, and then a second time, and the wind was more fierce. I reflected upon myself for my unquietness and the want of a resigned will to the will of God. And a third time [I] went and bewailed before God my anxious cares and the tumultuous workings of my own heart, begged a will fully resigned to the will of God, and thought that by the grace of God I was brought to say amen to whatever God should determine.

Upon my return to the company the wind was yet high; the Jesuit and my master said, "Come, we will go back again to the fort; for there is no likelihood of proceeding in our voyage, for very frequently such a wind continues three days, sometimes six."

---

81. The most likely father and daughter are Nathaniel Brooks (1664–?) and Mary Brooks (1696–?). After he was ransomed in 1706, Nathaniel returned to New France to look for his children. Mary converted to Catholicism and became a naturalized French subject in 1710 and then disappears from the records in New France.

82. Lake Saint Pierre is the name given to a very broad stretch of the Saint Lawrence River between Sorel and Trois-Rivières. It is about twenty-five miles long and in places eight miles wide.

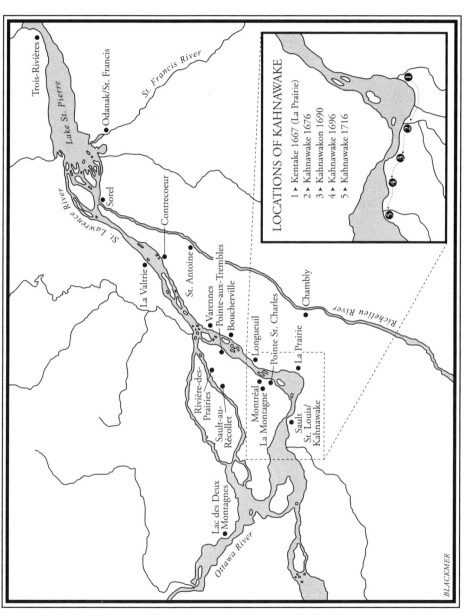

LOCATIONS OF KAHNAWAKE

1 ▶ Kentake 1667 (La Prairie)
2 ▶ Kahnawake 1676
3 ▶ Kahnawakon 1690
4 ▶ Kahnawake 1696
5 ▶ Kahnawake 1716

Trois-Rivières

Odanak/St. Francis

St. Francis River

Lake St. Pierre

St. Lawrence River

Sorel

Contrecoeur

La Valtrie

St. Antoine

Varennes
Pointe-aux-Trembles
Boucherville

Longueuil
Pointe St. Charles

Chambly

Richelieu River

La Prairie

Rivière-des-
Prairies

Sault-au-
Récollet

Montréal
La Montagne

Sault
St. Louis/
Kahnawake

Lac des Deux
Montagnes

Ottawa River

BLACKMER

MAP 4. The greater Montreal region, early 1700s.

After it continued so many hours, I said to them, "The will of the Lord be done," and the canoe was put again into the river[83] and we embarked.

No sooner had my master put me into the canoe and put off from the shore, but the wind fell, and coming into the middle of the river, they said, "We may go over the lake well enough." And so we did.

I promised if God gave me opportunity I would stir up others to glorify God in a continued persevering, committing their straits of heart to Him: He is a prayer-hearing God and the stormy winds obey Him. After we passed over the lake, the French wherever we came, were very compassionate to us.

[At Montreal]

When I came to Montreal, which was eight weeks after my captivity, [around April 25, 1704] the Governor de Vaudreuil redeemed me out of the hands of the Indians, gave me good clothing, took me to his table, gave me the use of a very good chamber, and was, in all respects relating to my outward man, courteous and charitable to admiration. At my first entering into his house, he sent for my two children,[84] who were in the city that I might see them and promised to do what he could to get all my children and neighbors out of the hands of the savages. My change of diet after the difficulties of my journeys caused an alteration in my body; I was physicked, and blooded,[85] and very tenderly taken care of in my sickness (figure 10).

The governor redeemed my eldest daughter [i.e., Esther] out of the hands of the Indians, and she was carefully tended in the hospital until she was well of her lameness and by the governor provided for with respect during her stay in the country. My youngest child [i.e., Warham] was redeemed by a gentlewoman [i.e., Agathe de Saint-Père] in the city as the Indians passed by. After the Indians had been at their fort and discoursed with the priests, they came back and offered to the gentlewoman a man for the child, alleging that the child could not be profitable to her, but the man would, for he was a weaver and his service would much advance the design she had of making cloth.[86] But God overruled so far that this temptation to the woman prevailed not for an exchange, for had the child gone to the Indian fort in an ordinary way, it [i.e., him] had abode there still, as the rest of the children carried thither do.

---

83. Either the Saint Lawrence or the Saint Francis River near where it flows into the Saint Lawrence.

84. Probably Esther and Warham.

85. In keeping with standard European medical practices, Williams was given purges and bled to restore his health.

86. Agathe de Saint-Père did in fact set up a business to weave cloth and employed several Deerfield captives in the operation.

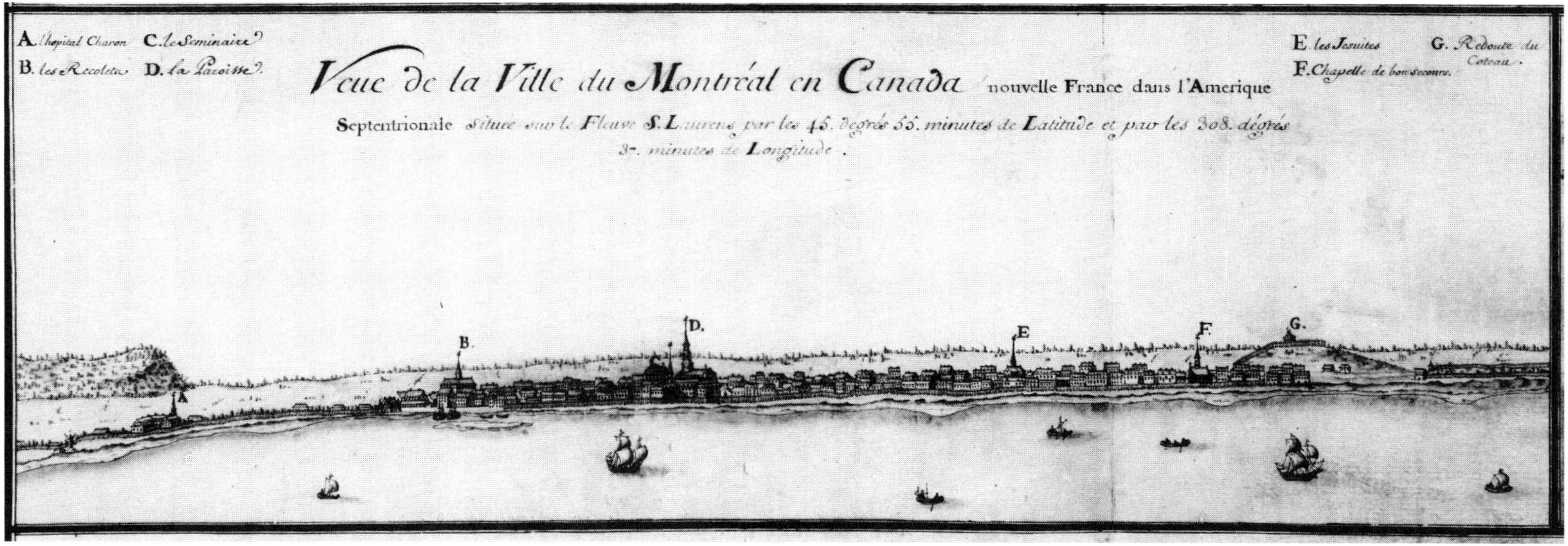

A. *Hopital Ouven*   C. *le Seminaire*   E. *les Jesuites*   G. *Redoute du Coteau*
B. *les Recolets*   D. *la Paroise*   F. *Chapelle de bonsecours*

Vcuc De la Ville du Montreal en Canada nouvelle France dans l'Amerique

Septentrionale *Situee sur le Fleuve S. Laurens, par les 46. degrés 55. minutes de Latitude et par les 308. degrés 3. minutes de Longitude.*

FIGURE 10. *Vue de Montréal* (View of Montreal). Watercolor, c. 1720, artist unknown. Montreal in the early 1700s was a medium-sized town surrounded by a palisade. Among the sites indicated in this view are (A) the general hospital, (C) the Seminary of the Sulpicians, and (D) the Church of Notre Dame. Photograph courtesy of the Edward E. Ayer Collection, The Newberry Library, Chicago.

The governor gave orders to certain officers to get the rest of my children out of the hands of the Indians and as many of my neighbors as they could. After six weeks, a merchant of the city obtained my eldest son,[87] that was taken, to live with him. He took a great deal of pains to persuade the savages to part with him. An Indian came to the city (Sagamore George of Pennacook)[88] from Cowass and brought word of my son Stephen's being near Cowass, and some money was put into his hand for his redemption and a promise of full satisfaction if he brought him; but the Indian proved unfaithful, and I never saw my child till a year after.[89]

The governor ordered a priest to go along with me to see my youngest daughter [i.e., Eunice] among the Maquas, and endeavor [for] her ransom. I went with him; he was very courteous to me, and, from his parish, which was near the Maqua fort,[90] he wrote a letter to the Jesuit to desire him to send my child to see me and to speak with them that took her to come along with it [i.e., her]. But the Jesuit wrote back a letter that I should not be permitted to speak with or see my child; if I came, that my labor would be lost, and that the Maquas would as soon part with their hearts as my child. At my return to the city I with a heavy heart carried the Jesuit's letter to the governor, who, when he read it, was very angry and endeavored to comfort me, assuring me I should see it [i.e., her], and speak with it [i.e., her]; and he would to his utmost endeavor its [i.e., her] ransom. Accordingly he sent to the Jesuits who were in the city and bade them improve their interest for the obtaining [of] the child.

After some days he [i.e., Vaudreuil] went with me in his own person to the fort. When we came thither, he discoursed with the Jesuits after which my child was brought into the chamber where I was. I was told I might speak with her but should be permitted to speak to no other English person there. My child was about seven years old; I discoursed with her near an hour; she could read very well and had not forgotten her catechism. And [she] was very desirous to be redeemed out of the hands of the Maquas and bemoaned her state among them, telling me how they profaned God's Sabbaths and said she thought that a few days before they had been mocking the devil, and that one of the Jesuits stood and looked on them.

I told her she must pray to God for His grace every day. She said she did as

---

87. Fifteen-year-old Samuel was ransomed by Jacques Le Ber (1633–1706), a merchant and seigneur who purchased letters of nobility in 1696. He was one of the wealthiest and most respected men in New France. Samuel was the oldest son taken captive, but actually he was the second oldest son after Eleazer (1688–1742), who was not captured.

88. George Tohanto (active 1695–1715) was a leader, or sagamore, of the Pennacooks and a kinsman of Wattanummon.

89. See the account in Williams, "What Befell Stephen Williams," 166–169.

90. The fort was built at the Mohawk village of Kahnawake.

she was able and God helped her. "But," says she, "they force me to say some prayers in Latin, but I don't understand one word of them; I hope it won't do me any harm." I told her she must be careful she did not forget her catechism and the Scriptures she had learned by heart. She told the captives after I was gone, as some of them have since informed me, almost every thing I spoke to her and said she was much afraid she should forget her catechism, having none to instruct her. I saw her once a few days after in the city but had not many minutes of time with her, but what time I had I improved to give her the best advice [that] I could.

The governor labored much for her redemption; at last he had a promise of it in case he would procure for them an Indian girl in her stead. Accordingly he sent up the river[91] some hundreds of leagues for one, but it was refused when offered by the governor. He offered them a hundred pieces of eight[92] for her redemption, but it was refused. His lady[93] went over to have begged her from them, but all in vain; it's [she's] there still and has forgotten to speak English. Oh! That all who peruse this history would join in their fervent requests to God, with whom all things are possible, that this poor child, and so many others of our children who have been cast upon God from the womb and are now outcast ready to perish, might be gathered from their dispersions and receive sanctifying grace from God!

When I had discoursed with the child and was coming out of the fort, one of the Jesuits went out of the chamber with me and some soldiers to convey me to the canoe. I saw some of my poor neighbors who stood with longing expectations to see me and speak with me and had leave from their savage masters so to do. I was by the Jesuit himself thrust along by force and permitted only to tell them [that] some of their relations they asked after were well in the city, and that with a very audible voice, being not permitted to come near to them.

After my return to the city I was very melancholy, for I could not be permitted so much as to pray with the English who dwelt in the same house. And the English who came to see me were most of them put back by the guard at the door and not suffered to come and speak with me. Sometimes the guard was so strict that I could scarce go aside on necessary occasions without a repulse; and whenever I went out into the city (a favor the governor himself never refused when I asked it of him) there were spies to watch me and to observe whether I

---

91. He sent up the Saint Lawrence River to the Great Lakes for an Indian girl.

92. The silver Spanish dollar, worth eight rials—hence piece of eight—was used as a coin in the cash-starved English colonies. It was worth six shillings.

93. Louise-Élizabeth de Joybert de Soulanges et de Marson (1673–1740) was the Canadian-born wife of Governor Vaudreuil.

spoke to the English. Upon which I told some of the English they must be care-ful to call to mind and improve former instructions and endeavor to stand at a further distance for a while, hoping that after a short time I should have more liberty of conversing with them.

But some spies sent out found on a Sabbath day more than three (the num-ber we, by their order published, were not to exceed together) of us in com-pany, who informed the priest. The next day one of the priests told me I had a greater number of the English with me and that I had spoken something re-flecting on their religion. I spoke to the governor that no forcible means might be used with any of the captives respecting their religion. He told me he al-lowed no such thing. I am persuaded that the governor, if he might act as him-self, would not have suffered such things to be done as have been done and that he never did know of several things acted against the English.

At my first coming to Montreal, the governor told me I should be sent home as soon as Captain Battis was returned,[94] and not before, and that I was taken in order to [secure] his redemption. The governor sought by all means to divert me from my melancholy sorrows and always showed a willingness for seeing my children. One day I told him of my design of walking into the city: he pleas-antly answered, "Go with all my heart." His eldest son[95] went with me as far as the door and saw the guard stop me. He went and informed his father, who came to the door and asked why they affronted the gentleman going out? They said it was their order. But with an angry countenance he said his orders were that I should not be stopped. But within a little time I had my orders to go down to Quebec.

Another thing showing that many things are done without the governor's consent though his name be used to justify them; *viz.,* I asked the priest, after I had been at Montreal two days leave to go and see my youngest child [i.e., Warham]. He said, "Whenever you would see it [i.e., him], tell me and I will bring it [i.e., him] to you, for," says he, "the governor is not willing you should go thither." And yet not many days after when we were at dinner, the gover-nor's lady (seeing me sad) spoke to an officer at table who could speak Latin to tell me that after dinner I should go along with them and see my two children. And accordingly after dinner I was carried to see them, and, when I came to the

94. Pierre Maisonnat, alias Baptiste (1663–1714), was a French privateer who operated along the coast of Acadia and New England. He had been captured by the English in 1702 and his return to New France was opposed by fishing and shipping interests in Boston. But in 1706, he would be exchanged for John Williams.

95. Louis-Philippe de Rigaud de Vaudreuil (1691–1763) began a distinguished career in the French navy in 1705 that would end with his promotion to vice admiral in 1753.

house,[96] I found three or four English captives who lived there,[97] and I had leave to discourse with them. And not long after, the governor's lady asked me to go along with her to the hospital to see one of my neighbors [who was] sick there.

One day one of the Jesuits came to the governor and told the company there that he never saw such persons as were taken from Deerfield. Said he, "The Maquas will not suffer any of their prisoners to abide in their wigwams while they themselves are at Mass but carry them with them to the church, and they can't be prevailed with to fall down on their knees to pray there, but no sooner are they returned to their wigwams, but they fall down on their knees to prayer." He said they could do nothing with the grown persons there, and they hindered the children's complying. Whereupon the Jesuits counseled the Maquas to sell all the grown persons from the fort—a stratagem to seduce poor children. Oh Lord! Turn the counsels of these Ahithophels[98] into foolishness, and make the counsels of the heathen of [no] effect!

Here I observed they were wonderfully lifted up with pride after the return of Captain Montinug from Northampton with news of success.[99] They boasted of their success against New England. And they sent out an army, as they said, of seven hundred men, if I mistake not, two hundred of which were French, in company of which army went several Jesuits, and said they would lay desolate all the places on [the] Connecticut River.[100] The superior of the priests[101] told me their general was a very prudent and brave commander, of undaunted courage, and he doubted not but they should have great success. This army went away in such a boasting, triumphant manner that I had great hopes God would discover and disappoint their designs; our prayers were not wanting for the blasting [of] such a bloody design.

---

96. Agathe de Saint-Père's house.

97. Among the nine New England captives living and working in Agathe de Saint-Père's house were two other Deerfield captives: Judah Wright (1677–1747), who was a weaver, and Ebenezer Sheldon (1677–1755). Both men returned to Deerfield.

98. The reference is to Ahithophel, the false counselor of King David who betrayed him and supported David's son Absalom in 2 Samuel 15–17.

99. On May 13, 1704, Jacques Testard de Montingy (1663–1737) led a party that attacked Pascommuck, a hamlet lying within Northampton that is today part of the town of Easthampton, Massachusetts. The raiders killed twenty, wounded fourteen, and captured three.

100. This is a reference to an expedition in the summer of 1704 against the frontiers of Massachusetts that was led by Jean-Maurice-Josué Dubois Berthelot de Beaucours (c. 1662–1750). His force contained about 100 to 125 French, most Canadian born, and perhaps 600 Native allies. The raid was a disappointing failure.

101. From 1701 to 1732, the superior of the Priests of the Congregation of Saint Sulpice, often called the Sulpicians, was François Vachon de Belmont (1645–1732).

The superior of the priests said to me, "Don't flatter yourselves in hopes of a short captivity, for," said he, "there are two young princes contending for the kingdom of Spain and a third that care is to be taken for his establishment on the English throne." [102] And [he] boasted what they would do to Europe; and that we must expect, not only [in] Europe, but in New England, the establishment of Popery. I said, "Glory not; God can make great changes in a little time and revive His own interest and yet save His poor afflicted people." Said he, "The time for miracles is past; and in the time of the last war the King of France was, as it were, against all the world and yet did very great things, but now the kingdom of Spain is for him, and the Duke of Bavaria,[103] and the Duke of Savoy,"[104] etc. And [he] spoke [in] a lofty manner of great things to be done by them and having the world, as I may say, in subjection to them.

I was sent down to Quebec in the company of Governor de Ramsey, governor of Montreal,[105] and the superior of the Jesuits,[106] and ordered to live with one of the council, from whom I received many favors for seven weeks. He told me it was the priests' doings to send me down before the governor came down, and that, if I went much to see the English, or they came much to visit me, I should yet certainly be sent away where I should have no [conversation] with the English.

[At Quebec]

After my coming down to Quebec, I was invited to dine with the Jesuits, and to my face they were civil enough. But after a few days a young gentleman came to my chamber and told me that one of the Jesuits (after we had done dinner)

---

102. The two princes contending for the Spanish throne were Philip Duke of Anjou (1683–1748), the grandson of France's Louis XIV, and the Archduke Charles of Austria (1685–1740), whose claims were supported by England, the Netherlands, and the Holy Roman Empire. The third prince referred to is James Edward Stuart (1688–1766), the son of the deposed James II of England who, after his father's death, was recognized by Louis XIV as James III and the rightful king of England. The English referred to him as the Old Pretender.

103. Elector Maximillian II Emanuel of Bavaria (1662–1726) supported the French during the War of the Spanish Succession (1702–1713), but after his defeat at Hochstadt in 1704, he was expelled from Bavaria and outlawed. He lived in France as a pensioner and did not return to Bavaria until 1715, after the war had ended.

104. Victor Amadeus (1666–1732) reigned as Duke of Savoy from 1675 to 1730. Initially he had allied with the French but switched sides in 1703 and at the end of the war was rewarded by the victorious allies with the crown of Sicily.

105. Claude de Ramezay (1659–1724) was the governor of the Montreal district of New France, which included the Island of Montreal and the surrounding parishes.

106. Father Vincent Bigot, whom Williams had already met at Saint Francis.

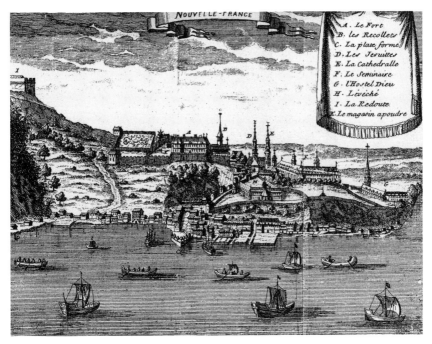

FIGURE 11. *A View of Quebec in 1700.* Engraving, c. 1700, artist unknown. This view of Quebec, which includes the Upper and Lower towns and the improvements to the fortifications made after the New Englanders' attack in 1690, shows the city as John and Stephen Williams saw it in the years 1704 to 1707. In particular, the Williamses were familiar with (A) the Chateau Saint-Louis, residence of the governor-general (called "Le Fort" in the key), (D) the Jesuit College, both a school and residence, and (F) the seminary. Engraving from Benjamin Sulte, *Histoire des Canadiens-Français 1608–1880* (Montreal, 1882), frontispiece. Photograph courtesy of René Chartrand.

made a few distichs of verses and gave them to his scholars [i.e., students] to translate into French. He showed them to me. The import of them was, that the King of France's grandson had sent out his huntsmen, and that they had taken a wolf, who was shut up, and now he hopes the sheep would be in safety (figure 11).

I knew at the reading of them what he aimed at but held my peace as though I had been ignorant of the Jesuit's intention. Observing this reproaching spirit, I said in my heart, "If God will bless, let men curse if they please," and I looked to God in Christ, the great shepherd, to keep His scattered sheep among so many Romish ravenous wolves and to remember the reproaches wherewith His holy name, ordinances, and servants were daily reproached. And upon an observation of the time of these verses being composed, I find that near the same time the bishop of Canada with twenty ecclesiastics were taken by the

English as they were coming from France and carried into England as prisoners of war.[107]

One Sabbath-day morning I observed many signs of approaching rain—a great moisture on the stones of the hearth and chimney-jambs. I was that day invited to dine with the Jesuits, and when I went up to dinner, it began to rain a small, drizzling rain. The superior told me they had been praying for rain that morning, "And lo," says he, "it begins to rain!" I told him I could tell him of many instances of God's hearing our prayers for rain. However, in the afternoon there was a general procession of all orders—priests, Jesuits, and friars—and the citizens in great pomp, carrying (as they said) as a holy relic, one of the bones of St. Paul.

The next day I was invited to the priests' Seminary to dinner. "Oh," said they, "we went in procession yesterday for rain, and see what a plentiful rain followed!" I answered we had been answered when praying for rain when no such signs of rain [or] the beginnings of rain had preceded, as now with them, before they appointed or began their procession, etc. However, they upbraided me that God did not approve of our religion in that He disregarded our prayers and accepted theirs. "For," said they, "we hear you had days of fasting and prayer before the fleet came to Quebec; God would not regard your prayers but heard ours, and almost in a miraculous way preserved us when assaulted and refused to hear your fast-day prayers for your preservation but heard ours for your desolation and our success."[108]

They boasted also of their king and his greatness and spoke of him as though there could be no settlement of the world but as he pleased, reviling us as in a low and languishing case, having no king, but being under the government of a queen.[109] And [they] spoke as though the Duke of Bavaria would in a short time be Emperor.[110]

From this day forward God gave them to hear sorrowful tidings from Europe, that a war was been commenced against the Duke of Savoy and so their enemies increased, their bishop taken,[111] and two millions of wealth with him. News every year more distressing and impoverishing to them; and the Duke

---

107. In July 1704, English warships captured at sea Bishop Jeanne-Baptiste de La Croix de Chevrières de Saint-Vallier (1653–1727) and several priests as they returned to New France. The bishop remained in England until the end of the war in 1713.

108. The French priest is referring to the defeat at Quebec in October 1690 of a New England army under Sir William Phips (1651–1695).

109. Queen Anne (1665–1714), the second daughter of James II, ruled from 1702 to 1714.

110. Elector Maximillian II Emanuel of Bavaria, an ally of the French, aspired to become the Emperor of the Holy Roman Empire, after the death of Emperor Leopold I (c. 1649–1705) who had been an ally of the English.

111. See note 107.

of Bavaria so far from being emperor that he is dispossessed of his dukedom; and France so far from being strengthened by Spain that the kingdom of Spain [is] like to be an occasion of the weakening and impoverishing their own kingdom—they themselves so reporting. And their great army going against New England turned back ashamed, and they discouraged and disheartened and every year very exercising fears and cares as to the savages who lived up the river [i.e., in the Great Lakes region]. Before the return of that army they told me we were led up and down and sold by the heathen as sheep for the slaughter, and they could not devise what they should do with us, we should be so many prisoners when the army returned.

The Jesuits told me it was a great mercy that so many of our children were brought to them, and that, now especially since they were not like speedily to be returned, there was hope of their being brought over to the Romish faith. They would take the English children born among them, and, against the consent of their parents, baptize them. One Jesuit came to me and asked whether all the English at Lorette,[112] a place not far from Quebec where the savages lived, were baptized. I told him they were. He said, "If they be not, let me know of it that I may baptize them for fear they should die and be damned if they die without baptism." Says he, "When the savages went against you, I charged them to baptize all children before they killed them, such was my desire of your eternal salvation, though you were our enemies."

There was a gentleman, called Monsieur de Beauville,[113] a captain, the brother of the Lord Intendant, who was a good friend to me and very courteous to all the captives; he lent me an English Bible, and when he went to France gave it to me.

All means were used to seduce poor souls. I was invited one day to dine with one of chief note. As I was going [I] met with the superior of the Jesuits coming out of the house, and he came in after dinner; and presently it was propounded to me, if I would stay among them and be of their religion, I should have a great and honorable pension from the king every year. The superior of the Jesuits turned to me and said, "Sir, you have manifested much grief and sorrow for your separation from so many of your neighbors and children; if you will now comply with this offer and proposal, you may have all your children with you, and here will be enough for an honorable maintenance for you and them."

---

112. The Huron village today known as Wendake.
113. Charles de Beauharnois de la Boische, Marquis de Beauharnois (1671–1749), was a French naval officer. Beauville was actually the title of his older brother, François de Beauharnois de la Chaussaye, Baron de Beauville (1665–1746), who was the intendant of New France, in charge of the legal and financial affairs of the colony, from 1702 to 1705. Charles de Beauharnois succeeded Vaudreuil as governor and served from 1726 to 1747.

I answered, "Sir, if I thought your religion to be true, I would embrace it freely without any such offer, but so long as I believe it to be what it is, the offer of the whole world is of no more value to me than a blackberry." And [I] manifested such an abhorrence of this proposal that I speedily went to take my leave and be gone.

"Oh, Sir," said he, "sit down, why [are you] in such a hurry. You are alone in your chamber; divert yourself a little longer," and fell to other discourse. And within a half an hour says again, "Sir, I have one thing earnestly to request of you. I pray pleasure me."

I said, "Let your Lordship speak."

Said he, "I pray come down to the palace tomorrow morning and honor me with your company in my coach to the great church, it being then a saint's day."

I answered, "Ask me anything wherein I can serve you with a good conscience, and I am ready to gratify you, but I must yet ask your excuse here," and immediately went away from him. Returning unto my chamber, I gave God thanks for His upholding me and also made an inquiry with myself whether I had by any action given encouragement for such a temptation.

[At Chateau Richer]

Not many days after and a few days before Governor de Vaudreuil coming down, I was sent away fifteen miles down the river that I might not have opportunity [to] converse with the English. I was courteously treated by the French and the priest of that parish. They told me he was one of the most learned men in the country.[114] He was a very ingenious man, zealous in their way, but yet very familiar. I had many disputes with the priests who came thither, and, when I used their own authors to confute some of their positions, my books, borrowed of them, were taken away from me, for they said I made an ill use of them. They, having many of them boasted of their unity in doctrine and profession, were loath I should show them from their own best approved authors as many different opinions as they could charge against us.

Here again, a gentleman in the presence of the old bishop[115] and a priest offered me his house and whole living with assurance of honor, wealth, and em-

---

114. Guillaume Gaultier (1653–1720) was born in Canada, but studied for the priesthood in France before returning to New France in 1675. He was the priest of Beaupré and Chateau Richer from 1678 until his death. Chateau Richer was a seigneurial manor belonging to Bishop Laval and from 1700 to 1710 a small Latin school was held in the church's presbytery.

115. François de Laval (1623–1708), the first bishop in New France, had resigned his office in 1685 but filled in for absent Bishop Saint-Vallier after the latter had gone to France in 1700.

ployment, if I would embrace their ways. I told them I had an indignation of soul against such offers on such terms as parting with what was more valuable than all the world, alleging, "What is a man profited if he gain the whole world and lose his own soul? Or what shall a man give in exchange for his soul?"

I was sometimes told I might have all my children if I would comply and must never expect to have them on any other terms. I told them my children were dearer to me than all the world, but I would not deny Christ and His truths for the having of them with me; I would still put my trust in God who could perform all things for me.

I am persuaded that the priest of that parish where I [was] kept abhorred their sending down the heathen to commit outrages against the English; saying it was more like committing murders than managing a war.[116] In my confinement in this parish I had my undisturbed opportunities to be humbly imploring grace for ourselves, for soul and body, for His protecting presence with New England, and His disappointing the bloody designs of enemies, that God would be a little sanctuary to us in a land of captivity, and that our friends in New England might have grace to make a more thankful and faithful improvement of [the] means of grace than we had done, who by our neglects find ourselves out of God's sanctuary.

On the twenty-first of October, 1704, I received some letters from New England with an account that many of our neighbors escaped out of the desolations in the fort, and that my dear wife was recarried and decently buried, and that my eldest son,[117] who was absent in our desolation, was sent to college and provided for, which occasioned thanksgiving to God in the midst of afflictions and caused prayers even in Canada to be going daily up to heaven for a blessing upon benefactors showing such kindness to the desolate and afflicted.

The consideration of such crafty designs to ensnare young ones and to turn them from the simplicity of the Gospel to Romish superstition was very exercising. Sometimes they would tell me my children, sometimes my neighbors, were turned to be of their religion. Some made it their work to allure poor souls by flatteries and great promises, some threatened; some offered abusive carriages to such as refused to go to church and be present at Mass; for some they industriously contrived to get them married among them. A priest drew up a compendium of the Romish Catholic Faith and pretended to prove it by Scriptures, telling the English that all they required was contained in the Scrip-

---

116. On this attitude toward Natives, see also, Letter from Claude de Ramezay, 83–86.
117. Eleazer Williams (1688–1742) was probably at school in Hadley, Massachusetts, at the time of the attack. He later attended Harvard and became the minister in Mansfield, Connecticut.

tures, which they acknowledged to be the rule of faith and manners, but it was by Scriptures horribly perverted and abused. I could never come to the sight of it, though I often earnestly entreated a copy of it, until I was [on] shipboard for our voyage to New England, but hearing of it, I endeavored to possess the English with their danger of being cheated with such a pretense. I understood they would tell the English that I was turned that they might gain them to change their religion.[118] These their endeavors to seduce to popery were very exercising to me.

And in my solitariness I drew up these following sorrowful, mournful considerations (though unused to and unskilled in poetry) yet in a plain style for the use of some of the captives who would sometimes make their secret visits to me, which at the desire of some of them are here made public.

Some Contemplations of the Poor and Desolate State of the Church at Deerfield

The sorrows of my heart enlarged are,
Whilst I my present state with past compare.
I frequently unto God's house did go,
With Christian friends His praises forth to show;
But now I solitary sit, both sigh and cry,
Whilst my flock's misery think on do I.
Many, both old and young, were slain outright,
Some in a bitter season take their flight;
Some burnt to death, and others stifled were:
The enemy no sex or age would spare.
The tender children, with their parents sad
Are carried forth as captives, some unclad.
Some murdered in the way, unburied left,
And some through famine were of life bereft.
After a tedious journey, some are sold,
Some kept in heathen hands, all from Christ's fold
By popish rage and heathennish cruelty
Are banished. Yea, some compell'd to be
Present at Mass. Young children parted are
From parents and such as instructors were.

---

118. See Williams, "What Befell Stephen Williams," 168.

Crafty designs are used by papists all
In ignorance of truth them to enthrall.
Some threatened are unless they will comply
In heathens' hands again be made to lie.
To some large promises are made if they
Will truths renounce and choose their popish way.
Oh Lord! Mine eyes on Thee shall waiting be
Till thou again turn our captivity.
Their Romish plots Thou canst confound, and save
This little flock, this mercy I do crave.
Save us from all our sins, and yet again
Deliver us from them who truth disdain.
Lord! For Thy mercy sake Thy covenant mind,
And in Thy house again rest let us find.
So we Thy praises forth will show, and speak
Of all Thy wondrous works, yea we will seek
The advancement of Thy great and glorious name;
Thy rich and sovereign grace we will proclaim.

The hearts of some were ready to be discouraged and sink, saying they were out of sight and so out of mind. I endeavored to persuade them we were not forgotten, that undoubtedly many prayers were continually going up to heaven for us. Not long after came Captain Livingston[119] and Mr. Sheldon[120] with letters from his excellency our governor to the governor of Canada about the exchange of prisoners, which gave a revival to many and raised expectations of a return. These visits from New England to Canada so often greatly strengthened many who were ready to faint and gave some check to the designs of the papists to gain proselytes.

But God's time of deliverance was not yet come. As to some particular persons, their temptations and trials were increased, and some abused because they refused a compliance with their superstitions. A young woman of our town met with a new trial. For one day a Frenchman came into the room where she was and showed her his beads and boasted of them, putting them near to her. She knocked them out of his hands on the floor, for which she was beaten

---

119. John Livingston (1680–1720) was a merchant from New York who lived in New England and had ties to New France. He offered to make use of these ties to secure the captives' return. He also served as a military officer during the War of the Spanish Succession.

120. Ensign John Sheldon (1658–c. 1733) of Deerfield made three trips to Canada from late 1704 to 1707 to obtain the release of captives.

and threatened with death and for some days imprisoned. I pleaded with God His overruling this first essay for the deliverance of some, as a pledge of the rest being delivered in due time.

I improved [i.e., implored] Captain de Beauville, who had always been very friendly, to intercede with the governor for the return of my eldest daughter, and for his purchasing my son Stephen from the Indians at St. Francis Fort, and for liberty to go up and see my children and neighbors at Montreal. Divine providence appeared to a moderating [of] my affliction in that five English persons of our town were permitted to return with Captain Livingston, among whom went my eldest daughter [i.e., Esther]. And my son Stephen was redeemed and sent to live with me. He was almost quite naked and very poor. He had suffered much among the Indians. One of the Jesuits took upon him to come to the wigwam and whip him on some complaint that the squaws had made that he did not work enough for them.[121]

As to my petition for going up to Montreal to see my children and neighbors, it was denied, as my former desire of coming up to the city before Captain Livingston's coming was. God granted me favor as to two of my petitions, but yet brought me by His grace to be willing that He should glorify Himself in disposing of me and mine as he pleased and knew to be most for His glory. And almost always before any remarkable favor I was brought to lie down at the foot of God and made to be willing that God should govern the world so as might be most for His own honor and brought to resign all to His holy sovereignty. A frame of spirit when wrought in me by the grace of God giving the greatest content and satisfaction, and very often a forerunner of the mercy asked of God or a plain demonstration that the not obtaining my request was best for me. I had no small refreshing in having one of my children with me for four months.

And the English were many of them strengthened with hopes that the treaty between the governments would issue in opening a door of escape for all. In August [1705], Mr. [William] Dudley and Captain Vetch[122] arrived, and great encouragements were given as to an exchange of all in the spring of the year; and some few again were sent home, among whom I obtained leave to send my son Stephen.

---

121. For Stephen's account of this incident, see "What Befell Stephen Williams," 168–169.

122. Samuel Vetch (1668–1732) was a Scot who settled in New York and became involved in illegal trade with New France. In 1705, he became involved with the efforts to secure the captives' return to further his trading interests and to spy on the French. In 1707 he went to England and became the leading advocate for a British invasion of New France. He served with the forces invading Acadia in 1710 and became the first governor of Nova Scotia.

[At Quebec]

Upon Mr. Dudley's and Captain Vetch's petitioning, I was again permitted to go up to Quebec. But disputing with a mendicant friar,[123] who said he was an Englishman sent from France to endeavor the conversion of the English at Quebec, who arrived at Canada while our gentlemen were there, I was, by the priests' means ordered again to return to Chateau Richer, and no other reason given but because I discoursed with that priest and their fear [that] I should prevent his success among the captives.

But God showed His dislike of such a persecuting spirit: for the very next day, which was September 20, Old Style, October 1st, New Style, the Seminary, a very famous building, was most of it burned down, occasioned by a joiner's letting a coal of fire drop among the shavings. The chapel in the priests' garden, and the great cross were burned down [and] the library of the priests burned up. This Seminary and another library had been burned but about three years before. The day after my being sent away by the priests' means from Quebec at first [i.e., previously], there was a thunderstorm and the lightning struck the Seminary in the very place where the fire now began.

[At Chateau Richer]

A little before Mr. Dudley's arrival, came a soldier into my landlord's house barefoot and barelegged, going on a pilgrimage to Saint Anne.[124] "For," said he, "my captain, who died some years ago, appeared to me and told me he was in purgatory, and told me I must go a pilgrimage to Saint Anne doing penance, and get a Mass said for him, and then he should be delivered." And many believed him and were much affected with it, [and] came and told me of it to gain my credit of their devised purgatory. The soldier told me the priests had counseled him to undertake this pilgrimage, and I am apt to think, ordered his calling in at my landlord's, that I might see and speak with him. I laughed at the conceit that a soldier must be pitched upon to be sent on this errand, but they were much displeased and lamented my obstinacy in that I would not be reclaimed from a denial of purgatory by such a miraculous providence.

As I was able, I spread the case before God, beseeching of Him to disappoint them in their expectations to proselyte any of the captives by this stratagem.

123. A Récollet friar. The Récollets were Franciscans.
124. The church of Sainte-Anne de Beaupré is about five miles from Chateau Richer. The church in Beaupré had been dedicated to Saint Anne, the mother of the Virgin Mary, in the seventeenth century and was immediately credited with miraculous healing powers.

And by the goodness of God it was not very serviceable, for the soldier's conversation [i.e., behavior] was such that several among the French themselves judged it to be a forgery. And though the captain spoken of was the governor's lady's brother,[125] I never more heard any concernment or care to get him out of purgatory.

One of the parish where I lived told me that on the twenty-second of July 1705, he was at Quebec, at the mendicant friars' church[126] on one of their feast days in honor of a great saint of their order and that at five o'clock Mass in the morning, near two hundred persons present, a great gray cat broke or pushed aside some glass, and entered into the church, and passed along it near the altar, and put out five or six candles that were burning, and that no one could tell which way the cat went out; and he thought it was the devil.

When I was in the city in September, I saw two English maids who had lived with the Indians a long time. They told me that an Indian had died at the place where they were; and that when sundry of his relations were together in order [to attend] his burial, the dead arose and informed them that at his death he went to hell, and there he saw all the Indians that had been dead since their embracing the popish religion, and warned them to leave it off or they would be damned too, and laid down dead again. They said the Indians were frightened and very melancholy. But the Jesuit to whom they told this [story] told them it was only a delusion of the devil to draw them away from the true religion, adding, that he knew for certain that all those Indians who had been dead, spoken of by that Indian, were in heaven, only one squaw was gone to hell, who died without baptism. These maids said also that many of the Indians much lamented their making a war against the English at the instigation of the French.

[Resisting Conversion]

The priests, after Mr. Dudley's going from Canada [October 12, 1705], were ready to think their time was short for gaining English proselytes and doubled their diligence and wiles to gain over persons to their persuasion. I improved all opportunities I could to write to the English that in that way I might be serviceable to them, but many or most of my letters treating about religion were intercepted and burned. I had a letter sent down to me by order of the governor that I had liberty of writing to my children and friends, which should be continued, provided I wrote about indifferent things and said nothing in them about

---

125. Pierre-Jacques Joybert (1677–1703), an officer in the colonial regulars, died of smallpox at Quebec in 1703.

126. The Récollets' chapel.

the points in controversy between them and us. And if I was so hardy as to write letters otherwise, they should endeavor to prevent their being delivered. Accordingly I found many of them were burned. But sometimes notice would be given to the English that there were letters written, but they were burned, so that their writing was somewhat useful though never perused by the English because they judged those letters condemned popery. Many of our letters written from New England were never delivered because of some expressions about religion in them.

And, as I said before, after Mr. Dudley's departure from Quebec endeavors were very vigorous to seduce [us]. Some were flattered with large promises, others were threatened and beaten because they would not turn. And when two Englishwomen who had always opposed their religion were sick in the hospital, they kept them night and day till they died, and their friends [were] kept from coming to visit them. After their death they gave out that they died in the Romish faith and were received into their communion. Before their death Masses were said for them and they [were] buried in the churchyard with all their ceremonies. And after this, letters [were] sent into all parts to inform the English that these two women turned to their religion before their death, and that it concerned them to follow their example, for they could not be more obstinate than those women were in their health against the Romish faith and yet on a deathbed [they] embraced it. They told the English who lived near that our religion was a dangerous religion to die in. But I shall hereafter relate the just grounds we have to think these things were falsehoods.

I was informed, there was an English girl bid to take and wear the cross and cross herself. She refused; they threatened her, and showed her the cross. At length she had her choice, either to cross herself and take the cross, or be whipped. She chose to be whipped, and they took up her clothes and made as though they would correct her. But seeing her choosing indeed to suffer rather than comply, they desisted and tied the cross about her neck. Some were taken and shut up among their religious, and all sorts of means used to gain them.

I received a letter from one of my neighbors[127] wherein he thus bewails:

I obtained leave of my master to go to the Maqua fort [i.e., Kahnawake] to see my children that I had not seen for a long time. I carried a letter from my master to show that I had leave to come. When I came to the fort, I heard that one of my children was in the woods. I went to see a boy I had there, who lived with one of the Jesuits. I had just asked him of his

---

127. This man was probably Martin Kellogg Senior (1658–1732), a captive whose daughters Joanna (1693–?) and Rebecca (1695–1757) and son Joseph (1691–1756) were at Kahnawake.

welfare: he said his master would come presently; he durst not stay to speak with me now, being in such awe of his master. On which I withdrew; and when his master came in, I went and asked leave of him to speak with my child and showed him my letter. But he absolutely refused to let me see or speak with him; and said I had brought no letter from the governor and would not permit me to stay in the fort, though I had traveled on foot near fifty miles for no other errand than to see and speak with my children.

The same person, with another Englishman last spring obtained leave of the governor-general to go to the same fort on the same errand and carried letters from the governor to the Jesuits that he might be permitted to speak with his children. The letter was delivered to the Jesuits, who told him his son was not at home but gone a-hunting, [when in fact] he was hid from them, as he heard afterwards. So the poor man lost his labor a second time. These men say that when they returned to Montreal, one Laland,[128] who was appointed as a spy always to observe the motions of the English, told them that one of the Jesuits had come in before them and had told the governor that the lad was gone out a-hunting. And that the Englishman who accompanied this poor man went out into the woods in hopes of finding the lad and saw him, but the lad ran away, and that he followed him and called after him, but he would not stop, but holding [out] a gun threatened to shoot him down if he followed him, and so was discouraged and turned back. And, says Laland, "You will never leave going to see your children and neighbors till some of you are killed." But the men told him it was an absolute lie, let who would report it, for they had neither seen the lad nor did they go into the woods to search after him. They judge this was told to the governor to prevent any English for the future going to see their children and neighbors.

Some of ours say they have been little better than absolutely promised to have their children who are among the savages in case they themselves would embrace popery. And that the priests had said they had rather the children should be among the Indians as they [were] than be brought out by the French, and so be in a readiness to return for New England.

A maid of our town was put into a religious house among the nuns for more than two years, and all sorts of means, by flatteries, threatenings, and abusive carriages, used to bring her to turn. They offered her money, which when re-

---

128. Jean LaLande (c. 1645–c. 1715) appears to have been a French soldier who arrived in New France in 1665. In the 1680s he and several other solders moved to New York and New Jersey, where they evidently engaged in the secret fur trade with New France. LaLande returned to Montreal around 1700 and served as an interpreter.

fused, especially the latter part of the time, they threatened her very much, sent for her before them, commanded her to cross herself. She refused. They hit her a box on the ear, bid her again; still she refused. They ordered a rod with six branches full of knots to be brought, and when she refused, they struck her on the hands with their renewing their commands, and she stood to her refusals till her hands were filled with wales [from] the blows. But one said, "Beat her no more; we will give her to the Indians if she won't turn." They pinched her arms till they were black and blue, and made her go into their church, and because she would not cross herself, struck her several blows with their hands on her face.

A squaw was brought in and said she was sent to fetch her to the Indians, but she refused. The squaw went away and said she would bring her husband with her tomorrow, and she should be carried away by force. She told me she remembered what I told her one day after the nuns had threatened to give her away to the Indians, that they only said so to affright her, that they never would give her away. The nuns told her she should not be permitted anymore to speak to the English and that they would afflict her without giving her any rest if she refused. But God preserved her from falling. This poor girl had many prayers going up to heaven for her daily and by name because her trials were more known to some of the English than the trials of others who lived more remote from them.

Here might be a history by itself of the trials and sufferings of many of our children and young ones who have been abused and after separation from grown persons made to do as they would have them.

[Samuel's Story]

I shall here give an account of what was done to one of my children, a boy between fifteen and sixteen years of age, two hundred miles distant from me, which occasioned grief and sorrow that I want words to utter, and yet he was kept under such awe that he never durst write anything to me for fear of being discovered in writing about religion. They threatened to put him to the Indians again if he would not turn, telling him he was never bought out of their hands but only sojourned with them, but, if he would turn, he should never be put into their hands any more. The priests would spend whole days in urging him.

He was sent to school to learn to read and write French. The schoolmaster sometimes flattered him with promises if he would cross himself, then threatened him if he would not. But when he saw flattering promises of rewards and threatenings were ineffectual, he struck him with a stick he had in his hand; and when he saw that would not do, he made him get down on his knees about an hour, and then came and bid him make the sign of the cross, and that without any delay. He still refused. Then he gave him a couple of strokes with a whip he had in his hand, which whip had three branches and about twelve great knots tied to it. And again bid him make the sign of the cross, and if it was any sin he would bear it himself. And said also, "You are afraid you shall be changed if you do it, but," said he, "you will be the same, your fingers won't be changed." And after he had made him shed many tears under his abuses and threatenings, he told him he would have it done; and so, through cowardice and fear of the whip, he made the sign, and did so for several days together, and with much ado, he was brought to cross himself.

And then the master told him he would have it done without his particular bidding him. And when he came to say his lesson and crossed not himself, the master said, "Have you forgot what I bid you do?

"No, Sir," said he.

Then the schoolmaster said, "Down on your knees." And so kept him for an hour and a half, till school was done, and so did for about a week. When he saw this would not do, he took the whip, "What! Won't you do it?" said he, "I will make you." And so again frightened him to a compliance.

After this, [he] commanded him to go to the church. When he refused, he told him he would make him. And one morning [he] sent four of the biggest boys of the school to draw him by force to Mass. These with other severities and witty stratagems were used, and I utterly ignorant of any attempt made upon him to bring him to change his religion. His fear was such that he never durst write any of these things least his letters should fall into their hands, and he should again be delivered to the Indians. Hearing of an opportunity of writing to him by one of the parish where I was, going up to Montreal, I wrote a letter to him and had by him a letter from my son, which I shall here insert.

Honored Father:—

I have received your letter bearing date January 11th, 1705/6, for which I give you many thanks with my duty, and my brother's. I am sorry you have not received all the letters I have writ to you, as I have not received all yours. According to your good counsel I do almost every day read something of the Bible and so strengthen my faith.

As to the captives newly brought, Lancaster is the place of two of them and Marlborough that of the third: the governor of Montreal has them all three. There is other news that will seem more strange to you: that two Englishwomen who in their lifetime were dreadfully set against the Catholic religion did on their deathbed embrace it. The one Abigail Turbet,[129] the other of them Esther Jones,[130] both of them known to you.

Abigail Turbett sent for Mr. Meriel[131] the Sabbath before she died, and said (many a time upon several following days) that she committed her soul into his hands and was ready to do whatever he pleased. She desired him to go to the Chapel Saint Anne and there to say a holy Mass for her that she might have her sins pardoned and the will of the Lord accomplished upon her. Her cousin, Mrs. Badston, now Stilson,[132] asked her whether she would be willing to do as she said. She answered, "Yes." And upon the Tuesday she was taken into the Catholic Church in the presence of John Laland, and Madam Grizalem, an Englishwoman,[133] and Mrs. Stilson, also with many French people besides.

She was anointed with oil on the same day, according to her will. Then upon Wednesday, an image of Christ crucified [was] brought to her. She caused it to be set up over against her at the curtains of her bed and looked continually upon the same. And also a little crucifix [was] brought unto her. She took it and kissed it, and laid it upon her stomach. She did also make the sign of the cross upon herself when she took any meat or drink. She promised to God that if she should recover she would go to the Mass every day. She, having on her hand a crucifix, saying, "Oh my Lord that I should have known thee so late!"

She did also make a prayer to the Virgin Mary the two last days of the

---

129. Abigail Cass Turbet (1674–1705) was captured, probably in August 1703, at Cape Porpoise, which is today part of Kennebunkport, Maine. French records indicate that she converted to Catholicism, received the sacraments of penitence and extreme unction from Father Meriel, and was buried in the cemetery of the church of Notre-Dame in Montreal.

130. Esther Ingersoll Jones (1665–1705) was captured on the May 19, 1704, raid on Pascommuck in Northampton, Massachusetts. French records indicate that she converted to Catholicism, received the sacraments of penitence and extreme unction from Father Henri-Antoine de Meriel, (1661–1713), a priest of the Congregation of Saint Sulpice, and was buried in the cemetery of Notre-Dame in Montreal.

131. Father Henri-Antoine Meriel (1661–1713) was born in France and came to Montreal in 1690. Because he spoke English, he played a central role in the efforts to convert New England captives to Catholicism.

132. Anne or Hannah Odiorne Batison (1673–?) was captured at Cape Porpoise along with her husband, John, and their two children, Mary and John, in August 1703. John died in captivity in 1704 and his wife and children converted to Catholicism. On October 4, 1705 (New Style) she married James Stilson, a captive from Marblehead, Massachusetts. They eventually returned to New England.

133. Madam Grizalem was Grizel Warren Otis (1662–1750). She was widowed and taken prisoner in the June 28, 1689, attack on Dover, Hew Hampshire. In New France she converted to Catholicism and married Philipe Robitaille in 1693. They lived in Montreal, where she assisted Father Meriel in his efforts to convert New England captives to Catholicism.

week. She could utter no word, but by kissing the crucifix [and] endeavoring the crossing herself, she gave an evidence of her faith. She died Saturday, the 24th of November [1705], at three o'clock in the afternoon. The next day the priest did commend that woman's soul to the prayers of the congregation in the Mass. In the afternoon she was honorably buried in the churchyard next to the church, close to the body of the Justice Pese's wife,[134] all the people being present at her funeral.

The same day in the evening Mr. Meriel, with an Englishwoman, went to Esther Jones. She did at first disdain, but a little [while] after she confessed there were seven sacraments, Christ's body present, the sacrament of the Mass, the inequality of power among the pastors of the church; and being returned to wait by her all night long, he read and expounded to her some part of the Catholic Confession of Faith to her satisfaction.[135] About midnight he asked her whether she might not confess her sins. "I doubt not but I may," said she, and two hours after, she made unto him a fervent confession of all the sins of her whole life. When he said he was to offer Christ to His Father for her, she liked it very well.

The superior of the nuns being come in to see her, she now desired that she might receive Christ's body before she died. She did also show Mrs. Stilson a great mind to receive the sacrament of extreme unction, and said that if ever she should recover and get home she would have reproached the ministers for their neglecting that sacrament so plainly commanded by St. James. In the afternoon after she had begged pardon for her wavering, and the Catholic Confession of Faith was read aloud to her in the hearing of Mr. Craston,[136] Mrs. Stilson, and another Englishwoman, and she owned the same. About seven o'clock the same day, she said to Mr. Dubison,[137] "Shall not they give me the holy com-

---

134. Justice Pese was probably a misnomer for justice of the peace, but who he or his wife might have been is unclear.

135. This sentence lays out a number of points in dispute between Catholics and Puritan New Englanders: Catholics believed in seven sacraments, the Puritans in two—baptism and communion; Catholics believed in the real presence of Christ's body in communion, the Puritans saw communion as a symbolic memorial; Catholics believed the Mass was a sacrifice and a sacrament, the Puritans did not; and Catholics believed in a hierarchical conception of the clergy and the primacy of the pope in Rome, the Puritans saw their ministers as equal and their clerical office dependent upon a specific relationship with a particular congregation.

136. Craston cannot be identified.

137. Dubuison was probably Robert Potier Dubuisson (1682–1744). Like Jean LaLande, Dubuisson's father had come to New France as a soldier and subsequently moved to New York around 1674 and then to Woodbridge, New Jersey, where Robert was born and where he learned to speak both English and Dutch. The family returned to New France in 1699 and after 1703 Robert was employed by the government.

munion?" But her tongue was then so thick that she could hardly swallow anything. She was then anointed with holy oil, but before, she said to Mr. Meriel, "Why have you not yet, sir, forgiven my sins?"

In the night following that priest and Mr. Dubison were continually by her and sometimes praying to God in her name and praying to the Virgin Mary and other saints. She said also, "I believe all. I am very glad Christ was offered to His Father for me." Six or seven hours before she died, a crucifix was showed to her by Mr. Dubison. She took it and laid it upon her heart, and kissed it, and then the nuns hung it with a pair of beads upon her neck. A little before she died, Mr. Dubison asked her to pray for him in heaven. She promised him.

So she gave up the ghost at ten o'clock the 27th of November [1705], while the high Mass was saying. She was soon commended to the prayers. On the fourth day of the week following [she] was buried after the Mass had been said for her. She was laid by Abigail Turbet.

January 23d, 1705/6

I have here transcribed the letter in the very words of it without the least alteration. The same [in] substance was sent to several other captives. When I had this letter, I presently knew it to be of Mr. Meriel's composing, but the messenger who brought the letter brought word that my son had embraced their religion. Afterwards, when some blamed him for letting me know of it because they said they feared my sorrow would shorten my days, he told me he thought with himself that, if he was in my case he should be willing to know the worst and, therefore, told me as he would have desired to have known if in my place. I thanked him, acknowledging it a favor to let me know of it, but the news was ready to overwhelm me with grief and sorrow.

I made my complaint to God and mourned before Him; sorrow and anguish took hold upon me. I asked of God to direct me what to do and how to write and find out an opportunity of conveying a letter to him and committed this difficulty to His providence. I now found a greater opposition to a patient, quiet, humble resignation to the will of God than I should otherwise have known, if not so tried. Here I thought of my afflictions and trials: my wife and two children killed, and many of my neighbors; and myself, so many of my children and friends in a popish captivity separated from our children, not capable to come to them to instruct them in the way they ought to go; and cunning, crafty enemies using all their subtlety to insinuate into young ones such principles as would be pernicious. I thought with myself how happy many others were, in that they had their children with them under all advantages to bring them up in the nurture and admonition of the Lord, while we were separated

one from another and our children in great peril of embracing damnable doctrines.

Oh, that all parents who read this history would bless God for the advantages
they have of educating their children and faithfully improve it! I mourned when
I thought with myself that I had one child with the Maquas [i.e., Eunice], a
second turned to popery [i.e., Samuel], and a little child [i.e., Warham], of six
years of age, in danger from a child to be instructed in popery, and knew full
well that all endeavors would be used to prevent my seeing or speaking with
them. But in the midst of all these, God gave me a secret hope that He would
magnify His power and free grace and disappoint all their crafty designs. When
I looked on the right hand and on the left, all refuge failed, and none showed
any care for my soul. But God brought that word to uphold me, "Who is able
to do exceeding abundantly above what we can ask or think." As also that, "Is
any thing too hard for God?" I prayed to God to direct me and wrote very short
the first time and in general terms, fearing lest if I should write about things in
controversy, my letters would not come to him. I therefore addressed him with
the following letter:

Son Samuel,

Yours of January 23d I received and with it had the tidings that you
had made an abjuration of the Protestant faith for the Romish,—news
that I heard with the most distressing, afflicting, sorrowful spirit that ever
I heard any news. Oh, I pity you; I mourn over you day and night! Oh, I
pity your weakness that through the craftiness of man you are turned
from the simplicity of the gospel! I persuade myself you have done it
through ignorance. Oh, why have you neglected to ask a father's advice
in an affair of so great importance as the change of religion? God knows
that the catechism in which I instructed you is according to the word of
God and so will be found in the Day of Judgment. Oh, consider and bethink yourself what you have done! And whether you ask me or not, my
poor child, I cannot but pray for you that you may be recovered out of
the snare you are taken in. Read the Bible; pray in secret; make Christ's
righteousness your only plea before God for justification. Beware of all
immorality and of profaning God's Sabbaths.

Let a father's advice be asked for the future in all things of weight and
moment. What is a man profited, if he gain the whole world and lose his
own soul? Or what shall a man give in exchange for his soul? I desire to be
humbled under the mighty hand of God thus afflicting me. I would not
do as you have done for ten thousand worlds. My heart aches within me,
but I will yet wait upon the Lord, to Him will I commit your case day and

night. He can perform all things for me and mine and can yet again recover you from your fall. He is a God, forgiving iniquity, transgression,
and sin. To the Lord our God belong forgiveness though we have rebelled.
I charge you not to be instrumental to ensnare your poor brother
Warham, or any other, and so add sin to sin. Accept of my love and don't
forsake a father's advice, who above all things desires that your soul may
be saved in the day of the Lord.

What I mournfully wrote, I followed with my poor cries to God in heaven
to make effectual, to cause in him a consideration of what he had done. God
saw what a proud heart I had and what need I had to be so answered out of the
whirlwind that I might be humbled before Him. Not having any answer to my
letter for some weeks, I wrote the following letter as I was enabled of God and
sent to him by a faithful hand, which by the blessing of God was made effectual
for his good and the good of others who had fallen to popery, and for the establishing and strengthening of others to resist the essays of the adversary to truth.
God brought good out of this evil and made what was designed to promote
their interest an occasion of shame to them.

Son Samuel,

I have waited till now for an answer from you, hoping to hear from
you why you made an abjuration of the Protestant faith for the Romish.
But since you continue to neglect to write to me about it as you neglected
to take any advice or counsel from a father when you did it, I cannot
forbear writing again and making some reflections on the letter you
wrote me last, about the two women. It seems to me from those words
of Abigail Turbet's in your letter, or rather of Mr. Meriel which you transcribed for him,—"Abigail Turbet sent for Mr. Meriel, she committed her
soul into his hands, and was ready to do whatever he pleased,"—I say, it
seems rational to believe that she had not the use of her reason; it's an
expression to be abhorred by all who have any true sense of religion. Was
Mr. Meriel a God, a Christ? Could he bear to hear such words and not reject them, replying, "Don't commit your soul into my hands, but see that
you commit your soul into the hands of God through Jesus Christ and do
whatever God commands you in His holy word."

As for me I am a creature and can't save your soul but will tell you of
Acts 4:12: "Neither is there salvation in any other, for there is no other
name under heaven given among men whereby we must be saved." Had
he been a faithful minister of Jesus Christ, he would have said, "Tis an
honor due to Christ alone." The holy apostle says, "Now unto Him that

is able to keep you and present you faultless before the presence of His glory with exceeding joy to the only wise God our Savior be glory and majesty, dominion and power, both now and ever. Amen." (Jude 24 and 25 verses).

As to what you write about praying to the Virgin Mary and other saints, I make this reply: had Mr. Meriel done his duty, he should have said to them, as 1 John 2:1–2: "If any man sin, we have an advocate with the Father, Jesus Christ the righteous, and He is the propitiation of our sins." The Scriptures say, "There is one God and one mediator between God and man, the man Christ Jesus." Yea, Christ said, "Go and preach, he that believeth and is baptized shall be saved." The apostle, in Galatians, 1:8, saith: "But though we or an angel from heaven preach any other gospel unto you than that we have preached to you, let him be accursed." They never preached [or] prayed to the Virgin Mary or other saints.

As you would be saved, hear what the apostle saith, Hebrews 4:13 etc: "Neither is there any creature that is not manifest in His sight, but all things are naked and opened unto the eyes of Him with whom we have to do. Seeing then that we have a great high priest that is entered into the heavens, Jesus the Son of God, let us hold fast our profession, for we have not a high priest that cannot be touched with the feeling of our infirmities but was in all points tempted like as we are, yet without sin. Let us therefore come boldly unto the throne of grace that we may obtain mercy and find grace to help in time of need." Which words do hold forth how that Jesus Christ is in every respect qualified to be a mediator and intercessor, and I am sure they can't be applied to any mere creature to make them capable of our religious trust.

When Roman Catholics have said all they can, they are not able to prove that the saints in heaven have a knowledge of what prayers are directed to them. Some say they know them one way, others say they have the knowledge of them in another way, and that which they have fixed upon as most probable to them is that they know of them from their beholding the face of God, seeing God, they know these prayers. But this is a great mistake. Though the saints see and know God in a glorious manner, yet they have not an infinite knowledge, and it does no ways follow that, because they see God, they know all prayers that are directed to them upon the earth. And God has nowhere in His word told us that the saints have such a knowledge.

Besides, were it a thing possible for them to have a knowledge of what prayers are directed to them, it does not follow that they are to be prayed to or have religious honor conferred upon them. The Romanists can neither give one Scripture precept or example for praying to them, but God has provided a mediator who knows all our petitions and is faithful and merciful enough, and we have both Scripture precept and example to look to Him as our mediator and advocate with the Father. Further it can't be proved that it's consistent with the saints being creatures as well as with their happiness to have a knowledge of prayers from all parts of the world at the same time from many millions together about things so vastly differing one from another. And then to present those supplications for all that look to them; it's not humility, but will worship. Colossians 2:18, "Let no man beguile you of your reward in a voluntary humility, worshipping of Angels." Verse 23: "Which things indeed have a show of wisdom, will worship and humility."

For what humility can it be to distrust the way that God has provided and encouraged us to come to Him in and impose upon God a way of our own devising? Was not God angry with Jeroboam for imposing upon Him after such a sort? 1 Kings 12:33: "So he offered upon the altar which he had made in Bethel the fifth day of the eighth month which he devised of his own heart." Therefore Christ saith, Mark 7:7: "Howbeit, in vain do they worship me, teaching for doctrines the commandments of men." Before the coming of Christ and His entering into heaven as an intercessor, Hebrews 7:25: "Wherefore He is able to save them to the uttermost that come to God by Him, seeing he ever liveth to make intercession for them." I say, before Christ's entering into heaven as an intercessor [there is] not one word of any prayer to saints. What reason can be given that now there is [need] of so many saints to make intercession when Christ as a priest is entered into heaven to make intercession for us?

The answer that the Romanists give is a very fable and falsehood, namely that there were no saints in heaven till after the Resurrection and Ascension of Christ but [they] were reserved in a place called *Limbus Patrum* and so had not the beatifical vision. See Genesis 5:24: "Enoch walked with God and was not, for God took him." If he was not taken into heaven, what can be the sense of those words "for God took him?" Again, 2 Kings 2:1: "When the Lord would take up Elijah into heaven by a whirlwind." Verse 11: "There appeared a chariot of fire and horses of fire and parted them both asunder, and Elijah went up by a whirlwind into heaven." Must the truth of the Scriptures be called in question to uphold their notions? Besides, 'tis not consistent with reason to suppose that Enoch and Elias, instead of having a peculiar privilege vouchsafed to them for their eminency in holiness, should be less happy for so long a time than the rest of the saints deceased who are glorified in heaven, which must be if they are yet kept, and must be till the Day of Judgment, out of heaven and the beatifical vision in an earthly paradise, according to some of the Romanists, or in some other place they know not where, according to others.

Religious worship is not to be given to the creature, Matthew. 4:9–10, and saith, "All these things will I give thee, if thou wilt fall down and worship me. Then saith Jesus to him, 'Get thee hence, Satan; for it is written, Thou shalt worship the Lord thy God, and him only shalt thou serve.'" That phrase, "and him only shalt thou serve," excludes all creatures. Revelations 22:8–9, "I fell down to worship before the feet of the angel which showed me these things. Then saith he to me, 'see thou do it not, for I am thy fellow servant, and of thy brethren the Prophets, and of them which keep the sayings of this book—worship God.'" Which plainly shows that God only is to be worshipped with a religious worship. None can think that Saint John intended to give the highest divine worship to the angel who saith, "Don't fall down and worship me; it's God's due, worship God." So Acts 10:25–26: "As Peter was coming in, Cornelius met him, and fell down at his feet and worshipped him, but Peter took him up, saying, 'Stand up; I myself also am a man.'"

See also Leviticus 19:10, the words of the Second Commandment (which the Romanists either leave out or add to the First Commandment, saying, "Thou shalt have no other gods before me," adding etc.). I say the words of the Second Commandment are, "Thou shalt not make to thyself any graven image, or any likeness of anything that is in heaven above, or that is in the earth beneath, or that is in the waters under the earth; thou shalt not bow down thyself to them nor serve them, for I the Lord thy God am a jealous God, etc." These words being inserted in the letter that came from your brother Eleazer in New England the last summer was the cause of the letter's being sent down from Montreal and not given to you when so near you, as I suppose there being no other clause of the letter that could be objected against and the reason why [I] found [it] at Quebec, when I sent it to you a second time [and] enclosed in a letter written by myself.

The brazen serpent made by divine appointment as a type of Christ, when abused to superstition, was by reforming Hezekiah broken in pieces. As to what the Romanists plead about the lawfulness of image and saint worship from those likenesses of things made in Solomon's Temple, it's nothing to the purpose. We don't say it is not lawful to make or have a picture, but those carved images were not in the Temple to be adored, bowed down to, or worshipped. There is no manner of consequence that because there were images made in Solomon's Temple that were not adored and worshipped that therefore it's now lawful to make and fall down before images and pray to them and so worship them. Religious worshipping of saints can't be defended from but is forbidden in the Scriptures, and, for fear of losing their disciples, the Romanists keep away from them the Bible and oblige them to believe as they say they must believe. As though there was no use to be made of our reason about our souls, and yet the Beroeans[138] were counted noble for searching the Scriptures to see whether the things preached by Saint Paul were so or no. They dare not allow you liberty to speak with your father or others for fear their errors should be discovered to you.

Again, you write that Esther Jones confessed that there "was an inequality of power among the pastors of the Church." An argument to convince the world that because the priests in fallacious ways caused a woman distempered with a very high fever, if not distracted, to say she confessed there was an inequality of power among the pastors of the church; therefore, all the world are obliged to believe that there is a pope; an argument to be sent from Dan to Beersheba,[139] everywhere, where any English captives are, to gain their belief of a pope.

Can any rational man think that Christ in the sixteenth chapter of Matthew gave Saint Peter such a power as the papists speak of, or that the disciples so understood Christ? When immediately there arose a dispute among them who should be the greatest in the Kingdom of Heaven? Matthew 18:1: "At the same time came the Disciples of Jesus, saying, 'Who is the greatest in the Kingdom of Heaven?' " The rock spoken of in the sixteenth of Matthew [is] not the person of Peter but the confession made by him, and the same power is given to all the Disciples, if you compare one Scripture with another [there is] not one word in any place of Scripture of such a vicarship power as of a pope, nor any solid foundation of proof that Peter had a greater authority than the rest of the Apostles. 1 Corinthians 4:6: "That you might learn in us not to think of men above that which is written." Yea, the apostle condemns them, 1 Corinthians 1:12, for their contentions, "one saying, I am of Paul, I of Apollos, and I of Caephas;" no more of Peter's being a foundation than any of the rest. "For we are built upon the foundation of the Apostles and Prophets,

---

138. The Beroeans were residents of a town in Macedonia where Saint Paul had success preaching the gospel at a Jewish synagogue. "These were more noble than those in Thessalonica, in that they received the word with all readiness of mind, and searched the scriptures daily, whether those things were so." Acts 17:11.

139. A reference to the boundaries of ancient Israel.

Jesus Christ Himself being the chief cornerstone." Not one word in any of Peter's epistles showing that he had greater power than the other Apostles.

Nay, if the Scriptures give any preference, it is to Saint Paul rather than Saint Peter. 1 Corinthians 3:10: "According to the grace of God which is given to me as a wise master builder, I have laid the foundation." 1 Corinthians 5:3–4: "For I verily as absent in body but present in spirit, have judged already as though I were present concerning him that hath so done this deed. In the name of our Lord Jesus Christ when ye are gathered together, and my spirit, with the power of our Lord Jesus Christ," etc. 1 Corinthians 7:1; "Now concerning the things whereof ye wrote to me;" application made not to Saint Peter, but Paul for the decision of a controversy or scruple. 1 Corinthians 11:2: "Now I praise you brethren that you remember me in all things and keep the ordinances as I delivered them to you." Either those spoken of, Acts 15, or in his ministry and epistles, 2 Corinthians 2:10, "For your sake forgave I it, in the person of Christ." 2 Corinthians 9:28: "That which cometh upon me daily, the care of all the churches." 2 Corinthians 12:11–12: "For in nothing am I behind the very chiefest of the Apostles, though I be nothing. Truly the signs of an Apostle were wrought among you, in all patience, in signs and wonders and mighty deeds," and in other places.

Again if you consult Acts 15 where you have an account of the first synod or council, you will find that the counsel or sentence of the Apostle James is followed, verse 19, "Wherefore my sentence is," etc., [but] not a word that St. Peter was chief. Again, you find Peter himself sent forth by other Apostles, Acts 8:14: "The Apostles sent unto them Peter and John." When the church of the Jews found fault with Peter for going in to the gentiles when he went to Cornelius, he does not say, "Why do you question me or call me to an account? I am Christ's vicar on earth." When Paul reproved Peter, Galatians 2, he does not defend himself by mentioning an infallibility in himself as Christ's vicar or reprove Paul for his boldness.

The Roman Catholic Church can't be a true church of Christ in that it makes laws directly contrary to the laws and commands of Christ. As for example, in withholding the wine or the cup from the laity in the Lord's Supper; [whereas] Christ commands the same to drink who were to eat. Their evasion that the blood is in the body, and so they partake of both in eating, is a great fallacy built on a false foundation of transubstantiation. For when men eat they can't be said to drink, which Christ commands, for Christ commands that we take the cup and drink, which is not done in eating; besides, the priests themselves won't be so put off. The words "This is my body" do only intend this doth signify or represent my body, which will appear if you compare Scripture with Scripture, for after the consecration the Holy Ghost calls it bread and the fruit of the vine. Exodus 12:11, "It is the Lord's Passover," that is, it represents it. In all the Evangelists you read of killing and eating the Passover a few lines or verses before these words, "this is my body," which plainly show that our Savior in the same way of figurative expression speaks of the Gospel Sacrament.

If these words were taken as the Romanists expound them, he must eat his own body himself, whole and entire in his own hands; and after that each one of the Disciples eat him entire, and yet he set at the table whole, untouched at the same time; contradictions impossible to be defended by any rational arguments. Yea, his whole body must be now in Heaven and in a thousand other places and in the mouth of every communicant at the same time, and that both as a broken and unbroken sacrifice and be subject to putrefaction. Christ is said to be a door, a true vine, a way, a rock. What work shall we make if we expound these in a literal manner as the Romanists do when they say "this is my body" is meant the real body of Christ in the Eucharist? It is said, 1 Corinthians 10:4: "And did all drink the same spiritual drink. For they drank of that spiritual rock that followed them—and that rock was Christ." Was Christ literally a rock, think you? Yea, it is absurd to believe that a priest uttering a few words over a wafer not above an inch square can make it a God or the body of Christ entire as it was offered on the cross. [It is] a blasphemy to pretend to a power of making God at their pleasure, and then eat Him and give Him to others to be eaten or shut Him up in their altars, that they can utter the same words and make a God or not make a God according to their intention, and that the people are obliged to believe that it is God and so adore it when they never hear any word of consecration nor know the priest's intention.

As to what you write about the holy Mass, I reply, it's wholly a human invention; not a word of such a sacrifice in the whole Bible; its being a sacrifice propitiatory daily to be offered, is contrary to the holy Scriptures. Hebrews 7:27: "Who needeth not daily, as those high-priests, to offer up sacrifice first for his own sins and then for the peoples', for this He did once when He offered up Himself." And yet the Romanists say there is a need that He be offered up as a sacrifice to God every day. Hebrews 9:12 "By his own blood He entered in once into the holy place, having obtained eternal redemption for us." And 25–28: "Nor yet that He should offer Himself often, as the high priest entereth into the holy place, every year with the blood of others. For then must He often have suffered since the foundation of the world. But now once in the end of the world hath He appeared to put away sin by the sacrifice of Himself. As it is appointed unto men once to die, but after this the judgment: so Christ was once offered to bear the sins of many." Hebrews 10:10: "By which will we are sanctified through the offering of the body of Jesus Christ once for all." Verse 12: "But this man, after He had offered one sacrifice for sins, forever sat down on the right hand of God." Verse 14: "For by one offering He hath perfected forever them that are sanctified." By which Scriptures you may see that the Mass is not of divine appointment but a human invention. Their evasion of a bloody and unbloody sacrifice is a sham. The holy Scriptures speak not one word of Christ being offered as a sacrifice propitiatory after such a sort as they call an unbloody sacrifice. All the ceremonies of the Mass are human inventions that God never commanded.

As to what in the letter about praying for the women after their death is very ridiculous. For as the tree falls, so it lies, as death leaves, judgment will find; no change after death from an afflicted to a happy place and state. Purgatory is a fancy for the enriching [of] the clergy and impoverishing the laity. The notion of it [is] a fatal snare to many souls who sin with hopes of easily getting priestly absolutions at death and buying off their torments with their money. The soul at death goes immediately to judgment and so to heaven or hell. No authentic place of Scripture mentions so much as one word of any such place or state. Mr. Meriel told me if I found one error in our religion it was enough to cause me to disown our whole religion. By his argument you may see what reason you have to avoid that religion that is so full of errors.

Bethink yourself and consult the Scriptures, if you can get them (I mean the Bible). Can you think their religion is right when they are afraid to let you have an English Bible? Or to speak with your father, or other of your Christian neighbors, for fear they should give you such convictions of truth that they can't remove? Can that religion be true that can't bear an examination from the Scriptures that are a perfect rule in matters of faith? Or that must be upheld by ignorance, especially ignorance of the holy Scriptures? These things have I written as in my heart I believe.

I long for your recovery and will not cease to pray for it. I am now a man of sorrowful spirit, and look upon your fall as the most aggravating circumstance of my afflictions, and am persuaded that no pains will be wanting to prevent me from seeing or speaking with you; but I know that God's grace is all-sufficient: He is able to do exceeding abundantly above what I can ask or think. Don't give way to discouragement as to a return to New England. Read over what I have written and keep it with you if you can; you have no friend on earth that wishes your eternal salvation more heartily than your father. I long to see and speak with you, but I never forget you. My love to you, and to your brother and sister and to all our fellow prisoners. Let me hear from you as often as you can. I hope God will appear for us before it be long.

There are a great many other things in the letter that deserve to be refuted, but I shall be too tedious in remarking of them all at once, yet [I] would not pass over that passage in the letter that Esther Jones confessed that there were seven sacraments. To which I answer that some of the most learned of the Romish religion confessed (without the distracting pains of a violent fever) and left it upon record in print that it can't be convincingly made out from the Scripture that there are seven sacraments, and that their most incontestable proof is from tradition, and by their traditions they might have found seventeen as well as seven, considering that four popes successively spent their lives in purging and correcting old authors. But no man can out of holy Scriptures prove any more than two sacraments of divine institution under the New Testament, namely, Baptism and the Lord's Supper.[140]

If you make the Scriptures a perfect rule of faith, as you ought to do, you can't believe as the Romish Church believes. Oh, see that you sanctify the Lord Himself in your heart and make him your fear and your dread. "Fear not them that can kill the body, and after that have no more that they can do, but rather fear him that has power to destroy soul and body in hell-fire." The Lord have mercy upon you and show you mercy for the worthiness and righteousness' sake of Jesus Christ, our great and glorious redeemer and advocate who makes intercession for transgressors. My prayers are daily to God for you, for your brother and sister, yea for all my children and Fellow prisoners.

I am your afflicted and sorrowful father,

John Williams.

Chateau Richer, March 22, 1706

God, who is gloriously free and rich in His grace to vile sinners, was pleased to bless poor and weak means for the recovery of my child so taken and gave me to see that He did not say to the House of Jacob, "Seek you me in vain." Oh, that

---

140. The Catholic Church recognized seven sacraments, not just two.

every reader would in every difficulty make Him their refuge! He is a hopeful stay. To alleviate my sorrow, I received the following letter in answer to mine.

Montreal, May 12, 1706

Honored Father,

I received your letter which was sent by _____, which good letter I thank you for and for the good counsel which you gave me; I desire to be thankful for it and hope it will be for the good of my soul. I may say, as in the Psalms: "The sorrows of death compassed me, and the pains of hell got hold on me. I found trouble and sorrow, then called I upon the name of the Lord. O Lord, I beseech Thee, deliver my soul! Gracious is the Lord and righteous, yea our God is merciful."

As for what you ask me about my making an abjuration of the Protestant faith for the Romish, I durst not write so plain to you as I would but hope to see and discourse with you. I am sorry for the sin I have committed in changing religion, for which I am greatly to blame. You may know that Mr. Meriel, the schoolmaster, and others were continually at me about it; at last I gave over to it, for which I am very sorry.

As for that letter you had from me, it was a letter I transcribed for Mr. Meriel. And for what he saith about Abigail Turbet and Esther Jones, nobody heard them but he as I understand. I desire your prayers to God for me to deliver me from my sins. Oh, remember me in your prayers! I am your dutiful son, ready to take your counsel.

Samuel Williams

The priest, Mr. Meriel, had brought many letters to him and bid him write them over and send them, and so he has done for many others. By this as also by Mrs. Stilson's saying she does not think that either of these women did change their religion before their death, [and] she affirms also, that oftentimes during their sickness, while they had the use of their reason, they protested against the Romish religion and faith. It's evident that these women never died papists, but that it was a wily stratagem of the priests to advance their religion, for letters were sent, immediately after their deaths to use this as a persuasive argument to gain others. But God in His providence gave in farther conviction of their fallaciousness in this matter.

For the last summer one Biggilow from Marlborough,[141] a captive at Montreal, was very sick in the hospital and in the judgment of all with a sickness to

---

141. John Bigelow (1675–?) of Marlborough, Massachusetts, was taken during the October 15, 1705, attack on Lancaster, Massachusetts. He appears to have returned to New England late in 1706.

death. Then the priests and others gave out that he was turned to be of their religion and taken into their communion. But contrary to their expectation he was brought back from the gates of death and would comply with none of their rites, saying, that, while he had the use of his reason, he never spoke anything in favor of their religion. And that he never disowned the Protestant faith, nor would he now. So that they were silenced and put to shame. There is no reason to think that these two women were any more papists than he, but they are dead and cannot speak. One of the witnesses spoken of in the forementioned letter told me she knew of no such thing and said Mr. Meriel told her that he never heard a more fervent and affectionate prayer than one which Esther Jones made a little before her death. I am verily persuaded that he calls that prayer to God, so full of affection and confession, the "confession made by her of the sins of her whole life." These two women always in their health, and so in their sickness, opposed all popish principles as all that knew them can testify so long as they could be permitted to go and speak with them. One of these women was taken from the Eastward, and the other namely, Esther Jones, from Northampton.

[At Quebec]

In the beginning of March 1706, Mr. Sheldon came again to Canada with letters from his Excellency our Governor, at which time I was a few days at Quebec.[142] And when I was there, one night about ten o'clock there was an earthquake that made a report like a cannon and made the houses to tremble. It was heard and felt many leagues all along the Island of Saint Lawrence and other places.[143] When Mr. Sheldon came the second time, the adversaries did what they could to retard the time of our return to gain time to seduce our young ones to popery. Such were sent away who were judged ungainable, and most of the younger sort still kept. Some [were] still flattered with promises of reward and great essays [were made] to get others married among them. One [was] debauched and then in twenty-four hours of time published, taken into their communion and married. But the poor soul has had time since to lament her sin and folly with a bitter cry and asks your prayers that God of His sovereign grace would yet bring [her] out of the horrible pit she has thrown herself into. Her name was Rachel Storer of Wells.[144]

---

142. John Sheldon made a second trip to Canada in January 1706 and returned with forty-five exchanged prisoners on August 1, 1706. He made a third trip to Canada in January 1707 and returned to Boston in September 1707.

143. The Island of Saint Lawrence is Ile d'Orléans, just down river from Quebec.

144. Rachel Storer (1687–?) was taken in an attack on Wells, Maine, in August 1703. She converted to Catholicism in April 1706 and immediately married Jean Berger. They moved to Boston around 1709. She was still living in Boston and known as Rachel Berger in 1729.

In April one Zebediah Williams of our town died.[145] He was a very hopeful and pious young man who carried himself so in his captivity as to edify several of the English and recover one fallen to popery taken [in] the last war. Though some were enraged against him on these accounts, yet even the French where he sojourned and with whom he conversed would say he was a good man, one that was very prayerful to God and studious and painful in reading the holy Scriptures, a man of a good understanding, [and] desirable conversation. In the beginning of his last sickness he made me a visit (before he went to the hospital at Quebec) to my great satisfaction and our mutual consolation and comfort in our captivity, as he had several times before, living not above two miles from me over the river at the Island of Saint Lawrence about six weeks or two months.

After his death the French told me Zebediah was gone to hell and damned. For, said they, he has appeared since his death to one Joseph Edgerly,[146] an Englishman who was taken [in] the last war, in flaming fire, telling him he was damned for refusing to embrace the Romish religion when such pains were used to bring him to the true faith and for being instrumental to draw him away from the Romish Communion, forsaking the Mass, and was therefore now come to advertise him of his danger. I told them I judged it to be a popish lie, saying I bless God our religion needs no lies to uphold, maintain, and establish it as theirs did. But they affirmed it to be true, telling me how God approved of their religion and witnessed miraculously against ours. But I still told them I was persuaded his soul was in heaven and that these reports were only devised fables to seduce souls.

For several weeks they affirmed it, telling me that all who came over the river from the island affirmed it to be a truth. I begged of God to blast this hellish design of theirs so that in the issue it might be to render their religion more abominable and that they might not gain one soul by such a stratagem. After some weeks had passed in such assertions, there came one into my landlord's house affirming it to be a truth reported of Zebediah, saying, Joseph Edgerly had been over the river and told one of our neighbors this story.

After a few hours I saw that neighbor and asked him whether he had seen Edgerly lately. He said, "Yes."

"What news told he to you?"

---

145. Zebediah Williams (1675–1706)—no relation of the Reverend John—and John Nims (1679–1762) had been captured in the meadows just north of the village of Deerfield on October 8, 1703. John Nims escaped with Joseph Petty in May 1705.

146. Joseph Edgerly (1677–?) was taken prisoner during the July 18, 1694, raid on Oyster River, today part of Durham, New Hampshire. During his years in Canada he apparently did not convert to Catholicism but did forget much of his knowledge of English. He returned to New England with John Williams in November 1706.

"None," said he.

Then I told him what was affirmed as a truth; he answered [that] Edgerly said nothing like this to him, and he was persuaded [that] he would have told him if there had been any truth in it.

About a week after this came one John Boult from the Island of Saint Lawrence, a lad taken from Newfoundland, a very serious, sober lad of about seventeen years of age. He had often before come over with Zebediah to visit me. At his coming in, he much lamented the loss of Zebediah and told me that for several weeks they had told him the same story, affirming it to be a truth, and that Edgerly was so awakened by it as to go again to Mass every day, urging him since God in such a miraculous way offered such conviction of the truth of their religion and the falsehood and danger of ours, to come over to their religion or else his damnation would be dreadfully aggravated.

He, said he, could have no rest for them day and night, but, said he, "I told them their religion was contrary to the word of God, and therefore I would not embrace it, and that I did not believe what they said." "And," says he to me, "one day I was sitting in the house and Edgerly came in, and I spoke to him before the whole family in the French tongue, for he could not speak much English, and asked him of this story. He answered, 'It's a great falsehood,' saying, 'He never appeared to me, nor have I ever reported any such thing to any body.' And that he had never been at the Mass since Zebediah's death." At the hearing of which, they were silenced and put to shame. We blessed God together for discovering their wickedness, and disappointing them in what they aimed at, and prayed to God to deliver us and all the captives from delusions, and recover them who had fallen, and so parted.

After which I took my pen and wrote a letter to one Mr. Samuel Hill, an English captive taken from Wells who lived at Quebec, and his brother Ebenezer Hill[147] to make a discovery of this lying plot to warn them of their danger and assure them of the falsehood of this report, but the letter fell into the hands of the priests and was never delivered. This Edgerly came home with us so that they gained nothing but shame by this stratagem. God often disappoints the crafty devices of wicked men.

[Return to New England]

In the latter end of summer they told me they had news from New England by one who had been a captive at Boston, who said that the ministers at Boston

---

147. Samuel Hill (1668–?) was captured at Wells, Maine on August 10, 1703 and his brother Ebenezer (?–1758?) was taken at Saco, Maine, on the same day. They returned from Canada in November 1706.

had told the French captives[148] that the Protestant religion was the only true religion, and that as a confirmation of it, they would raise a dead person to life before their eyes for their conviction, and that having persuaded one to feign himself dead, they came and prayed over him and then commanded him in the name of Christ (whose religion they kept pure) to arise. They called and commanded, but he never arose, so that instead of raising the dead they killed the living, which the bereaved relations discovered. I told them, it was an old lie and calumny against Luther and Calvin new vamped and that they only changed the persons and place, but they affirmed it to be a truth. I told them I wondered they were so fond of a faith propagated and then maintained by lying words.

We were always out of hopes of being returned before winter, the season proving so cold in the latter end of September, and were praying to God to prepare our hearts with all holy submission to His holy will to glorify His holy name in a way of passive obedience in the winter. For my own part, I was informed by several who came from the city that the lord intendant[149] said if more returned and brought word that Battis [i.e., Baptiste] was in prison, he would put me into prison and lay me in irons.[150] They would not permit me to go into the city, saying I always did harm when I came to the city, and if at any time I was at the city, they could persuade the governor to send me back again.

In the beginning of last June the superior of the priests came to the parish where I was and told me he saw I wanted my friend, Captain de Beauville, and that I was ragged. "But," says he, "your obstinacy against our religion discourages [us] from providing better clothes." I told him it was better going in a ragged coat than with a ragged conscience.

In the beginning of last June [1706] [there] went out an army of five hundred Maquas and Indians with an intention to have fallen on some English towns down the Connecticut River, but lighting on a Schaghticoke Indian, who ran away in the night, they were discouraged, saying he would alarm the whole

<hr>

148. The French captives were probably Acadian colonists and soldiers captured in a raid launched from Boston in late spring of 1704. See also Letter from Claude Ramezay, 83–86.

149. It could be either Jacques Raudot (1638–1728), who served as intendant of New France from 1705 to 1711, or his son Antoine-Denis Raudot (1679–1737), who served conjointly as intendant of New France from 1705 to 1710.

150. The refusal of Massachusetts authorities to exchange Captain Baptiste, Pierre Maisonnat, remained a sticking point. Williams's reiteration of the importance of Maisonnat to the French and to his own release provided political cover for Governor Dudley of Massachusetts, who eventually agreed to exchange the French privateer for Williams, despite strong opposition in Boston to Maisonnat's release.

country.[151] About fifty as some say, or eighty as others, returned; thus God restrained their wrath.

When they were promising themselves another winter to draw away the English to popery, [there] came news of an English brigantine [was] a-coming and that the honorable Captain Samuel Appleton, Esquire[152] was coming [as] ambassador to fetch off the captives, and Captain John Bonner[153] with him. I cannot tell you how the clergy and others labored to stop many of the prisoners; to some liberty, to some money, and yearly pensions were offered, if they would stay. Some they urged to tarry at least till the spring of the year; telling them it was so late in the year they would be lost by shipwreck if they went now; some younger ones they told if they went home they would be damned and burned in hell for ever, to affright them; day and night they were urging them to stay. And I was threatened to be sent aboard without a permission to come ashore again if I should again discourse with any of the English who were turned to their religion.

At Montreal especially, all crafty endeavors were used to stay the English. They told my child,[154] if he would stay he should have an honorable pension from the king every year and that his master, who was an old man and the richest in Canada, would give him a great deal, telling him, if he returned, he would be poor, for, said they, "your father is poor, [he] has lost all his estate, it was all burned." But he would not be prevailed with to stay. And others were also in like manner urged to stay, but God graciously broke the snare and brought them out. They endeavored in the fall of the year to have prevailed with my son to have gone to France when they saw he would not come to their communion any more.

One woman belonging to the Eastern parts, who had by their persuasions married an English captive taken in the last war, came away with her husband,

---

151. This would have been an Indian from the Native village in Schaghticoke, New York, which was allied with the English. The Natives in this raiding party may have feared that the Schaghticocke would warn the English. For whatever reason, this expedition never reached its intended target, for there is no evidence that a party of this size attacked towns along the Connecticut River in western Massachusetts in the summer of 1706.

152. Samuel Appleton (1654–1725) was a member of the Governor's Council of Massachusetts. He arrived in October 6, 1706 to arrange for the return of English captives. In 1707 he led one of the Massachusetts regiments that attacked Port Royal in Acadia.

153. John Bonner (1643–1726) was a Boston mariner and cartographer. His presence strongly suggests that Massachusetts authorities remained interested in learning all they could about the approaches to and the defenses of Quebec. In 1711 Bonner was the chief pilot for the ill-fated expedition under Admiral Hovenden Walker (c. 1656/1666–1725) that attempted to capture Quebec by sailing up the Saint Lawrence River.

154. Samuel Williams still lived with the wealthy Jacques Le Ber, who was dying.

which made them say they were sorry they ever persuaded her to turn to their religion and then to marry. For, instead of advancing their cause by it, they had weakened it, for now they had not only lost her, but another they thought they had made sure of. Another woman belonging to the Eastward, who had been flattered to their religion, to whom a Bible was denied till she promised to embrace their religion and then had the promise of it for a little time, opening her Bible while in the church and present at Mass, she read the fourth chapter of Deuteronomy and received such conviction while reading that before her first communion she fell off from them and could never be prevailed with any more to be of their religion.

We have reason to bless God who has wrought deliverance for so many, and yet pray to God for a door of escape to be opened for the great number yet behind, not much short of a hundred, many of which are children, and of these not a few among the savages and having lost the English tongue, will be lost and turn savages in a little time unless something extraordinary prevent [it].

The vessel that came for us, in its voyage to Canada struck on a bar of sands and there lay in very great hazard for four tides, and yet they saw reason to bless God for striking there, for had they got over that bar, they should at midnight in a storm of snow have run upon a terrible ledge of rocks.

We came away from Quebec, October twenty-five [1706] and by contrary winds and a great storm we were retarded, and then driven back nigh the city, and had a great deliverance from shipwreck, the vessel striking twice on a rock in that storm. But through God's goodness we all arrived in safety at Boston, November twenty-one, the number of captives, fifty seven, two of which were my children. I have yet a daughter of ten years of age [i.e., Eunice] and many neighbors whose case bespeaks your compassion and prayers to God to gather them, being outcasts ready to perish.

At our arrival at Boston, we found the kindness of the Lord in a wonderful manner in God's opening the hearts of many to bless God with us and for us wonderfully to give for our supplies in our needy state. We are under obligation to praise God for disposing the hearts of so many to so great charity and under great bonds to pray for a blessing on the heads, hearts, and families of them who so liberally and plentifully gave for our relief. It's certain that the charity of the whole country of Canada, though moved with the doctrine of merit, does not come up to the charity of Boston alone, where notions of merit are rejected, but acts of charity performed out of a right Christian spirit from a spirit of thankfulness to God out of obedience to God's command and unfeigned love and charity to them that are of the same family and household of faith. The Lord grant that all who devise such liberal things may find the accomplishment of the promises made by God, in their own persons and theirs after them from generation to generation.

[News of Detroit]

I shall annex a short account of the troubles beginning to arise in Canada. On May sixteen [1706] arrived a canoe at Quebec that brought letters from Mississippi written the May preceding giving an account that the plague was there, and that one hundred and fifty French in a very little time had died of it, and that the savages called the Lezilouways[155] were very turbulent, and had with their arrows wounded a Jesuit in five places and killed a Frenchman that waited on him. In July news came that the nations up the river were engaged in a war, one against the other, and that the French living so among them, and trading with them were in great danger, that the Michel-macquinas had made war with the Mizianmies, and had killed a mendicant friar and three other Frenchmen and eleven savages at a place called the Straits where they are settling a garrison and place for traffic; the Michel-macquinas had taken sixteen Frenchmen prisoners and burned their trading-houses. These tidings made the French very full of perplexing troubles, but the Jesuits are endeavoring to pacify them. But the troubles when we came away were rather increasing than lessening, for the last letters from the French prisoners at Mitchel-macquina report that the savages had sent out two companies, one of a hundred and fifty and another of a hundred and sixty, against the savages at the Straits, and they feared they would engage as well against the French as the Indians.[156]

---

155. Lezilouways were probably the Illinois. The event being referred to cannot be identified.
156. This news that Williams relays came from Detroit. The Mitchel-macquinas were Ottawas from Michilimackinac. They had attacked the Miamis, whom Williams calls Mizianmies. The Miamis were living in a village near Detroit where Ottawas, Miamis, and other Native allies of the French had recently moved. One French soldier and a Récollet priest were killed, but none was captured or burned. The skirmish arose out of tensions and mistrust following the Natives' move from the Jesuit mission and trading post at the Straits of Michilimackinac to the new Récollect mission and trading post at Detroit. French officials soon calmed the dispute.

FIGURE 12. The Reverend Stephen Williams (1693–1782). Oil painting, c. 1755, attributed to Joseph Badger. Because of his capture in 1704 and later service as a chaplain on military expeditions in 1745, 1755, and 1756, Williams became a symbol of New England's decades-long contest with the Catholic French in Canada. He also maintained a lifelong interest in the Protestant missionary efforts among Natives in the Northeast. Photograph courtesy of the Pocumtuck Valley Memorial Association, Memorial Hall Museum, Deerfield, Massachusetts.

What Befell Stephen Williams in His Captivity, c. 1707

Stephen Williams

S TEPHEN WILLIAMS (1693–1782) was a ten-year-old boy when he was captured along with his father, John Williams, and 110 others at Deerfield. As such, he was of prime age for adoption into a Native community. Almost all of the captives who lived out their lives in New France in either a French or a Native community were under thirteen years old when captured (appendixes C and D). However, Stephen did not follow the path of his younger sister Eunice. He returned to Massachusetts, where he went on to become a minister in Longmeadow.

Stephen probably wrote the following account of his captivity experience not too long after his return in 1705 and the subsequent publication of his father's *The Redeemed Captive Returning to Zion* in 1707. In places his narrative parallels and his phraseology echoes that of his father's narrative. At the same time his vivid descriptions and his characterization of a fish "as large as I am," suggests that the narrative was composed not long after his ordeal, when he was in his mid-teens. Later, he appears to have made some additions and may have intended to include this narrative in his never-completed history of the "remarkable providences of God" during the wars with the Indians.[1] During his lifetime, Stephen might have shared his account with acquaintances and then passed it on to his descendants (figure 12).

This account of Stephen's captivity focuses on his interactions with his Pennacook and Abenaki captors. Unlike most of the Deerfield captives, including his father, who soon found themselves in the hands of the French, Stephen spent most of his time with Natives, none of whom seemed particularly eager to convert him to Catholicism. In fact his master, the Pennacook leader Wattanummon (c. 1660–1712), left Odanak soon after his arrival because he "could not comply with [the] rites and customs" of the Catholics. Partly for this reason the religious questions that dominate John Williams's narrative are largely

---

This version of "What Befell Stephen Williams in his Captivity" is based on the original manuscript, which is in the Williams Family Papers, box 1, folder 10, Pocumtuck Valley Memorial Association in Deerfield Reproduced with permission of the P.V.M.A.

1. Stephen Williams Diary, January 6, 1729, typescript transcription, microfilm edition, Historic Deerfield Library.

absent here. Even though Stephen was the son of a minister and became one himself, the traditional Puritan stock of biblical quotations and providential deliveries is very restrained. What emerges most from this text is a set of very human issues: the experience of captivity through the eyes of a child. Stephen is cold, hungry, and lonely. He misses his beloved father. He is afraid and resentful of his masters and what he sees as their strange ways. Nonetheless, he adapts and survives.

It is clear, however, despite the misery, that Stephen's Pennacook masters—Wattanummon and his kinsman George Tahanto—were trying to incorporate him into their family. He certainly received better treatment than the two adult male captives who were worked as slaves and allowed to starve to death. Stephen received medical attention, food, and some education about Pennacook customs. When he was well he was put to work, but he did no more than what other Pennacooks did. But Stephen was not the stuff of which a good Pennacook was made. Unlike other captive children, such as Joseph Kellogg, who seems to have enjoyed life among the Natives, Stephen resented it.

Stephen's ineptness—he got lost in the woods, he failed to perform basic tasks assigned to him—makes it clear that not everyone could adapt to Native life. While Stephen's depictions of his master lack the vitriol found in other accounts, such as Mary Rowlandson's captivity narrative, he clearly did not want to stay with them. Like his father, he obstinately refused to cooperate with his captors any more than he had to. When he worked, he did not always do a good job. He seemed to give his Pennacook masters more trouble than he was worth.

His desire to get away from his Pennacook masters was so strong that Stephen, like Quentin Stockwell, relished the attentions of every French colonist he met. In his quest for comfort, he was drawn to French companionship time and again. Unwittingly, this put him at the center of a series of power struggles between Pennacooks and French. Their alliance was not an easy one, and Stephen had a knack for bringing out the mistrust and clashing cultural values embedded within it.

In the end, Stephen's perspective provides a rare example of how captivity was experienced by a child. As a remarkably candid account of what happened, Stephen's narrative adds to our picture some of the raw material from which published captivity accounts were fashioned. At the same time, his text reveals that he reviewed a copy of his father's *Redeemed Captive* to refresh his memory of some of the experiences they had shared. However, because *What Befell Stephen Williams* was not "improved" for publication, like *The Redeemed Captive,* it is easier to read through Stephen's experiences and come to some understanding of his Pennacook captors as well as the boy captive.

The first printed version appeared in 1837 as an appendix to a biographical sketch of the Reverend John Williams written by a collateral descendant, Stephen West Williams.[2] Stephen West Williams reprinted the sketch in 1853 when he appended the narrative to his republication of John Williams's *The Redeemed Captive*.[3] The Deerfield historian George Sheldon published an annotated version in 1889.[4] All of these versions of the narrative printed in the nineteenth century contain some errors.

§

What Befell Steven Williams in his Captivity

On the last [day] of February 1703/4[5] the French and Indians came and surprised our fort[6] and took it. And after they had broken into our house and took us prisoners, they barbarously murdered a brother and sister of mine as they did several of our neighbors.[7] They rifled our house and then marched away with us that were captives, and set our house and barn afire as they did the greatest part of the town. When the greatest part of the enemy were gone out of town there came some English from the next town that drove those Indians that remained in the town away, but they [i.e., the English] were quickly driven back again by the rest of the army. Nine of them were slain as they retreated. Then they [i.e., the French and Indians] marched a little further and stopped, for they had several wounded men that hindered them. There they told us that if the English pursued them they would kill us, but if otherwise they would not. But they quickly proved themselves liars for before they departed from that place they barbarously murdered a child of about two years old.[8]

---

2. Stephen West Williams, *A Biographical Memoir of the Rev. John Williams, first minister of Deerfield, Massachusetts with a slight sketch of ancient Deerfield, and an account of the Indian wars in that place and vicinity; with an appendix containing the journal of the Rev. Doctor Stephen Williams, of Longmeadow, during his captivity, and other papers relating to the early Indian wars in Deerfield* (Greenfield, Mass.: C. J. J. Ingersoll, 1837).

3. John Williams, *The Redeemed Captive Returning to Zion,* ed. Stephen W. Williams (Northampton, Mass.: Hopkins, Bridgman and Company, 1853), 144–152.

4. [Stephen Williams], *What Befell Stephen Williams in his Captivity,* ed. George Sheldon (Deerfield: Pocumtuck Valley Memorial Association, 1889).

5. The English still used the Julian calendar, which began the new year on March 25 rather than January 1; thus, dates in English documents between January 1 and March 25 were often written with both years.

6. The palisade surrounding the center of the village of Deerfield.

7. John Junior (1698–1704) and Jerusha, aged 1 1/2 months.

8. The victim was Marah Carter (1701–1704).

There my master took away my English shoes and gave me Indian ones[9] in the room of them which I think were better to travel in (map 3). Then we marched 5 or 6 miles further where we took up our lodging.[10] Then one English man ran back to Deerfield[11] which provoked them much: they told us if any more ran away they would burn the rest. There they slew our Negro man.[12] The next morning [March 1] we traveled about 2 or 3 miles [and] then they murdered my ever-honored mother[13] who having gone over a small river[14] [in] which water running very swift flung her down. She being wet was not able to travel any further. We traveled 8 or 9 miles further and lodged that night. There some of them were disturbed for some had five or six captives and others none. Then they called the captives together to make a more equal distribution but I remained with my former master.[15] Here they searched me and took away my silver buttons and buckles which I had on my shirt. Before we came to a small river named the West River about thirty miles above Deerfield they murdered 3 or 4 more persons.[16] When [March 3] they came to the West River where they had sleighs and dogs with which they drew their wounded men they traveled, (we thought) as if they designed to kill us all, for they traveled 35 or 40 miles a day.[17] There they killed near a dozen of [the] women and children, for their manner was if any loitered to kill them.[18] My feet were very sore so that I was afraid they would kill me also. We rested on the Sabbath day [March 5]. They gave my father liberty to preach. There we sang a psalm for they required of us a song.

The next day [March 6] we traveled a great way farther than we had at any time before. About the middle of the day some that were in the rear fired at

---

9. The Indian shoes that Stephen received were undoubtedly winter moccasins, often called Indian stockings by the English. Winter moccasins covered the foot, ankle, and lower calf and kept the wearer warmer and drier than did low-cut leather shoes.

10. The camp was on Petty Plain, across the Deerfield River in what is today Greenfield, Massachusetts.

11. The man who escaped was Joseph Alexander (1681–1761).

12. Frank, husband of Parthena, who had been killed along with John and Jerusha.

13. Eunice Mather Williams (1665–1704) was the daughter of the Reverend Eleazer Mather and the granddaughter of the Reverend John Warham. She married John in 1687. Stephen was one of their eleven children.

14. The Green River.

15. Wattanummon (c. 1660–1712).

16. The victims were most likely Hannah Carter (seven months), Jemima Richards (c. 1694–1704), and Waitstill Warner (1679–1704).

17. The actual distance was more like twelve to eighteen miles.

18. The victims were four women: Hepzibah Belding (c.1650–1704), Mary Frary (c. 1640–1704), Mehitable Nims (1668–1704), Hannah Carter (1674–1704)—mother of the two slain Carter girls—and three young children who were probably Mary Alexander (1702–1704), Abigail Hoyt (1701–1704), and Benjamin Hurst (1702–1704).

some geese that flew over which put them into a considerable fright, for they thought the English were come up with them. Then they began to bind the prisoners and to prepare themselves for battle. But when they understood what the matter was they shot a volley for joy, boasting that the English could not overtake them. I coming to my honored father he told me he was taken lame in his ankle, which he sprained in the fall of the year. He said likewise he thought he should be killed, and if I should live to get to Canada, to tell them who I was etc., which then did terrify me much, but it pleased God to strengthen him to perform his journey.

The next day [March 7] was a tempestuous day and I froze my great toe of my left foot. The day after [March 8], which was Wednesday, my master bid me go down to the river with him very early in the morning, which startled me, for he did not use to be so early. There the river parted, and I went up one branch, [and] my father with my brothers and sisters the other (map 3).[19] I never saw my father for 14 months after. I did not eat anything in the morning yet must travel all day; yea I traveled till about 9 o'clock at night without one morsel of victuals. I traveled about 50 miles that day and night. For my supper I had one spoonful of Indian corn, in the morning 5 or 6 kernels, but must travel. Then we left the river and traveled till about noon on the west side of the river and then we came to two wigwams, where were signs of Indians but no Indians. In those wigwams they left their packs and went a-hunting if perhaps they might find some moose buried in the snow by the hunting Indians, but could not find any.

I wandered about and lost myself and helloed. My master came to me and was very angry with me, threatened to kill me. He lifted up the breech of his gun in order thereto but God kept back his hand for which I desire His name might be praised. The Indians will never allow a body to hello in the woods. Their manner is to make a noise like wolves or owls or other wild creatures when they would call to one another.

My master sent the Indian lad and I to those wigwams but he himself took his gun and went a-hunting. Now there were only we three in company, we had left all the army. We made a fire but had no victuals to dress, only a moose's paunch and bones which the hunting Indians had left. We took that paunch and boiled [it], without cleansing of it, for what was in it served for thickening the broth. There we tarried that night and the next day till about noon. Then there came an Indian girl and brought us some moose's meat dried, which I thought was the best victuals ever I ate. We traveled with that Indian girl about

---

19. Stephen's father and siblings went up the White River while Wattanummon and Stephen continued up the Connecticut River and then up the Wells River.

10 miles [to] where [there] was two wigwams. My master that left us the day before was got there. While we tarried here the French that were in the army passed by.

Within a day or two we traveled seven or eight miles northward to a place where they had killed some moose, where they made wigwams; for their manner was when they killed any moose to move to them and lie by them till they had eaten them up. Now there were two Englishmen of our town in company with me, who came from the army, to wit Deacon Hoit[20] and one Jacob Hix, a soldier.[21]

Now my master was not yet come to his own family from hence he went to look for his family and within a day or two sent for me. I thought this was hard to go away alone, that is to any English persons. Here I left Deacon Hoit and Jacob Hix. And Deacon Hoit I never saw more for he was dead before I came from hunting. I went with the messenger and after a tedious day's travel came to my master's family. He gave me to his brother, with whom I continued 2 or 3 months thereabouts hunting moose, bears, and beavers.

When I first arrived here, they were extraordinary kind, took care of my toe that was frozen, would not suffer me to [do] any work, [and] gave me a deer skin to lie on and a bear's skin to cover me withal. But this did not last long, for I was forced to carry such a pack when I traveled that I could not rise up without some help, was forced to cut wood, and carry it sometimes a considerable way on my back. After that manner I lived till their hunting time was over, without any society but these inhuman pagans.

Then we traveled with a design to go to Cowass [today Newbury, Vermont], where was their rendezvous. But before we had got quite there we met some Indians that stopped us. They told us that all the Indians were coming away from Cowass, which within a day or two came to us. Now the reason of their deserting the land was this: there came one Englishman with six of our Indians and destroyed a family of Indians about 20 miles below Cowass.[22] Here we stayed where these Indians met us a month or six weeks. [We] suffered much for want of provision for there was not much to be got a-hunting then, and if there was anything it was as nothing amongst so many. The chief of our provisions was roots of several sorts and bark of trees.

---

20. David Hoyt (1651–1704) was a deacon in Deerfield's church and lieutenant of its militia company.

21. Jacob Hickson (1683–1704) of Hadley was one of the twenty militiamen from other towns stationed in Deerfield as so-called garrison soldiers.

22. Caleb Lyman (1678–1742) and five Mohegans from Connecticut killed seven Pennacooks and took their guns, furs, and canoes in June 1704. They earned bounties for the six scalps that they brought back.

Here I met the above said Jacob Hix. Deacon Hoit was already dead for want of provision. This Hix looked like a ghost. [He] was nothing but skin and bone. [He] could scarce go, yet had no victuals but what he got himself, for he had been at Cowass with the Indians a-planting corn, where he suffered much for want of provision. I was better of it than they [were] for whiles I was hunting we had meat enough, but neither bread or salt to eat with it. There was a company now: one Mrs. Bradley of Haverhill[23] and one Hannah Eastman,[24] one Daniel Ardery of Haverhill,[25] and one Mrs. Jones[26] and Margaret Higgens, her maid,[27] who were taken at Northampton farms [i.e., today Easthampton].

Now from hence we set away for Canada. My master had so much lumber[28] to carry that we were forced to carry a pack a mile or two and go back and fetch another, which was very tedious. Jacob Hix died at the first carrying place of the French River.[29] This was an exceeding tedious march to me we being so laden; the other Indians left us. I suffered much in this journey, for when we came to the French River it was as much as our canoe would carry our lumber; the water was so shallow, so that I was forced to travel afoot on the bank without any shoes. My feet were much galled and one or two of my toes almost cut off with the stones. I had little or any thing to eat. My master killed a duck one day in the river and for my part I had the guts, which I laid on the coals without cleansing them, which seemed a sweet morsel to me. They did eat skins and etc., but when we arrived at the lake [i.e., Lake Champlain] we were supplied with fish and fowl, for there is a great number both of fish and fowl.

The Indian boys do kill the geese with their bows and arrows. They are so bold, fish can be easily taken with hooks. One day as we sailed on the lake two young Indians shot a fish with a bullet and took it into the canoe; it was as large as I am.

---

23. Hannah Heath Bradley (c.1670–1761) had already been captured, along with the famous Hannah Dustan, in 1697. Returned in 1699, she was again captured in the February 8, 1704, raid on Haverhill after killing one Native attacker by pouring boiling soap on him. Pregnant, she gave birth in captivity. Her baby died while she was working the fields at Cowass. Her husband, Joseph, joined John Sheldon's 1706 mission and returned with Hannah, who fought off a third attempt to capture her that same summer by shooting one of her attackers dead. The rest fled.

24. Hannah Green Eastman (?–?) was captured with Hannah Bradley and eventually redeemed by her husband, Jonathan.

25. Daniel Avery (?–?). Nothing further is known of him.

26. Esther Ingersoll Jones (1665–1705) was captured in the May 13, 1704, raid on Pascommuck (now Easthampton, Mass.). Her husband and two children were killed in the raid. She died in Montreal in December 1705, ostensibly after having converted to Catholicism. This incident is discussed in Samuel Williams's letters to John Williams; see "The Redeemed Captive," 136–139, 150.

27. Margaret Huggins (1686– ?) was Esther's niece. She was rebaptized a Catholic in September 1706. Nothing further is known of her.

28. Useless odds and ends, not sawn wood.

29. The French River is now known as the Winooski River.

I arrived [at] Chambly[30] in August, which was about half a year from the time I was taken. The French were kind to me [and] gave [me] bread which I had not eaten in a great while. They told me my father and brothers and sisters were got to Canada, which I was glad to hear of for I was afraid my youngest brother was killed.[31]

While I tarried here a Frenchman came and desired the Indians to let me go with him, which they did. I went with the Frenchman who gave me some victuals, and made me lie down in his couch, which my master's son perceiving told his father who thought he did it to hide me and did design to steal me, upon which he came and fetched me away and would not let me go to the fort any more for which I suffered. While I was here the French dressed my feet that were wounded at which the Indians seemed to be vexed.

From hence we went towards Sorel,[32] but tarried a day or two near a Frenchman's house about 8 miles from Chambly, who was kind to me and would have lodged me in his house but the Indians would not allow of it, mistrusting he would convey me away in the night privately. From hence we went to Sorel and as soon as we had landed, there came a woman across the river on purpose to bring me some victuals and seemed to pity me.

Here we tarried a day or two. My master bid me go to the fort a visiting which was about four score rod off. I went and at a Frenchman's persuasion tarried all night and till next day about noon, when my master came for me. He was very angry with me, and after that would never suffer me to go to a French house alone.

From this place we went to Saint Francis, the Indian fort (figure 10).[33] My master could not comply with their rites and customs, whereupon he went to Albany,[34] and gave me to his kinsman Sagamore George.[35]

Now this George when I was at Cowass told the French governor that I was his prisoner, whereas then he had nothing to do with me, whereupon the Gov-

---

30. Fort Chambly had been a French post since 1665. A new fort had been built in 1702. The expedition that attacked Deerfield had gathered at Chambly.

31. John Williams describes what happened to four-year-old Warham Williams (1699–1751) in his account, "The Redeemed Captive," 104, 116. Warham returned with his father and eventually became minister of Watertown, Massachusetts.

32. Sorel, like Chambly, began as a French fort in 1665 but by 1704 was a settlement as well.

33. Odanak is the Abenaki name for this village. Saint Francis was the name of the Jesuit mission in the village.

34. Wattanummon undoubtedly went to the Native village of Schaghticoke, founded by refugees from the Connecticut River valley in the aftermath of King Philip's War on land just northeast of Albany, within the jurisdiction of New York colony and under the supervision of the Five Nations of the Iroquois League.

35. George Tohanto (active 1695–1715), a cousin of Wattanummon.

ernor improved [i.e., empowered] one Mr. Chambly,[36] a captain, to buy me,
who made a bargain with George, gave him earnest money. Now [I] being put
into his hands he was not willing that the French should know it. But having a
desire to go to Chambly, the place where Monsieur Chambly lived, [he] took
me with him, but within ten miles of Chambly left me alone in the woods,
while he with those that were with him went to Chambly. After he came from
Chambly, we went a-hunting [and] caught about 80 beaver in the brooks which
run into the river between Chambly and Sorel.[37] After we had done hunting,
we went again to Saint Francis fort where I continued till toward spring, and
then removed because the smallpox was among the Indians and my master's
children had not had it, so that he removed.

But while I continued there, Monsieur Chambly[38] heard that I was with
Sagamore George and came to buy me. I seemed to be willing to go with him
at which the Indians were much disturbed, and would not let me go because I
showed a forwardness to go. [They] did likewise threaten to kill me, did complain to the Jesuit[39] who came and said to me, "What no love Indian? They
have saved your Life" and etc.

It is no wonder that children that are small will not speak to their friends
when they come to see to them but they will scoff and deride them, because the
Indians have taught them so, [and] will be angry if they do otherwise. While I
lived here I observed that some English children would scoff at me when before
the Indians worse than the Indian children. But when alone they would talk fa-
miliarly with me in English about their own country and etc., whereas [when]
before the Indians they would pretend they could not speak English.[40] Here the
Indians did say something to me about religion but not much, being Eastern Indians were not so zealous as the Maquas are. (I with a young woman etc.)[41]

---

36. Probably Joseph-François Hertel de la Fresnière (1642–1722), father of the French commander of the Deerfield raid. Joseph-François had inherited the seigneury of Chambly through
marriage and was living there at the time the Deerfield captives passed by. Another son, René
Hertel de Chambly (1671–1723), had been on the raid but was not involved in ransoming captives.
John Williams also mentions this incident in "The Redeemed Captive," 118.

37. The Richelieu River.

38. Joseph Hertel de Saint François, another son of Joseph-François, lived on a seigneury next
to the Abenaki village and probably informed his father about what was happening there.

39. The Jesuit was Jacques Bigot (1651–1711), who had been working as a missionary to
Abenaki peoples since 1679, often in cooperation with his brother Vincent Bigot (1649–1720).
Jacques oversaw the establishment of the Saint Francis mission at Odanak and worked there until
illness forced him to leave in 1708. He died in Quebec.

40. Compare these statements with those of Joseph Kellogg, "When I Was Carried to Canada," 185, and Williams, "The Redeemed Captive," 109.

41. It is unclear what Stephen intended by this sentence fragment, which was clearly added to
the manuscript by him at a later date.

The French governor[42] after he heard I was in the country, because of my father's entreaties, was often sending to the Indians to buy me who were quite wearied out because of the many messages he sent. The governor was not willing to give above 30 crowns[43] whereas they stood for 40. At length being wearied out my master went to the Jesuit [i.e., Jaques Bigot] and got pen and ink and paper and would have me to write to my father, for we had heard that he was turned, and had 200 pounds a year allowed him which I believed some of them believed.[44] After he [i.e., George Tohanto] had got paper he takes another Indian with him that could speak good English who were to indite [i.e., interpret] for me.

The substance of the letter was this: that if he did not buy [me] before spring they would not sell me afterwards and that he must give 40 crowns for me. They carried it to the Jesuit, who could speak English, to read to see whether I had written as they ordered me. And when they found I had, they were well pleased. My master had a mind to go a-hunting and would have taken me with him, but because he had sent such word, that they must buy [me] by such a time, he left me at home that I might be ready if they should send to buy me.

And when Captain Livingston[45] and Mr. Sheldon[46] were come to Canada my mistress thought there would be an exchange of prisoners, and lest the French should then take me away for nothing, she removed up in the woods about half a mile from the river,[47] that if they came, they might not find me.

On a certain day my mistress went to a French house to get victuals, and ordered me to spend my day getting wood loads, but it proved a tempestuous day and we had half a cart load of wood at the door, which is a great deal for Indians to have, so that I did not get any. When she came home, being disturbed by the French, [and] asked what I had been doing, they replied nothing. At which she was very angry. "I will not beat you myself," says she, "for my husband ordered me to the contrary, but will tell the Jesuit the next time he comes." Now they were not gone so far but that the Jesuit knew where they

---

42. Governor Philippe de Rigaud de Vaudreuil (c. 1643–1725).

43. Crown refers to the French *écu à couronne,* which was worth about five English shillings. Forty crowns was therefore equal to about 10 pounds sterling.

44. The offer of money in exchange for his conversion was made to John Williams, who declined it; see "The Redeemed Captive," 125–126, 128.

45. John (Johannes) Livingston (1680–1720) was the eldest son of Robert Livingston, the prominent fur trader and diplomat of colonial Albany. A merchant and military officer, John had settled in Connecticut.

46. John Sheldon (1658– c. 1733) was an ensign in Deerfield's militia company. He made three journeys to Canada starting in late 1704 to redeem captives, three of whom were his children. This was his second trip. He died in Hartford a wealthy man and the owner of seven slaves.

47. Probably the Saint Francis River.

went. [He] often visits them. Within a day or two, the Jesuit comes. She was as good as her word [and] did complain. He takes me out and whips me with a whip with six cords [of] several knots in each cord. After a few days he comes again and brings me a letter from my father by which I understood he was a prisoner as well as I, which I told the Indians, who said they believed it. He likewise said in his letter that the governor of New England[48] would take care we should be redeemed.

While I lived here I made about fourscore weight of sugar with the sap of maple trees for the Indians. My mistress had a mind to go to Sorel, and because there was a barrel of sap to boil she sent me to the sugar place over night to boil it, that so we might go in the morning. I went and kept a good fire under the kettle, little thinking of its coming to sugar till it was spoiled for want of stirring. For the manner is to stir it when it comes almost to sugar. For which they were very angry and would not give me any victuals.

It being now spring we went in canoes to Sorel, and so soon as we had got there the woman that brought me victuals across the river when I was there before, came and desired the Indians to let me go to the fort, which they consented to. I went but remembering the bad effect of tarrying all night before durst not do so again, without the Indians' leave. I went to the Indians and carried them some victuals and asked them to let me lie at the fort, which they granted. I kept here about a fortnight and lay at the fort every night. The French were very kind, provided victuals for me, and would give me some to carry to the Indians, which pleased them well.

As we went back to Saint Francis fort we met a French canoe who told us that the French governor would come to Saint Francis fort quickly, upon which my mistress said to me "your time is short [that] you have to live with me." Truly I hoped it was. When we came to Saint Francis we went to [my] master's island where I began to make preparation to plant corn, but before we began to plant the governor came and bought me, after a long parley, for 40 crowns. With him I went to Sorel where I met with Captain Livingston and several captives. Captain Livingston told me I should go home to New England with him which revived me much to think of going home. But the governor quickly altered his mind [and] said I must not go.

From hence I went down to Quebec with the Lord Intendant.[49] When I came to Quebec I found several English people that were prisoners there. One

---

48. Joseph Dudley (1647–1720), who was governor of Massachusetts.

49. François de Beauharnois de la Chaussaye, Baron de Beauville (1665–1746), was intendant of New France from the fall of 1702 to the fall of 1705, when he returned to France, served as intendant of the important port city of Rochefort, and died in his home city of Orleans. The intendant had oversight of legal and financial affairs.

Mrs. Hill[50] took care of me [and] cut my hair for me. (Now my hair was like an Indian one side long and the other short). She got me a shirt and a pair of breeches and a jacket and stockings and etc. for me. From hence on the 11 of May I was sent to live with my father at Chateau Richer.

While I lived here the French were very courteous and kind to me, as they were to my father. This seemed almost home to me because I was got to my father who I had not seen for 14 months. When Mr. Dudley[51] came to Canada my father and I were sent for up to Quebec. When we were at Quebec Captain Courtemanche[52] took us to his house, entertained us very nobly. He said he received kindness at New England. While we were at Quebec the Seminary, a famous building was burned. And upon Mr. Dudley and Captain Vetch's[53] petitioning, the governor gave me liberty to come home.

Accordingly I came away on the 12 of October 1705, but I left my honored father and brothers and sisters behind. And after a tedious voyage I arrived safe at Boston in New England, which was on the 21 of November 1705. And I desire that the name of God may be praised and adored for his wonderful goodness to me in sparing my life when I was as it were at the brink of eternity and that he stayed the hands of those that [took] up their weapons to slay me with.

Finis

N B. that while with Indians I was in great danger of being drowned several times.[54]

---

50. Elizabeth Austin Hill (c. 1675–c. 1745) was captured at Wells in August 1703 with her family. Her husband, Samuel, returned to Massachusetts on parole after the visit by Sheldon and Livingston to negotiate further prisoner exchanges. He returned to Quebec and, with his family, came back to Massachusetts on the *Hope* in 1706. The Hills returned to their family farm at Saco.

51. William Dudley (1686–1749) was the eighteen-year-old son of the governor of Massachusetts.

52. Augustin Legardeur de Courtemanche (1663–1717) was a prominent officer and nobleman in New France. He had escorted Livingston and Sheldon back to New England in May 1705, doing some spying for the French at the same time. However, he caused a scandal in New France when, ostensibly falling ill while in Boston, he asked to be taken back by ship (with William Dudley and Samuel Vetch) rather than go overland, thus revealing the seaward approach to Quebec to the English. He ended his life as a post commander in Labrador.

53. Samuel Vetch (1668–1732) was a merchant who captained the ship that brought Courtemanche to Quebec. Vetch and Dudley came to spy out ways to attack Quebec as well as negotiate further prisoner exchanges. In the next five years, Vetch went on to promote two (failed) attempts to conquer Quebec and participated in the successful conquest of Acadia.

54. Stephen added this note to the manuscript at a later date.

LETTER FROM JOHN WILLIAMS TO STEPHEN WILLIAMS, 1729

T HE REVEREND John Williams of Deerfield wrote the following letter to his son the Reverend Stephen Williams exactly a quarter century after the raid and approximately three months before his death in June 1729. At the time, Stephen was collecting material on the 1704 Deerfield raid and other incidents for a history of what he describes as "the remarkable providences of God towards the people in that place in the wars with the Indians." [1] The letter details how several individuals and families avoided capture on the morning of February 29, 1704. It also refers to an at-present lost account that John Nims of Deerfield wrote for Stephen Williams about his capture in October 1703 and his subsequent captivity.

Like the other materials in this volume that Stephen Williams collected or wrote, the contents of this letter were never published. It provides another example of the "unimproved" raw materials that ministers and others used to compose captivity narratives and accounts of God's providence. Here Deerfield's residents do not willingly submit to their fate but strive to avoid capture at all costs, which in some instances involved unheroic flight and the abandonment of family and neighbors. None of the incidents mentioned in the letter was recounted by John Williams in *The Redeemed Captive Returning to Zion*.

§

Deerfield March 11, 1728–9 [2]

Dear Son, [3]

I have wrote down the names of three [that] were omitted, but [I am] like to have made a blunder. In writing down by the side you may easily see what it

---

The original John Williams to Stephen Williams, Deerfield, March 11, 1728/1729, Gratz Collection, Historical Society of Pennsylvania, Philadelphia. Reproduced by permission of the Historical Society.

1. Stephen Williams Diary, January 6, 1729, typescript transcription, microfilm edition, Historic Deerfield Library.

2. The English still used the Julian calendar, which began the new year on March 25 rather than January 1; thus, dates in English documents between January 1 and March 25 were often written with both years.

3. John's son, the Reverend Stephen Williams (1693–1782), who was then the minister in Longmeadow, Massachusetts.

FIGURE 13. Esther Meacham's gravestone, schist, c. 1751, probable carver Gershom Bartlett. This gravestone marks the burial and commemorates the life of Esther Williams, John Williams's oldest daughter, who was thirteen when she was captured in 1704. She returned to New England in the spring of 1705. Ten years later, in 1715, she married the Reverend Joseph Meacham and settled with him in Coventry, Connecticut. Though she died many years after the 1704 raid, the Williams family's captivity and the fact that they were "wonderfully preserved & Redeemed" are prominently featured on her grave marker. Photograph by Linda Pagliuco, courtesy of Antiquarian & Landmarks Society, Hartford, Connecticut.

is. I think it not worth the while to write about my deliverance at Sugar Loaf Brook[4] being in a great hurry at present for I am to preach tomorrow at Northampton. I blocked out Philip Mattoon[5] on one side finding he was down on the other side. Mr. Richards and his wife[6] escaped out at a small gate and ran down to Harrow Meadow and so escaped to Hatfield.[7] John Allison and his wife[8] escaped out the great gate [illegible] Meadow, went and ran to Hatfield. She was frozen in her feet very much and Ebenezer Brooks[9] and family went down into their cellar and so did Sergeant Munn[10] in his house run down into the cellar and so were not found [and] the houses left unburned. [illegible] Belden[11] run out of a little gate eastward up the mountain and escaped to Hatfield. Deacon Sheldon,[12] Godfrey Nims[13] and a soldier escaped to Captain Wells's fort.[14] You know the circumstances of their surprising the fort.

Abigail[15] has been ill with a canker in her throat and a fever but it [is now] better. Mr. Grant[16] has sent the accounts as you will find. I sent you John Nims's

---

4. John was almost captured by a raiding party near Mount Sugar Loaf (which today is South Deerfield) on October 12, 1693. Martin Smith (?–1704) was captured the next day. See Williams "Daniel Belding's 1696 Captivity," 59n33.

5. Philip Mattoon (1680–1704) was killed in the attack not, as is sometimes claimed, on the march to Canada.

6. John Richards (c. 1662–?) and Abigail Parsons Munn Richards (1662–?) lived near the south end of the stockade. He arrived in Deerfield sometime before 1698. He was addressed as "mister" and served as schoolmaster. Abigail had married John Munn in 1680 and was widowed in 1684. She married John Richards in 1686.

7. Hatfield is twelve miles south of Deerfield.

8. John Allison (?–1722) and his wife, Mary Jeffreys Allison (1669–1730), were among Deerfield's humbler residents. In 1712 John was employed to sweep the meeting house, a form of work relief in many New England towns.

9. Ebenezer Brooks (1662–after 1720), his wife, Elizabeth Belding Brooks, and two sons survived the attack in a structure very close to the stockade's north gate.

10. Benjamin Munn (1683–1774), his wife, Thankful Nims Munn, and their infant daughter, Thankful, survived the attack in a structure near the stockade's south gate.

11. This appears to be a reference to Daniel Belding (1648–1731), and/or his son Nathaniel (1675–1714), who had been captured in 1696. Stephen Williams wrote an account of his captivity ("Daniel Belding's 1696 Captivity," 54–60.)

12. John Sheldon (1658–c. 1733) was the builder of the house that survived the attack and came to be known as the Old Indian House, whose battle-damaged front door is still preserved.

13. Godfrey Nims (? –1705) lived in a house near the south end of the stockade. The other members of his family were killed or captured.

14. The garrisoned house of Captain Jonathan Wells (1659–1739) was south of the main stockade.

15. Abigail Williams (1708–1787) was Stephen's half-sister, the daughter of the Reverend John Williams and his second wife, Abigail Allen Bissell Williams (1673–1754).

16. Mr. Grant was probably Ebenezer Grant (1706–1783) of East Windsor, Connecticut. After graduating from Yale in 1726, he returned home and quickly established himself as one of the region's leading merchants, trading with Boston, England, and the West Indies.

account of his captivity[17] and the circumstances of his being taken. I, your brother and sisters salute you and daughter[18] and all the children.

I am your loving father

J. Williams

[P.S.] Jonathan[19] will very probably disoblige me if he fails me for I am not like to have any other help. It's now so late before I heard of his changing his mind I had I know not which way to [illegible] myself.

---

17. John Nims (1679–1762) was captured along with Zebediah Williams (1675–1706) in Deerfield's North Meadows on October 8, 1703. Nims was one of the three men who escaped in 1705 with Joseph Petty. His account of his captivity cannot now be located. The Reverend John Williams talks about the fate of Zebediah Williams in "The Redeemed Captive," 152–153.

18. Stephen Williams's wife and John Williams's daughter-in-law, Abigail Davenport Williams (1696–1766).

19. The identity of this individual is not known.

JOSEPH PETTY'S 1705 ESCAPE, C. 1729

JOSEPH PETTY

NOT ALL of the captives taken at Deerfield in 1704 patiently awaited their redemption and return to New England. In the spring of 1705 three of them—Thomas Baker (1682–1753), Martin Kellogg (1686–1753), and Joseph Petty (1672–1746), along with another Deerfield man captured in October 1703, John Nims (1679–1762)—took matters into their own hands. All four were located on the Island of Montreal and had freedom to move about, enabling them to meet in early May and plan their escape. Despite the odds against their success, they left Montreal on May 14 Old Style (May 25 New Style)[1] and managed to reach Deerfield around June 8 Old Style (June 19 New Style), "more dead than alive from hunger and fatigue," according to local tradition, and "guided more by instinct than reason, in making their way towards home."[2] Their twenty-five-day journey had taken them up Lake Champlain, across the Green Mountains, and down the Connecticut River.[3]

The most detailed account of their journey comes from a letter written years after the event by Joseph Petty and addressed to the Reverend Stephen Williams, then the pastor of a church in Longmeadow, Massachusetts. Though this letter is literally a story in which the end of a period of captivity is narrated, it was intended for inclusion in a collection of stories about captivity. It was apparently written in response to an inquiry Williams wrote as he gathered material in 1729 for his projected work on "remarkable providences of God" during the wars with the Indians.[4] The original letter cannot be located, but it survives as a photocopy and in a printed version in George Sheldon's *History of Deerfield*.[5]

Joseph Petty to Stephen Williams [n.p., n.d.] (photocopy), Wars, box 1a, folder 12, Pocumtuck Valley Memorial Association, Deerfield, Mass. Reproduced with permission of the P.V.M.A.

1. The English still used the Julian calendar. It was eleven days behind the newer and improved Gregorian Calendar, which is basically the same calendar in use today. All dates that appear in this document are from the Julian calendar and thus are in Old Style.

2. George Sheldon, *A History of Deerfield, Massachusetts*, 2 vols. (Deerfield: privately printed, 1895–1896), 1:351–352.

3. A brief notice of their escape appears in *Boston News Letter,* June 18, 1705.

4. Stephen Williams Diary, January 6, 1729, typescript transcription, microfilm edition, Historic Deerfield Library.

5. Joseph Petty to Stephen Williams, [n.p., n.d.], Wars, box 1, folder 12, Pocumtuck Valley Memorial Association, Deerfield, Mass., and Sheldon, *History of Deerfield,* 1:353–354.

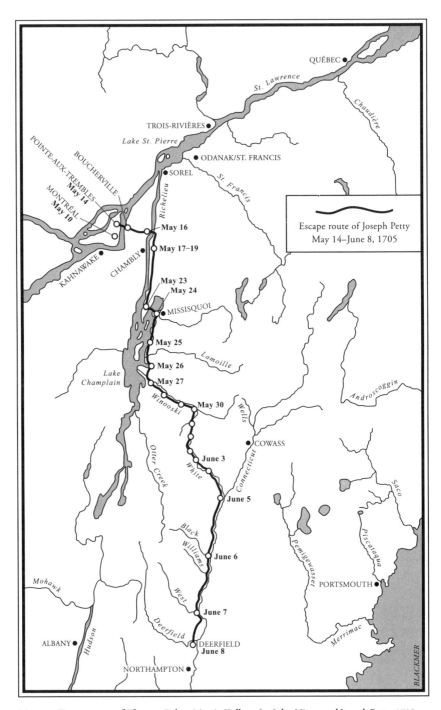

MAP 5. Escape route of Thomas Baker, Martin Kellogg Jr., John Nims, and Joseph Petty, 1705.

Like the account of Daniel Belding's 1696 captivity and Stephen Williams's account of his own captivity from 1704 to 1705, Petty's letter provides another revealing glimpse into the raw material for a published captivity narrative. It too lacks clerical "improvements" pointing to evidences of God's providence in every mundane occurrence and does not present their escape as a time of trial in which their faith was tested. The existing account is a fairly straightforward, surprisingly detailed report of their escape from Montreal and the journey south. Only near the end does Petty acknowledge "the good hand of divine providence (which watched over us all the way)" and praise God for their deliverance.

After their return to Deerfield, these men drew upon the skills and knowledge that they had acquired during their march north and escape south. Martin Kellogg became a scout and was captured in a fight near Cowass (today, Newbury, Vermont) in 1708. The next year some of his fellow escapees were undoubtedly among the four or five former captives from Deerfield who were part of Francis Nicholson's army poised to invade New France because they "knew the territory." In 1712, Captain Thomas Baker, Lieutenant Martin Kellogg, and Lieutenant Samuel Williams led a scouting party that surprised Wattanummon, Stephen Williams's captor, and killed him in a fight along the Pemigewasset River in New Hampshire (map 5).[6]

The experience of captivity and their escape continued to set apart the lives of several of these men. Joseph Petty, the author of the letter, moved north to establish a new frontier community at Northfield, Massachusetts, in 1715. Martin Kellogg settled in Wethersfield, Connecticut, far from the frontier, but served as an interpreter, militia captain, and for a time, a teacher at the Indian mission in Stockbridge, Massachusetts. Thomas Baker married another captive but had a hard time settling down, moving from Northampton to Brookfield and then Mendon, Massachusetts, and on to Newport, Rhode Island, before finally establishing himself in Dover, New Hampshire. Only John Nims returned to the relatively sedentary life of a Deerfield farmer.

---

6. Evan Haefeli and Kevin Sweeney, *Captors and Captives: The 1704 French and Indian Raid on Deerfield* (Amherst: University of Massachusetts Press, 2003), 195, 201, 205–206.

§

The Reverend
Mr. Stephen Williams
At Springfield, Longmeadow

Reverend Sir:

Upon your desire, I now present you with a narrative of my escape from Canada, though it is now so long since that I may possibly forget some particulars. But the account as near as I can remember is as follows *viz:*

About thirteen months after I was taken from Deerfield (which you well remember) four of us consulted [about] methods to make our escape. Sometime in May upon their great procession day[7] we had liberty to go in and about the city of Montreal, and there we happened all to meet together, and John Nims and I informed the other two[8] of our design to make our escape. This was on a Thursday [May 10] and we agreed that the other three were to come down to where I lived which was about 9 miles from the city [map 4].[9] What was something remarkable: the guns and provisions which I had designed to bring with us was in another room from where I lodged which exercised my mind very much [concerning] how I should come at them since I lodged in another room with the people of the house. And what still oppressed my spirits more was that coming in from work at noon I found a bed and sick person placed in that room where the guns and provisions were. I thought now it was impossible to escape but upon my return at night I found the sick person removed and my bed brought into that room which much revived me.

On the Sabbath [May 13] following I was to go to the city again to conclude further about our escape and having confirmed all matters I returned at night and found my landlord's son there [who] was designed to lodge with me which again dashed my spirits much for now I thought it impossible for me to escape from him. But while I sat pausing what to do I remembered that I was to set up a sign by the river for the other three to know where the house was. And I thought I would go and do that. Which when I had done [it], upon my return I found my landlord's son moving off and would not stay though much persuaded to tarry. Although it was very dark, he did go which again revived me.

---

7. They met on Thursday, May 21, 1705 New Style, which was the Feast of the Ascension, the day on which Catholics celebrate Christ's ascension into heaven. It was May 10 Old Style.

8. Thomas Baker and Martin Kellogg, who had been taken captive on February 29, 1704.

9. Petty was apparently staying at Pointe-aux-Trembles, which was on the south shore of the Island of Montreal 9 miles below the village of Montreal.

And about break of day the other three came and I handed them two guns and some provision.

We took a canoe and passed the river by sun rising, and though the people lived on the other side,[10] we passed by them undiscovered [map 5]. This was on Monday morning [May 14] the [sun about two hours high and on Wednesday at night][11] we arrived at [the] Chamblee River about 9 miles below the fort.[12] There we made a raft and went over, and the next day we traveled up against the fort and stopped to get some provision, killed a calf and dried it. But Friday and Saturday [it] rained so hard that we could not travel which then we judged made against us, but in providence we found it otherwise, for those that pursued us were in this time returned.

On the Sabbath [May 20] following we set out for the lake [i.e., Lake Champlain] and arrived there on Wednesday [May 23] about noon. There we found two canoes which we judged our pursuers had left. One of these we took and came along with our journey and came along that day and all night and the next day. At night [we] left our canoe. We came along on the east side of the lake until we came to the mouth of the Mesisecou [i.e., Missisquoi] River. We went up this river all night for it comes along the same course as the east shore of the lake, and next morning we found a small run of water which led out of the river into the lake which we made use of to waft us into the lake again. There is extraordinary good land on each side of this river all the way we went as far as we could perceive.

This day [May 24] we traveled on the lake till night and lay by the lake. But next morning the wind was so high against us that we left our canoe and traveled on the side of the lake that day. The next day being Saturday we struck across [to] the French River falls[13] and arrived there on Sabbath [May 27] about 9 in the morning. This [river] we traveled up about 2 or 3 days and left it and struck away for the branches of the White River and on the next Sabbath [June 3] about 9 in the morning we came to the White River.

Now our provision was spent excepting some small matters we had left to fish with, and that day we spent in getting provision and supplied ourselves for

10. Boucherville is located on the south bank of the Saint Lawrence River opposite Pointe-aux-Trembles.

11. This is our rephrasing of what appears to be a garbled chronology in the text. When George Sheldon published the letter in his *History of Deerfield*, he dealt with this problem by leaving out words. Here we draw on the photocopy of the original.

12. The Chamblee River was the Richelieu River. The fort is Fort Chambly, located on the east bank of the Richelieu River.

13. The French River is the Winooski River. The falls of the Winooski is today the location of the city of Winooski, Vermont.

that night and part of the next day which was all the provision we had until we came to Deerfield, excepting the leg of a tortoise and a small hook fish which we brought along a little way. The next night [June 5] we came to the mouth of the White River and made a fire and designed to lodge there, and we set one to fish for us. But by reason of [the] flies he was soon discouraged. As soon as he came up I was going down to the river to drink and espied an Indian on the east side of the Great River[14] coming to drink which made me stop and hide myself until he was gone off.

For fear of discovery we made off that night and the next day our provision all being spent sometime and we weak and faint, we thought [it] best to make a raft upon which we came down that day and the next night on [the] Connecticut River. The next day [June 6] also we still continued our course on the raft and on Thursday about 9 or 10 in the morning we came to the great falls.[15] There we let go our raft and went below the falls and made another and came that day [June 7] to the lower end of the Great Meadow or the place now called the canoe place.[16] There we lodged that night and the next morning we came on our raft to the meadow where the fort is now.[17] There we left our raft and came on foot that day into Deerfield about twilight in the evening, and thus through the good hand of divine providence (which watched over us all the way) we safely arrived to our own native land again and were joyfully received and well taken care of by our friends. Upon which I cannot but say that we have reason to praise God for our deliverance and never forget his benefits.

Thus Sir I have given you a brief and as exact a relation [as I] can [tell], since 'tis so long a time passed since, and if it may be of any service I rejoice and subscribe myself yours to command,

Joseph Petty

---

14. The Great River is the Connecticut River. This particular location is today White River Junction, Vermont.

15. The location of the great falls is today Bellows Falls, Vermont.

16. The location of the Great Meadow is today Putney, Vermont.

17. The fort Petty refers to is Fort Dummer, which was built in 1724, two miles south of the present location of Brattleboro, Vermont.

When I was Carried to Canada, c. 1740

Joseph Kellogg

ORE THAN death itself, the New England captives feared conversion to Catholicism. Yet some of them did convert. Because few of the converts returned home, however, relatively little is known about how the conversion process worked. Until recently the major source has been John Williams, who had plenty of reasons to portray the process in as negative a light as possible. This manuscript, which has not been published before now provides a rare first-hand account of how one captive, the boy Joseph Kellogg, converted.

Joseph Kellogg (1691–1756) was one of the forty-one children captured in the 1704 raid. The Kellogg family was deeply affected by the event. His five-year-old brother Jonathan was killed in the raid. Captured, in addition to Joseph, were his father, Martin, his brother Martin Junior (age seventeen) and his sisters Rebecca (age eight) and Joanna (age ten). Martin Senior was quickly ransomed and returned. Neither the French nor the Natives had much interest in holding a forty-five-year-old man. But the children were a different story.

The young Kellogg captives were taken into the Iroquoian villages around Montreal. Martin apparently went to Sault-au-Récollet, the others to Kahnawake. All of them learned Mohawk and served as interpreters and go-betweens later in life. Joanna and Rebecca married into the community at Kahnawake. Joanna never came back. Rebecca, however, did return to New England decades later. Martin Junior escaped with Joseph Petty in 1705.[1] He returned to Canada at the end of the war and persuaded Joseph to return to New England. Kinship ties prevailed. Joseph, who had not yet married, returned in 1714 with his brother.

Shortly after his return, Joseph was appointed a sergeant and interpreter for the province of Massachusetts. He quickly rose in rank and influence on the western frontier, becoming a captain and a justice of the peace. He married

---

Joseph Kellogg, "When I was Carryed to Canada . . . ," mss. in folder "Papers Relating to the 1704 Attack on Deerfield," case 8, box 28, The Reverend John Williams and Family, Gratz Collection, Historical Society of Pennsylvania, Philadelphia. Reproduced by permission of the Historical Society.

1. See Petty, "Joseph Petty's 1705 Escape," 175–180.

Rachel Devotion of Suffield, Connecticut, and brought up his family in her hometown rather than expose them to the dangers of the frontier. Joseph and Rachel had three daughters and two sons, one of whom evidently endorsed this account at the end. Joseph's rank and connections helped him enlist the government of Massachusetts in a successful effort to persuade his sister Rebecca to return in 1729. His career as a frontier diplomat continued until 1756, when he died in Schenectady, New York, while serving on an expedition against the French.

This manuscript offers an explanation for why he and other English captives, including his younger sisters, converted to Catholicism. It exposes the vigorous efforts of several Frenchmen to convert the captives. Some were Jesuits, but others, referred to as "priests," were probably Sulpicians, members of the French religious order that dominated the Island of Montreal. Kellogg's account is not so much a narrative as a list of the arguments and techniques used to procure a conversion. As such it offers a rare glimpse of how the theological struggles of post-Reformation Europe adapted to the colonial American frontier.

§

When I was carried to Canada, I was forced by my master to go to church. He forced me to cross myself when I was unwilling. He threatened to beat me and would by force take my hand and make it for me. [He] would deny me victuals unless I would conform to them [i.e., Catholic religious practices].[2]

By the priests' means all the grown persons were put away. Then they used all their art to make us in love with their religion. [The priests] were often crying against our religion. [They] told us our Bibles were defective and did not contain all. [They] showed us so many leaves as contained the Apocrypha books and said the English had taken all that out of their Bibles.[3]

[They] told us the rise of our religion was [caused by] King Henry the Eighth's wickedness. [They said] that he killed two wives and married his own daughter.[4] [They said] that he had six wives one after another, for which wick-

---

2. It is unclear exactly who Kellogg's master was, but he was an Iroquoian warrior.

3. The Apocrypha are religious texts generally dated to the period between the Old and New Testaments. Some Christians consider certain Apocrypha to be part of their sacred scripture. Others, including many Protestants, do not. In 1546, the Council of Trent affirmed that they were part of the Catholic canon. Parts of the Apocrypha support belief in Purgatory (2 Maccabees 12:39–45), which Protestants oppose. However, the priest was mistaken because both the Geneva Bible, which was the English version favored by the Puritans, and the King James version of the Bible include the Apocrypha.

4. Henry Tudor (1491–1547) became King Henry VIII of England in 1509. His first wife, Catherine of Aragon, gave birth to a daughter (later Queen Mary) but no son. Desperate for a male

edness he was excommunicated by the pope and that then by means of Luther's[5] and Calvin's[6] apostasy he made himself lord and master of Religion.

They said Calvin and Luther were very wicked [and] that Luther himself said he had eaten a bushel of salt with the Devil. [They said] that Calvin was enraged because, when a canon expecting a bishopric, he failed in it and in discontent he ran away and took a nun with him with whom he lived in whoredom, and that for these wickednesses he was whipped and branded at Geneva.

[They] often told us their religion was confirmed by miracles. [They] told us such and such miracles were wrought by them. [They] would call persons who would swear that such miracles were wrought on them. One priest Monsieur Rene told me he had heard of great miracles wrought by Saint Katherine (here note that this Saint Katherine was a Maqua squaw that was dead and sainted)[7] but he did not believe them and was struck deaf. And after sometime he thought how he had reproached her and went to her tomb. [He] confessed his sin and asked her pardon and prayed that he might be restored. [He] was immediately cured. A nun at Montreal [who] was very sick and had a grievous pain in her side sent for a tooth of Saint Katherine's and a dish, which she used to use. She put [the tooth] into her mouth and drank in the dish and was cured.

Near a twelve-month after I had lived with them, I was taken sick with the

---

heir, Henry sought to have the pope approve a divorce so he could get a new wife. When the pope refused to support him, Henry broke with the Catholic Church (1529), and became head of the Church of England. Henry's action started England's Protestant Reformation and freed him to marry Anne Boleyn, who bore another daughter (later Queen Elizabeth). Henry had Anne Boleyn executed for infidelity (1536) and married Jane Seymour, who bore a son (later King Edward VI) but died of complications from the birth. Henry went on to marry Anne of Cleves, whom he immediately divorced (1540), Catherine Howard, whom he also had executed for infidelity (1542), and Catherine Parr, who survived him. None of his wives was his own daughter.

5. Martin Luther (1483–1546), an Augustinian monk and professor at the University of Wittenberg in Saxony, Germany, is credited with starting the Protestant Reformation through his opposition to the idea that the Church could sell an "indulgence" to reduce the time a soul would spend in Purgatory before going on to Heaven. Lutheranism is the term for the brand of Protestantism he inspired. He married a former nun.

6. John Calvin (1509–1564) was the son of a French lawyer who became the leading theologian of the Protestant Reformation. Geneva, Switzerland, was the base from which he disseminated his religious ideas, setting the tone of Protestantism in those areas not dominated by Lutherans. Calvinism had a great influence on English Puritans. Calvin married a widow.

7. Pierre Rémy (1636–1706) was a Sulpician priest who served the church in Lachine, a French village near Kahnawake, for many years and was an early promoter of Catherine's saintliness. Catherine Tekakwitha (1656–1680) was a Mohawk woman who converted to Catholicism and moved to Kahnawake. There her rigorous piety and refusal to marry impressed several French priests. Almost as soon as she died, they began a movement to make her a saint. Though often referred to and treated as a saint, Catherine Tekakwitha was only recently beatified (1980) and has not yet been formally canonized.

smallpox. When my distemper was at the height, and my sores white and just ready to run, a Jesuit came to me.[8] [He] told me my case was very hazardous, and that he had used all ordinary means but without success. But, when he was looking over his medicines, some of the relic of this saint often came into his hand. But though he knew the great virtue in them, he dare not give them [to] me, because I was not a Roman Catholic in heart. [He] told me I was near dying. [He said] that if I would now promise that I would confess and be a Roman Catholic if upon taking some of these relics I should have help, he would give them to me. So I promised him. He gave me something under the name of the relics of the rotten wood of the coffin, after which I slept better and grew better. When I was recovered, he told me of the promise that I had made, and how angry God would be with me if I did not make good my promises.

They told me of a saint that had been dead above a hundred years [whose] body was yet whole, only one arm that the pope had cut off for a relic. [They told me] that when they were going to cut it off many years after his death, he pulled in his arm to oppose or hinder it, but that they spoke to him and told him, that what they were doing was by order of his superior, and that he was to obey, and thereupon he yielded. When it was cut off, it bled as much as though he had been alive. This saint they say in his life had wrought more miracles than ever Christ had done, when he was in the world.[9]

For the proof of their [belief in] transubstantiation (that Christ's body could be in heaven and in the host [at the same time])[10] they told me that a boat's crew were in a great storm drove off from the ship. In the time of the tempest this Saint Xavier was with them praying to God sometimes kneeling, sometimes walking. The captain was concerned about the men in the boat, but Saint Xavier assured the men in the ship, that the men in the boat would come again in a little time. And so it happened. When the captain asked them how it had been with them, they said very well, they had an excellent steersman: that was Saint Xavier that all the while was a pilot to them so that this same saint's body was at the same time in the ship and boat at a distance.

---

8. Probably Pierre Cholonec (1641–1723), another promoter of the cult of Catherine Tekakwitha and her first biographer. A Jesuit who worked at several of the Iroquoian missions after his arrival in New France 1674, he had known Tekakwitha personally.

9. Francis Xavier (1506–1552), a founding member of the Society of Jesus, was born in Spain and carried the Jesuit mission to Asia, first to India, then Indonesia, Japan, and finally China, where he died. His body was brought back to the Portuguese colony of Goa in India. In 1614 his right arm below the elbow was cut off and sent to Rome. He was canonized in 1622.

10. Transubstantiation, also known as the doctrine of the real presence, claims that in the course of the Catholic Mass, bread and wine are transformed into the body, blood, and spirit of Jesus Christ. The host is the wafer of bread used in the Mass.

The priest told me he could by the host or sacrament cast out devils at any time.[11]

They kept telling me and the other children that unless I really hated my father and mother I could not be saved. [They] told me that I must do it, that it was the word of God, and showed me the text.[12]

They told me a pretence of Calvin's working a miracle that he killed instead of raising of the dead.[13]

The priest always humored me, giving me anything if I complied with them.

The Indians prohibited the children speaking together in the English tongue. If we did speak it must be in the Maqua language.[14]

After I was wrought upon by their insinuations to be a Roman Catholic, they would often tell the children that I was converted and ask me to persuade them to their ways. The priests persuaded the Indians to marry the English, propounded such and such to them, and though the Indians at first unwilling, they persuaded them to it, to secure them there.[15]

They persuaded me to go to Montreal, and in the Jesuits' church[16] with a lighted wax candle in my hand to read over their creed, and on my knees to promise God and the church to live and die in their religion and land. And several of them that are yet with the Indians are such as by the instigations of the priests and Jesuits have on their knees promised God and the Virgin Mary to live and die with the Indians, and are by them threatened with eternal damnation if they break their vow.

They promised me and so others that are yet there that forgetting all

---

11. This is a reference to exorcism, a means of curing people who are deemed possessed by the devil. Puritans believed possession could be cured only by praying and fasting.

12. This may be a reference to Matthew 10:35–37 "For I have come to set a man against his father, and daughter against her mother, and a daughter-in-law against her mother-in-law; and a man's foes will be those of his own household. He who loves father or mother more than me is not worthy of me; and he who loves son or daughter more than me is not worthy of me."

13. This is a classic piece of anti-Protestantism, which John Williams denounces in "The Redeemed Captive," 154.

14. Mohawk, or a closely related Iroquoian language. See also Stephen Williams's experience at Odanak in Williams, "What Befell Stephen Williams," 167.

15. Few male English captives married into the Native communities, and none that we know of from Deerfield did. The only Deerfield captive who married into the Sault-au-Récollet community was Hannah Hurst (1695– ?). The remaining marriages between women from Deerfield and Native men took place at Kahnawake.

16. The Jesuits did have a residence in Montreal by 1704 and it undoubtedly had a chapel, but as a rule they did not minister to the churches in Montreal. It is possible that Kellogg, like other New England captives, mistook for Jesuits the Sulpician priests, who did have a seminary in Montreal and did minister to churches in the Montreal area.

for Christ we should be sure of heaven when we died. They brought me the book of the saints' lives and then read to me the holy lives and happy deaths of many English. [They] told [me] it was but a little while and all the English were [i.e., would become] good Catholics, and not the name of a Protestant among them. [They said] that Protestants had that name from protesting against the right way.

The Indians indulge the English boys abundantly, let them have the liberty they will, while they outwardly conform to them, and so an easy way of life and libertinism is more prevailing with them than any affection they have to religion.

For the proof of their purgatory one of them assured me that after his mother had been dead many years she appeared to him one night and told him that she was in great distress in purgatory, but [he] must not fail of getting so many masses and prayers said for her and then she should be delivered. [He said] that after so many masses and prayers [were] said for her she appeared to him again in the same place, and with a shining countenance, telling him she was now happy in paradise, and told him what was become of many that had been dead some years before.[17]

A Jesuit told me that there was but one true religion in the world, and that among the English there were a great many religions. He told me that I ought to believe him because he was more learned and had more knowledge than I had, and that he had quitted all to come and instruct the poor people in the right way. He told me that miracles were one great mark of the true church, and though there were none in our country, yet I should see one there [in New France]. The worms were eating their grain. They went in procession saying their prayers and sprinkling holy water. Within a little time all the worms were all gone away.[18]

These are some few short hints of the many artifices used to persuade the English children to stay there. They have craftily wrought upon many English to marry in the country, and now oblige them by their promises before marriage to stay there. They pretend that some scores of the English are naturalized, which as to many of them is either altogether false, or obtained of them by a list of their names for other ends to be presented to their King.[19] They

---

17. See also the stories of visits from souls in Purgatory in Williams, "The Redeemed Captive," 131.

18. These processions to protect the crops were a common part of rural Catholicism. They appear in other captivity accounts.

19. Dozens of English captives were naturalized by Louis XIV in 1710, among them Joseph Kellogg himself. Others were naturalized in 1713. Conversion to Catholicism was a precondition for naturalization.

won't suffer married persons to bring away their children born in the country, and so constrain the parents to tarry.[20]

This I suppose is Captain Kellogg's account. I found it among my father's papers.

---

20. This was the law of New France. It prevented some captives, especially women, from trying to leave. Others returned but left behind family members. Sometimes a captive's child migrated down to New England, leaving the parent behind, as did Aaron Denio (1704–1780), son of Abigail Stebbins De Noyon (1687–1740) and Jacques De Noyon (1668–1745).

FRENCH NARRATIVES

A Letter Concerning the Mission of Lorette in New France, 1710

Louis d'Avaugour

THE FOLLOWING narrative is a letter describing life in the Huron community of Lorette, from which came some of the raiders who attacked Deerfield. The author was a Jesuit priest, Louis d'Avaugour (1669–1732). More than just a report on conditions at the Lorette mission during the War of the Spanish Succession (1702–1713), the letter is also a work of propaganda. D'Avaugour wanted to convince his readers that the Jesuit missions play a vital role in helping New France survive. For him, Lorette is an example of how Catholic piety, political loyalty, and military effectiveness are linked together in the service of New France. At the same time, this account is the only contemporary narrative presenting the captors' side of the Deerfield raid.

The central figure of the narrative is a young Huron man named Thaovenhosen (c. 1680–?). Since there is no v in the Huron language, the name is possibly a misprint for Tsauoenhohoui, Saouhenhohi, or Isawanhoni, all forms of a name associated with Huron leaders from later periods of the community's history. The man described here seems to be carving out a leadership position at Lorette, which required a combination of religious, military, and political authority. Like other members of the community at Lorette he appears to be living in a world that was shaped by Huron traditions and the Catholic teachings of the missionaries. Still, it is important to remember that Thaovenhosen did not write this account. Apart from this narrative we know very little about Thaovenhosen's life.

More is known of Louis d'Avaugour. He entered the Jesuit order at the relatively advanced age of twenty-seven at a time when most novices were around seventeen. Trained in Paris, he arrived in Quebec in 1699. He was posted to Lorette, his first mission, in 1705, not long after the Deerfield raid. He stayed at Lorette until about 1720, when he was sent west to the Illinois mission. In 1726 he was recalled to France to serve as the procurator of the Jesuit missions in

Ruben Gold Thwaites, ed., *The Jesuit Relations and Allied Documents: Travels and Explorations of the Jesuit Missionaries in New France, 1610–1791*, 73 vols. (Cleveland: Burrows Brothers, 1896–1901). The letter is at 66:147–173.

New France and Louisiana. He died in Paris. During the fifteen years he spent at Lorette he had ample time to get to know Thaovenhosen and the roughly 150 other Huron inhabitants of the village. Because primary documentation is very scarce for the community, d'Avaugour's account is the closest we can get to the details of their life at this point in time.

Though European missionaries expected those who converted to Christianity to make a radical break with their past, it was not so easy to separate the "Christian" from the "traditional" in their lives. This account provides an excellent case in point. On the surface one sees a community intensely dedicated to the seasonal round of Catholic devotion. They go to church regularly; they respect their Jesuit priests; and they fervently pray to figures approved by Church authorities: Jesus Christ, the Virgin Mary, and a select few saints. But if one looks beyond the particular names and religious authorities involved, there are remarkable continuities with pre-Christian times. Both systems fit into the seasonal pattern of the Hurons' lives as they moved from hunting to fishing, farming, gathering plants, and back again. The Christian All Souls Day seems much like the traditional Huron Feast of the Dead, when those who had died during the past year were disinterred, reburied, and commemorated. And both systems accepted that individuals of extraordinary spiritual power had a special leadership role to play in the community. Here, however, conflict could arise between claims of Christianity and those of Huron traditions as the story of Thaovenhosen reveals.

D'Avaugour's letter was designed to be published and read by an international audience. Originally written in Latin, it would have been accessible to educated Catholics across Europe. The Jesuits had been writing, usually in French, and publishing accounts of their missionary work—now known as *The Jesuit Relations*—since their first missions to New France in the early seventeenth century. The purpose of letters like this one was to inspire support for the Jesuit missions financially and politically by recounting the progress of Catholicism abroad. The Jesuits were highly educated men, able to learn the languages of the Native peoples they worked with. They were also excellent writers and observers. They described the difficulties and challenges of their mission as well as the successes. Much can be learned from their work, but its context must always be kept in mind. This version of the letter is based on an English translation printed at the turn of the last century.

§

Your Reverence[1] asks me to give you information respecting the state of our Mission of Lorette. I comply with your request in this letter—wherein, although you will read nothing that is brilliant or magnificent, as may be related of other missions, yet you will learn, I think, with pleasure what kind of life our Hurons lead here, and what practices of piety they daily perform. I write this with all the more confidence, because I have had but little share in what I am about to relate. The whole merit is due, after God, to the care and ability of Reverend Father De Couvert,[2] who was recently compelled by ill health to return to Quebec, that he might be more conveniently cared for in our college.[3] Appointed in his place, although unequal to the task, I shall narrate what I have seen and discovered in this village of Lorette.

Some there are who think, and therefore write, that the soil of Canada is thoroughly sterile and unfruitful; that the heralds of the Gospel reap therefrom hardly any fruit in return for long and painful labor. This single village of Lorette can teach them otherwise. In fact, I make bold to say that all the other missions of Canada are by no means as fruitful as this one. Drunkenness,—a vice inborn in barbarians, and spread far and wide by the greed of European traders,—and the corrupt morals and criminal examples of Europeans, deplorably oppose the Gospel. These obstacles are, however, surmounted, although not everywhere with the same promptness and facility. They have been thoroughly abolished and destroyed in the village of Lorette, where the savages enjoy the most ample liberty, and have made it a custom to practice piety openly and in security.

[Life at Lorette]

Every day at early morn, as soon as they awake, they repair to the church, to pay their homage to the Lord Christ on the *throne of his grace.* Neither age nor

---

1. Joseph-Louis Germain (1633–1722). Born in Auvergne, he entered the Jesuit order in 1656 and taught in various places in France until he joined the Canadian mission in 1687. He spent most of his time in Quebec, where he taught at the college until his death. From September 11, 1710, until October 1, 1716 he served as the superior of the Jesuit mission in Canada. He probably solicited this report shortly after taking up his post.

2. Michel-Germain de Couvert (1653–1715), who was born in Bayeaux and trained in Paris, arrived in New France in 1690. He had worked at the Lorette mission since 1691 and served as its superior since 1694. He presided over the mission's 1697 move from Ancienne Lorette to its final location, once called Jeune Lorette, then Village-des-Hurons, and now Wendake. He died in Quebec.

3. The Jesuit College in Quebec, founded in 1635, was the only institution of higher learning in the colony. It was also a central residence for Jesuits in the colony.

sex, neither rigorous December nor the burning dog-days can deter any from this pious duty. The very children vie in outstripping their seniors. What laborer for souls would not readily forget all his trials on beholding the peaceful throng in the early morning, and often before sunrise, prostrate before the altar, lisping with tender accents the praises of Christ? I have often found savages in the coldest winter, kneeling and praying before the door of the church, waiting until it should be opened. As soon as it is opened, they approach; and each one prays separately, some of them during a whole hour. At sunrise, or shortly after, the signal is given for saluting the Mother of God in the words of the Angel. They regard this as a religious duty, and are careful not to omit it, wherever they may be. Half an hour later, Mass is celebrated, at which they all assist.

The concourse is the same on working-days and holy days, their ardor the same. Their modesty is so remarkable that the French passing through the village admire it—to their own confusion, when they compare themselves and their behavior with these barbarians. When Mass is finished, they leave, if it be a working-day, to labor at home or in the fields. In the evening, at sunset, the signal is given for prayer. All gather in the chapel, where prayers are offered up in common for the whole village. Each family also recites prayers privately at home, after which each one, with a pious kiss, venerates the most holy wounds of Christ.

The order is the same for feast-days and working-days, except for the labor which the holiness of the day prohibits. All are present in the morning at the sacrifice of the Mass, which is celebrated in behalf of the whole village. Nearly all assist at the Mass of a second priest, and not a few at another if there be a third celebrant. While the first Mass of all, which is called "the Mission Mass," is being said, they sing sacred hymns written in the vernacular tongue, and adapted to the feasts which are then being celebrated,—with a harmony truly beautiful, and not at all barbarous. Toward noon they assemble in the chapel for vespers,[4] which likewise consist in the singing of pious hymns. In these they use the cadence and the airs prescribed by ecclesiastical law, and practiced in the churches of Europe. To avoid all idleness, from which vice barbarians have most to suffer, some of the men go to the river to snare fishes with their treacherous hooks; others pursue wild beasts in the neighboring forest. All at the same hour, before the sun sets, repair to the chapel to attend evening prayers and to hear the instruction.

On the greater feast-days, no one leaves the village after vespers. Meanwhile, lest there be occasion for idleness or weariness, the priest will explain some equally useful and pleasing story taken from the sacred pages, or from the lives

---

4. A late afternoon or early evening worship service.

of the saints. Or he will arrange among the children a competition bearing on the Christian doctrine, and will feast their rustic eyes on this agreeable sight; or he will devise something else of this kind, that is wont to attract the people. Somewhat more time is spent in public prayers; the evening prayers begin a little earlier, and end with the solemn benediction which the priest, raising aloft the most blessed Sacrament, imparts to the adoring multitude. Thus, Reverend Father, the Hurons of Lorette have their day divided and ordered, as Your Reverence especially desired to know.

If you inquire what are their yearly occupations, these vary with the different seasons. After having gathered in the crops, they occupy themselves with hunting the beaver, whose richly-furred and highly-prized skins form the chief staple of Canadian commerce. This hunting lasts two or three months. When the Feast of All Saints[5] draws nigh, all the hunters return home to attend the divine mysteries, and relieve by pious prayers the souls of the dead, a duty which they perform with remarkable piety and attention. The feast-days over, they immediately return to the forest and to their hunt, laboring thereat until the beginning of December. Then, leaving the forest, they come home again to celebrate the feast-day of the Virgin conceived without stain;[6] also that of St. Francis Xavier,[7] whom they honor with a special zeal as being, besides St. Joseph,[8] another guardian and patron of the Canadian missions. All, by the sacrament of penance, discharge the debts that they have contracted toward God,—doing so a few days before the feast itself, that they may have more leisure to examine their consciences and prepare their souls for the sacrament. This also gives the priest greater facility for hearing each one of them—which is done less conveniently and usefully when they flock in crowds to the sacred tribunal of penance.

The remainder of December and the month of January—until the day sacred to the Mother of God purified in the temple[9]—they spend partly in fishing, partly in the easier hunting of partridges, hares, and other game of that kind, during which time they seldom spend the night out-of-doors. If bitter cold or rain keep them indoors they then busy themselves in netting their raquettes

---

5. All Saints Day is November 1 and commemorates the lives of all holy individuals, not just recognized saints.

6. December 8 is the Feast of the Immaculate Conception, which is the Catholic doctrine that Mary was conceived free from original sin so that she was pure enough to be the mother of Jesus.

7. December 3 is the feast day of Saint Francis Xavier (1506–1552), a Spaniard who helped Ignatius Loyola found the Jesuits and spent his clerical career as a missionary in Asia.

8. The husband of Mary, mother of Jesus.

9. February 2 is Candlemas Day, which traditionally honored Mary's purification after the birth of Jesus. Modern observances emphasize the presentation of Jesus when he was taken to the Temple by his parents according to Jewish custom.

[i.e., snowshoes], which they use in fearlessly treading the snow when pursuing the larger animals through the forest or over plains covered with deep snow. When they have recognized the footprints or the haunts of those creatures, they migrate thither with their whole families; and they do not revisit their village and their homes before the vernal breadth of the zephyrs has begun to melt the snow.

Having returned to this village and being restored by the Paschal food,[10] they sow their fields with Indian corn. Then they resort to the rivers' banks in quest of fish, or strip the aged trees in the forest, with whose bark they build their light canoes. After framing their vessels, they gather, toward the end of August, quantities of a plant useful in pharmacy and of no mean value in Europe, which druggists call "Capillaire."[11] Meanwhile the Indian corn ripens, and is cut toward the 13th of September. After this follows the beaver hunt, which, as I have just said, continues to the 1st of November.

In these occupations their piety shines forth, as well as their extreme docility in obeying the priest who presides over the mission. Such docility maintains them in concord, and in the practice of every virtue. Before leaving the village to work in the woods or in the fields, they never fail to pass by the chapel, and there to salute Christ in the most holy sacrament. On returning, they do the same before entering their huts. If they have to spend the night out of the village, if they have to travel anywhere, if they depart in a band for the chase, they notify the priest thereof and seek his advice. Nor do they hesitate to give up their hunt or any other work, if they see that it does not quite please him or meet with his approval. In all other matters they show him equal obedience and docility, and they venerate him and listen to him as no less than a father and guide (figure 14).

But this conduct is easy when they are at home, and stimulated by mutual example; the difficulty and trouble become far greater when they leave for Quebec, which is not very distant. There other savages meet them, and invite them to drink; there grasping tavern-keepers urge them, and well-nigh drag them into their wine-shops. Nevertheless, during the five years that I have spent here, I have seen no one, I will not say drunk, but even tainted with the least suspicion of having tasted wine—either among the traders with whom they deal, or the tavern-keepers, or the savages of other missions.

Sometimes the French insist, and complain of their excessive scrupu-

---

10. Paschal is a reference to the celebration of Easter, a moveable feast day that cannot come before March 23 or after April 25.

11. "Maidenhair" ferns, used for medicinal purposes.

losity: "For," say they, "what crime is there if by the way, or when weary from one's journey, or for a guest's or friend's sake, one quaff a cup of wine?" These men of Lorette answer very freely: "It is just as thou sayest, brother; but we have promised Mary that we would never drink even a single cup. We thereby expiate our former misdeeds when, ignorant of true piety and

FIGURE 14.   Huron woman and man. Watercolor, eighteenth century, artist unknown. The clothing reflects Huron adoption and adaptation of European fabrics. The woman's skirt and the man's shirt were made of European cloth. The blankets were also European, as was the man's hat. The leggings and moccasins were made of skins and, like the beadwork and jewelry, would have been fashioned according to Huron traditions. City of Montreal, Records Management and Archives.

of religion, we were wont to gorge ourselves with wine. Now we have adopted other customs and other ideas." I saw some of them, in the house of the governor and viceroy of Canada, utterly refuse a goblet of wine offered them, and not drink it until a priest of our society ordered them to do so. Not long ago, a French merchant spoke to me as follows: "We cannot, my father, help admiring the temperance and constancy of the Lorette Hurons. Recently we happened to come upon their band, and we all spent the night in the same place, in the cabins that they usually construct. They never could be induced by us to taste a drop of wine, even to touch it with their lips, being satisfied with bread and a little tobacco, which we willingly gave them."

[Hurons at War]

On the other hand, this piety of the Lorettans—so exact, so abstemious from intoxicating liquor—does not at all diminish the warlike spirit which these savages commonly possess; it merely imposes moderation and certain limits upon their martial ardor. Accordingly, they never take up arms unless at the governor's pleasure. When they have to fight, they often serve as an example and a cause for shame to their other countrymen. When a certain village of the English [i.e., Deerfield] was being assaulted, and a troop of cavalry sent to defend it was approaching, the French, with the Lorettans and Abenakis alone sustained and repelled the onset, the other savages having been shamefully put to flight. "And this is not surprising," said our Hurons, "For who can be strong knowing that he is the enemy of God; and that, after losing this mortal life, he must enter into everlasting death?"

The French captains enlist no soldiers more willingly than those from the village of Lorette. "For," they admit, "we know with certainly that in the fray they will never desert the standard, or yield before the enemy's attack." And as greatly as the French esteem them, so highly do they esteem the French; and they revere above all King Louis of France, on account of both his noble deeds, and the zeal for the extension and protection of religion of which they know him to be eminent. Before they march to war, and, if occasion require it, to certain death, they endeavor to strengthen or recover God's friendship by laying their sins at the priest's feet; and they diligently preserve the grace received in the sacrament—as I personally discovered in the war quite lately waged, during which I was in their midst.[12]

A savage who had escaped from the English camp made his way to Quebec,

---

12. These are the preparations to resist the projected English invasion of 1709.

and announced that the enemy was at hand with three thousand men.[13] The Marquis de Vaudreuil,[14] the commander of the war, judged it best not to wait for the English. He therefore hastily gathered two thousand men, partly French and partly savages. The Lorettans, thinking that they had been overlooked because they had not been enlisted with their countrymen, sent to me one of their chiefs, who complained of the injustice, as they amicably styled it. I answered him that a captain would soon come from the governor; in fact, he came at the very moment, and invited the inhabitants of Lorette to join the war. Thereupon great joy was felt in the whole village. No one of an age to fight was missing, not even two old men aged sixty years.

Meanwhile, a sudden report came that the enemy was nigh. The call to arms was sounded. But our Hurons—whom, as a mark of honor, our governor had chosen for his bodyguards and sentinels—would not set out until they had all assisted at the divine rites, although it was in the dead of night. The same piety shone in their conduct throughout the whole expedition and elicited great admiration, with due praise, on the part of the French. The same spirit persevered after the whole army had reached Chambly,[15] where all the troops had to assemble. There they performed morning and evening prayers,—both publicly, as is the custom in the village of Lorette, and privately; they shunned the nightly gatherings and dances of the other savages, although they were their kindred and friends; they visited them by day, and everywhere gave examples of modesty and piety. So excellent was their behavior that, when the troops were disbanded after the victory, the Lorette Hurons went by no other name than "the holy savages;" and that Father Valland,[16] Superior of the Residence of Montreal,—on his way through Quebec, where I chanced to be,—embraced me affectionately and said: "My Father, congratulate yourself; for thou hast as many saints as thou hast Hurons at Lorette." (In truth, when lately, on the Nativity of the Blessed Virgin,[17] they all approached the holy table, I hardly found, in most

---

13. In 1709 an army of fifteen hundred English colonists and six hundred Native allies assembled at Albany to invade New France by way of the Lake Champlain route guarded by Fort Chambly. John Williams and several other former Deerfield captives joined the expedition, which failed to advance on Canada.

14. Philippe de Rigaud de Vaudreuil (c.1643–1725), governor-general of New France from 1703 to 1725.

15. Fort Chambly had been a French post since 1665. A new fort had been built in 1702.

16. François Vaillant de Gueslis (1646–1718) entered the Jesuit order in 1665 and arrived in Quebec in 1670. His first mission was Lorette, in 1675 and 1676. Thereafter he was involved in missionary, diplomatic, and military activity with the Five Nations of the Iroquois League until 1693, when he established a residence for the Jesuits at Montreal. Further missions took him to Detroit and the Senecas before returning to Montreal in 1706. D'Avaugour undoubtedly met him sometime between 1706 and 1717, when Vaillant returned to France.

17. The feast of the Birth of the Virgin Mary is September 8.

of them, cause for needing the sacrament of penance; and almost the entire village might have partaken of the holy banquet without having confessed.)

The same piety that exists in the living shines forth in the dying. During the five years that I have spent here, not a single soul has departed this life otherwise than is the wont of the predestined: in full possession of the mind, even to the very last breath; assiduous in practicing the Christian virtues with tongue and heart; enjoying perfect tranquility, and entirely submissive to the divine command, whether to live or to die; finally, pronouncing the most holy names of Jesus and Mary, and dying while devoutly kissing the wounds of their crucified immortal Savior.

[The Story of Thaovenhosen]

They preserve the same serenity of a peaceful mind in accidents, however painful and unexpected. A young man named Paul, whom his imprudent and unknowing brother killed through a lamentable mistake, may serve as an example of this. They were paddling in a canoe, when they observed a flock of ducks. Both fired their guns; but Paul's brother, who was behind, discharged his into the head of his brother—who, falling in his blood, begged to be carried to the shore and that a priest be called. But, as the priest lived far away, he said: "Summon to my aid Thaovenhosen," that warrior chief, not more remarkable and famous for his skill in battle than for his Christian piety. As soon as the dying youth beheld him, he said: "My uncle"—Thus are the captains of troops called by the younger men—"help me, I pray, that I may make good use of the few moments that are left me." It would be difficult to relate with what affection, with what earnestness of voice and mind, Thaovenhosen breathed into the ears of the dying man an act of Contrition; with what words he incited him to faith, hope, charity, and conformity to the divine will. While his lips were imprinting a pious and last kiss on the wounds of Christ offered to his veneration, he ceased to speak and to live.

He seemed to have foreseen the death that threatened him, so changed was he from what he had been before. He would linger in the sacred house for a longer time; shun all pleasures, even those that were permitted and harmless; observe a singular moderation and modesty, in whatever he did or said; spurn martial glory, and I know not what ornaments of savage warfare with which the victors love to adorn their persons, and which they seek; and mention in frequent speech the heavenly rewards. Thus did God prepare that soul destined unto himself.

And since I have mentioned Thaovenhosen, whom the whole country considers as a model of Christian integrity, I will add a few words to manifest the distinguished virtue of the man. There is nothing barbarous in him, save his origin. His mind is broad and elevated, conceiving nothing base, nothing unworthy of an honest and wise man; his countenance breathes modesty, dignity, uprightness. The fame of his virtue is so great that none hesitate to commend themselves to his prayers, and they acknowledge that through these they have obtained many favors from God. They say that the sight of him kindles their piety, and revives the extinct or slumbering ardor of their charity.

To the French as well as to the savages, he is an incentive to live well and fight well. He is all covered with honorable wounds received in battle; and, if the French Mars had found ten such as he in the other nations of Canada, long ago no enemy of the French, no Iroquois would have been left. His remarkable kindness and gentleness—with which the Christian law inspires him, and by which he conquers every one—has abated naught of the bravery of the warrior, or of the boldness of the Huron. As soon as the news of war was heard, he was the first to take up arms, the last to lay them aside. Wherever he fought, the enemy was routed, defeated, and slaughtered; and great was his share in the victory won over the English when their great village which I mentioned before, was stormed;[18] more than a hundred prisoners were taken in it, and distributed among the allied savages who had taken part in the war.

The great chief of the Lorette Hurons had fallen in battle. It is the custom among the Canadians[19] to seek, as it were, expiation and consolation for the death of their chiefs by the slaughter of some captive. A relative of the dead man presents himself, and demands the prisoner; on the latter being handed over, his owner destines him to the flames, and prepares to satisfy his barbarous cruelty by torturing the wretched man. Thus the custom of the nation regulates. Meanwhile, the others murmur; the elders, although reluctantly, keep silence; the young men clamor for this right of arms, this reward of victory, this sole consolation for the chief and afflicted family.

Thereupon Thaovenhosen rising, although not yet honored with the dignity or the title of chief, makes a speech in the assembly of the notables, and boldly pleads for the life of the captive. He prays, he entreats them to remember that they are Christians and citizens of the village of Lorette; that dire cruelty is unbecoming to the Christian name; that this injury cannot be branded upon the reputation of the Lorettans without the greatest disgrace. The nephew of the dead man insists; his relatives urge his claim; they allege the custom, stating that clemency shown toward a single head will bring ruin to all; that the enemies will grow more ferocious, and more audacious to harm

---

18. The attack on Deerfield on February 29, 1704.
19. Here "Canadians" refers to the Native, not European, population of New France.

them, through hope of impunity. "I also," said he, raising his voice, "am related to that chief whose fall in battle we mourn, and whose death you would avenge by an unworthy cruelty. To me also is the captive due; I claim him as my own, and I contend that such is my right. If any one lays hands on him against my will, let him look to me for chastisement." Astounded at this speech, the assembly was mute, and no one dared to decide upon any greater severity toward the captive.

Thus does this remarkable man make use of his authority for the welfare of the unfortunate; he energetically devotes it also to the protection of religion,— on behalf of which he burns with such zeal that he highly esteems the King of France, on the ground that he had heard that he was an excellent defender of the Catholic ancestral religion. In the village of Lorette, he lends great assistance to the priest who presides over the mission. Whatever the Father ordains, whatever he considers useful for all, he intrusts to this man, and confidently relies on him to have it taken care of and fulfilled. For my part, I doubt not that he possesses a special gift of prayer, and that he has God always before his eyes; the most holy name of JESUS is ever on his lips, and, although he pronounces it in a low voice, he cannot help its being heard by passers-by. Behold the fruits borne by this Canadian soil!

These would be more blessed and more abundant still, if the triple tares were absent which, thanks be to God, have been totally uprooted from the field of Lorette—I mean drunkenness, superstition, and lewdness. Such is the threefold stain of our missions, the first and chief one of which is drunkenness. It was the latter which destroyed that fairest mission, which took its name from the Sault.[20] The same will ruin the others, unless the King's foresight put a curb upon the greed of the traders, through whom liquor distilled and decocted by fire is forced upon the savages. If a remedy be not applied to that evil, we shall soon have to deplore not only the loss of religion, but the total overthrow of the French Colony.

For nothing else than religion retains the savages in their fidelity to the French; that being lost, they will flock to the neighboring heretics,[21] from whom they make a much greater profit than from the French, and much more easily dispose of their goods. The motive of eternal salvation is the only one to prevent them from dealing with those with whom they know there is no hope in that direction. This link once broken, care for salvation and religion once re-

20. The Jesuit mission at Sault Saint Louis in the Mohawk village of Kahnawake. *Sault* is French for waterfall or rapids.

21. "Heretics" is a reference to the Protestant colonists in New York and New England.

laxed by drunkenness and its accompanying plagues, and all is over with the colony of the French in Canada; the labor of so many years, of so many wars, of so many priests will be lost. You know this, my Father; Reverend Father De Couvert knows it—who for seventeen years was superior of the Mission of Lorette; from him, who now lives in Quebec, you may learn more.

Heaven grant that I may guard and—if it be granted—may increase that which was so happily begun by him, and brought to the maturity that we here behold. For this object I need the special help of heavenly grace, which I earnestly beg your Reverence to obtain for me by your prayers to God, and by your most holy sacrifices.

> Your Reverence's
> Servant in Christ,
> LOUIS D'AVAUGOUR, S.J.[Society of Jesus]

From the village of Lorette,
October 7, 1710.

FIGURE 15. Jean-Baptiste Hertel de Rouville (1668–1722). Oil painting, prior to 1713, artist unknown. This portrait was probably painted around 1712 when De Rouville was promoted to captain. When he was made a knight of the order of Saint Louis in 1721, the insignia of the order was added to the portrait. Photograph courtesy of the McCord Museum of Canadian History, Montreal, M966.62.1.

HERTEL MEMOIRE, C. 1712

J OSEPH-FRANÇOIS Hertel de la Fresnière (1642–1722) is a famous figure in
French Canadian history. He rose to prominence from a humble origin:
his father was a common soldier and early immigrant to New France who
died when Joseph-François was only nine years old. Often called "the Hero,"
Joseph-François made his reputation as a soldier fighting against the Iroquois
and English enemies of New France. His deeds gained such fame and proved so
useful to New France that he was eventually ennobled for his services. Hertel's
rise to glory is the quintessential, but exceptional, success story of colonial
French Canada.

This memoir of service narrates the exploits of Joseph-François and his
sons. Because one of his sons, Lieutenant Jean-Baptiste Hertel de Rouville
(1668–1722) (figure 15), commanded the French raiders at Deerfield and three
or four of his other sons participated in the attack, this memoir contains a description of the assault. The fact that it gives more detail on the Deerfield raid
than any other single event suggests the raid's importance to the entire Hertel
family. Such a memoir of service was composed by French officers when they
were being considered for some sort of special honor, either the Cross of Saint
Louis or, in Hertel's case, letters of nobility. This document is an edited draft
that passed down within the family until, at the end of the nineteenth century,
it was submitted for publication in an antiquarian journal. The location of the
original is currently unknown.

The memoir is of interest today because biographical narratives from New
France are rare. Unlike New England Puritans, who wrote constantly, New
France's colonists rarely wrote unless they had to. This narrative served at least
two purposes, both tending to promote the prestige of the Hertel family. The
memoir was composed in 1712, as Joseph-François Hertel finally made a successful case for ennoblement. Joseph-François's son, Jean-Baptiste Hertel de
Rouville, appears to have built on this distinction that his father achieved to
make his own case for a Cross of Saint Louis, which he received in 1721, the
first in his family to attain this honor.

A. C. de Lery MacDonald, "Services of the Hertel Family," *Canadian Antiquarian and Numis-
matic Journal* 1, no. 1 (July 1889): 5–9. We have translated the document from the original French,
drawing on MacDonald's editorial notes to create a coherent text. As such, it is not a definitive
version of the text but an interpolation of an edited draft that cannot be found in the original.

While much of the memoir is devoted to recounting battles, note that there are also two captivity stories tucked into it. Both Joseph-François and his eldest son, Zacharie-François (1665–1752), spent several years as captives among the Iroquois. These captivity experiences gave these Hertel men a familiarity with Native languages and customs that enabled them to work closely with Native warriors on their many military expeditions. Other sons, including Jean-Baptiste Hertel de Rouville, developed ties to Natives by living near them in places such as Odanak. The Hertels played an important role in New France's history not only because they willingly fought for their king but because they were able to collaborate with Native warriors.

Governors of New France had been working to secure for Hertel letters of nobility since 1689. Promised in 1691, the letters never arrived. Another request in 1694 was refused when it seemed that Hertel was unable to pay for the required stamp. Nonetheless, the family behaved as if they were nobles, using the title of esquire (*ecuyer* in French), marrying into noble families, and above all serving as officers in the colonial regulars in the wars against the king's enemies. By 1704, Joseph-François was too old to go on raids, but his son Jean-Baptiste was not. Accompanied by younger brothers, Jean-Baptiste Hertel de Rouville led a number of raiding parties against New England.

Together with the support of the governors of New France, the deeds of the Hero and his sons eventually persuaded the French government to grant the Hertels letters of nobility. It was a notable achievement, but it came at a high cost. Joseph-François and several of his sons were wounded, sometimes seriously, and two sons were killed. Because of their extraordinary rise from the status of commoners to nobility and fame, the Hertels are often held up as an example of the sort of social mobility possible in French Canada. However, only eleven Canadian families were ennobled in the history of New France, and the Hertels, who achieved this status in 1716, were the last. Determined to preserve their status, Hertels continued to serve in the French military until the conquest of New France in 1760. The path to nobility was not easy.

§

Memoire of the Services of Sir Hertel the elder and his sons

Sir Hertel is 70 years old. He has been a *lieutenant réformé*[1] in the *troupes de la marine*[2] for 17 years.

He has ten sons, all of them serving in the *troupes,* to wit one *lieutenant-en-pied,* a *lieutenant réformé,* an ensign, two *ensigns réformés* and the others cadets in the companies, of which the youngest is between 24 and 25.[3]

Sir Hertel the elder began to bear arms in 1657 at the beginning of the first wars against the Iroquois.[4]

He was wounded and taken prisoner by these Natives in 1659 and remained a slave among them for about two years. He ran the risk of being burned alive. One of his hands was crippled by the bad treatment he received from those barbarians.

After his return, and the war against them still continuing, he took part in all of the war parties that were made by either the governors or other officers, as well as a number of small skirmishes to repulse the incursions that they made on our homes.

He had the honor of accompanying Monsieurs De Tracy[5] and De Courcelle[6] in the two different expeditions they made against the villages of the Iroquois.

---

1. Military rank was an important mark of status. In Canada, the only soldiers to command were the *troupes de la marine* (see note 2). Since the companies of soldiers were small, few men could hold high rank and many prominent individuals held comparatively low rank. Each company had a captain, lieutenants, ensigns, and cadets (officers in training). Since there were not enough positions for all the men who wanted them, New France's governors used half-pay, or *réformé,* positions to give as many men as possible a ranked position.

2. The *troupes de la marine* were a newly created military force of regular soldiers under the command of the minister of the marine. They were distinct from the *troupes de terre,* who made up the regiments of France's European land army. The *troupes* served in small companies as regular soldiers for the navy, in ports and in the colonies. The first companies of *troupes de la marine* came to New France in 1683.

3. This youngest son would have been Pierre Hertel de Moncours (1687–1739), who had probably been on the Deerfield raid and went on to command forts on Lake Champlain and at what is now Green Bay, Wisconsin.

4. The French-Iroquois Wars covered much of the seventeenth century: 1642–1653, 1658–1667, and 1682–1701.

5. Alexandre de Prouville de Tracy (c. 1600–1670) was a lieutenant-general in the French army who was appointed governor-general of all the French colonies in America in 1663. From 1664 to 1667 he led French forces against the Dutch in the Caribbean (1664) and against the Iroquois in North America (1666) before returning to France.

6. Daniel de Rémy de Courcelle (1626–1698) was governor of New France from 1665 to 1672.

He also accompanied Count Frontenac when he went to establish Fort Frontenac and forced the Iroquois to sue for peace, and in all the other voyages that he made from this fort.[7]

Monsieur De La Barre[8] gave him the command of all the Algonquin, Nippising and Timiskaming Indians when they also went to the Iroquois' borders to force them to sue for peace in 1684. It was on this expedition that the two oldest sons of Sir Hertel began to carry arms, the one aged 18, the other 16.[9]

Monsieur the marquis de Denonville[10] gave him the command of the same Indians in the campaign against the Senecas,[11] the oldest of his sons served him as lieutenant and two accompanied him as cadets.

The same Monsieur de Denonville honored him many times with the command of war parties, French as well as Indian, wherein he fulfilled his duty well. Among other notable deeds, when Fort Saint Francis[12] was besieged by the enemy he came to its relief with only sixteen men, of whom two were his sons. With this small relief force, he attacked the enemy and forced them to abandon the siege.

Monsieur Count Frontenac demonstrated his confidence in him upon his [i.e., Frontenac's] return from France, when he put him at the head of a party of 50 French and as many Indians to attack the English in the government of Boston. He took possession of an entrenched fort, burned twenty-two houses, killed about a hundred people, and took 60 prisoners.[13] On his retreat he was pursued by two hundred and forty men, whom he repulsed, making himself master of the battlefield, where he rested. After two hours of combat, the enemy left twenty dead, and according to the report of a Frenchman taken several days before during the retreat, they had over sixty wounded. He lost in this fight one of his nephews killed[14] along with two other Frenchmen and 3

---

7. Louis de Buade de Frontenac et de Palluau (1622–1698) was governor-general of New France from 1672 to 1682; he returned to France, then served again as governor-general from 1689 to 1698. Fort Frontenac was built on Lake Ontario in 1673.

8. Joseph-Antoine Le Febvre de La Barre (1622–1688) was governor-general of New France from 1682 to 1685.

9. Zacharie-François and Jacques Hertel de Cournoyer (1667–c. 1725).

10. Jacques-René de Brisay de Denonville (1637–1710) was governor-general of New France from 1685 to 1689. His expedition against the Senecas was in 1687.

11. The westernmost of the Five Nations of the Iroquois League.

12. In the summer of 1688 raiding parties from the Iroquois League—Mohawks were specifically mentioned—"ravaged" the countryside at Saint François, Rivière de Loups, Sorel, Contrecoeur, and Saint Ours.

13. This was the March 27, 1690, raid on Salmon Falls, New Hampshire. English records indicate that thirty-four residents were killed and fifty-four captured and twenty homes destroyed.

14. Louis Crevier (c. 1669–1690), son of the seigneur of Saint Francis, who owned the land that Odanak was established on.

Indians, his eldest son who served him as a lieutenant was wounded, from which he is still very crippled, and three Indians also wounded. He had with him two others of his sons and two nephews.[15]

After this expedition, having learned that Sirs De Courtemanche[16] and De Port-Neuf[17] commanding a party of two hundred men were about to attack the fort at Ques-que-bay[18] he went to join them with those who followed him and was not unhelpful in the taking of that fort.

Several days after his return the English having come to besiege Quebec[19] he immediately came to its defense with four of his sons. He and his sons strove to prove their zeal for the service, taking part in all of the actions of the siege.

In 1691, his eldest having recovered somewhat from his wound, was part of a detachment commanded by a *lieutenant-en-pied* which was overwhelmed after a long fight with a great number of enemies and taken prisoner. He was a slave of the Iroquois for three years.

That same year another of his sons was wounded in Sir De Valrennes' fight[20] with the English and Iroquois; another of his sons took part in the same engagement.

During all the wars no war party or expedition was made without the father or some of his sons being part of it. In 1704 the governor general[21] honored Sir De Rouville[22] with the command of a party of 200 men, which included three of his brothers.[23] He captured the fort of Guerefil,[24] where there were one hundred twenty-seven armed men, at the break of day. In this assault and in a fight undertaken while retreating with his rear guard of thirty men against over

---

15. The eldest son was Zacharie-François Hertel (1665–1752).

16. Augustin Legardeur de Courtemanche (1663–1717). This is the same man who appears in Williams, "What Befell Stephen Williams," 170.

17. René Robinau de Portneuf (1659–1729).

18. The fort at Falmouth, Maine, on Casco Bay, was taken after a five-day siege in May 1690. About a hundred English were killed or captured.

19. A New England expedition led by Sir William Phips (1657–1695) laid siege to Quebec in October 1690.

20. Philippe Clément du Vuault de Valrennes (1647–c.1708) served in the *troupes de la marine* in New France from 1685 to 1693, before retiring to France because of wounds. The battle was near Fort Chambly on August 11, 1691. Valrennes's men attacked a force of Mohawks, Mahicans, and Anglo-Dutch colonists led by Major Peter Schuyler (1657–1724) as they retreated from a successful raid on the French at La Prairie.

21. Philippe de Rigaud de Vaudreuil (c.1643–1725) was governor-general of New France from 1703 to 1725.

22. Jean-Baptiste Hertel de Rouville (1668–1722).

23. While this memoire written eight years after the 1704 Deerfield raid claims that three brothers accompanied de Rouville, Vaudreuil's April 1704 letter claims that four brothers accompanied him. See Letter from Philippe de Rigaud de Vaudreuil, 81.

24. Deerfield, which regularly appears in the French sources as Guerefil.

a hundred, he killed one hundred fifty people, took one hundred seventy prisoners. His lieutenant[25] was killed along with eleven other of his men. He was wounded along with twenty-two others, including three officers and one of his brothers who served as his aide.

He [Vaudreuil] honored him [De Rouville] with the joint command along with Sir Deschaillon[26] of a party of three hundred men who attacked an enemy village of over thirty houses. He had with him two of his brothers of which one was killed[27] while breaking down the door of a guardhouse.

In 1709 he was honored again with the command of a party of one hundred fifty men.[28]

Monsieur the governor general [Vaudreuil] so honored this family that he did not allow any party to be sent against the enemy without one of its members. Again it was Sir De Rouville who went with one hundred thirty men, Indians and French, to reconnoiter the retreat of the enemy who had come to attack this colony by way of Lake Champlain. He had with him one of his nephews who is a cadet in the *troupes*.[29]

Sir De la Fresnière his eldest has for the last three years been in command of Fort Frontenac where he distinguishes himself as much in his management of the Indians as his command of the fort.[30]

---

25. François-Marie Margane de Batilly (1672–1704).

26. Jean-Baptiste de Saint-Ours Deschaillons (1669–1747) was the son of a prominent nobleman who pursued a career as an officer in the *troupes de la marine*. Though he shared command with De Rouville, the August 29, 1708, raid on Haverhill was his most notable military exploit. It was not a successful raid.

27. René Hertel de Chambly (1675–1708).

28. De Rouville raided Deerfield again in late June 1709, but only managed to ambush some militiamen outside the village.

29. In October 1711 Francis Nicholson (1655–1728) gave up a plan to invade New France by way of Lake Champlain after hearing that the British fleet that was supposed to attack Quebec by ascending the Saint Lawrence River had turned back following a disastrous shipwreck.

30. This is a reference to Zacharie-François Hertel, who asumed his father's title of de la Fresnière. He commanded Fort Frontenac from 1708 to 1712.

MOHAWK NARRATIVES

FIGURE 16. Bell, Saint Francis Xavier Church, Kahnawake. This bell, which sits today on the floor in the nave of the Catholic church in Kahnawake, is believed to be the bell in the story of the bell. Photograph by Kevin Sweeney.

THE STORY OF THE BELL, 1882

MRS. E. A. SMITH

T HIS DOCUMENT is an early transcription of an oral tradition still present at Kahnawake (figure 16). With the probable exception of the final paragraph, it is not a word-for-word version of what was said. The transcriber, "Mrs. E. A. Smith," did some interpolation of her own as she wrote the story up. It is hard to imagine that a Mohawk would have so condescending an attitude toward the spirituality of his or her own ancestors as is evident in the text. Instead, the author's attitude reflects an elite disdain for popular religious attitudes and practices that seem somewhat naïve or unorthodox to someone more learned in theology. These interpolations may well be the result of conversations between Mrs. Smith and the local priest. The account's representation of the Mohawks as somewhat childlike as well as its clear admiration for the near saintlike character of "Father Nicolas" can thus be considered a reflection of the mentality of the priest and writer rather than the Mohawks.

The identity of the writer is something of a mystery. Most likely it was Elizabeth Oakes Smith (1806–1893), a writer, speaker, and women's rights activist born in what is now Maine in 1806. She spent most of her literary career in New York City. Challenging the established social order also led her to question her religious origins. Raised a New England Congregationalist, she turned first to Unitarianism and then to Catholicism later in her life. This religious journey, as well as a lifelong interest in history, seems to have drawn her to the story of the bell. In 1875 she published a dramatic retelling of the story in the widely read *Potter's American Monthly*. Perhaps this text represents notes she took on a trip to Canada before she wrote her published version. It resembles the published version, though it differs in the attention that it pays to the Mohawks' actions. Perhaps 1882 was the date she turned the manuscript in to the Bureau of American Ethnology, which was not established until 1879. Neither the bureau nor any other organization has previously published this manuscript.

The text is not an accurate recounting of historical facts. As the historian Geoffrey Buerger has established, there is no evidence to support the basic story of the bell. There was in fact no bell in Deerfield to be taken. Hertel de Rouville's

Mrs. E. A. Smith, "Legend of the Deerfield Massacre and the events leading to it, including the story of the bell in the town of the church at Deerfield, and its transfer to the Mission at Caughnawaga, 1882," manuscript, Bureau of American Ethnology, copy in curatorial files, Pocumtuck Valley Memorial Association, Deerfield, Mass.

rank is misrepresented, and he did not travel in a carriage. No Jesuit, nor any other Catholic priest, joined the raid on Deerfield. Furthermore, the French soldiers on the raid, as well as the Native warriors, used snowshoes. The anecdote about rushing forward in spurts is an interesting interjection of a piece of local Deerfield lore about the attack that dates to at least the mid 1700s.[1] In the end, the blurring of chronology—the quick leap from the time of the mission's founding in 1669 to the Deerfield raid in 1704—and the ubiquitous presence of Father Louis Nicolas (long after he had died) clearly indicate that this story's function is more mythical than historical. Buerger makes a compelling case that the story originated with the Reverend Eleazer Williams, Eunice Williams's great-grandson (1788–1858) and passed from him into the legends of New England, Canada, and eventually the Mohawk community at Kahnawake.[2]

Buerger suggests that the tale was popular among American writers for its anti-Catholic overtones. But there are also reasons why aspects of it would have made sense to Mohawks. The story clearly resonated at Kahnawake because it recounted an important period of the community's history in terms that made sense in the nineteenth century. This can be said about both the overall structure of the story and the individual misrepresentations. For example, the anecdote about snowshoes shows Mohawk men to be wiser and more adept at life in the forests than the French.

The story helps define Kahnawake's role in the colonial wars. Important for this effort is the role of "Father Nicholas." While no Jesuit from Kahnawake accompanied the Deerfield raid, by having him lead a "division" of men on the raid, the author reinforces the Jesuits' leadership role of the Mohawk community. This portrayal points up the importance of the Jesuits in maintaining alliances between Natives and the French, something they had been arguing for since the seventeenth century. At the same time, it highlights the autonomy of Kahnawake. Mohawks join the raid of their own volition and for their own reasons and under their own leader, albeit a Jesuit. And Kahnawake's leader is considered important enough by the author of the text to deserve the special dignity of riding in a carriage with a French nobleman.

In addition to what the story can reveal about Mohawk identity in the nineteenth century, clear Mohawk motifs convey certain cultural truths about the

---

1. For the first known incidence of this lore see [Lucy Watson], "Mrs. Lucy Watson's memory & account of New Settlers in the American Woods 1762, Chiefly Walpole, N[ew] H[ampshire]." "Lucy Watson's Acct of New Settlers of Walpole N.H. were related to her son. John F. Watson, in the year 1825 when in the 71st year of her age . . . ," 2–3, Watson Family Papers, box 2, Winterthur Library, Winterthur, Del.

2. Geoffrey E. Buerger, " "Out of Whole Cloth: The Tradition of the St. Regis Bell" unpublished paper in the collections of the Pocumtuck Valley Memorial Association, Deerfield, Massachusetts.

Mohawks' involvement in the raid, even if the details are not supported by the record. Notice for example the important role of women and children in the religious and political life of the community. The prominent place they have in the adoration of the bell echoes the central role that women played in the communal and spiritual life of Kahnawake.

Above all, the "Story of the Bell" is a parable of mourning warfare. If it is remembered that, while Mohawk warriors probably did not go to Deerfield in 1704 to get a bell, they most certainly went to take captives, then the story can be seen as an allegory about captive taking. Here again, women played a central role. While they do not go off to war, they are part of the decision-making process. More important, they are the ones who accept the bell into their community, just as they did war captives. The moral of the story is that something of great spiritual and economic significance had been stolen from the community and the Mohawks had a righteous desire to get it back. Whether a bell or a girl like Eunice Williams, what the Mohawk men took back from Deerfield restored the community, just as a mourning-war raid for captives was supposed to. In the end, then, this ostensible act of Catholic devotion can also be seen as the pursuit of a very ancient Mohawk tradition.

The Legend of the Deerfield Massacre and the events leading to it

Caughnawaga[3]

Collector Mrs. E. A. Smith 1882
Bureau of American Ethnology

In the year 1669 the Jesuit Fathers founded the mission of St. Francis Xavier des Pres in Lapraire. It was in 1676 removed to Rivière du Portage and in 1690 near the rapids at Sault St. Louis [and] in 1718 to Caughnewage village. The mission continued in their charge until 1783, when Father Huguet died.[4] It was then continued by secular clergy until 1855 when Father Antoine[5] (Omblat Marie

---

3. This is the old spelling of Kahnawake, the Mohawk town where the Jesuit mission of Sault Saint Louis was located.

4. Joseph Huguet (1725–1783). Born in Belgium, he entered the Jesuit order in 1744 and came to Canada in 1756. He was the last Jesuit to be in charge of the mission at Kahnawake, serving there from 1759 to 1783.

5. Joseph-Eugène Antoine (1826–1900) was born in France. He worked at Kahnawake from 1851 until 1864, when he returned to oversee the Oblates' missions in America and Europe. He died in Paris.

Imacul)[6] was appointed in the place of Père Marcours.[7] Since the death of the former it has been in the charge of Père Burtien.[8] (C.M.B.)[9] Having been for so many years under the influence of the Church it is not strange that the old legends have been forgotten, and replaced by those of a religious character.

The situation of Caughnewage is one of the most beautiful to be found on the banks of the noble St. Laurence and the village one of the most picturesque in the country. The beautiful church so interwoven among these many legends stands on a little cape which extends slightly into the river. Adjoining the church are the ruins of an old French fort, and the home of cher père Burtien, the old curé[10] who exhibits with pride to his visitors the writing desk, chair and bedstead once occupied by Charlevoix.[11]

The legend regarding the bell of this old church runs as follows:

"Père Nicolas"[12] having gathered together a large number of Indians whom he had succeeded in converting, established them in a village called Sault Saint Louis upon the banks of the Saint Laurance.

After having built the church and its belfry all completed, father Nicolas in one of his sermons explained to his humble followers that a bell was as necessary to a belfry as was a priest to a church and exhorted them to amass as large a quantity of skins and furs as possible to send in exchange for one to France. This was accordingly done and soon the worthy ecclesiastic learned that the

6. The Oblates of Mary Immaculate is a religious order founded in Provence, France, in 1816. Designed to restore devotion to the Catholic Church after the disruptions of the French Revolution, it has been involved in missionary work in France and abroad.

7. Père is French for "father." Joseph Marcoux (1791–1855) was born in Quebec. After studying in Quebec's seminary, he was ordained and sent to the mission at Saint Regis in 1813. In 1819 he was transferred to Kahnawake, where he stayed until his death.

8. Nicholas Burtin (1828–1902) was born in Alsace, France. He joined the Oblates of Mary Immaculate and worked at Kahnawake from 1857 to 1892, when he retired to Quebec, where he died.

9. This should probably read O.M.I. rather than C.M.B., since Nicholas Burtin was a member of the Oblates of Mary Immaculate.

10. "Dear Father Burtien, the old priest." Burtin was an avid historian of Kahnawake and its most famous resident, Catherine Tekakwitha (1656–1680). He hosted a variety of visitors and seems to have specialized in passing on bits and pieces of local lore. See Edward James Devine, *Historic Caughnawaga* (Montreal: The Messenger Press, 1922), 411–416.

11. Pierre-François-Xavier de Charlevoix (1682–1761) was a famous historian of New France. Born in France, he entered the Jesuit order in 1698. He came to Quebec in 1705 to teach at the Jesuit College until 1708, when he returned to France. In 1720 he was back in New France on a mission to discover the "Western Sea" that took him out west to the great Lakes, down to New Orleans, then back to France by way of Saint Domingue (today's Haiti). On his return, Charlevoix published his travel journal and began to write histories of Japan, Saint Domingue, Paraguay (all areas of Jesuit missions), and, most important, New France. From 1742 to 1749 he served as procurator of the Jesuit missions in New France and Louisiana. He died in France.

12. Louis P. Nicolas (1634–1682) was born in France and entered the Jesuits at Toulouse in 1654. He arrived in New France in 1667 and was dead by the time of the 1704 Deerfield raid.

bell had been bought and placed on board the *Grand Monarque*[13] which was bound for Quebec.

It happened that all this occurred during the war between the French and the English and the consequence was that the *Grand Monarque* never reached its destination. It was taken by a New England cruiser, conducted to Salem [Massachusetts] where it was sold for the benefit of those who had captured it.

The bell was bought by the village of Deerfield upon the Connecticut River where a church had just been built of which the preacher was no other than the great John Williams. With great pains the bell was placed in the belfry tower of that little church.

When Père Nicolas received the news of this great misfortune he assembled the Indians together [and] recounted to them the unhappy situation of the bell, retained in purgatory in the hands of heretics and he begged of them to go recover it. The Indians deplored together over the fate of the poor bell which had not even been baptized, for although ignorant of what the bell was like they knew that Père Nicolas preached and said mass in the church and they supposed that some similar relation existed between the belfry and the bell. The chase was abandoned and gathered upon the banks of the river they sought to devise means for its deliverance. The women who had heard that the voice of the bell could be heard beyond the roaring of the rapids and that it was sweeter than song were all melancholy and submitted to rude penances to obtain deliverance for the bell or to abate its sufferings.

At last the day of deliverance came. The Marquis de Vaudreuil, governor of Canada,[14] resolved to send an expedition against the British colonies of Massachusetts and New Hampshire.[15] The command was given to Major Hertel de Rouville[16] and one of the priests of the Jesuit College at Quebec sent word to Père Nicolas by a pious traveler of the projected expedition.

The Indians were immediately assembled together in the church where Père Nicholas in a solemn discourse introduced the traveler as a messenger of good tidings.

They were then informed of all the preparations for war which were being made at Quebec and were urged to join the expedition. At the close of the dis-

---

13. No ship *Grand Monarque* has been found sailing to New France in this period. An alternative version of this tale claims Grand Monarque was the name of the bell itself; see Elizabeth Oakes Smith, "The Crusade of the Bell," *Potter's American Monthly* 4, no. 43 (1875): 518–520.

14. Philippe de Rigaud de Vaudreuil (c. 1643–1725) was governor-general of New France from 1703 until his death.

15. Technically the colonies were still English. They would not be British until the Union of the Crowns of Scotland and England in 1707.

16. Jean-Baptiste Hertel de Rouville (1668–1722) commanded the raid on Deerfield, but he was a *lieutenant reformé,* not a major.

course the whole assembly arose and sounded the war-cry. They then returned to their homes [and] began putting on their war paint, for all had decided to join the expedition. It was in the heart of winter when they started to join the army of Monsieur de Rouville at Fort Chambly.[17] Père Nicolas marched at their head with a banner surmounted by a cross and as they were leaving the women sang a sacred hymn which had been prepared for the occasion by the good father.

After a fatiguing day's march they arrived at Chambly at the moment when the French soldiers mounted with their [illegible] were leaving for Lake Champlain.

The Indians followed in the track of the trains with all the perseverance natural to their character. Father Nicolas was seated in the carriage of Monsieur de Rouville. In this order the Indians followed in silence until all the army were united upon the banks of [Lake] Champlain which as it was completely frozen over was chosen as the route.

Thinking only of the captivity of their unhappy bell, the Indians showed no symptom of regret, fatigue or fear during the long and painful route, while the French soldiers suffering from cold and wading through the thick snow looked with envy upon the patient Indians who clad in snowshoes seemed to glide over the moving surface.[18]

When they had arrived at the point where today stands the beautiful city of Burlington the order for a general halt was given in order to make preparations for penetrating into the forests which separated the army from the inhabitants of Massachusetts. Monsieur de Rouville left Père Nicolas to conduct his division, and at the head of his own directed the way upon Deerfield. Nothing the troops had suffered before could compare to the fatigues of this long march.

Long before the expedition had arrived at its destination the poor Père Nicolas had fallen sick from the effects of this long crusade but notwithstanding his failing health and bleeding feet he still pressed on recalling the many martyred saints and the persecution of a crowd of fathers[19] and sustained by the hope of delivering the bell.

In the eve of February 20th 1701[20] the expedition arrived within two miles of Deerfield without having been discovered.

Monsieur de Rouville ordered his men to stop and rest until midnight when

---

17. Fort Chambly had been a French post since 1665. A new fort had been built in 1702. The expedition that attacked Deerfield had gathered at Chambly.

18. In fact, the French on the 1704 expedition did have snowshoes.

19. A reference to the early Fathers or leaders of the Christian Church.

20. The actual date was February 29, 1704 Old Style. For the French it would have been March 11, 1704 New Style.

he gave the order to attack the village. The surface of the snow was frozen and cracked underneath their feet. With remarkable sagacity in order to deceive the English garrison, Rouville ordered his troops to run swiftly a few paces and then pause abruptly. By this ingenious precaution the sentinels of the village supposed that the noise was occasioned by the snow in falling from the trees whose branches were being swayed by the wind. At last the alarm was given and a terrible battle took place which resulted in the garrison being dispersed and the city taken.

At the break of day although weary with the fatigues of the night the Indians surrounded Père Nicolas and begged him to conduct them to the bell that they might offer it their homage and express their veneration for it. Père Nicolas was somewhat disconcerted at this request for Monsieur de Rouville and several Frenchmen, who were present began to laugh immoderately. But the good Father did not discourage the idea entirely.

As the Indians had never heard a bell, he sent one of the soldiers to go and ring it. The sound of the bell in the silence of a cold morning and in the midst of the calm of the woods rose clear and sonorous. To the ears of the simple Indians it was the voice of an oracle. They were filled with astonishment and fear. The bell was taken down and arranged upon a scaffolding in such a manner that eight men could carry it. In this fashion the Indians started for their homes glorying in the miraculous organ. But they found that it was too heavy a burden for the rough way and severe weather so by the advice of Père Nicolas they buried it temporarily on the banks of Lake Champlain until they could return with better means for its transportation.

When the snow and ice had disappeared Père Nicolas assembled anew his followers at the church and having procured a yoke of oxen they started again in quest of the bell.

During the interval the women and children had been informed of its marvelous power and awaited its arrival as one of the greatest events.

One evening when conversing upon this subject a beautiful sound was heard in the woods which every instant became louder and louder. The astonished listeners at last exclaimed, "It is the bell! It is the bell!" Then the oxen surrounded by Indians were to be seen coming out of the woods. There was the bell balancing inside of the framework on the top of which in a large seat and covered with garlands rode the good father Nicolas. Even the oxen were laden with flowers. In such a triumphfull march in the calm of twilight the distant murmur of the rapids making a counterbass to the accords of the bell, the cortege entered Caughnewage and this is the legend of the bell.

"And how much of this legend is historically true?" said I to my friend "Alexandre" a born resident of Caughnewage.

"But very little I fear," replied he "but of the large bell which is now ringing I can give you the exact history which is this. Over fifty years ago my father in company with several other chiefs went over to England to present some grievances to King George.[21] The visitors were very kindly received and when leaving were requested to name some present they would like to take home as a keepsakes, one chose a large violin, another a big brass kettle for maple sugar, and my father suggested that we needed a new church bell.[22] The requests were granted and all commended the wisdom of my father's choice. Long ago it sounded the old man's funeral knell but still the bell continues its invitation to prayers, *Entendez la maintenant c'est pour les vêpres. Ecountons la.*"[23]

---

21. King George IV (1762–1830). He ruled as regent for his mentally ill and blind father (George III) from 1811 until his death in 1820. Thereafter George IV was king in his own right, until his death in 1830.

22. In the fall of 1829 a delegation from Kahnawake went to England to appeal for the return of a bordering strip of land the community had been claiming since 1762. They did not get the land, but they were promised a bell, which arrived in 1832.

23. "Listen to it now. It's [ringing] for vespers. We hear it." Vespers is the evening prayer service.

THE FAIR CAPTIVE: THE LIFE AND CAPTIVITY OF MISS EUNICE WILLIAMS, 1842

CHARLES B. DE SAILEVILLE

NO DEERFIELD captive has inspired more stories than Eunice Williams (1696–1785). The daughter of the Reverend John Williams, she was taken captive with the rest of her family. Unlike her relatives, however, she never returned from captivity. Instead, she forgot how to speak English, converted to Catholicism, and married a Mohawk man. She did visit her relatives in Massachusetts and Connecticut many years later, but she had to communicate with them through an interpreter.

Because Eunice left so little documentation and because she was a member of the important Williams family, her story has fired the imagination of a host of writers, artists, and historians to this very day. The lack of explicit information leaves much room for imagination. The drama of her fate—the complete absorption into Mohawk society—gives much to think about. Most of the writing about Eunice comes out of New England, where Eunice's Anglo-American descendants have agonized about her fate ever since her father published *The Redeemed Captive*.[1] Recently, the Yale historian John Demos labelled her the "Unredeemed Captive" in his prize-winning book about her.[2] Demos's book in turn has inspired the composition of a cantata[3] and an opera.[4]

The story that appears here, however, comes from the Mohawk side of the Williams family, which still has roots in Kahnawake today. Eunice Williams had three children, one son and two daughters. Only one of her daughters had a child, a son named Thomas. Thomas married the granddaughter of another

---

Charles B. de Saileville, "A History of the Life and Captivity of Miss Eunice Williams, Alias, Madam De Roguers, Who Was Styled 'The Fair Captive' " (1842), Neville Public Museum of Brown County, microfilm, State Historical Society of Wisconsin, Area Research Center, Green Bay. Reproduced with permission of the Neville Public Museum

1. John Williams, *The Redeemed Captive Returning to Zion* (Boston: B. Green, 1707).
2. John Demos, *The Unredeemed Captive: A Family Story from Early America* (New York: Knopf, 1994).
3. *One Blood*, composed by Marjorie Merryman, 2000
4. *The Captivation of Eunice Williams*, composed by Paula M. Kimper, libretto by Harley Erdman, 2004.

New England captive, Silas Rice. They had thirteen children, one of them a boy named Eleazer, whose lasting legacy was to reunite the histories of Deerfield and Kahnawake.

Eleazer Williams (1788–1858) grew up to become a controversial figure.[5] When he was twelve, his father placed him in the care of a Williams relative in Longmeadow, Massachusetts, to ensure that he received an education. There, Eleazer learned much about the local interest in the history of the Deerfield raid and the fascination with the story of Eunice. Evidently impressed by the status of the clergymen he came to know, Eleazer decided to become a minister himself. However, it soon became clear that his American relatives would never let a Mohawk boy preach to one of their congregations. Eleazer then joined the Episcopal Church and began a career as a missionary to the Oneidas. After several years of success, he helped broker a move by some Oneidas to Green Bay, Wisconsin, but soon thereafter lost the support of both the Oneidas and the Episcopal Church (figure 17).

At this point, Eleazer's life took its most famous and controversial turn. After his father died in 1848, Eleazer let it be known that he was not a Mohawk, nor even a Williams. In fact, he claimed, he was none other than the son of Louis XVI and therefore the Lost Dauphin of France. He allowed a story to circulate that he had been smuggled out of revolutionary France and hidden away in the safe obscurity of Kahnawake. Some Americans believed him. Many others did not. The scandal it caused colors any understanding of his life (figure 18).

Eleazer spent the last years of his life living in poverty on the Mohawk reservation of Saint Regis [today Akwesasne]. There he assembled a wide-ranging collection of papers related to various aspects of his life. Not least of these were stories related to the Deerfield raid of 1704. Aware of New Englanders' interest in this story, Eleazer often drew on his knowledge of Mohawk oral traditions to solicit the attention and interest of prominent New Englanders, including the famous historian Francis Parkman.[6] The excerpt from a manuscript biography of Eunice Williams that follows was a product of Williams's engagement with his ancestors' history and is found among his papers. Ostensibly composed by a Frenchman named Charles B. de Saileville and edited by Eleazer, it has never been published.

---

5. For an instructive analysis of his life and legacy, see Geoffrey E. Buerger, "Eleazer Williams: Elitism and Multiple Identity on Two Frontiers," in *Being and Becoming Indian: Biographical Studies of North American Frontiers*, ed. James A. Clifton (Chicago: Dorsey, 1989), 112–136.

6. As a boy, Francis Parkman met Eleazer. In his account of the 1704 Deerfield raid, Parkman airs his suspicion that Eleazer had invented the Bell of Saint Regis story and that neither he, nor the story, was to be trusted. See Parkman, *A Half Century of Conflict in France and England in North America*, 2 vols. (New York: Library of America, 1983), 2:396–397.

It is very likely that Charles de Saileville is a pseudonym for Eleazer Williams. No American or Canadian records from the period document the existence of a Charles de Saileville. His name appears only on the manuscript biography of Eunice Williams and in two letters addressed to Eleazer Williams. All of these materials are among the papers of Eleazer Williams. One of these letters, purported to have been written by De Saileville, acknowledges Eleazer's role in providing the materials that De Saileville used to compose the biography.[7] The sentiments in this letter and in the manuscript biography mirror those of Eleazer Williams. The author is a pious man whose stated purpose in writing the biography was to demonstrate that Eunice had lived a life of exemplary piety and not that of a "savage," as Deerfield's local historians were claiming. These goals were identical to those of Eleazer, who at this point in his life sought to be on good terms with his white, Protestant American kinfolk.

To appeal to nineteenth-century New Englanders, the biography attempts to make Eunice's abandonment of her native Anglo-Protestant culture palatable to those she left behind. One strategy for doing this is to turn on the Jesuits. The Jesuits, more than Catholicism itself, are portrayed as the true source of falsehood. New England Protestants would certainly agree, though they would have had more difficulty accepting Eleazer's ecumenical vision of the many virtues Catholicism shared with Protestantism. Also, the story defends and explains the customs of Eleazer's Mohawk ancestors. In the story of the Mohawk woman going to Deerfield seeking a replacement for the child she had lost, he is passing on a fundamental motif of Iroquoian mourning-war culture. According to these traditions, war was waged in part to gain captives who could then be adopted to fill the places left empty by people who had died an untimely death. This practice was a major motive for the Mohawk warriors who attacked Deerfield in 1704 and explains why so many of the captives who did stay in New France remained with the Mohawks. It is hard to find a more sympathetic account of the process than what is here. Overall, the story downplays the differences in race, culture, and religion that kept a man like Eleazer on the margins of Anglo-American society.

Given Eleazer's skill at embroidering history (especially when it would redound to his benefit), there is good reason to suspect that much of what he passed off as Mohawk tradition about the Deerfield raid actually began with him. This is most probably true of the Story of the Bell, as well as this narrative

---

7. Charles de Saileville to Eleazer Williams, Burlington, Vermont, June 12, 1842, Eleazer Williams Papers, Missouri Historical Society, photostat copy, Williams Papers, box 20, folder 8, Pocumtuck Valley Memorial Association, Deerfield, Mass.

of the life of Eunice Williams. Eleazer had a talent for including in his stories just enough semblance of fact to make them seem plausible. He holds to certain conventions of scholarship, using footnotes with references to books and manuscript sources. But his scholarship is not reliable. Many of the sources he

FIGURE 17. The Reverend Eleazer Williams (1788–1858). Oil painting, 1836, George Catlin. Born into the Catholic faith at Kahnawake and educated as a Congregationalist in New England, Williams joined the Episcopal Church in 1815 and was ordained a deacon in 1826. By this time he was engaged in missionary work, land speculation, and other more grandiose schemes involving the Menominees and Oneidas in the area around Green Bay, Wisconsin. Eventually, they rejected his self-proclaimed leadership. The artist, George Catlin, made his reputation painting American Indians. Wisconsin Historical Society, 1942.156

cites do not exist. Yet some do. The subtle mix of the true with the patently false has to be acknowledged. There are some facts cited that are not as clear-cut as they seem. But also they are not totally invented. Someone who did not know the history could think them believable.

FIGURE 18. The Reverend Eleazer Williams (1788–1858). Oil painting, 1853, Giuseppe Fagnini. In 1839 Williams began to suggest that he was the "Lost Dauphin of France," Louis XVII, son of Louis XVI and Marie Antoinette. After the death of his father, Thomas Williams, in 1848, he openly claimed to be heir to the French throne and tricked his mother into signing an affidavit that stated he was adopted. This painting emphasized those facial features that would promote his claim. National Portrait Gallery, Smithsonian Institution, Gift of Mrs. Lawrence M. C. Smith, NPG 75.40.

Names and details give the impression of historical accuracy. It is quite possible that a Mohawk man in Kahnawake at the time would bear the name Paul. Jean-Baptiste Hertel de Rouville did command the raid on Deerfield, but he was a half-pay lieutenant, not a colonel. There is no evidence that he turned in a written report of this expedition. Eunice did have a sister named Esther who returned to New England with John Livingston and John Sheldon in 1705. In the 1730s the French built Fort Saint Frédéric at Crown Point and began to patrol the lake with boats. But in 1704 Crown Point was not yet a French post, nor were there any French boats (known as bateaux) on Lake Champlain. Philippe de Rigaud de Vaudreuil was governor-general of New France from 1703 to 1725 and he did have a wife, though she was mostly in France after 1709 and therefore could not have had extended contact with Eunice. Claude de Ramezay was the governor of the Montreal region from 1704 to 1724. Jean Bochart de Champigny had been intendant of New France from 1686 to 1702, but then he left Quebec for France and was not around to work for Eunice's release as the biography claims. Guillaume de Lorimier de la Rivière was the name of a French noble officer stationed in the Montreal region from 1691 to 1709, but there is no indication he took any particular interest in the fate of New England captives like Eunice. The Carignan-Salières regiment was in New France only from 1665 to 1668. Other references to events and individuals have no apparent basis in fact. There is no evidence that Eunice was ever known as Madam D. Roguere, nor is that name even found in New France at the time. No evidence supports the claims that Eunice or any other war prisoner was styled the "Fair Captive" by anyone in New France. There was no Chevalier du Portail in New France in 1705, nor was there a Lieutenant Laval who was taken captive and interrogated by the English in 1707. Bouchel was not a name to be found in New France at this time, though there were plenty of Bouchers. And in fact, there was no artillery unit in the colony for a Bouchel or anyone to command until 1750.

The real value of this biography is not its relation of factual details or its literal historical accuracy. As with the Story of the Bell, this story conveys a certain cultural truth. While details may be wrong, the tone and tenor of the story do accurately reflect some of the concerns of Mohawk culture. As such, it can be seen as representing a Mohawk perspective, or interpretation, of what happened and why. Only the first two chapters of the manuscript have been reproduced here because these deal most directly with Eunice Williams's captivity and adoption into the Mohawk community. The original manuscript is part of the collections of the Neville Public Museum of Brown County, Green Bay,

Wisconsin. It is also available at the State Historical Society of Wisconsin, Area Research Center, Green Bay, Wisconsin.[8]

§

A History of the Life and Captivity of Miss Eunice Williams, alias, Madam D. Roguere who was styled "The Fair Captive"

The Life and Captivity of Miss Eunice Williams

CHAPTER I

The memorable catastrophe which befell the town of Deerfield by a detachment of three hundred French and Indians under Colonel Hertel de Rouville[9] in 1704 has often been reiterated by historians, and orally by the fathers and matrons in New England to the rising generation.

In the narrative of the Reverend Mr. Williams's captivity it is to be seen, that one of his daughters named Eunice, was left and died among the Indians.

The object of this is to give a brief narrative of her life and death.

At the time of her captivity, she had just entered her seventh year. Young as she was, yet she retained, and was able during her life to relate the particulars of that eventful day, when she and her father's family fell into the hands of the enemy.[10]

It would appear that the first indications of her alarms and fears about the French and Indians was on the day of fasting and prayer, which is alluded to by her father in his narrative. In the evening of that day he assembled the younger part of the family for religious instruction, and after having explained to them the reason for the appointment of that day of humiliation, fasting and prayer; he adverted to the necessity of it at that particular juncture. He said that hitherto the inhabitants of the New England colonies had only heard the rumours of wars in Europe, but that now many of the frontier towns, were suffering from its direful effects. And that Deerfield as well as other frontier towns was exposed to the attacks of the enemy. And it behoved them to prepare them-

---

8. All footnotes that appear hereafter are from De Saileville's original document, with the exception that additions by the editors appear in square brackets.

9. [Lieutenant Jean-Baptiste Hertel de Rouville (1667–1722) commanded the French forces that attacked Deerfield on February 29, 1704.]

10. Her memory undoubtedly was greatly assisted to many facts, by the recapitulation of them by her adopted mother and others.

selves to meet with Christian fortitude, whatever trials and afflictions God may, in his infinite wisdom, see fit to bring upon them. And that this preparation must be by repentance. "My children," said he, "if you love God with all your hearts, and dedicate yourselves to him, both soul and body, he will, by his almighty arm protect you, so that no harm shall befall you. If you do this, you will be able to say, 'God is my refuge, I will trust and not be afraid, for the Lord Jehovah is my everlasting strength.' "

He then recapitulated the sufferings of the people in several places by the irruption of the enemy—their hideous appearance and their cruelty, which were attributed to their ignorance of the Christian faith. These were represented in somewhat lively colors, which made a deep impression upon little Eunice who was then sitting near her father. She often said during her life, the exhortation of her father that evening, was so extraordinary and so affectionate that all the anxieties, trials and sufferings, which she endured, and even time, were incapable of erasing them from her mind.

The evening previous to her captivity, her beloved mother[11] as usual made her kneel by her side, and say her prayers, after which she went to bed with her sister Esther.[12] The next morning by the dawning of the day, she was awakened by the roar of musketry, and the war-whoops of the savages. And immediately she heard the forcing of the front door by the enemy; upon which, with throbbing heart and trembling voice she asked her sister what that might be. It was answered, the enemy, the Indians had now come, and upon that, they rose to dress themselves, but were hindered by an Indian who now thrust himself into the room. After having brandished his tomahawk over their heads he pushed them out into a larger room, where they beheld their father who was already bound in the midst of about twenty Indians, while others of the family were permitted to put on their clothes. Little Eunice now surveyed those who were pictured to her imagination only a few days before by her father, but who now appeared in reality, and that in a terrific manner. Their appearance was truly

---

11. She was the only daughter of the Rev. Eleazer Mather, first Pastor of the church in Northampton, by his wife Esther the daughter of the Rev. and famous John Warham, formerly a minister in Exeter in England, who came to New England in 1630, and was settled as one of the ministers in Dorchester. Rev. Dr. Thomas Prince [1687–1758] observations to the third edition of *The Redeemed Captive* p. 220 E. Hoyt's *Antiq[uarian] Researches or Indians Wars* [1824] p. 187 note 130.

12. Esther and five others from Deerfield were redeemed under the negotiation of Messers. [John] Livingston [1680–1720] and [John] Sheldon [1658–c. 1733], with whom they returned to New England in 1705. She was married to the Rev. Joseph Meachem [1685–1752] of Coventry Connect[icut]. Rev. Drs. Strong & McClure Funeral Sermons. Redeemed Captive, p. 65. [Strong and McClure are probably Nathan Strong (1748–1816) and David McClure (1748–1820). The reference to funeral sermons is unclear.]

frightful, with painted faces of various colours, with instruments of death in their hands, such as guns, tomahawks, war clubs, and scalping knives.

The terror and confusion that reigned in the house, by breaking the chests and closet doors for plunder, and the yells or war-whoops of the savages, and the thunder of the musketry without, were enough to move the stoutest heart. Yet the little band now collected in one room were unmoved and listened to the pious exhortations of their head, which were uttered at intervals, and were as follows "to trust in God and submit cheerfully to his merciful dealings.—That his ways were perfect and all his works righteous." At length the enemy hurried Mr. Williams out of the house and as he got to the door, he turned his face once more to his beloved family, of whom two were already in the eternal world,[13] and he was heard with, "I commend you all to God and to the word of his grace."

Eunice was soon carried out by one of the warriors, who placed her on the bank of snow near the gate outside of the fort, and then returned to the house for plunder. Not many minutes after this, she saw an Indian woman advancing towards her from a different direction, with quick steps, and when within a few feet of her, she stopped and surveyed her [and] with a smile took the shivering child up into her arms. This was no other than the Indian woman who afterwards she styled her mother. She carried the child to the bank of the river, where she took off one of her own blankets, wrapped her with it, and made a motion to her to keep herself there, and returned to the fort. While here she saw some of the captives passing at a little distance from her.[14]

The sun was now rising with all his glory, but the scene before her was terrific beyond description. The flames of the church[15] and other buildings rose up in columns and the whole heavens as it were, were illuminated by them. The horrors of that scene can never be realized, never even imagined, but by the survivors; the last awful struggles of those who remained amid the burning fragments of their houses, until they were reduced to the appalling alternative of the flames or the bayonets of the French soldiery and the tomahawks of the Indian warriors. Their only requiem was the roaring of the flames and the yells of the savages, and the agonizing screeches of mutual misery and mutual terror. There were witnessed woes such as human nature is rarely called upon to endure. There were uttered plaints more heart rending, than agony is often called upon to utter. There were severed ties, the tenderest that link one human being to another on earth. The mother there clung to the in-

13. John & Jerusha were dragged to the Door & murdered.
14. [Women rarely accompanied war parties, but it did happen. See Introduction, 2.]
15. [The meeting house was not burned.]

fant until she saw it perish on her bosom, and soon followed it, in one wild and distracted utterance of its father's name! There did the husband and father breathe his last aspiration for the wife of his bosom, and the child of his heart. "It were almost too much," says one "to dwell on such a theme. The heart grows liquid while the thoughts revolve upon them. Peace to the dead, and grace and consolation to the living. Comfort to the mourner, and resignation to the surviving relatives."

All this and much more were presented to the eye and imagination of little Eunice, who was still in full view of the fort. Although unable to see what was passing within, she heard all the noise, terrific as it was. Yet she was composed in a great measure, because her father had told them to be submissive to the will of heaven. But when she saw her beloved mother passing at a little distance from her and walking over a deep snow, she was moved to tears, and at that moment the Indian woman returned with a heavy load of plunder. After wrapping the child, and placing it upon the load she commenced to cross the meadows with such speed as to be a few minutes in front of the French column, which was now on retreat. And when they had reached the high grounds, her mistress, (as she may now be termed) entered into a thicket of pines and made a stop, and there she began to dress the child with warmer clothes. She made Eunice try several pairs of moccasins before she found one that fitted her feet, and gave the child some bread and biscuits, which she had brought from the fort.

Here again she saw some of the captives passing by, and the troops at that moment halted opposite them in the meadow, and heard the vociferous voices of the French commanders and Indians chiefs, who now began to move gradually back towards the town, and others who had gone on were returning in a great haste, and soon heard a heavy fire of the musketry which continued for a time at intervals. Her mistress having once more placed her on her pack, she travelled as fast as her legs would carry her. As they passed by the captives, she heard some of their exclamations, "O Eunice, or poor Eunice." At the lodging place that night she saw her father, and one of her brothers, but no communication passed between them.

The army being composed of French, Iroquois and Abenakis Indians, and each party usually encamped by themselves, her mistress being of the Iroquois,[16] she of course lodged with that party, but her father and others of the family were in the hands of the Abenakis.

The incidents which occurred on this journey of hers are many and worthy

---

16. [This biography uses Mohawks and Iroquois interchangeably to refer to the Mohawks who lived at Kahnawake.]

of notice, but we shall pass them over, only [mentioning] such as are most remarkable and interesting.

She being an uncommonly handsome child, did not escape the acute eyes of some of the French officers, who styled her the "Fair Captive." Not only they [noticed her], but [she] even attracted the attention of the ferocious warriors.[17] Her mistress had obtained a pledge from one of them (a distant relation of hers) that she and her daughter as she now called Eunice, should not suffer for want of fire and food on the way.

There was another female in the party who also had a little captive boy, and these two were now associated and appeared to take great pleasure and delight in nourishing and cherishing each other with their prizes.

Every night a little bower, either with spruce, hemlock, or pine branches was prepared by the young warrior for their lodging place, who commonly with one or two of his comrades, occupied and lodged on one side of the place.

The death of her mother was unknown to her for several days, and the awful tidings were communicated to her by one of the female captives. "Eunice" said she, "you appear to be kindly treated by the enemy, for which I heartily rejoice, but O your poor mother is gone." "Gone where?" exclaimed Eunice. "She is dead," continued the female, "she was killed in the brook." At this Eunice wept and enquired where her father was. She was told he was still in the rear. Eunice now became inconsolable and was often in tears, and this was observed by her mistress, but unable to ascertain the cause of it, till one of the Abenakis or Saint Francis Indians, who spoke a little English, inquired of her why she cried so much [asking] whether she was cold or sick. She replied, "No, no, but my mother, O my poor Mother, dead in the snow." It was then for the first time that her mistress became acquainted [with] who the parents were of her little captive. She had already become so attached to the child as to be moved whenever she saw it [i.e., Eunice] was in tears, and would endeavour to console it [i.e., Eunice], by every means in her power. On these occasions, Paul, the young warrior, was called upon to amuse her, whose kindness and attention to the child had already gained her affections.

She saw her father at or near the White River for the last time on their journey. He was sitting with some of the captives on the bank of the river, and the moment she discovered him, she extended her little arms and cried "Father, father, let me come!" She was then sitting on Paul's back, who stopped and observed the motions of the child. He to gratify her, advanced towards the

---

17. Chevalier *Du Portail's* Letter, from Chambly in 1705 to Madam *Vaudrueil*. Lieut. *Laval's* Statement to Col. Schuyler of Albany when he was a prisoner in 1707. [The letter from Du Portail to Madam Vaudreuil and Laval's Statement cannot be located.]

group. Her father spoke to her with placid countenance. He told [her] that he was glad to see her alive, and that good care was taken of her: "Be content," said he, "my child be resigned to God's will. He will save and protect you—pray much. We are going to Canada, and if I live I shall see you there." The last words were consoling to her, having the hope that where she was going she would meet her father.

The army here separated, as they were now suffering for the want of provisions. The party which our little captive accompanied consisted of five or six warriors, a French lieutenant and two soldiers who were slightly wounded. They took their course for Lake Champlain, which they gained in a few days at Saint Frederick or Crown Point.[18] This party all were young and great hunters, who procured on the way more meat than the party could consume. They crossed the lake and made their headquarters in the vicinity of the above mentioned place, till the opening of the navigation on the lake.

In the meantime the warriors employed themselves in the chase, by which they were abundantly supplied with meat of various kinds, which induced Laval, the French lieutenant, to say, "We were in a continual feast."[19]

Eunice was now more or less an object of attention from the whole party.

Each vied to learn [i.e., to teach] her their respective language. She was caressed by the three Frenchmen to amuse her. But Paul was her favourite, he who bore her most of the way on their journey to that place. When she was afflicted, he alone could console [her], and when in anger appease her wrath. While here, she was much amused with the employment of her mistress, which was making sugar from maple trees. The two French soldiers acted as her assistants. Paul would often lead the "Fair Captive" from tree to tree, to taste the sweetness of the Indian beer as he called it, while her mistress in caking off her sugar made many little cakes in various shape for her, with which she was highly pleased and delighted. Relating to this part of her journey, she often declared, that the kind treatment which she received from every person in that party made her forget that she was a captive.

The warriors having employed themselves for more than two weeks in making their canoes finally embarked, and descended Lake Champlain. As they entered the River Richelieu,[20] they met a batteau with troops on board and several French officers. The little captive was accosted by one of them, in her own language, with; "My little girl where are you from?" No reply was made.

---

18. [The party would have arrived at Lake Champlain via the Winooski River which enters to lake far to the north of Crown Point (see map 3).]

19. Laval's Statement to Col. Schuyler.

20. This river flows from Lake Champlain in a northerly course; to its confluence with the St. Laurence at Sorel or William Henry.

Again, "I say, little girl, what is the name of the place where you are from?" She now answered, "Deerfield." After a few minutes he again accosted her, saying, "little girl will you accept this from me," which was a dozen or more hard biscuits and a fine silk handkerchief.

At the same time the Indians received two or three bottles of rum, and proceeded on their course.[21]

On their arrival at the Fortress of Chambly,[22] the commanding officer invited the warriors into the fort, and on their return, a quantity of provisions were sent to them, upon which they immediately began to prepare to depart for their canton.

Here Eunice was visited by Monsieur Chambly[23] and an officer, by whom she was informed that her father passed at that place a few days before, and had gone to Saint Francis.

This intelligence was highly gratifying to her, as it awakened the idea of seeing her father before long. The party here left their canoes and travelled by land to La Prairie, [and] thence to Kahnadaquenga [i.e., Kahnawake], the chief village of the Iroquois [figure 19].

Chapter II

"The Fair Captive" having now arrived in New France, and the village and headquarters of those who had torn her away from her native country, and murdered some of her family, the survivors were scattered, and in a state of captivity in a strange country; all these were sufficient to produce a melancholy gloom in her tender mind. "It was a day of darkness and anxiety with me," as she said, "But hope, yes that most consoling word hope, sustained me from sinking under the might of despair; and having this hope, that sooner or later I should be relieved from my situation, and be joined once more with my father and the rest of the family. It dispelled those heavy clouds which hung over me, and above all, was I comforted when I reflected that all the events passing before me were under the control of that merciful God, in whom my father had so repeatedly exhorted me to trust, and to submit to His holy and blessed will."[24]

---

21. Laval's Statement.

22. [Fort Chambly had been a French post since 1665, but its fort remained wooden until 1710 when the stone fortress implied in this text was constructed.]

23. [Joseph-François Hertel (1642–1722) was the seigneur of Chambly and the father of Jean-Baptiste Hertel, who had led the French raiders against Deerfield.]

24. John Stacy's Letter to President E. Wheelock [1711–1779]. [John Stacy, born in Ipswich, Massachusetts, April 11, 1736, was taken captive September 19, 1756, and was reported to be living with Indians in New France. In 1773 the Reverend Thomas Kendall (1745–1836) stayed with a man named Stacy at Kahnawake.]

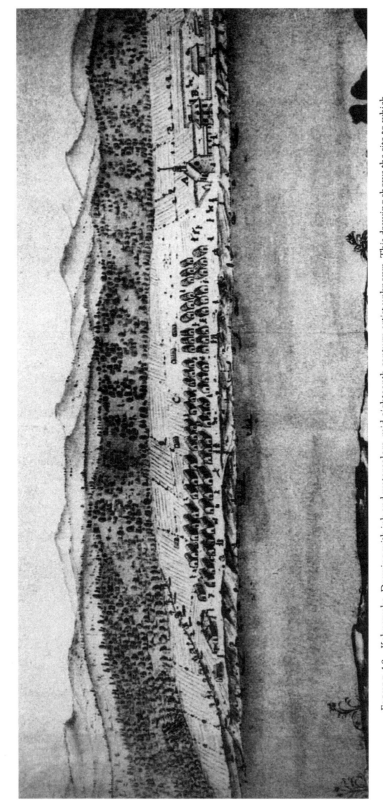

FIGURE 19. Kahnawake. Drawing with ink and watercolors, mid-eighteenth century, artist unknown. This drawing shows the site to which the community moved in 1716 and at which Eunice Williams and the other Deerfield captives adopted into the community lived out their lives. The sketch shows (A) the church, (B) the missionary's house, and (C) the Mohawks' longhouses. Traditional housing remained the norm at Kahnawake well into the eighteenth century. The mission, while prominent, was separated from the village proper. Cliché Bibliotèque nationale de France, Cabinet des Estampes, Paris.

In the metropolis of the domesticated Indians of New France,[25] she found, three sorts of captives, *viz:* English, Dutch, and of the Five [Iroquois] Nations of New York, who in dress as well as herself, appeared like one of the villagers. The relations of her adopted mother took much notice of her, and the children were instructed to treat her as one of the family. Her mother was one who may be termed ambitious and high minded. By her industry and economy, she was living in a comfortable manner, and her little girl was always neatly dressed after their fashion.

It may not be improper to state here the cause and the object which induced her to follow an army to such distance, when she must have known that such an undertaking was attended with many hardships and exposure to many dangers. But all these were overlooked by her; and the obstacles and the dangers, which might have been presented to the imagination of a person of less courage would not make her shrink from the task, but she surmounted them all to attain her object.

Two years previous to the expedition she lost an only child (daughter) on account of which she became inconsolable. She was so much borne down with it, that some of her relations predicted that she could not survive long. It was visible in her countenance that she was on the decline; she had lost the vivacity which was a peculiar trait in her character before she was bereft of her child.

To place one in the room of that which she had lost was the reason of her undertaking such a long, tedious and dangerous journey. From the time she heard that an irruption was to be made into the English colonies by an army of French and Indians, there was a visible alteration in her countenance, and she soon made known her determination to follow them, and the object she had in view. To dissuade her from this, her husband as well as her relations made strong efforts, but without effect. Paul, a young warrior, a connection of hers, was one of the volunteers, who engaged to be her protector, and on her part she promised in case of an accident to take care of him. Such was the cause which in all probability saved from the tomahawk and scalping knife little Eunice.

One of the Jesuits stationed in the canton visited the family at a certain time, and seeing the captive girl proposed to make her a Christian by baptism as he had done to others. Her adopted mother replied that she believed the child was as much Christian as he was. The father asked rather in an angry tone, how that might be? She replied, that she had been informed that the father of the child was an English minister, and that no doubt she had been baptised. "Minis-

---

25. [This is a reference to the Natives who lived in villages near the French settlements. Because they were resident or domiciled in New France, the French called them *sauvages domiciliés*.]

ter, minister!" exclaimed the Jesuit, "he who is now with the Marquis De Vaudreuil[26] of Montreal, and who Monsieur De Rouville mentioned in the report
of his expedition, that he was looked upon by the captives as a saint!" She answered undoubtedly he was the man, as she knew but one Protestant minister
was taken in that expedition. "Ah!" said he, "he is called a saint by his deluded
followers, when he is nothing but an arch-heretic. His baptism is nothing, as he
is not a minister of the true Church—he has no authority to administer that
holy ordinance. If he has baptised her, the holy Roman Church will never recognize it as valid baptism."[27]

Although the woman herself being in communion with the Church of
Rome, yet she was unwilling at this time for the child to receive baptism—and
for the reason above stated. It is said however, that it was more on the account
of the uncertainty of its [i.e., Eunice's] continuance in that canton, as a prisoner,
in consequence of great exertions made at this time by certain liberal officers of
the army whose politeness and refined feelings carried them far into detesta-
tion of the practice of permitting the Indians to retain persons of a civilized nation as prisoners when taken by them. The governor general and his lady,[28] the
intendant[29] of the colony, were among the number who made efforts to redeem Eunice from the hands of the Indians, but in the end all proved abortive.
The Jesuits were far otherwise; no stone was left unturned, no stratagem however impious, says Monsieur De Lorimier,[30] but what was resorted to, with a
view to detain the unhappy captives. They told the Indians, "that it was merito-
rious in the sight of God for any to be made an instrument of detaining, and
making them members of the true Catholic Church."

With such intimations as these, of course, the Indians cooperated with the
Jesuit Fathers, to hinder and prevent, if possible, the captives being either delivered to the governor or to their friends. With this view they were sometimes
taken to their hunting grounds, where they generally fared much better than in
the village. These were the reasons in two or three instances why Eunice could

---

26. [Philippe de Rigaud de Vaudreuil (c.1643–1725) was the governor-general of New France
from 1703 to 1725.]

27. [In fact, Jesuits did recognize baptisms performed by Protestant ministers and baptized
English captives only if they felt they had not yet been baptized. See the Jesuits's discussion with
John Williams on this topic in Williams, "The Redeemed Captive," 125.]

28. [Louise-Élizabeth de Joybert de Soulanges et de Marson (1673–1740) was the Canadian-
born wife of Philippe de Rigaud de Vaudreuil.]

29. M. de Champigny. [Jean Bochart de Champigny (c. 1645–1720) was intendant of New
France from 1686 until 1702, when he returned to France.]

30. [Guillaume de Lorimer de la Rivière (1657–1709) was a captain in the *troups de la marine*
stationed in the Montreal area.]

not be seen by her father, as she had been carried into a distant part of the country.

The subject of initiating Eunice into the Catholic Church by baptism was once more revived by the Jesuit Fathers, who were well versed in managing the Indians in the most difficult cases, and they now succeeded in obtaining the consent of her mother, although she was strongly advised by the Chevalier de Ramezay,[31] governor of Montreal, to oppose the Jesuits in this matter. "The father of the child," said he, "is a Protestant minister, and no doubt he had administered that ordinance upon his child, and as he was opposed to the ministration of the Jesuits, it would be ungenerous, yea most cruel it must be to his feelings to have an ordinance repeated, after he had performed it himself, and above all upon his own child, and that too, by those of whom he considered were in error, and that in the sight of God, no one had a stronger claim upon her than he had. It [i.e., Eunice] was his. It [i.e., Eunice] was what God had given him, and he had still a right to direct its [i.e., Eunice's] eternal interest. Although a prisoner, and as a prisoner, it [i.e., Eunice] was public property—property of the King. Therefore it [i.e., Eunice] ought to be given up to the officers of the government and that it had been hitherto conceded by the Indians in the colony, that all the white prisoners taken, were to be given up to the governor general—and he on the other hand, had engaged to them, that all those taken by them [i.e., Indians in the colony] of the Indian tribes, they might do with as they pleased."[32]

All this, and much more were said on the subject but the Jesuits had obtained a promise and it must be carried into effect.

Eunice was, therefore, rebaptized by the name of Mary, and on the occasion a high mass to the Holy Ghost was celebrated, by the superior of the missions.[33] An officer[34] of the regiment of Carignan[35] happened to be at the place, and hearing of what had transpired, was extremely exasperated against the Jesuits of that mission. A warm and obstinate debate ensued between them, for rebap-

---

31. [Claude de Ramezay (1659–1724) was the governor of the district of Montreal from 1704 to 1724.]

32. [The Indians had not conceded that all the white prisoners taken were to be given up to the governor general. As a rule, French officers did not—could not—interfere with Natives' control of their captives.]

33. [Vincent Bigot (1649–1720), who had worked with the missions to the Abenakis in Maine, served as superior-general of the Jesuit missions in New France from 1704 to 1710. There is no record that this Mass was performed.]

34. This was Lieut. Col. Bouchel of the royal artillery. [This individual cannot be identified. The first artillery unit arrived in New France in 1750.]

35. [The Carignan-Salières Regiment was stationed in New France from 1665 to 1668.]

tizing a child of a Protestant minister and a prisoner. "To call ourselves Christians, an enlightened and polite nation, as we do," said he, "and to be guilty of such an ungenerous and illiberal act as this, we are unworthy of those high titles." "To you fathers as an order of Jesuits, I fear this act of yours will leave an indelible stain of infamy and disgrace upon you in the view of the Protestants and some the Catholics. The validity of his baptism you will not admit, and that, because he is a heretic and layman. And I would ask, has not the Catholic Church acknowledged that baptism of heretics to be valid? Yes, this is her [i.e., the Church's] sentiment. As to his being a layman, we will admit he is—and consequently his baptism is not to be valid. And I would ask again, are those savages all in sacerdotal orders, whom you have requested to baptise the enemy, before they imbued their hands in the blood of their victim? The Church also I know allows all lay Catholics either male, or female to baptise in case of necessity. And now is their baptism more valid than that of the Protestant minister? If our Church allows the validity of lay-baptism, then his baptism in her view is good, and I verily believe in the sight of God, and Christ, it is an acceptable performance, and that too according to the design of that holy institution. Therefore, by your repeating that holy ordinance on the captive girl you have committed the heinous sin of sacrilege."

The instruction of the novitiates[36] was consigned to one of the Jesuits in the mission who was borne down with ill health, whose appearance commanded respect and commiseration from all who approached him. Tall in stature, with a pale countenance, emaciated body, and his eyes only indicated there was life, and his whole demeanour [was] so humble, gentle and condescending as to draw forth from his catechumen, both love and veneration. There was a strong indication in his deportment, that his thoughts were absorbed in things of eternity.

His religious instructions were limited [and] principally confined to the creed, the Lord's Prayer, and the mutilated form of the Ten Commandments. His exhortations and reproofs were in accordance with the spirit and temper of Him who gave them.

With such a teacher was Eunice first initiated into the Romish Church, whose instruction in the first rudiments of Christianity were of course the same as that any of the Protestant ministers would inculcate upon his pupils, and much of what she heard from the Jesuit she recognized to be the same that she had been taught by her honoured father.

---

36. [Novitiates is generally used to refer to those who are new members of a religious order. Here it appears to mean more loosely one who is undergoing training prior to conversion to Catholicism.]

Comparing in this way what little she knew of the great principles of the Christian faith paved the way to the belief that the difference between the Catholics and Protestants was not so great as some would believe; that both believed in the fundamental principles of the Christian religion, upon which they depended for salvation. With no other instructor than the Jesuits, and the knowledge which she acquired from them was but small indeed and living as she did at first, under the cloud of ignorance, she was incapable of discerning between truth and error. Hence she was gradually led to embrace those corruptions, both in doctrine and worship, which so abundantly abounds in the Church of Rome.

With all her strictness in adhering to the peculiarities of that church, yet in its denunciations against the heretics Eunice never could join with, as her own views were liberal towards them, and she would not confine heaven as a place only for the Roman Catholics, but she believed that all who are holy and live in obedience to God's commandment and are godly in all their works towards their fellow men are also accepted as the children of God. All these appeared in her at this early period of her life. Her liberality towards heretics was attributed by one to her having relations among them; another observed that her liberality was equally great towards the heathen. "It seems then," says the Jesuit father, "she includes both, and would have them to go to heaven, if so, it is because that her religion is pure in its kind. God is love, and this love of his is as universal as the world."

The two interviews she had with her father (as stated in *The Redeemed Captive*) were often referred to by her as serious and solemn moments, whilst she listened to his pious and godly exhortations. Whenever she would rehearse them in broken sentences, it was with faltering voice and with tears in her eyes. Her favourite sentences were, "Fear God and keep His commandments. Remember your creator in the days of your youth. Serve Him with perfect heart, and daily worship Him in spirit and truth. Look to Jesus as your only saviour. Receive Him in your heart of faith. Trust in His all atoning blood for pardon, and cleansing of your sins. And let this blessed saviour be ever precious with you. Let God your heavenly father be always in your thoughts and strive in all that you do, to please Him, and if you do this in sincerity, He will be with you and bless you. In the hour of death He will be your support and joy, and if you are truly His child by grace He will receive you into His everlasting kingdom in the regions of bliss."

As her father was a man of integrity, so he was sincere in his profession; as a Christian, he was consistent, and strictly adhered to the precepts of the religion he professed; and as a minister, he was ever ready to defend the faith which was once delivered to the saints. Fidelity to his divine master and "to make full proof of his ministry" induced him to embrace every opportunity of seeing and conversing with the unfortunate captives to console them in their afflicted state, and to confirm them in the faith of the gospel. From this circumstance, and [because of] his office as a Protestant minister, he was watched with a jealous eye by the Jesuits and other ecclesiastics. His occasional interviews and his religious communications with them at length exasperated the Jesuits to that degree as to induce them to make strong efforts to deprive the captives [of] this intercourse, but it was only partially effected.

An order was obtained from the governor prohibiting them to assemble more than three at a time. This was merely to gratify the Jesuits and to put an end to their importunities, as he had nothing to fear from the captives.

Although surrounded as he was by the enemies of this religion and restrictions put upon him of praying and conversing with his fellow captives, yet he was undaunted by the menaces of the popish priesthood and continued whenever an opportunity presented, to exhort them to hold fast the faith which they had received [and] to keep themselves from the pollutions of the world, and from being entangled with false doctrines.

It was soon discovered by the Jesuits that the restrictions which had been put upon him did not answer to the full extent it was intended by them. And that they may be more successful in their attempts to convert the heretical captives and to remove the obstacles in their way, they besought the governor once more, to send Mr. Williams to a distant part of the colony, to which with much reluctance he finally consented. The priest of Chateau Richer had been sounded, who consented to receive him as his boarder. Thus the wishes of Mr. Williams and the captives were frustrated and compelled to submit to the operations of inscrutable providence.

By the cruelty of these proceedings, the feelings of the captives as well as the liberal part of the Roman Catholics were shocked. The excellent character of the sufferer, and the noble spirit which he exhibited in the hour of trial, produced a strong sensation in his favour, and rendered the Jesuits odious; so that these intrigues and ill treatment, tended to strengthen, rather than to weaken the faith of the captives.

Previous to Mr. Williams's departure from Montreal, he expressed to the governor his desire to see his daughter Eunice, upon which an officer was dispatched to the Indian village to bring her. But on his arrival he found she had been taken by a hunting party up the Great River,[37] about twenty leagues.

37. [A reference to the Saint Lawrence River or possibly the Ottawa River.]

After this she heard only occasionally from her father, while he was in the country.

On the arrival of Mr. [John] Williams at Quebec he found that by the last order of the governor general he was to remain in that city with one of the council. So he did. When this gentleman was informed that he [i.e., Williams] was sent down thither by the intrigues of the Jesuits, he appeared to be greatly exasperated. This gentleman, although a Roman Catholic, his language was decidedly against them, representing them as hypocrites and deceivers, men of the world who were for aggrandisement of their order, saying that the order of Saint Sulpicious and of the Franciscan friars were much better ecclesiastics, and were of more real service to the French colony at large, and that their zeal for God was according to the dictates of religion.

Mr. Williams attracted the attention of the ecclesiastic orders wherever he went, and this may be attributed to his pious examples and firmness in the doctrines and worship of the Reformed Church[38] and his good sense and extensive acquaintance with books which enabled him to meet his opponents at all times without being dismayed. As he was held by the captives in high estimation, so the Jesuits supposed wherever he must be he was the obstacle in their way of making converts of the unfortunate captives, and his disputation while at Quebec with some of those Fathers, particularly an Irish Jesuit, produced a sensation once more among them, and which eventuated in his being sent to the place of his former destination, Chateau Richer. This conference took place in [the] Bishop's Palace and in presence of several ecclesiastics and civilians who were entertained at times in English and Latin. Although the Irish Jesuit preferred in English dress [i.e., preferred to debate in English], yet his opponent would gradually fall back into the Latin, as he wished that the auditors should be the judges of the strength of their arguments. Mr. Williams's acquaintance with the works of the ancient fathers astonished them.

One of the friars of the Franciscan order being present, remarked that his learning was sufficient to make a good Catholic bishop.

In the few days after this Mr. Williams went down to Chateau Richer, where he was received with much kindness by the parish priest, who was of the order of Saint Sulpicious.[39] During his residence with this friendly ecclesiastic he was treated with great hospitality.

In regard to Eunice, the customs, manners, and habits of the people with

---

38. [Reformed Church refers to the faith of the New England Puritans.]

39. [The priest at Chateau Richer from 1678 to 1720 was Guillaume Gaultier (1653–1720). See Williams, "The Redeemed Captive," 126.]

whom she was now living had in a measure become familiar with her. The Iroquois village being in the vicinity of the French, and their intercourse with them, being frequent some of them were induced to adopt their customs and mode of living. Eunice with her mother lived in a small stone building[40] and the order and neatness within exceeded that of many of the French.

They spent their time according to the season, alternately in the canton or in the chase.

In the spring, they planted their maize, beans, and potatoes and etc. and cultivated them during the summer, and in autumn after having gathered the fruits of their labour, they departed for hunting grounds.

In these excursions, Eunice was greatly amused with the objects which met her eye, either the cataracts on the rivers, or the lofty mountains whose towering tops were at times covered with clouds or the beasts of the forests which presented themselves here and there before them.

Her living when in the forests was with the best. In no instance as she recollects did she suffer for want of food, but on the contrary was always plentifully supplied.

Being remarkably delicate in her constitution and incapable of carrying any heavy burden, strict regard was paid to her in these journeys. No remarks were made when in travelling if she carried nothing but a few articles of her clothing and a little basket containing her needlework, while others of her sex and of the same age were born down with heavy packs.

As we have observed that her family spent their summers principally in the canton in these times the younger part of the community were catechized by one of the Jesuits, and Eunice was one of those who attended strictly and made great proficiency, in which she displayed the strength of her mind and memory.

As the catechism which she was taught abounded with the peculiar tenets of the Romish church, so she was gradually initiated into its mysteries and corruptions.

At a proper age according to the customs of that church she was admitted into the communion, and her preparation for the eucharistical feast was by fasting and prayer. From this period may be dated her great regularity in devotional exercises, and as she advanced in years her piety increased. From the circumstance, she was eventually looked upon as a person eminent in the Christian faith, and one who lived and walked in accordance to her profession.

---

40. [Houses were not built of stone at Kahnawake until the late eighteenth-century. Until then the community retained the traditional Iroquois longhouses made of wood. See figure 19.]

Although the Church was overloaded with ceremonies, and her ministers enforced them upon its members with the most intolerant zeal, yet she strictly observed them.

Catharine Tekawitawa [41] a Mohawk convert who was sainted by the Jesuits, was held up to her view, more than any of the scripture saints, or even the perfect pattern of her saviour.

---

41. [Catherine Tekakwitha (1656–1680) was a Mohawk woman who converted to Catholicism and moved to Kahnawake. There her rigorous piety and refusal to marry impressed several French priests. Almost as soon as she died, they began a movement to make her a saint. Though often referred to and treated as a saint, Catherine Tekakwitha was only recently beatified in 1980 and has not yet been canonized.]

A DIFFERENT VIEW: A DESCENDANT RECOUNTS THE 1704 ATTACK, 1995

TAIAIAKE ALFRED

O N FEBRUARY 13, 1995, Taiaiake Alfred came to Deerfield to make a presentation to the guides and employees of Historic Deerfield, Inc., and the Pocumtuck Valley Memorial Association. Taiaiake was born in Montreal in 1964, grew up in the Mohawk community of Kahnawake, and earned a Ph.D. in political science at Cornell University. He is a writer, philosopher, activist, and professor at the University of Victoria with his own website (http://www.taiaiake.com/). His scholarly work includes *Heeding the Voices of Our Ancestors: Kahnawake Mohawk Politics and the Rise of Native Nationalism* (Toronto: Oxford University Press, 1995), and *Peace, Power, Righteousness: An Indigenous Manifesto* (Toronto: Oxford University Press, 1999).

Taiaiake's talk at Deerfield forms part of his effort to educate the broader public about Native issues and, in this instance, the history and culture of Kahnawake. What follows is an excerpt from a longer talk, which was recorded and archived in the library at Historic Deerfield. The rest of the talk focuses on how Kahnawake's identity has been shaped by its location between two colonial powers, first the French and English empires, now the nations of Canada and the United States. It has been a difficult existence.

Though Kahnawake is located just across the Saint Lawrence River from Montreal, its people, like Taiaiake, are predominantly English-speaking. This fact has set them apart from their French-speaking neighbors in what is now Canada's Province of Quebec. In 1990 tensions over land rights led to an armed stand-off first with the Quebec police force, then with the Canadian army that lasted all summer.

For Taiaiake, the great theme of Kahnawake's history has been persistence and survival under colonial conditions. One important element of that theme in the seventeenth and eighteenth centuries was the absorption of captives from other communities into Kahnawake in order to maintain its population—the

---

Gerald R. [Taiaiake] Alfred, Mohawk Community at Kahnawake [sound recording], 1995, guides training, April 13, 1995, Historic Deerfield Library. Transcription made with the speaker's permission and assistance.

fundamental strength of its community. Within this context he recounted the Mohawk story of the bell. This version of the story is particularly important. It is told directly by a Mohawk, but it is told to a Deerfield audience knowledgeable about the 1704 raid and captives, such as Eunice Williams, taken by men from Kahnawake. Scholar, Mohawk, and educator, Taiaiake here not only recounts a venerable Mohawk tradition; he expounds on it to take into consideration the concerns of the Deerfield audience. Why were captives taken? What happened to them after they were captured?

More than just the latest recorded version of a Mohawk oral tradition, then, this is an informed commentary on the issues raised by the story from a contemporary Mohawk perspective. What Taiaiake stresses here is the Mohawks' ability and desire to assimilate all sorts of people into their community. Whether Native, European, or African in origin, once they were adopted into a Kahnawake family they were Mohawk. Some accepted this practice more than others, as he notes by contrasting Eunice Williams with John Smith, but the important point is that the Mohawks themselves decided who was a Mohawk. Race did not matter. Culture and community membership did. Further on in his talk Taiaiake emphasizes that the legacy of colonialism means that now Mohawks are preoccupied with racial definitions of who is and is not Mohawk.

All of this from a man who, as he discovered, is also a descendant of Eunice Williams and of Puritans. In his person and his experience, then, Taiaiake embodies the legacy of both the English colonists at Deerfield and the Mohawk warriors who attacked them in 1704.

§

I'll tell you the story from our side of the raid on Deerfield. Then we can compare notes. It is a very simple story from our perspective. The Jesuits promised us a bell for our church. Part of the deal in converting over to Christianity [was] that we would have a nice new church and we would have a nice place to worship in our new faith. In the understanding of our people it was a bargain made on both sides. So the Jesuits promised a bell from France which was forthcoming. The bell was in a ship destined for Quebec and thence to Montreal [but] an English pirate took that ship and took the bell and sent it to Deerfield illegally.

The Mohawk people found out about this fact and developed the will to come and return to Kahnawake—its rightful place—this bell which had been taken by the English enemies. And they weren't going to let anything get in the way. I'm giving you the side of the story that the people in Kahnawake understand. So they rounded up some French people to support them and they came

FIGURE 20. Bullet pouch (Great Lakes region), wool sash (Anishinaabe), tobacco pouch (Mohawk), and gorget (Mohawk), mid-eighteenth century. Eunice Williams remained in Kahnawake and married Arosen, a Mohawk. Four times, in 1740, 1741, 1743, and 1761, they traveled south to visit kin in Massachusetts and Connecticut,. During these visits Arosen gave the items shown here to his brother-in-law the Reverend Stephen Williams. A gorget was a symbol of status worn on the chest. These gifts document the persistence of bonds between Mohawk families and their English kin in New England. Photograph courtesy of the Pocumtuck Valley Memorial Association, Memorial Hall Museum, Deerfield, Massachusetts.

FIGURE 21. Ball, Barnes, Horne, and Williams children, Kahnawake, 1967. Connections between the communities of Kahnawake and Deerfield persisted throughout the 1800s and the 1900s. In 1967 the Ball family of Deerfield visited Kahnawake, and their children Carol, Shelly, and Terry posed for this photograph with their Mohawk cousins. At the center of the photograph, which was taken in front of the Catholic Church of Saint Francis Xavier, is the bell and seated on the bell is Steven Williams. Photograph courtesy of Harriet Ball.

FIGURE 22. I. K. Williams (on the left) visiting Deerfield, 1973. In 1973 Deerfield celebrated the three hundredth anniversary of its incorporation as a town. A large contingent of Mohawks came down from Kahnawake to participate in the commemoration. Among the visitors was Dr. Ignatius Karoniaktatie Williams (1902–1976), a direct descendant of Eunice Williams. After becoming a doctor in the mid-1920s, he lost his Indian status and right to remain in Kahnawake; because he was a university-educated professional, the Canadian government no longer considered him to be an Indian. Eventually, "I. K." or Karoniaktatie, as he preferred to be known, regained his Indian status, and from 1969 to 1976 he served as staff physician at Saint Catherine's Hospital in Kahnawake. Photograph courtesy of Joseph Peter Spang.

down to get their bell in 1704. [They] dragged the bell all the way back to Kahn-awake and it's still sitting there. People who have been to Kahnawake can go in the church and see the bell. Now I don't know if that [story] is historically, fac-tually, empirically verifiable, but that's the understanding and as far as I know that is the truth in our community with regard [to] the raid on Deerfield.

It is interesting and somewhat ironic given everything that I sense here and the interesting history that I read in the museums and the displays that I see that there is no mention [in the story of the bell] of the fact that they took cap-tives [and] there is no understanding of the significance of Eunice Williams, and there is [in Kahnawake] no relationship made to the type of issues that people here [in Deerfield] think are important [regarding] the raid. So, it is a completely different perspective on this intersection and interaction between [the] two peoples. The French are unimportant. The only thing that is impor-tant is the fact that the Mohawk people rectified an unjust situation. That's all they [i.e., the Mohawks] see in it, and I think they took some captives while they were here [i.e., Deerfield] to fill some spots within their society.

It is important to understand the concept of the Iroquoian [mourning war] that I referred to earlier. Daniel Richter wrote an excellent article on the mourn-ing war explaining in a very concise, lucid way what the mourning war meant to Iroquoian peoples.[1] [It was] a very significant element in their societies. One of the central facts to explain warfare in this era among the Native peoples, and the Iroquois in particular, was that they saw the need to fill places within their societies and their families and their lives [by replacing people who] had been lost through death, through disease and through warfare with other peo-ple, not necessarily people of their own race, in the way that we understand race today, [and] not necessarily their own people, their own family. In the Iro-quois conception there were names—there were places within the Iroquois society—that needed to be filled by individuals and in a utilitarian sense there were jobs that needed to be done. There was a society that needed to be upheld and run. And the Iroquois people needed a significant amount of individuals to fulfill those roles within that society. And so the mourning war refers to the fact that a family in a mourning situation undertook to either capture children [or] capture replacement members, [to] fill these roles in family and society. So you find numerous captivity narratives throughout the history of the relationship where people were taken in and treated as sons, as daughters, [and] as chiefs in some instances who in fact were British soldiers the week before or a couple of months before.

---

1. Daniel Richter, "War and Culture: The Iroquois Experience," *William and Mary Quarterly*, 3rd ser., 40 (1985): 528–559.

There is an interesting story, one in particular, [that] I really recommend to you—it is published by the Ohio Historical Society—the captivity narrative of James Smith, [who was called] Scoouwa.[2] He was a British soldier captured . . . [in 1755 in central Pennsylvania and] . . . brought up to Detroit and over to Montreal. And he basically [wrote] an [account] of his experiences with these people who happen to be Mohawks of Kahnawake documenting their lifestyle, their traveling habits, their language and their worldview at the time.

One particular segment is very informative as to the view of the Mohawks and Iroquois people towards adoptive captives. Eunice Williams being one of them and all of [the] people from Deerfield would have gone through, I would sense, the same trial. [There] is no denying that it was a brutal existence by our standards today. James Smith was taken in by a very prominent member of the society—it seems a sachem—a leader within the Mohawk community [who] was moving through the area as our people did, following the cycles of the season from Kahnawake and Montreal down to the Ohio Valley up to Detroit and moving over. . . . Soon after he was taken, he underwent an adoption ritual which involved the women the of the party or the village stripping him of his clothes, pulling out all of his hair [and] washing him ceremoniously, or unceremoniously, depending on your viewpoint in the river. [He went] through a whole day-long ceremony, whereby in the end, the chief gave a moving speech indicating that all the white blood had been washed out of this man's veins. He was in fact no longer a white man, he was a member of his family; he was his son. He was painted up as the ceremony was going on in the fashion of a Mohawk warrior. He was given the clothes and the ornaments of a Mohawk warrior and instructed that he should forget his prior existence that his mind had to come over now to the Mohawk community. And he was a member of a proud nation and a proud family. And he should take pride in that fact and make the best of his existence and learn his responsibilities within Mohawk society.

And James Smith . . . did very well in taking on his responsibilities: he survived the winter. He [also] managed to fool—it turns out in the end—his captors. He learned the rudiments of the language. He was able to communicate. He assumed a position of trust within the community, and in the end I say fooled them, because when he got to Montreal [in 1759] he [attempted] to jump on the first ship he could and [return] to New York [which he eventually did by an overland route.]

There were a lot of people for example who didn't fool anyone who were

2. James Smith (1737–1814) was taken captive in Pennsylvania in 1755 while working with a party cutting a military road. He remained with the Indians for four years and later wrote an account of his captivity: Smith, *An Account of Remarkable Occurrences in the Life and Travels of Col. James Smith* (Lexington, Ky.: John Bradford, 1799).

actually converted and assimilated—reverse assimilation—into the Mohawk community; Eunice Williams being one of them. Eunice Williams for those of you who don't know was taken in 1704 at seven years of age along with a lot of other people from this community [i.e., Deerfield] to Kahnawake. There is some indication that people were taken to other Native communities because, of course, there were Abenaki and other Native people who participated in this raid and they wanted their share, and I assume that some captives were taken to different Native communities. Some no doubt had [been] ransomed off or traded for captives in other Native communities, and so the people who were taken here no doubt scattered throughout the Iroquois world and even beyond.

Eunice Williams was significant because I think she is illustrative—she is an archetype—of the captive who had become successful, completely successful in a way that James Smith did. The women for various reasons and sometimes if the captor took a serious liking or saw something in the child which was reminiscent of his own child or of his niece or nephew that had been lost didn't have to go through the trials that the older people did and so all indications are from reading James Smith's captivity narrative that Eunice Williams was one of those who was very well treated, taken in from the beginning and taken good care of by the captors. And I think the results show: she stayed with us until she was eighty-nine years old and died a member of our community. And most of you know that she forgot her prior existence. She forgot to speak English and she spoke Mohawk. And in our community the Williams name is carried on.

Eunice Williams is remembered no differently than any other ancestor. We have a number of non-Native ancestors who are like Eunice Williams who were captives. The Rice brothers from Albany are prominent.[3] In fact an older man, McComber,[4] from this part of the country, was taken at twenty-seven-years-old, integrated, and I think McComber, Rice, and Williams are three of the biggest family names in Kahnawake today. So [Eunice] Williams wasn't unique, but she is illustrative, I think.

Actually, McComber's is a story that I should tell you because it is very inter-

---

3. The Rice brothers, Silas (1695–1779) and Timothy (1697–1777), were taken prisoner during the August 8, 1704, raid on Westborough, Massachusetts, and remained with the Mohawks. Silas was renamed Jacques Tannhahorens, and Timothy, who became a grand chief, was known as Jacques Oserokohton.

4. Jarvis or Gervais McComber (c. 1778–1866) moved to Kahnawake on his own around 1805 from southeastern Massachusetts. He may have been born in Scotland. He was baptized a Catholic in 1805 and married into the Mohawk community. The belief that he was a captive rather than someone who had voluntarily joined the community at a later date reflects the important role of incorporating captives into this and other Native communities in the Saint Lawrence valley.

esting. He was taken at twenty-seven-years of age, from this area. He was a soldier, captured and brought to the community and decided to stay. I guess he liked it, because he had twenty-seven children, starting at the time he was twenty-seven with three different wives. Needless to say his legacy lives on.

Most captives were not as prolific. Most captives who came to the community integrated within the society along the ideals that I portrayed to you in the story of James Smith. They didn't keep a detailed journal; there [are] no documented remembrances in the community, because of course at the time, and still to a large extent now, we are an oral society. Our history is in the stories of our people and in the remembrances of our families. I cannot refer to a document which tells us that Eunice Williams came to our community and went through certain trials, was adopted into the families of so and so. All we know in fact in any empirical sense that would be comparable to the type of records that Europeans kept were the records in place now at the church that the Jesuits kept. The Jesuits of course had their own interests in documenting and having people come over from heathenism and Protestantism to Catholicism.

The first thing they did when Eunice Williams came to Kahnawake was [to] give her a French Catholic name Marguerite. They let her keep her last name, Marguerite Williams. She was given Kanenstenhawi[5] which is a Mohawk name. My sense is that she probably spoke Mohawk very quickly because the everyday language in that community up until the 1940s was Mohawk, primarily. My sense is that name that she was known as was Kanenstenhawi [which was] probably a nickname but that was her real name. She quickly forgot her English background aside from the fact that she paid visits, not too successful I understand, back to the community of her ancestors, and had some sense of connection to the community here in Deerfield. But as with many of the other captives there is no sense of specialness.

There is no unique sense of the captives who came to Kahnawake which may surprise some of you. There is no sense that there is a special connection to Deerfield because most of the people are not conscious of the fact that these ancestors came from a particular community. They know that our people engaged in a mourning war; they know that people come from different racial backgrounds. There are white, black, white and black, and different Native nations who have been adopted into our society, but there is no attention paid to the individual character—individual aspects—of that history, and it may sound clichéd somewhat to those of you who have been paying attention to Native history for a long time that there is a collective sense—a collective history—and we share this history.

---

5. Kanenstenhawi means "she brings corn."

So too it came as somewhat of a surprise to me when Suzanne [Flynt][6] was at the Cultural Center and I was doing research on my own family tree, my genealogy, and she was looking in particular for someone who was descended from Eunice Williams and [said] won't it be nice to find someone who was descended from Eunice Williams. And low and behold on my computer screen was, eight generations back, Eunice Kanenstenhawi Williams. And at the time I had no conception who Eunice Williams was, the importance of Eunice Williams in the community or of her family, or in fact that I was a descendant of Puritans. It was quite a shock for me. But the fact is that on my little card file on my computer it said Eunice Kanenstenhawi Williams. And this is the actual Jesuit writing [in] the letters [of] archaic French but it translates as "taken in 1704 from Deerfield by the Iroquois." And that's all our community knows about Eunice Williams except for what I am going to tell them when I come back.

But in a sense that is the entire remembrance among those people in Kahnawake who pay attention to history and that's a minority. The people who pay attention to history know about Eunice Williams and [Timothy] Rice and the other captives coming, but like I said, it is a very different understanding and appreciation of history. I'm not sad to report [this] but it is something interesting for you to think about that there is not this level of interest. I have a feeling that if Donald [Friary][7] came to speak on Eunice Williams at Kahnawake, even with his excellent abilities and magnetic personality, I don't know how many people would show up to hear [and to learn] about it. But there are people who are descended of Eunice Williams—I am not unique. Eunice Williams had two children[8] [and] numerous [great]-grandchildren and multiply that by the generations and—I'd say—you have hundreds of people who are direct descendants of Eunice Williams in our community today. Some of them even look like John Williams I am convinced.

---

6. Suzanne Flynt has been the curator of the Memorial Hall Museum of the Pocumtuck Valley Memorial Association in Deerfield, Massachusetts, since 1982.

7. Donald R. Friary served as executive director of Historic Deerfield, Inc., from 1975 to 2002.

8. Eunice had at least three children who survived childhood, two daughters and a son.

ABENAKI NARRATIVES

FIGURE 23. Elizabeth Sadoques (1897–1985), photograph, possibly mid-1920s, photographer unknown. She was born in Keene, New Hampshire, where her father and mother settled in the late 1800s. He worked as a fancy basket maker. Elizabeth Sadoques graduated from high school in Keene and became a registered nurse in 1919. Photograph courtesy of Lynn Murphy.

THE HISTORY AND TRADITIONS OF EUNICE WILLIAMS AND HER DESCENDANTS, 1922

ELIZABETH M. SADOQUES

E LIZABETH MARY SADOQUES was born in 1897, grew up in Keene, New Hampshire, and died in 1985. She was the great-great-granddaughter of a woman who was part of a group of Abenakis who visited Deerfield in 1837. That visit, and a subsequent one the next year, drew the attention of the local media and ministers. Newspaper accounts documented the visit. In Deerfield there was much excitement because one of the Abenaki women claimed that she was descended from Eunice Williams. Deerfield's minister, the Reverend John Fessenden, was inspired to preach a sermon admiring "the workings of that mysterious providence, which has mingled your blood with ours."[1] The following year Abenakis visited Northampton as well (figure 23).

For both the people of Deerfield and the Sadoques family, the relationship to Eunice formed a compelling connection. Speaking in 1922 to the members of Deerfield's local historical society, the Pocumtuck Valley Memorial Association, Elizabeth Sadoques emphasized her people's abiding sense of their ancient ties to the land now a part of the United States. Her ancestor Eunice Williams embodied these ties for Sadoques. At the same time, she claimed that Eunice was not all that Abenakis and Americans had in common. Sadoques was at pains to set the event in the context of a continuing series of exchanges involving land, trade, religion, and politics, stretching back to the 1620 arrival of the Pilgrims and continuing to the present.

Sadoques's account does not present a generic "Native" version of events. Instead, it reflects the perspective of her people, the Abenakis, and the more

---

Elizabeth M. Sadoques, "The History and Tradition of Eunice Williams and Her Descendants," 1922. The manuscript of her February 28, 1922, talk to the Pocumtuck Valley Memorial Association remains in the hands of her family and is reproduced here with the permission of Lynn Murphy.

1. John Fessenden, *A Sermon, Preached to the First Congregational Society in Deerfield, Mass., and in the Hearing of Several Indians of Both Sexes, Supposed to be Descendants of Eunice Williams daughter of Rev. John Williams, First Minister of Deerfield, August 27, 1837* (Greenfield, Mass.: Phelps and Ingersoll, 1837).

particular concerns of her family. In her discussion of Eunice and Kahnawake, for example, she claims for the Abenakis people and places associated with the Mohawks. This action is an important reminder of the differences, political as well as cultural, among Native peoples. Her hostility to the Jesuits who set up a mission at Odanak in 1701, however, derives largely from the fact that she was a Protestant. Her family, the Sadoques, along with the Wajoos, whose visit to Deerfield is described in this account, were among the first converts to Protestantism at Odanak. In 1837, a local man who had graduated from Dartmouth College, Pierre-Paul Osonkilaine Masta, began building a Protestant chapel that divided the community of Odanak. The ensuing controversy may have played roles in the Wajoos' visits to New England in 1837 and 1838, and in the Sadoques family's subsequent relocation to New Hampshire, where Elizabeth was born.

For Sadoques's Deerfield audience, the interest was somewhat different. Deerfield's residents had been fascinated for two centuries with the plight of the captives who never returned. Their interest in the talk focused primarily on Eunice Williams. Their perspective is evident in the revisions made to Sadoques's manuscript when it was published in 1929 in the Pocumtuck Valley Memorial Society's *Proceedings*. Whereas Sadoques begins her manuscript with a broad sketch of the history of the relations between Natives and Europeans, the published version condenses this section and puts it toward the end, placing her discussion of the captive Eunice at the front instead. The published version also emphasizes the differences between Abenakis and Anglo-Americans. It drops Sadoques's mention of "strange men" and instead inserts "White-men" in several places were it had not been in the manuscript. Such changes reflect a sense of racial distinctiveness that undercuts the sense of commonality emphasized in the original manuscript. In short, for the people of Deerfield in 1922, Sadoques's talk was configured in ways to reinforce their sense of being different and victimized, rather than similar and victimizers.[2]

Now is time to look anew at the original version of Sadoques's address. The version of the address that follows is based on the original manuscript.

Children love stories, and the children of the forests who inhabited this country before the coming of the white-man, loved their stories which told of hunting, traveling and warfare. Then it was told around the camp-fires that "Awa-nooti,"

---

2. Elizabeth M. Sadoques, "History and Traditions of Eunice Williams and Her Descendants," *Pocumtuck Valley Memorial Association History and Proceedings* 6 (1929): 128.

strange men, were coming in great numbers from across the great river, the ocean. Still later various events which occurred in colonial days were related. As this was their only means of preserving great deeds and events, each story was cherished and handed down from father to son.

So as a child, I heard the same stories of hunting the great bear and moose; of travels down long streams and thundering rapids or through peaceful valleys and blue mountains unencumbered with cares. Now a very beautiful portion of this country which is now the New England states and including the St. Lawrence River valley was the territory of the Algonquian Indians of which there are many divisions, the Abenaki being one division or tribe.[3] This great family of allied tribes were from the same stock, spoke the same language of which there are many dialects.

At the present time the old Indian names throughout New England and a part of Canada are quite readily translated through the Abenaki language—my native tongue. Your neighbor "Wachusetts," small mountain, and your Connecticut, "Quanitagook," long river, as also your Pocumtuck, "river with many turns," are words very familiar to me.

These were the people who greeted the Pilgrims in 1620 and who accepted Champlain[4] in his journeys down the St. Lawrence River in his attempts to find China. The English came here for freedom in religion and that was their one desire while the French who at that time were under control of the Jesuit priests came to convert the Indians to their religion and incidentally to so control their savage minds to *their* wills.

The Jesuits had great success with the Eastern Indians[5] but their attempt to Romanize the Mohawks was vastly different. They met with disfavor and finally were compelled to establish a mission principally for their Mohawk converts on the Algonquian territory which was the St. Louis Mission or Caughnawaga.[6] This proves the result of the Jesuit influence over the Algonquians as exemplified by their tolerance for an age old enemy.

Then there came a time when the Indians in Massachusetts were sorely grieved. The English were coming in ever increased numbers always crowding the aborigines from their once peaceful hunting grounds. Finally King

---

3. Algonquian is one of the linguistic families of Native America, much as Indo-European is in Eurasia. Algonquians included all the various peoples living along the coast of North America from the Carolinas up through Canada and from there out west to the Great Lakes. Mohawk belongs to the Iroquoian family of languages.

4. Samuel de Champlain (c.1570–1635) was a famous explorer and a founder of the French settlements in Canada.

5. The English referred to Abenaki Indians in Maine as the Eastern Indians.

6. The Jesuit mission at Sault Saint Louis was located in the Mohawk town of Kahnawake. Caughnawaga is an older English spelling of the Mohawk name for their village.

Philip[7] broke the treaty his father[8] had made with the settlers and began ravaging every town and hamlet they could find until finally they were defeated and their allies fled to Canada for protection under the Jesuits. Here they were sheltered and converted thus making of themselves slaves to the Jesuits' desires as were the French.

About the year 1700 the mother countries—France and England—were at odds, and the French seeing the opportunity to use their Indian allies in New France ordered their soldiers to lead the unbroken spirits of the savages against the English settlers who had their lands. The result was many cruel massacres and the taking of many captives to Canada.

The most important to us is the memorable sack of Deerfield in 1704 over 200 years ago. I'll not repeat the story here as you are all so well acquainted with it, but I will add that among the many captives taken to Canada was one, Eunice Williams, of whom I will tell a tradition that has existed in my family for two centuries. I will tell it exactly as mother tells it and which was told [to] her by her mother.

Many years ago, when there existed a great number of wars between the French and English, a number of captives were brought to Canada from the land of the "Bostonias," the name given the English settlers. Counted among them were two small children, a brother and sister, who were brought to the camp-fires of the Abenaki. The boy[9] was given up but the little girl was adopted into the tribe and grew up as an Indian child later marrying an Indian brave.

This child came from a long way down the "Quanitagook," Connecticut, from a place where there lived a number of Williamses, Williamsecook, and her name was Eunice Williams as was also her granddaughter, who is my mother's great-great-grandmother.

Eunice of Williamsecook tells this story of her grandmother to her son Louis and to her grandson John Wajoo, [meaning] mountain, with whom she lives at St. François the old village of the Abenaki tribe.[10] She remembered her grandmother Eunice perfectly and heard her say many times that she had on several occasions returned to her kinsfolk at Williamsecook.

---

7. Metacom (?–1676), the leader of the Wampanoags, who was called King Philip by the English, led his people and other Natives in a series of attacks on the English from 1675 to his death in 1676 that came to be known as King Philip's War.

8. Massasoit (?–1661) was the leader of the Wampanoags who greeted the first settlers of Plymouth Colony and maintained peaceful relations with them. Traditionally he is assumed to be the father of Philip, though some claim he was Philip's grandfather.

9. The boy being referred to is Stephen Williams (1693–1782).

10. Eunice of Williamsecook (c. 1750–1848), Louis Wajoo or Watso (1778–1885), and John or Jean Wajoo or Watso (1818–1868) as well as other relatives of Elizabeth Sadoques are discussed in greater detail in the notes to the following essay by Marge Bruchac.

It was a custom with the Abenaki that during the warm summer months, they would leave their gardens and with a few provisions, as corn and beans, take their children for a holiday. Several families would go together in parties and travel through lakes and down long rivers. When nightfall came they would make camp and if the place was beautiful they would remain there until they were again so inclined to move on.

So it was on such a joyful expedition in 1837[11] that Eunice of "William-secook" traveled with her son, grandson and wife with their small children, together with other families from St. Francis. This party decided to take the journey down the Connecticut in an attempt to find the place where Eunice's grandmother was captured many years before.

After several days journey down the "Quanitigook" they finally located what was known to them as "Williamsecook" and there camped, giving Eunice an opportunity to find her relatives, who received and treated her kindly. She was shown many things among which was the house[12] the door of which had resisted the attacking Indians on that memorable night of the sack of Deerfield in 1704.

At this time Eunice of Williamsecook was old as she must have been since her only son and grandson, accompanied her. She was content to return to St. Francis, having accomplished the same visit her grandmother Eunice of Deerfield had traveled so many years before.

These were the party of Indians of whom the Reverend Mr. Taylor spoke of at the Deerfield church in August 1837 as mentioned in Miss Baker's book.[13]

On their journey back to Canada or very shortly after, a son was born to Eunice's grandson, John Wajoo, who was called William in memory of their visit to the Williamses. A few years later when Eunice of Williamsecook was very old and blind, a daughter was born to John Wajoo at St. Francis, and Eunice, holding this baby in her arms said, "This child will be called Eunice, as I was called by my grandmother, Eunice Williams the white papoose."

History tells us that Eunice was taken by a Maqua or Mohawk but we know

---

11. It is worth noting that 1837 and 1838 were the years of the *Patriote* Rebellion in Lower Canada and even though fighting did not break out until the fall of 1837, tensions had been building all summer. Unwilling to take sides in a fight that was not theirs, the Abenakis of Odanak did their best to stay out of the conflict. Visiting New England in 1837 and 1838 was one safe way to do so.

12. This was the Ensign John Sheldon House, which stood until it was torn down in 1848. The door was saved and became a relic of the 1704 raid.

13. John Fessenden (1799–?), Deerfield's minister from 1830 to 1840, not John Taylor (1762–1840), who ministered at Deerfield from 1787 to 1806, was the author of the sermon. Sadoques was misled by C. Alice Baker, *True Stories of New England Captives Carried to Canada during the Old French and Indian Wars* (1897; repr., Bowie, Md.: Heritage Books, 1990), 393, which claims it was John Taylor who gave the sermon.

that the Reverend John Williams was taken by an Abenaki as also was his son Stephen and brought to St. Francis. If the Williams house was attacked by Abenakis why should she be taken by a Mohawk unless they merely used that story the better to keep her from being returned to her people. Even so Eunice may have been taken to Caughnawaga and from there placed with the Abenaki since no records exist at Caughnawaga of her baptism or marriage.

When Sheldon[14] went to Canada to negotiate the exchange of captives Eunice very easily could have journeyed from St. Francis at news of his coming and there talk with him since the Abenaki village is only a day's journey, 60 miles as measured by the Indians.[15] They could have come in a very short time.

The Reverend James Deane,[16] missionary to the Indians at Caughnawaga and St. Francis in 1773 [and 177]4, knew Eunice well. No doubt the missionary saw Eunice at St. Francis, the little village of my ancestors, and talked with her and her children.

Nehemiah Howe[17] in the story of his captivity states that he met at Crown Point an Indian called "Amrusus" who said he was the husband of she who was called Eunice Williams. The name Amrusus is strictly Algonquin in construction and accent and translated in the Abenaki language is the name Ambrose called "Ambroasis."

Last summer I visited the old village of St. Francis, the home of my forefathers, but the circumstance of my visit did not permit me to look into any records, as I am of Protestant faith and the high wall between the Roman and Protestant division which now exists would prove to be a great obstacle in my attempt.

However, I discovered an old copy of [the] History of the Abenaki written by one of the Roman priests, Father Maureau, and in his story I find that a Eunice Williams was named as one who was captured during the French and Indian

14. Ensign John Sheldon (1658–c. 1733) made three trips to Canada in 1705, 1706, and 1707 to negotiate for the return of English captives.

15. Such a day's journey would have been by water along the Saint Lawrence River.

16. James Deane (1748–1823) was born in Groton, Connecticut, but lived at a mission to the Oneidas as a young boy, where he learned their language. Graduating from Dartmouth College in 1773, he was immediately sent to Kahnawake and Odanak to recruit Natives from those villages to attend Dartmouth. Returning in 1774, he went on to serve in the American Revolution as an officer, Indian agent, and translator. He received a large grant of land in Oneida County, New York, at the war's end.

17. Nehemiah Howe (1693–1747) was captured at what is now Pultney, Vermont, by Abenakis from Odanak. After meeting Arosen at Crown Point he was taken to Quebec, where he was questioned, then put in the French prison. There he (like many other prisoners) died of disease. While in prison, he kept a journal, which was published in Boston in 1748.

wars.[18] She married into the tribe and to this day her descendants live at St. Francis. In the New England States there are several descendants one of which is my aunt Eunice previously mentioned as being named by Eunice of Williamsecook and whose daughter also is named Eunice and lives at present just outside of Boston and her sister Mary who is my mother.

I will state in closing that they, too, in response to the voice of their ancestors, have traversed the same course down the Quanitagook and here settled not far from its shores, here rearing their children, near the great river of their forefathers.

Annual Meeting of the Pocumtuck Valley Memorial Association, 1922.

---

18. Joseph Pierre Anselm Maurault (1819–1870). Maurault, who was born in the province of Quebec and grew up there, began serving the Catholic mission at Odanak in 1841. Beginning in 1842, when he became a priest, he also served a neighboring French Canadian community. This post placed him at the center of conflicts over land and religion between French and Abenakis, Protestants and Catholics until he died of pneumonia. His *Histoire des Abénakis, depuis 1605 jusqu'à nos jours* (Sorel, Que.: L'Atelier typographique de la Gazette de Sorel, 1866), 320, mentions that Eunice Williams was captured and assimilated into the Mohawk community of Kahnawake.

ABENAKI CONNECTIONS
TO 1704: THE SADOQUES FAMILY
AND DEERFIELD, 2004

MARGE BRUCHAC

MARGE BRUCHAC is a scholar, consultant, historical interpreter, and traditional storyteller of Abenaki Indian descent. Born in 1953 in Saratoga Springs, New York, she grew up in Greenfield Center, New York, and was graduated from Smith College. She is now a doctoral candidate in anthropology at the University of Massachusetts in Amherst and a Five College Fellow at Amherst College. Her research, as the following essay shows, focuses on hidden histories, stories, language, material culture, and the continuing survival of Native peoples and culture in their traditional homelands. For years she has been active in the field of public history, serving as an adviser to the Wampanoag Indian Program at Plimouth Plantation, a member of the Five College Native American Indian Studies Curriculum Committee, and a trustee of Historic Northampton.

Bruchac brings Elizabeth Sadoques's story up to the present, when Abenaki Indians became involved in the commemoration of the three hundredth anniversary of the 1704 Deerfield raid. Her own work was an important part of this involvement, which included consulting, along with other Native descendants of 1704 Deerfield raiders, on a museum exhibition as well as a Web site. Both are dedicated to setting the event within a context that incorporates all of the peoples involved. The museum exhibit was mounted at the Flynt Center in Deerfield. The Web site created by the Pocumtuck Valley Memorial Association is at http://www.1704.deerfield.history.museum/. It is the product of a collaborative effort of individuals and scholars from a variety of communities. This multicultural perspective, along with text, interactive maps, images, and links to various sources that a viewer can navigate at will give the site its distinctive quality.

Bruchac wrote the following essay for a special issue of the magazine *Historic Deerfield*, titled "Rediscovering 1704," that was published in the spring of

Marge Bruchac, "Rediscovering 1704," *Historic Deerfield* 4, no. 1 (Spring 2004): 21–24. Reproduced here in an expanded version with permission.

2004. In it, she situates the work of Elizabeth Sadoques by demonstrating the ongoing connections between Abenaki peoples and southern New England. Bruchac points out the significance and persistence of relationships between Abenakis and other New Englanders. Instead of dwelling on past wars, she draws our attention to the exchanges of gifts, knowledge, and medical care that continue even today.

Bruchac's essay and her work on the museum exhibition and the Web site remind us that physical objects—a landscape, baskets, an old door, gravestones, a shoe—can provide access to the past in ways that texts cannot. Interpreting artifacts may be more of a challenge, but if examined closely, they too have their stories to tell. In this way, people who otherwise have no written historical voice can speak to history. Now a history that for so long has been dominated by a single text, John Williams's *Redeemed Captive Returning to Zion,* can be understood through a range of different elements. None alone is authoritative or definitive. History lies in the combination and juxtaposition of these different avenues to the past and in the inclusion of Native voices that were left out of earlier conversations.

When Elizabeth Sadoques came to Deerfield in 1922 to relate her family's oral history, she was viewed as an exotic outsider. Local museums made no further attempt to maintain contact, in large part because the dominance of Eurocentric histories and the discourse of Indian disappearance led many historians to assume that contemporary Native oral histories were either unreliable or irrelevant. Some eighty years later, Bruchac has demonstrated that the Watso and Sadoques families have both broad and deep connections to the landscape of Deerfield, reaching back to a point that precedes the founding of the town. Furthermore, much of the documentation for Sadoques's story of the family's visit in 1837 can be found in previously overlooked materials stored in Deerfield's own archives, information about Indians that has been, literally, hiding in plain sight.

§

Deerfield, August 15, 1837: A Visit

On August 15, 1837, twenty-five Saint Francis Abenaki Indians,[1] traveling by horse and wagon, arrived in Deerfield and set up camp within the bounds of the

---

1. The name Abenaki, as a derivation of Wôbanakiak, meaning "people of the dawn," refers in this instance to the Native American Indian people of Vermont, New Hampshire, and southern Canada, sometimes called "Western Abenaki" or "Saint Francis Abenaki." This family group came from the village of Saint Francis, also called Odanak, on the Saint Francis River near the

village, where they stayed for several weeks. Some of them were already known to Deerfield residents, but one, an eighty-six-year-old woman named Eunice, had never been to Deerfield before. She called the town "Williamsecook," an Abenaki locative form that indicates "the Williamses' place," and told Deerfield residents that she had undertaken the trip to honor her grandmother and to visit the graves of her great-grandparents. The *Greenfield Gazette and Mercury* reported:

> Our people were thrown into a state of considerable emotion last Monday evening and Tuesday, by the encampment of a body of Indians from Canada, about twenty five in number who . . . passed through the village and went to Deerfield where they encamped, and still remain. . . . They are of the Saint Francis tribe, in Canada, and are descendants of Eunice Williams, daughter of the Reverend John Williams, who, it will be recollected, was, with his family, carried captive when Deerfield was destroyed in 1704. One of the party, a woman of 86 years, the mother of the rest, is grand daughter to Eunice.[2]

The elderly Abenaki woman, who was known to her family as "Eunice of Williamsecook," was warmly greeted by white members of the Williams family who "were not slow to admit their [the Indians'] claim, but uniformly called them 'our cousins.' "[3] Only a few of these individuals were mentioned by name in Deerfield's records, but other surviving documents and oral histories reveal the identities of several. Eunice of Williamsecook was accompanied by her granddaughter (who is sometimes identified as her daughter), thirty-nine-year-old Marie Eunice Agent, and Marie Eunice's husband, fifty-nine-year-old Louis Otondosonne Watso.[4] The Watsos' nineteen-year-old son, Jean Baptiste (John)

Saint Lawrence, north of Montreal. Since the generic term *Indian* was so widely used in early documents and family reminiscences, I use either *Indian* or *Native* in place of the more modern term *Native American.* No insult is implied or intended by the use of *Indian.*

2. *Greenfield Gazette & Mercury,* August 29, 1837.

3. John Fessenden, *A Sermon, Preached to the First Congregational Society in Deerfield, Mass., and in the Hearing of Several Indians of Both Sexes, Supposed to be Descendants of Eunice Williams daughter of Rev. John Williams, First Minister of Deerfield, August 27, 1837* (Greenfield, Mass.: Phelps and Ingersoll, 1837), 4.

4. Louis was apparently the first member of his family to adopt the surname Watso, meaning "mountain." His descendants kept the name in later generations with alternate spellings that include Watzeau, Watsaw, Wadso, Wajoo, and Wajo. See Nancy LeCompte, "Case Study—Chief Louis Watso: Parents, Siblings, Spouses, and Children, Facts, Oral Tradition, and Conclusions," http://www.avcnet.org/ne-do-ba/cs_d08_1.html#6, accessed January 15, 2004. In 1922, Watso's great-granddaughter Elizabeth Sadoques said that Louis Otondosonne Watso (c. 1778–1885) was a son-in-law of Eunice of Williamsecook (c. 1750–c. 1840). The spread in ages and the family tra-

Watso, brought his wife of the same age, Marguerite (Margaret) Obomsawin, who was pregnant. Marie[5] Saraphine (Sophie) Watso Denis-Paul, Louis Watso's twenty-eight-year-old daughter from his first marriage to the late Marie Marguerite Taxus, came with her six-year-old son, Ambroise Denis-Paul. The fact that Abenaki people routinely traveled in extended family groups from shared places of residence suggests the identity of a few of the other relatives in the party. Louis Watso's next eldest daughter, twenty-seven-year-old Marie Anne, and his unmarried sister, sixty-year-old Marie Helaine Watso, lived with him at Odanak. Marie Eunice and Louis Watso likely also brought their twin sons, fifteen-year-old Simon and Joseph Louis, and their sixteen-year-old daughter, Suzanne.[6]

The records indicate that these Abenaki Indians were treated very hospitably by Deerfield residents, who paid them numerous visits, purchased their baskets, shared food with them, and invited them into their homes. In case the resonances between the 1837 visit and the events of 1704 were not obvious, it should be noted that the same issues of the *Greenfield Gazette and Mercury* that described the Indian encampments included large advertisements for a new biographical memoir of the Reverend John Williams written by Stephen West Williams.[7] The elderly Eunice was offered indoor lodging, but she preferred to

---

dition of passing on the name Eunice from grandmother to granddaughter suggest that Marie Eunice Agent (1798–1848) may be a granddaughter of Eunice of Williamsecook. Records at Odanak indicate that Marie Eunice Agent's father was Pierre Michel Agent (?–1822) and her mother was a woman baptized as Marie Angelique, whose parents and dates are unknown.

5. The use of the personal name Marie was common in northeastern Native villages with Catholic missions, where women would be baptized with the name of the holy mother Mary (spelled as Marie in French, Mali in Abenaki), followed by a middle name (e.g., Saraphine, Sophie) that might shift into a phonetic variant for everyday use, and a family surname that might relate to either the mother's or the father's side. These names were also used in combination with Native names, and all could change with over time. For Native families, multiple names reflected the realities of multiple identities and family alliances. See Alice Nash, "The Abiding Frontier: Family, Gender and Religion in Wabanaki History, 1600–1763" (PhD diss., Columbia University, 1997).

6. Recorded dates for the other family members mentioned include Marie Saraphine Watso (c.1809–1882), Jean Baptiste Watso (1818–1868), Suzanne Watso (c.1821–1891), Simon Watso (1822–?), and Joseph Louis Watso (1822–1902). It should be noted that Abenaki written records before 1759 are scarce because many were destroyed when the church was burned during a British raid led by Robert Rogers. Statistics after that date come from family papers, oral traditions, and various other sources, including a handwritten document titled "Abenaquis Indian Marriages St-Francois-du-Lac" (1796–1805), Abenaki tribal census lists for 1822, 1841, 1844, 1845, 1850, 1851, and records of the Anglican Church and Congregational Church, at Saint Francis Reserve Odanak, Quebec.

7. *Greenfield Gazette & Mercury,* August 29, September 5, 1837. The preface to a volume containing a later edition notes: "A great and growing interest in antiquarian research evinces the eagerness with which the present generation seek after the particular history of their ancestors, and the desire they feel of becoming acquainted with their privations and sufferings, their hardships and dangers, in transmitting to them the beautiful heritage they now enjoy." John Williams, *The*

stay with her kin in the Indian camp. The Abenaki had brought canoes, which they took out on the Connecticut River, and decades later, an elderly Jonas Wilder would recall his childhood memories of this visit: "While I was at Bloody Brook [today, South Deerfield], the Williams Indians came down from Canada, and camped on the river bank. A real pretty young squaw took me out on the river in a birch bark canoe, and we had a good time." [8]

Although Native families such as these were frequently seen traveling through New England towns in the early nineteenth century, they were not, as is so often assumed, gypsies, paupers, or the "last of their kind," eking out a living on the fringes of Yankee society. The 1837 visitors, for example, were described by a Greenfield newspaper reporter as "comfortably well off for Indians, having several horses and wagons, and a goodly supply of blankets and buffalo robes," at a time when few people in Deerfield owned horses, let alone wagons.[9] The Abenaki would later recall the whole of the nineteenth century as a time when they traveled with complete freedom through familiar territory in New England, New York, and Canada, "camping where they so desired and resting when so inclined." [10]

Our Blood Is Mingled

The Reverend John Fessenden,[11] the minister of the First Church of Deerfield, prepared a special sermon, preaching from "ACTS, XVII. 26. *And hath made of one blood all nations of men for to dwell on the face of the earth.*" In his prefatory remarks, he noted that the Abenaki camp had been crowded by visitors, "almost denying them time to take their ordinary meals." The inconvenience was more than compensated for by the ready trade in Indian baskets.[12]

During a time of racial intolerance and religious diversity, Deerfield's minister chose a universalist theme: "Revelation gathers all the scattered kindreds of

---

Redeemed Captive, ed. Stephen West Williams (1707; Northampton, Mass.: Hopkins, Bridgman and Co., 1853), iii.

8. Jonas Wilder, "Reflections of a Nonagenarian," *History and Proceedings of the Pocumtuck Valley Memorial Association* 4 (1912–1920): 43.

9. *Greenfield Gazette and Mercury,* August 15, 1837.

10. Elizabeth M. Sadoques, "History and Traditions of Eunice Williams and her Descendants," *History and Proceedings of the Pocumtuck Valley Memorial Association* 7 (1921–1929): 126.

11. John Fessenden (1799–?) was born in Dedham and was graduated from Harvard University in 1818 and Cambridge Theological Seminary in 1821. He was a tutor at Harvard from 1825 to 1827. A Unitarian, he served as minister of Deerfield's First Church from 1830 to 1840. During his ministry a group of parishioners seceded and formed an orthodox Congregational society. His Unitarian faith with its universalist view of salvation and belief in the brotherhood of mankind clearly shaped his sermon on this occasion. —eds.

12. Fessenden, *Sermon Preached,* 4.

the earth, into a common family . . . finds the same life-blood circulating through the veins of every human creature, whether his skin be blanched like the snows . . . or darkened to a sable hue . . . purifies and reconciles all the discordant and conflicting customs and religions . . . as brethren of a single, united, harmonious household." [13] He declared this Indian visit to be a "remarkable illustration of the truth declared in our text, by which the blood of two races so distinct and unlike, and once so hostile and irreconcilable, has been blended together." [14]

The Reverend Fessenden reminded his listeners that the Pocumtuck Indians, whom he likened to the "Canaanites and Amelekites," [15] had long since been overcome and their land rightly claimed by God's chosen people as in scripture. He hoped that ill feelings about the bloody past could be exchanged for "the hand of friendship" and "the pipe of peace." Referring to the battle-scarred door of the Sheldon House, he noted: "I would say as ye have buried the hatchet whose traces still remain visible on the ancient portal, to remind us of by-gone days of blood and violence, of suffering and captivity, so sleep the sword by which those wrongs,—if wrongs they were,—have been fully avenged." [16] Such gracious words of reconciliation were, in a sense, easy to offer, since so many of the original Native inhabitants of the valley had, by the 1830s, left Deerfield. One can only wonder what the reaction might have been if these Native visitors had intended to take up permanent residence.

These same Indians were not well received in Northampton. In 1838, a reporter for the *Northampton Courier* disparaged them as a "slothful, ragged, dirty, squalid race, appearing to have adopted the vices of the whites without seeming to emulate any of their virtues. The lofty bearing and noble demeanor of the primitive Indians are gone, and nothing is left but the abject and debased exterior of the red man." [17] A reporter from the *Hampshire Gazette* seemed offended at their popularity. Noting, "Visitors have enthronged their encampment from all quarters," he went on to imply that Eunice of Williamsecook was deluded: "We do not think there is any evidence that she is descended from Eunice Williams except her word." [18]

Many New England newspaper writers had little tolerance for Indians, during an era when politicians supported the forcible removal of American Indians

---

13. Fessenden, *Sermon Preached*, 10–11.
14. Fessenden, *Sermon Preached*, 13.
15. According to the Bible, the Canaanites and Amelekites were the original inhabitants of the land God promised to the ancient Israelites.
16. Fessenden, *Sermon Preached*, 14.
17. *Northampton Courier*, June 6 1838.
18. *Hampshire Gazette*, June 6 1838.

to lands west of the Mississippi, when James Fenimore Cooper's 1826 *Last of the Mohicans* was a best-seller, and when audiences could watch a fictional "Last of the Wampanoags" dying on stage nightly in the famous stage play *Metamora,* which ran almost continuously from 1829 to 1872.[19] One can only wonder whether the Northampton writer had history or fiction in mind when he complained that the Abenaki were "a wretched remnant of a race of noble and proud Red men, who once tenanted this fair valley, and whose stealthy tread and uplifted tomahawk, carried death to hearts terrified by their appalling war-cry."[20] These stereotypical images, oft-repeated in fiction, drama, and historical writing, obscured more realistic portrayals of Native peoples. In this light, encounters with living Indians could be an unwanted reminder of a people who had refused to vanish under the onslaught of colonization. Throughout the nineteenth century, the lives of many Native peoples in New England were poorly documented, unless they were intriguing, dramatic, or destitute enough to catch the eye of white historians.[21] While New Englanders were inventing stories about the "last of the Indians," the Indians themselves carried on with their ordinary lives.[22] Ironically, theater reviewers noted that Native people sometimes attended dramatic productions on Indian themes, "adding a most picturesque feature by their presence."[23]

---

19. John Augustus Stone wrote "Metamora, Last of the Wampanoags," loosely based on the events of Metacom's Rebellion or King Philip's War (1675–1677), as an American dramatic vehicle for the Shakespearian actor Edwin Forrest. See Jill Lepore, *The Name of War: King Philip's War and the Origins of American Identity* (New York: Alfred A. Knopf, 1998), 191–226.

20. *Northampton Courier,* June 6 1838.

21. For a discussions of how Native people were routinely ignored as part of a regional discourse of disappearance, see Donna K. Baron, J. Edward Hood, and Holly V. Izard, "They Were Here All Along: The Native American Presence in Central New England in the 18th and 19th Centuries," research summary for Old Sturbridge Village, Sturbridge, Mass., 1994; and Thomas L. Doughton, "Unseen Neighbors: Native Americans of Central Massachusetts, A People Who Had Vanished," in *After King Philip's War: Presence and Persistence in Indian New England,* ed. Colin G. Calloway (Hanover, N.H.: University Press of New England 1997), 207–230.

22. Robert F. Berkhofer and Mary Ann Weston both suggest that the misidentification and marginalization of Indians, as the predominant literary style throughout the nineteenth and early twentieth centuries, made it nearly impossible to report accurately on Native issues in the news. Generic traits were assigned to all Indians; cultural, linguistic, and other differences were often misreported, and Native peoples were expected to assimilate white cultural norms or disappear. See Robert F. Berkhofer, *The White Man's Indian: Images of the American Indian from Columbus to the Present* (New York: Vintage Books, 1978); and Mary Ann Weston, *Native Americans in the News: Images of Indians in the Twentieth Century Press* (Westport, Conn.: Greenwood Press, 1996). These tropes bled into academic historical writing as well. See Donald L. Fixico, "Ethics and Responsibilities in Writing American Indian History," in *Natives and Academics: Researching and Writing About American Indians,* ed. Devon A. Mihesuah (Lincoln: University of Nebraska Press, 1998), 84–99.

23. "Many a time delegations of Indian tribes who chanced to be visiting the cities where acted this character—Boston, New York, Washington, Baltimore, Cincinnati, New Orleans—at-

The relationship of the Nonotuck, Woronoco, Agawam, Quaboag, and Sokoki Indians to the Deerfield landscape long predated the events of 1837 and 1704. Many members of those groups had folded in among their northern Abenaki neighbors in the aftermath of the French and Indian wars. As just one example, the contemporary Abenaki family name of Sadoques originated with a man named Shattoockquis, who, on November 10, 1665, signed off on a deed for land in Quaboag (now Brookfield) along with the Pocumtuck sachem Mettawampe.[24] By 1685, Shattoockquis was the leader of a group of Connecticut River valley Indians who went through a series of relocations, first to Saint Francis, then to the refugee village at Schaghticoke, New York, and then back to Saint Francis.[25] This pattern was so typical of valley Indians that it would not be at all outlandish to suggest that Shattookquis, or his close relatives, participated in the raid on Deerfield. The ethnohistorian Gordon Day surmised that the origin of this family name was either *msátegwés,* meaning "big river person," or *msádokwés,* meaning "big rump person." Shattoockquis's signature on the Brookfield deed may hold the clue—it shows a hump-backed, short-legged animal. Although it most resembles a fox, family traditions suggest that it might also represent a beaver.[26]

By the early nineteenth century, many Abenaki Indians, and their cousins from the south, regarded the landscape around Deerfield as a homeland they had been forced to leave. For millennia, New England's Native peoples had preserved memories of ancient and historic events by recounting oral traditions while traveling through the landscape where events took place, thus nar-

---

tended the performance, adding a most picturesque feature by their presence, and their pleasure and approval were unqualified." William Alger, *The Life of Edwin Forrest, the American Tragedian* (Philadelphia: J. B. Lippincott 1877), 240.

24. Harry Andrew Wright, *Indian Deeds of Hampden County* (Springfield, Mass., 1905), 57–59.

25. Although there is not yet a comprehensive written history of the movements of the Native peoples of this region during the eighteenth and nineteenth centuries, some aspects of the Connecticut River valley Indian diaspora are discussed in Peter Thomas, "In the Maelstrom of Change: The Indian Trade and Cultural Process in the Middle Connecticut River Valley, 1635–1665 (Ph.D. diss., University of Massachusetts, 1979); Colin G. Calloway, *The Western Abenaki of Vermont, 1600–1800: War, Migration, and the Survival of an Indian People* (Norman: University of Oklahoma Press, 1990); Gordon Day, *The Identity of the Saint Francis Indians, Canadian Ethnology Service,* Paper no. 71 (Ottawa: National Museum of Man, 1981); Evan Haefeli and Kevin Sweeney, "Revisiting the Redeemed Captive: New Perspectives on the 1704 Attack on Deerfield," in *After King Philip's War: Presence and Persistence in Indian New England,* ed. Colin G. Calloway (Hanover, N.H.: University Press of New England 1997), 29–71; James Spady, "As If In a Great Darkness: Native American Refugees of the Middle Connecticut River Valley in the Aftermath of King Philip's War," *Historical Journal of Massachusetts* 23, no. 2 (1995): 183–197. Also see the character narratives written by Marge Bruchac, "Atiwans," "Mashalisk," "Umpanchela," "Wattanummon," and "Weetanusk," for *Raid on Deerfield: The Many Stories of 1704,* http://www.1704.deerfield.history.museum/people/index.jsp.

26. Day, *Identity of the Saint Francis Indians,* 86–87.

ratively naming, and claiming, familiar space.[27] Even after people had moved away from places like Pemawatchuwatunck, the hill in the shape of a beaver now called the Pocumtuck Range, the stories continued to be told, sometimes encoded in names like Amiskwolowoakoaik, meaning "people of the beaver-tail hill."[28] Some of the newest stories involved captives, since events of the eighteenth century had forged some lasting relationships between captors, captives, and their descendants. In later generations, when Native and non-Native people met face-to-face in once-contested lands, the social activities that Euro-Americans might well have perceived as simple courtesy—welcoming, visiting, exchanging gifts, sharing food, and publicly acknowledging relationships—likely served to reinforce Native peoples' sense of emotional attachments to these Indian places that had become Euro-American space.

Connecting Deerfield Objects and Abenaki Family Stories through Time

The Abenaki Indians who circulated throughout New England, upstate New York, and southern Canada in the nineteenth and twentieth centuries kept the memory of their visits to Deerfield alive through family stories. Louis Watso's great-granddaughter Elizabeth Sadoques explained it like this: "Eunice of Williamsecook tells this story of her grandmother to her son Louis and to her grandson John Wajoo, [meaning] mountain, with whom she lives at St. François the old village of the Abenaki tribe. She remembered her grandmother Eunice perfectly and heard her say many times that she had on several occasions returned to her kinsfolk at Williamsecook."[29]

The white-girl captive Eunice Williams started a naming tradition that has persisted to the present among her Abenaki descendants. In 1837, Eunice of Williamsecook told the people of Deerfield that she had been named after her grandmother, Eunice Williams. She passed the name Eunice on to Marie Eunice Agent, who became Louis Watso's wife. Louis and Marie Eunice Watso's son, Jean Baptiste Watso, and his wife, Marguerite Obomsawin, who

---

27. For a discussion of Abenaki and Pocumtuck oral traditions about the local landscape, see Marge Bruchac, "Earthshapers and Placemakers: Algonkian Indian Stories and the Landscape," in *Indigenous Archaeologies: Decolonizing Theory and Practice,* ed. Claire Smith and H. Martin Wobst (New York: Routledge, 2005), 56–80.

28. For example, in the beaver hill story associated with the Pocumtuck Range, a giant beaver builds a dam that floods the landscape before he is killed and transformed into the mountain in the shape of a beaver. See Phinehas Field, "Stories, Anecdotes, and Legends, Collected and Written Down by Deacon Phinehas Field," *History and Proceedings of the Pocumtuck Valley Memorial Association* 1 (1870–1879): 63. For the reference to the people called the Amiskwôlowôakiak, see Gordon M. Day, *The Mots Loups of Father Mathevet,* Publications in Ethnology no. 8 (Ottawa: National Museum of Man, 1975), 56.

29. Sadoques, "History and Traditions of Eunice Williams," 258.

were expecting a child while they were at Deerfield, continued the tradition of naming children for long-past relatives. When a boy was born on the return trip north, he was baptized "William," in memory of that trip to see the Williamses; when a girl was born a few years later, she was named "Eunice." Another one of Louis Watso's grandchildren, Ambroise, who, at six years old, was the youngest visitor to Deerfield in 1837, had been named, according to Sadoques family tradition, after Eunice Williams's husband, Amrusus.[30] Those three names, Eunice, Ambroise, and William, have been repeated through the Abenaki generations to the present.

Some skeptics have questioned how an Abenaki family could claim a connection to Eunice Williams, given the understanding that, in 1704, Eunice was adopted and married into the Kanienkehaka Mohawk community at Kahnawake. Eunice could easily have had relatives in other tribes, since social interactions, political alliances, and outmarriages were common among Catholic Indians and the members of the Seven Nations Confederacy.[31] The Sadoques family story reveals that Eunice's granddaughter established an Abenaki line of descent, and that these Abenaki descendants then reinforced their attachments to Deerfield by regular visiting and repeated use of the name Eunice, a practice that continues even today.

During the late nineteenth century, when C. Alice Baker and Emma Coleman were tracking the captives' stories, they took an interest in Eunice's Mohawk relatives living at Kahnawake but ignored the Abenaki Indians who had visited them, such as Louis Watso and his children.[32] In an 1890 letter

---

30. Eunice Williams's husband has been variously identified in primary sources as Amrusus, De Rogeurs, Tairagie, Toroso, Auresa, and Arosen. Elizabeth Sadoques wrote in 1922: "Nehemiah Howe in the story of his captivity states that he met at Crown Point an Indian called 'Amrusus' who said he was the husband of she who was called Eunice Williams. The name Amrusus is strictly Algonquin in construction and accent and translated in the Abenaki language is the name Ambrose called 'Ambroasis' " (Sadoques, "History and Traditions of Eunice Williams," 260). In 1897, C. Alice Baker wrote: "It is with diffidence that I have declined to accept the name Amrusus, and prefer to await further knowledge . . . Rev. G. L. Forbes, a scholarly man, an adept in the Iroquois language, curé of Caughnawaga and a diligent student of the records, says that the name Amrusus does not appear there. 'Toroso' and 'Amrusus,' writes Mr. Forbes, 'are certainly corrupt names. They are not Iroquois at all. They remind one of 'Arosen' and 'Tekentarosen,' which are Iroquois, and proper names of men. The records of Caughnawaga have been carefully studied in the hope of finding a name suggestive of Amrusus or Toroso. Arosen and Tekentarosen occur as masculine names, but nowhere in connection with Eunice Williams or her children." See Baker, *True Stories of New England Captives* (1897; Bowie, Md.: Heritage Books, 1990), 381.

31. One other consideration that must be taken into account is the fact that not all Native people were Christian, and not all marriages were recorded by the church. Unwed partnerships, illegitimate children, and polygamy were also sometimes found; these practices were known to the Native community but unrecorded in Catholic Church records.

32. In 1897, C. Alice Baker remarked on the 1837 visit: "The possibility that the old squaw was a granddaughter of Eunice is refuted by what we now know of her posterity." Baker, *True*

to C. Alice Baker, the Reverend Edwin Benedict, an Abenaki minister in the Anglican Church at Odanak, recalled that "Eunice Williams M [married] an Abenaki—Her descendants are here now. Their Indian name is Watso as they spell it now—It was Wajo. . . . Old Wajo died in Lake George in 1880 where Bishop John Williams saw him in 1878." [33]

When George Sheldon accessioned one of the 1837 baskets into Memorial Hall Museum, he neglected to indicate the name or tribal identity of the maker, labeling it only as a basket "given to 21 year old Catherine Williams, gifted by her daughter, Helen Sheldon Wells." [34] Until fairly recently, most of the Native artifacts in New England museums, including thousands of Native-made baskets, were identified only by the names of their white owners, a practice that obscured the artistic and social traditions involved in indigenous basketry.[35] In the mid-1990s, when curator Suzanne Flynt turned over this particular ash-splint storage basket, she was still able to read faint writing on the bottom. The basket was made by Marie Saraphine (Sophie) Watso Denis-Paul as a gift for twenty-one-year-old Catherine Williams. So as not to forget the friendship with this Indian woman whom she acknowledged as a distant cousin, Catherine had penciled an inscription that reads: "Basket Given me September 1837 / By Sophie one of the St. Francis Indians / Connected with the Williams family" (figure 24).

Another related object in the collections of Historic Deerfield is an herbar-

---

Stories, 393–94. What Baker failed to mention is that "what we now know" is based on mission records that were woefully incomplete. Baker and Forbes could find no written records of Eunice's baptism, or marriage or the births of any of her children. Baker, *True Stories*, 380–86. Furthermore, Father J. Guillaume Forbes at Caughnawaga (now Kahnawake) had cautioned Baker about the veracity of some of the Mohawk claims of descent: "The fact that the children of Louis issued from Marie Kahentaieronni and now Marie Kahnetaieronni's great grand children call themselves by the name of Williams is not sufficient proof of their having Williams blood." See Forbes to Baker February 5, 1897 and February 6, 1897, Baker Papers, Pocumtuck Valley Memorial Association, Deerfield, Mass.

33. Even though many Deerfield residents had witnessed the 1837 visit and other interactions with Abenakis in Deerfield in the nineteenth century, none of their recollections made it into the published histories or museum interpretations at the Pocumtuck Valley Memorial Association until the late 1990s. C. Alice Baker corresponded with the Abenaki schoolteacher and minister Edwin Benedict, but she failed to follow his lead regarding the Watso family's history. See E. Benedict to C.A. Baker, [Pierre]ville [P.] 2 Canada Feb 17, 1890, Baker Papers, Pocumtuck Valley Memorial Association.

34. Memorial Hall accession catalogue, Pocumtuck Valley Memorial Association.

35. For a discussion of the symbolism and social beliefs involved in making, decorating, selling, and giving as a gift Northeastern Algonkian Indian basketry during the nineteenth century, see Ann McMullen and Russell Handsman, *A Key into the Language of Woodsplint Baskets* (Washington, Conn.: American Indian Archaeological Institute, 1987).

FIGURE 24. Splint basket, ash, 1837, made by Sophie Watso. This basket was made by twenty-six-year-old Marie Saraphine Watso, nicknamed Sophie, and presented to twenty-one-year-old Catherine Williams at the time of Watso's visit to Deerfield in late August and early September of 1837. To remember this visit and to acknowledge their kinship, Catherine penciled on the bottom of the basket the following inscription: "Basket given me September 1837 / By Sophie one of the St. Francis Indians / Connected with the Williams family." Photograph courtesy of the Pocumtuck Valley Memorial Association, Memorial Hall Museum, Deerfield, Massachusetts.

ium of indigenous medicinal plants compiled by Dr. Stephen West Williams. In an 1849 article for the American Medical Association, Williams noted, "When the tribe of Indians from Canada were here in 1837, Louis Watso, their doctor, gave me an account of the principal medical plants they use in their practice."[36] "Indian Doctors" like Watso treated both Native and non-Native patients with various herbal medicines.[37] The stimulant *Asarum canadense,* commonly called Canadian snakeroot or wild ginger, was known to the Abenaki as *skogabedakwa,* "snake head plant." Although Williams was keen to learn about Native medicine, he was a bit skeptical about taking it.

---

36. Stephen W. Williams, *Report on the Indigenous Medical Botany of Massachusetts,* American Medical Association Transactions (Philadelphia: American Medical Association 1849), 916.

37. Some of Watso's medicinal knowledge, including the use of wild ginger, spruce gum, and pine fungus, was passed on to his granddaughter Mary Watso; some notes are still in private family collections. Several contemporary over-the-counter herbal remedies sold in Canada, such as "Fortin's Fir Compound" for bronchitis and flu symptoms, are based on Native remedies that

When a company of Indians from Canada were in Deerfield, in the year 1837, I was much affected with palpitation of the heart, and they were much offended with me because I would not take one of their preparations which contained a large proportion of this snakeroot. They use it extensively in many complaints.[38]

Williams's skepticism may have resulted, in part, from the threat Watso's visits posed to his medical practice. In the 1840s, Williams wrote:

Within a year or two I have seen hundreds of my fellow citizens chasing after a part of a tribe of Indians who came here to make us a visit from Canada, for the cure of their diseases. They pretended to be able to cure all diseases by their simple remedies and the people believe them. The chief of their tribe was called a physician.[39]

Dr. Louis Watso's remedies were apparently efficacious in preserving his own health, since he was said to have been exceptionally resilient—in his eighties and nineties he was still hunting in the Adirondack Mountains and around Lake Champlain, and "on his hundredth birthday he was skating on the lake." He lived to the age of 107.[40] Watso's many relatives made their homes across New England, often settling in Abenaki homelands near tourist resorts in the Adirondacks, the Green Mountains, and the White Mountains. His granddaughter, Mary Watso, eventually moved with her husband, Israel M'Sadoques, to Keene, New Hampshire. Mary Watso M'Sadoques, and her sister Eunice

---

were originally marketed by Indian doctors and doctresses. Fortin's contains fir-tree gum (koakh8akwpego in Abenaki) mixed with the bark of red spruce (mskask), hemlock (alnizedi), and prickly ash (kagowakw).

38. Williams, *Report on the Indigenous Medical Botany of Massachusetts,* 883.

39. Original letter in Williams Papers, box 15, folder 1, Pocumtuck Valley Memorial Association.

40. A 1922 article about Louis Watso notes, "The old chief of the Banaca [Abenaki] tribe lived to be 107 Years and five months old. The man possessed the true Indian features and physical development, as shown when on his hundredth birthday he was skating on the lake . . . He was wounded in the leg the bullet being kept there the rest of his life, because of his refusal to have it removed. . . . During the latter part of his life he walked from this village to Saratoga to attend the funeral of his sister who lived to be a hundred and one. . . . Watso is said to have been one of the most famous Indian Chiefs in this part of the state." *Lake George Mirror,* June 3, 1922. Louis Watso was married at least three times: first, on October 14, 1807, to Marie Marguerite Taksus (c.1792–1814), the daughter of Joseph Taksus (also spelled Taxus or Toxsoose) and Marie Louise Vincent. When his first wife died, Louis Watso married Marie Eunice or Anniese Agent (1798–1848) on November 28, 1814. After she died, he married Marie Louise Wanlinas. Although there are numerous descendants, only the Sadoques family has kept the tradition of their relationship to Eunice Williams alive in the oral tradition.

passed on the family oral histories of the *ngonniak* ("those who came before") to their daughters, including a girl named Elizabeth.[41]

Deerfield, February 28, 1922: A Meeting

By 1922, Mary and Israel's M'Sadoques' daughter, Elizabeth Sadoques, was employed as a practical nurse for the aging painter Abbott Handerson Thayer. On March 5, 1921, Thayer's young assistant, Elizabeth B. Fuller,[42] wrote to her mother in Deerfield: "The nurse we have is a pure blood indian and has ancestor named Eunice Williams who was taken capture from Dfd. Very interesting I think—she is a charmer from the word go and very refined." [43]

Fuller's mother, Mary Williams Field Fuller,[44] seized the opportunity to speak to the Abenaki nurse and was excited to realize that they were distant cousins: "By 1921 the tribe had forgotten the name of Williams, although still continuing the name of Eunice, and when in that year my daughter, Elisabeth met in Dublin, New Hampshire an Indian girl by the name of Elisabeth Sadoques, they soon discovered they were both descendants of that far away Robert of Roxbury." [45] Fuller insisted that Elizabeth Sadoques come to Deerfield.

On February 28, 1922, when the Pocumtuck Valley Memorial Association held its annual meeting in Deerfield, the agenda included the usual—elections of officers, financial reports, readings from letters, and committee appointments. A turtle shell and bowl, recently unearthed from a Pocumtuck Indian

41. After the M'Sadoques family moved to Keene, New Hampshire, they were advised to change their name to Sadoques to make it easier for Americans to pronounce. Five of the Sadoques daughters, Ida Ann (1886–1981), Maude (1889–1993), Margaret (1891–1993), Agnes (1894–1979), and Elizabeth (1898–1985), all well-educated women, were collectively known as "the aunts." Both of Elizabeth's daughters became historians. Claudia Mason Chicklas has worked with the Ware Historical Society and the New England Native American Institute. The late Mali Mason Keating made a series of recordings for the Vermont Folklife Society in Montpelior. See Mali Keating, "North American Passage: The 19th Century Odyssey of an Abenaki Family," in *Visit'n: Conversations with Vermonters* (Vermont Folklife Center) 7 (November 2001):24–31.

42. Elizabeth B. Fuller (1896–1979) was an artist who was born and died in Deerfield. She was a direct descendant of Dr. Thomas Williams (1718–1775), a first cousin, once removed, of the Reverend John Williams of Deerfield.

43. Fuller Papers, in collections of Pocumtuck Valley Memorial Association Memorial Libraries, Deerfield, Mass.

44. Mary Williams Field Fuller (1863–1951) was a direct descendant of Dr. Thomas Williams.

45. Mary Williams Field Fuller, "The Williams Family in Deerfield," *History and Proceedings of the Pocumtuck Valley Memorial Association* 8–9 (1950):100. Robert of Roxbury was Robert Williams (1607–1693), who emigrated from Norwich, England, to Roxbury, Massachusetts, in 1637. He established the family from whom most of the prominent Williamses in western Massachusetts were descended. He was the Reverend John Williams's grandfather.

gravesite, were exhibited. The books of Mary P. Wells Smith[46] were praised for stimulating interest in Deerfield traditions. In the evening, after supper, an Abenaki Indian woman from Keene, New Hampshire, presented a paper on her family history titled, "History and Traditions of Eunice Williams and Her Descendants." It was considered a "rare addition to the early history of Massachusetts."

Miss Elizabeth Mary Sadoques recited excerpts from "a tradition that has existed in my family for two centuries," promising to "tell it exactly as mother tells it and which was told [to] her by her mother." She recalled a white child whose "name was Eunice Williams" and the Abenaki "granddaughter who is my mother's great-great-grandmother." She recounted the family story of a "joyful expedition in 1837" when Eunice of Williamsecook found "her relatives, who received and treated her kindly," and "was shown . . . the house the door of which had resisted the attacking Indians on that memorable night of the sack of Deerfield in 1704."[47] By 1922, the Sheldon House, also known as the "Indian House," was long gone, but the door had been preserved, and so she made a point of viewing it.

The Sadoques family story, in an edited form, was published in the Pocumtuck Valley Valley Memorial Association proceedings, the first time it had been put into writing. In later years, Elizabeth would recall with fondness the treatment she received in Deerfield, while puzzling over the fact that, although there would be Mohawk guests in later years, no one at the museums evinced any further interest in Abenaki history. Another seventy-five years would pass before anyone rediscovered the connections between the documents and artifacts in Deerfield's own museums and the family traditions that Elizabeth Sadoques shared.

Part of the problem may be laid at the doorstep of Deerfield's influential historian, George Sheldon, who believed that the Pocumtuck and all of their descendants had vanished and argued that the Abenaki had been merely foreign puppets of the French. As an amateur archaeologist, Sheldon eagerly excavated Native gravesites in Deerfield, including more than twenty on his own home lot, but he staunchly opposed any efforts to work with or provide assis-

---

46. Mary P. Wells Smith (1840–1930) wrote *The Boy Captive of Old Deerfield* (Boston: Little Brown, 1904) and *The Boy Captive in Canada* (Boston: Little Brown, 1905), fictionalized accounts of Stephen Williams's captivity written for a youthful audience.

47. Sadoques, "History and Traditions of Eunice Williams," 259. The door referred to in the quotation is the front door of the Ensign John Sheldon House that survived the 1704 raid. When the house was torn down in 1848, the door was saved and is on display in the Memorial Hall Museum in Deerfield. It is the best-known relict associated with the February 29, 1704, raid.

tance to living Native peoples. The Abenaki visitors warranted only a single sentence in Sheldon's *History of Deerfield*; they, and Fessenden's sermon, were listed by the wrong date.[48]

Deerfield, 2003–2004: Making Connections

In 2003, when Elizabeth Sadoques's daughter, Claudia Chicklas, and grand-daughter, Lynn Murphy, visited Deerfield, and in 2004, when their observations were added to the exhibit "Remembering 1704: Context and Commemoration of the Deerfield Raid," these Abenaki women were seen not as exotic outsiders but as respected informants. The social relations of the 1837 visit, the 1922 talk, and the 2004 commemorative events began to be recognized as important pieces of the local history, fleshed out by Elizabeth Sadoques's oral traditions and the surviving artifacts. By making room for these traditions in the histori-cal narrative, Deerfield's museums were able to expand, and complicate, our view of the past, but this is just one Native family's story—imagine how many others have yet to be explored.

The traditions of Native connections to the valley have been literally hiding in plain sight, obscured for too many years by the assumption that Native oral histories were unreliable. Native stories—whether about a giant beaver in the hills that make up the Pocumtuck Range or about Native families visiting Deer-field in the nineteenth century—were tossed into the category of myth. The written truths embedded in Native stories, even when verifiable, are amplified by the performative experience of sharing them. In much the same way that Europeans have taken literary license to evoke their connections with the past, Native family stories have flexible rules of performance, and they need not be strictly linear accounts. As Lynn Murphy puts it:

> We know that antiquity exists, but we prefer to tell the old stories as though they happened yesterday. I've seen this consistently happen in my family. My grandmother told stories that were centuries old with my grandfather in them. The immediacy of having it be your uncle instead

---

48. George Sheldon's take on the "Indian Question" was that no redress was due Native peo-ple for any past injustices. He argued against history by claiming that "In no case, can the origin of Indian hostilities in New England be traced to any claimed infringement by the whites on the ter-ritory of the Natives, with the single exception of the Eastern war of 1723." See George Sheldon, *A History of Deerfield, Massachusetts*, 2 vols. (Deerfield, Mass.: privately printed, 1895–1896), 1:670. Fessenden's sermon was listed as being given in 1835 instead of 1837 in *A History of Deerfield*, 2:804.

of long ago and far away made the stories more believable to the kids. Europeans get all tied up in the issue of linear history . . . it's really about place, and time, and family.[49]

In 2004, history circled back on itself when members of the Watso and Sadoques families came back to Deerfield to commemorate the events of 1704 along with other Native peoples, including three music and dance troupes from the communities who had sent raiders to Deerfield three centuries earlier: the Thunderhawk Dancers from Kahnawake, Mikwôbait Dancers from Odanak, and Andicha n'de Wendat from Wendake. Lynn Murphy, Elizabeth Sadoques's granddaughter, commemorated the past, and forged a reconnection, by crafting a reproduction of the basket that her ancestor Sophie Watso made in 1837. The Pocumtuck Valley Memorial Association accepted this new/old basket to display not as an artifact of a vanished race but as an artifact that testifies to the persistence, and the connectedness, of Native families, and Native memories, in a very familiar place.

---

49. Conversation with Lynn Murphy, February 11, 2001.

APPENDIX A

Identities of Native Peoples

	Odanak Abenakis	Pennacooks	Kahnawake Mohawks	Iroquois of the Mountain	Hurons
John Williams's Name	Indians	Eastern Indians	Maquas	Maquas	Maquas
Alternative Names	Canada Indians North Indians Sokokis	Penikokes Penask Openangos	Iroquois of the Sault French Mohawks	Iroquois of the Mountain French Mohawks	Wendats Lorretans French Mohawks
Modern cultural and linguistic categories	Algonquian Mostly Western Abenakis	Algonquian Western Abenakis	Iroquoian Iroquois	Mostly Iroquoian Iroquois, Hurons	Iroquoian Huron
Location	St. Francis River	Vermont New Hampshire Southeastern Maine	Near Montreal	Montreal Island	Quebec
Principal villages	Odanak	Pennacook Pigwacket Cowass	Kahnawake	La Montagne Sault au Récollet Lac des Deux Montagnes	Lorette

Source: Identities of Indians from John Williams's *The Redeemed Captive* (1707). Adapted from Colin G. Calloway, *The Western Abenakis of Vermont, 1600–1800* (Norman: University of Oklahoma Press, 1990), 8–9.

APPENDIX B

List of the 1704 Deerfield Captives

Name	Age	Fate
Mary Alexander	36	Returned to Deerfield
Mary Alexander	2	Killed on the march
Joseph Alexander	23	Escaped on the march
Sarah Allen	12	Naturalized[a] 1710, married 1710, remained in New France
Mary Allis	22	Returned to Deerfield
Thomas Baker	21	Escaped from New France
Simon Beamon	47	Returned to Deerfield
Hannah Beamon	58?	Returned to Deerfield
Hepzibah Belding	54	Killed on the march
John Bridgeman	30	Escaped in the Meadows
Nathaniel Brooks	39	Returned to Deerfield
Mary Brooks	40	Returned to Deerfield
Mary Brooks	7	Naturalized 1710, remained in New France?
William Brooks	6	Fate unknown
Abigail Brown	25	Returned to Deerfield
Benjamin Burt	23	Returned to New England
Sarah Burt	22	Returned to New England
John Burt	21	Returned to Deerfield
Hannah Carter	29	Killed on the march
Hannah Carter	7 months	Killed on the march
Mercy Carter	10	Married, remained in Kahnawake
Samuel Carter Jr.	12	Remained in New France
John Carter	8	Naturalized 1710, married 1718, remained in New France
Ebenezer Carter	6	Returned to New England
Marah Carter	3	Killed on the march
John Catlin	7	Returned to Deerfield
Ruth Catlin	20?	Returned to Deerfield
Elizabeth Corse	32?	Killed on the march
Elizabeth Corse	8	Naturalized 1710, married 1712, remained in New France
Daniel Crofoot	3	Fate unknown
Jacques De Noyon	36	Remained in New France
Abigail De Noyon	17	Naturalized 1710, remained in New France
Sarah Dickinson	24	Returned to New England
Joseph Eastman	20	Returned to New England
Mary Field	28	Returned to New England
Mary Field	6	Married, remained in Kahnawake
John Field	3	Returned to New England
"Marguerite Field"	3	Married 1722, remained in New France

Name	Age	Fate
Mary Frary	64?	Killed on the march
Thomas French	47	Returned to Deerfield
Mary French	40	Killed on the march
Thomas French Jr.	14	Returned to Deerfield
Mary French	17	Returned to New England
Freedom French	11	Naturalized 1710, married 1713, remained in New France
Martha French	8	Naturalized 1710, married 1711, remained in New France
Abigail French	6	Remained in Kahnawake
Mary Harris	9	Married, remained in Kahnawake
Samuel Hastings	20	Naturalized 1710, returned to New England
Elizabeth Hawks	6	Killed on the march
Mehuman Hinsdale	31	Returned to Deerfield
Mary Hinsdale	23	Returned to Deerfield
Jacob Hickson	21	Died of starvation in Vermont
David Hoyt	52	Returned to Deerfield
Abigail Hoyt	44	Returned to Deerfield
Sarah Hoyt	17	Married 1712, returned to Deerfield
Jonathan Hoyt	15	Returned to Deerfield
Ebenezer Hoyt	8	Killed on the march
Abigail Hoyt	2	Killed on the march
Elizabeth Hull	15	Returned to Deerfield
Sarah Hurst	40	Naturalized 1710, married 1710, returned to New England
Sarah Hurst	18	Returned to New England
Elizabeth Hurst	16	Naturalized 1710, married 1712, returned to New England
Thomas Hurst	12	Naturalized 1710, married 1718, remained in New France
Ebenezer Hurst	5	Naturalized 1710, probably returned to New England
Hannah Hurst	8	Naturalized 1710, married 1712, remained with Iroquois of the Mountain
Benjamin Hurst	2	Killed on the march
Martin Kellogg	45	Returned to New England
Martin Kellogg Jr.	17	Escaped from New France
Joseph Kellogg	12	Naturalized 1710, returned to New England
Joanna Kellogg	11	Married, remained at Kahnawake
Rebecca Kellogg	8	Married, returned to New England
John Marsh	24	Returned to New England
Sarah Mattoon	17	Returned to Deerfield
Mehitable Nims	36	Killed on the march
Ebenezer Nims	17	Married 1712, returned to Deerfield
Abigail Nims	3	Married 1715, remained in New France
Joseph Petty	31	Escaped from New France
Sarah Petty	31	Returned to Deerfield
Lydia Pomroy	20	Returned to New England
Joshua Pomroy	28	Returned to New England
Esther Pomroy	27?	Killed on the march
Samuel Price	18?	Naturalized 1710, returned to New England
Jemima Richards	10	Killed on the march

Name	Age	Fate
Josiah Rising	9	Married 1715, remained in New France
Hannah Sheldon	23	Returned to Deerfield
Mary Sheldon	16	Returned to Deerfield
Ebenezer Sheldon	12	Returned to Deerfield
Remembrance Sheldon	11	Returned to New England
John Stebbins	56	Returned to Deerfield
Dorothy Stebbins	42	Returned to Deerfield
John Stebbins Jr.	19	Returned to Deerfield
Samuel Stebbins	15	Returned to New England
Thankful Stebbins	12	Naturalized 1710, married 1711, remained in New France
Ebenezer Stebbins	9	Naturalized 1710, remained in New France
Joseph Stebbins	4	Married 1734?, remained in New France
Elizabeth Stevens	20	Naturalized 1710, married 1706, remained in New France
Ebenezer Warner	27	Returned to Deerfield
Waitstill Warner	24	Killed on the march
Sarah Warner	4	Returned to Deerfield
Waitstill Warner	2	Fate unknown
John Williams	39	Returned to Deerfield
Eunice Williams	39	Killed on the march
Samuel Williams	15	Returned to Deerfield
Esther Williams	13	Returned to New England
Stephen Williams	10	Returned to New England
Eunice Williams	7	Married 1713, remained in Kahnawake
Warham Williams	4	Returned to New England
Frank	?	Killed on the march
John Wilton	39	Returned to New England
Judah Wright	26	Returned to Deerfield

Note: Two additional French men whose names are unknown were taken and returned to New France.

ᵃ Indicates that the individual in question became a naturalized French subject.

Source: This table is largely based on Stephen Williams's list of captives and their fates, which is reproduced in George Sheldon, *A History of Deerfield, Massachusetts*, 2 vols. (Deerfield: privately printed, 1895–1896), 1:308–309. Where this table diverges from Williams's list, it follows Marcel Fournier, *De la Nouvelle-Angleterre à la Nouvelle-France: L'histoire des captifs anglo-américains au Canada entre 1675 et 1760* (Montreal: Société généaologique canadieen-français, 1992). It also omits Philip Mattoon, who is listed among those killed in Deerfield in two sources from the period.

APPENDIX C

Fates of the 1704 Deerfield Captives

	Females			Males			Totals
	Over 21	20–13	Under 13	Over 21	20–13	Under 13	
Numbers taken	23	12	24	24[a]	12	17	112[a]
Died on march	10		6	3		2	21
Escaped				4	1		5
Returned by 1707	12	8	1	14	7	5	47
Returned by 1714	1	2			3	2	8
Returned Later			1		1		2
With French		2	8	3[a]		6	19[a]
With Natives			7				7
Fate Unknown			1			2	3
While in Canada							
Converts		3	11		3	5	22[b]
Naturalized	1	3	7		2	5	18
Married	1	3[c]	14[c]		1[c]	4[c]	23

[a] Includes three French men who "had lived in Deerfield for some time."

[b] This is an underestimate. It includes only those captives for whom a record of baptism exists and those captives at Kahnawake—Abigail French, Mary Field, and Eunice Willams—for whom other evidence of their embrace of Catholicism exists. It excludes three other females known to have been at Kahnawake and four people who were naturalized but for whom no record of baptism exists.

[c] Includes a captive who married another Deerfield captive.

Sources: Emma Lewis Coleman, *New England Captives Carried to Canada between 1677 and 1760 during the French and Indian Wars*, 2 vols. (Portland, Maine: Southworth Press, 1925); Marcel Fournier, *De la Nouvelle-Angleterre à la Nouvelle-France: L'histoire des captifs anglo-américains au Canada entre 1675 et 1760* (Montreal: Société généaologique canadieen-français, 1992).

APPENDIX D

Fates of New England Captives Taken between 1703 and 1712

	Females				Males				Totals
	Over 21	20–13	Under 13	UK	Over 21	20–13	Under 13	UK	
Numbers taken	42	23	56	2	66	28	53	13	286[ab]
Died before 1713	13	16	8		9	1	3		35
Escaped					6	1			7
Returned	28	6	10		44	18	23	2	141
With French		6	23		3[a]	5	14	1	52[a]
With Kahnawake Mohawks			6				4		10
With Iroquois of the Mountain			3				1		4
With Abenakis at Odanak									3[b]
Fate unknown	1		6	2	4	3	8	10	34

Note: A total of 372 captives were taken in New England between 1703 and 1713. The table above includes the 286 on whom we have the most information. It is known that of the remaining 86, 26 were killed almost immediately after they were captured, leaving 60 additional individuals unaccounted for.

[a] Includes 3 Frenchmen who "had lived in Deerfield for some time".

[b] Three individuals, presumably children, sex unknown, who remained at Odanak after the 1714 trip by John Stoddard and John Williams.

Sources: See sources cited in Appendix C, and Samuel Penhallow, *History of the Indian Wars*, ed. Edward Wheelock (1726; 1924; repr. Williamstown, Mass.: Corner House, 1973); Sylvester Judd, *History of Hadley including the Early History of Hatfield, South Hadley, Amherst and Granby, Massachusetts* (Springfield, Mass.: H. R. Huntting, 1905); John Pike, "Journal of the Rev. John Pike," *Proceedings of the Massachusetts Historical Society, 1875–1876* (Boston, 1876), 117–151; George Sheldon, *A History of Deerfield, Massachusetts*, 2 vols. (Deerfield: privately printed, 1895-1896); Stephen Williams, "An Account of Some Ancient Things," in John Williams, *The Redeemed Captive Returning to Zion*, ed. Stephen W. Williams (1853; repr., Cambridge, Mass.: Applewood Books, 1987), 156–161.

SUGGESTED READINGS

Below is a list of readings for those wishing to pursue further the topics raised in this collection. For the sake of convenience, we have listed only works in English, but French-language works can be found in the footnotes and bibliographies of several of the titles listed below. The list is only suggestive, not definitive. It is intended merely as a starting point for those working their way from the Deerfield-related events presented in this collection to the broader historical and cultural context of captivity in northeastern North America in the 1600s and 1700s.

SETTING

Batinski, Michael C. *Pastkeepers in a Small Place: Five Centuries in Deerfield, Massachusetts.* Amherst: University of Massachusetts Press, 2004.

Cronon, William. *Changes in the Land: Indians, Colonists, and the Ecology of New England.* New York: Hill and Wang, 1983.

Main, Gloria L. *Peoples of a Spacious Land: Families and Cultures in Colonial New England.* Cambridge: Harvard University Press, 2001.

Melvoin, Richard. *New England Outpost: War and Society in Colonial Deerfield.* New York: Norton, 1989.

Sheldon, George. *A History of Deerfield, Massachusetts,* 2 vols. Deerfield: privately printed, 1895–1896.

THE RAID

Buerger, Geoffrey E. "Out of Whole Cloth: The Tradition of the St. Regis Bell." Paper presented at the Mid-Atlantic Conference for Canadian Studies, Bucknell University, 1986. Copy in the Pocumtuck Valley Memorial Association Library, Deerfield, Mass.

Demos, John. *The Unredeemed Captive: A Family Story from Early America.* New York: Knopf, 1994).

Haefeli, Evan, and Kevin Sweeney. *Captors and Captives: The 1704 French and Indian Raid on Deerfield.* Amherst: University of Massachusetts Press, 2003.

Parkman, Francis. *A Half Century of Conflict.* Vol. 2 of *France and England in North America.* New York: Library of America, 1983.

Steele, Ian K. *Warpaths: Invasions of North America.* New York: Oxford University Press, 1994.

CAPTIVITY

Axtell, James. *The Invasion Within: The Contest of Cultures in Colonial North America.* New York: Oxford University Press, 1985.

Baker, C. Alice. *True Stories of New England Captives Carries to Canada during the Old French and Indian Wars.* Bowie, Md.: Heritage Books, 1990.

Coleman, Emma Lewis. *New England Captives Carried to Canada between 1677 and 1760 during the French and Indian Wars.* 2 vols. Portland, Me: Southworth Press, 1925.

Colley, Linda. *Captives: The Story of Britain's Pursuit of Empire and How Its Soldiers and Sailors Were Held Captive by the Dream of Global Supremacy, 1600–1850.* New York: Pantheon Books, 2002.

Foster, William Henry. *The Captors' Narrative: Catholic Women and Their Puritan Men on the Early American Frontier.* Ithaca: Cornell University Press, 2003.

Haefeli, Evan, and Kevin Sweeney. *Captors and Captives: The 1704 French and Indian Raid on Deerfield.* Amherst: University of Massachusetts Press, 2003.

Starna, William, and Ralph Watkins. "Northern Iroquois Slavery," *Ethnohistory* 38, no. 1 (winter 1991): 34–57.

Vaughn, Alden, and Daniel K. Richter. "Crossing the Cultural Divide: Indians and New Englanders, 1605–1763," *American Antiquarian Society Proceedings* 90 (1980): 23–99.

Captivity Narratives: Editions of Texts

Calloway, Colin, ed. *North Country Captives: Selected Narratives of Indian Captivity frm Vermont and New Hampshire.* Hanover, N.H.: University Press of New England, 1992.

Rowlandson, Mary. *The Sovereignty and Goodness of God.* Ed. Neal Salisbury. Boston: Bedford Books, 1997.

VanDerBeets, Richard, ed. *Held Captive by Indians: Selected Narratives, 1642–1836.* Knoxville: University of Tennessee Press, 1994.

Vaughn Alden T., and Edward W. Clark, eds. *Puritans among the Indians: Accounts of Captivity and Redemption, 1676–1724.* Cambridge: Harvard University Press, Belknap Press, 2005.

Captivity Narratives: Scholarly Studies

Baum, Rosalie Murphy. "John Williams's Captivity Narrative: A Consideration of Normative Ethnicity." In *A Mixed Race: Ethnicity in Early America*, ed. Frank Shuffleton. New York: Oxford University Press, 1993. 56–76.

Burnham, Michelle. *Captivity and Sentiment: Cultural Exchange in American Literature, 1682–1861.* Hanover, N.H.: University Press of New England, 1997.

Castiglia, Christopher. *Bound and Determined: Captivity, Culture-Crossing, and White Womanhood from Mary Rowlandson to Patty Hearst.* Chicago: University of Chicago Press, 1996.

Derounian-Stodola, Kathryn Zabelle, and James Arthur Levernier. *The Indian Captivity Narrative, 1550–1900.* New York: Twayne, 1993.

Ebersole, Gary. *Captured by Texts: Puritan to Post-Modern Images of Indian Captivity.* Charlottesville: University of Virginia Press, 1995.

Haefeli, Evan, and Kevin Sweeney. "*The Redeemed Captive* as Recurrent Seller: Politics and Publication, 1707–1854," *New England Quarterly* 77 (2004): 341–367.

Namias, June. *White Captives: Gender and Ethnicity on the American Frontier.* Chapel Hill: University of North Carolina Press, 1993.

Strong, Pauline Turner. *Captive Selves, Captivating Others: The Politics and Poetics of Colonial American Captivity Narratives.* Boulder, Colo.: Westview Press, 1999.

NEW FRANCE

Eccles, William J. *The Canadian Frontier.* Albuquerque: University of New Mexico Press, 1974.

Frégault, Guy. *Canadian Society in the French Regime.* Ottawa: Canadian Historical Association, 1981.

Dechêne, Louise. *Habitants and Merchants in Seventeenth-Century Montreal.* Trans. Liana Vardi Montreal and Kingston: McGill-Queen's University Press, 1992.

Greer, Allan. *The People of New France.* Toronto: University of Toronto Press, 1997.

Dale, Miquelon. *New France, 1701–1744: "A Supplement to Europe."* Toronto: McClelland and Stewart, 1987.

Moogk, Peter N. *La Nouvelle France: The Making of French Canada—A Cultural History.* East Lansing: Michigan State University Press, 2000.

MOHAWKS

Buerger, Geoffrey E. "Eleazer Williams: Elitism and Multiple Identity on Two Frontiers." In *Being and Becoming Indian: Biographical Studies of North American Frontiers,* ed. James A. Clifton. Prospect Heights, Ill.: Waveland Press, 1989. 112–136.

Alfred, Gerald R. "Taiaiake." *Heeding the Voices of Our Ancestors: Kahnawake Mohawk Politics and the Rise of Native Nationalism.* Toronto: Oxford University Press, 1995.

Greer, Allan. *Mohawk Saint: Catherine Tekakwitha and the Jesuits.* Oxford: Oxford University Press, 2005.

Richter, Daniel. *The Ordeal of the Longhouse: The Peoples of the Iroquois League in the Era of European Colonization.* Chapel Hill: University of North Carolina Press for the Institute of Early American History and Culture, Williamsburg, Va., 1992.

———. "War and Culture: The Iroquois Experience," *William and Mary Quarterly,* 3rd ser., 40 (1985): 528–559.

Snow, Dean R. *The Iroquois.* Cambridge: Blackwell, 1994.

ABENAKIS

Calloway, Colin. *The Western Abenakis of Vermont: War, Migration, and the Survival of an Indian People, 1600–1800.* Norman: University of Oklahoma Press, 1990.

Foster, Michael K., and William Cowan, eds. *In Search of New England's Native Past: Selected Essays by Gordon M. Day.* Amherst: University of Massachusetts Press, 1998.

Haviland, William A., and Marjory W. Power. *The Original Vermonters: Native Inhabitants Past and Present.* Hanover, N.H.: University Press of New England, 1981.

Morrison, Kenneth M. *The Embattled Northeast: The Elusive Ideal of Alliance in Abenaki-Euramerican Relations.* Berkeley: University of California Press, 1984.

Wiseman, Frederick Matthew. *The Voice of Dawn: An Autohistory of the Abenaki Nation.* Hanover, N.H.: University Press of New England, 2001.

INDEX

Numbers in italics refer to figures and maps.

Le Moyne de Maricourt, Paul, 81, 81n10
Leopold I, Holy Roman Emperor, 124n110
Levasseur de Néré, Jacques, *108, 110*
"The Life and Captivity of Miss Eunice
  Williams" (De Sailleville), 9, 223–33,
  235–43
  adoptive mother, 229, 230, 231, 235–36
  assimilation into Kahnawake, 241–42
  Catholicism, conversion to, 237–39, 242–43
  Deerfield, vulnerability of, 227–28
  Deerfield raid, 228–30
  New France, journey to, 231–33
  scholarship, reliability of, 30n51, 223–26
  Williams, John, portrayal of, 232, 239–41
Livingston, John, 129, 129n119, 168, 168n45,
  169, 228n12
Livingston, Robert, 168n45
Lorette, village of, 7, 19–20, 112, 125, 191
Lorette Hurons, 5
  bravery, 198–99
  female captives, preference for, 10–11
  mixed spirituality, 192
  mourning-war tradition, 201–2
  occupations, 195–96
  piety, 193–95, 196–98, 199–200
  See also Hurons
Lorimer de la Rivière, Guillaume de, 236,
  236n30
Louis XIV, King of France, 5, 122n102, 186n19
Luther, Martin, 154, 183, 183n5
Lyman, Caleb, 164, 164n22

Maisonnat, Pierre, 91, 120, 120n94, 154,
  154n150
Maqua, 96n19
  See also Hurons; Mohawks
Marcoux, Joseph, 216n7
Margane de Batilly, François-Marie, 4, 64n6,
  82, 82n13, 97n27, 210, 210n25
Margane de Lavaltrie, Charles Séraphin, 82,
  82n14
Margane de Lavaltrie, François, 82, 82n15
Marsh, John, 281
Massachusetts legislature, 66
Massasoit (Wampanoag leader), 258n8
Masta, Pierre-Paul Osonkilaine (Abenaki),
  256
Mather, Cotton, 35n2, 85, 85n1, 89
  captivity narratives, political use of, xiv,
  13–14
  The Redeemed Captive Returning to Zion and,
  10, 11, 90
Mather, Eleazer, 89, 228n11
Mather, Esther, 228n11

Mather, Increase, xiv, 10, 13, 35n2, 89, 90
  addendum to Stockwell's captivity
  narrative, 36, 47–48
Mather, Samuel, 35, 35n1, 36
Mattoon, Philip, 173, 173n5, 282
Mattoon, Sarah, 55, 281
Maurault, Joseph Pierre Anselm, 260–61,
  261n18
Maximillian II Emanuel of Bavaria, 122n103,
  124n110
McComber, Jarvis, 250–51, 250n4
Meacham, Esther (Williams), 104–5, 104n54,
  130, *172*, 228n12, 282
Meacham, Joseph, 104n54, *172*, 228n12
Meadows Fight, 6, 65, 65n12, 97
Memorial Hall Museum (Deerfield), *17*
Mercure galant (Paris newspaper), 19
Meriel, Henri-Antoine, 137, 137n131, 139,
  150, 151
Metacom (Wampanoag leader), 257–58,
  258n7
"Metamora, Last of the Wampanoags"
  (Stone), 268, 268n19
middle sort, 73
Mitchel-macquinas, 157, 157n156
Mohawk narratives, xiv, 23–26
  See also "The Life and Captivity of Miss
  Eunice Williams"; Story of the Bell
Mohawks. *See* Kahnawake Mohawks
Mohegans, 164, 164n22
Montbeton de Brouillan, Jacques-François,
  111n76
Montreal (New France), *115*, 116, *117*, 118–22
mourning-war tradition, 5, 201–2, 223,
  248–49
M'Sadoques, Israel (Abenaki), 274–75
Munn, Benjamin, 173, 173n10
Munn, Thankful, 173n10
Munn, Thankful Nims, 173n10
Murphy, Lynn (Abenaki), 277–78

Narrangasett, 2, 28n4
Native narratives, xiv–xv, 21, 23–27
  See also Abenaki narratives; Mohawk
  narratives
New Netherland, 59n29
Nicholson, Francis, 177, 210, 210n29
Nicolas, Louis P., 216, 216n12, 217, 218, 219
Nims, Abigail, 7, 281
Nims, Ebenezer, 281
Nims, Godfrey, 51, 51n13, 173, 173n13
Nims, John, 18, 152n145, 174n17, 177
  escape of, 175, *176*, 178–80
Nims, Mehitable, 102, 102n42, 162n18, 281

Nine Years' War (1689–1697), 3
nobility
 Hertel family, 105, 106
 military rank and, 80
nogging, 64n7
Northampton Courier, 26, 267, 268
Northampton (Massachusetts), 1–2, 26
 Abenakis' visit to (1837), 267–68
Northeast (circa 1660–1725), *xxii*
Northfield (Massachusetts), 8, 40n18, 57n17
Norwottucks, 28n4
Notre Dame, Congregation of, 58n25
Notre-Dame-de-Liesse-de-Rivière-Ouelle de
 Quebec
 votive painting, *22*
Nova Scotia, 86n9
Noyon, Abigail de, 280
Noyon, Jacques de, 3, 107n63, 280

Oblates of Mary Immaculate, 216n6
Obomsawin, Marguerite (Abenaki), 265,
 270–71
Odanak, village of, *110*, 166–69, 256
 See also Fort Saint Francis
Odanak Abenaki, 4, 6, 7, 11, 26
 See also Abenaki
Oka, 7
Old Indian House, *17*, 65n8, 173n12, 259,
 259n12, 276n47
oral traditions
 English captivity narratives, 16
 Native narratives, 21, 23
Oserokohton, Jacques (Mohawk), 250n3
Oso. *See* Sault Saint Louis
Otis, Grizel Warren, 137, 137n133
Owaneco (Mohegan), 42n27

Parkman, Francis, 222, 222n6
Parr, Catherine, 183n4
Parthena (John Williams's slave), 96, 96n21
Partridge, Samuel, 14, 63, 69n10, 71
 Deerfield raid, account of, 63–66
 lament of, 72–77
Paschal, 196n10
Pascommuck, 121n99, 165n26
Pennacooks, 3, 4–5, 7, 159–60, 163–64
Peskeompscut, 2, 40
Petty, Joseph, 8, 18, 152n145, 175, 177, 281
 escape of, 175, *176*, 177–80
Petty, Sarah, 281
Phélypeaux, Jérôme, Comte de Pontchartrain
 et de Maurepas, 19, 79, 80–82, 85
Philip, Duke of Anjou, 122n102
Phillips, Rita, 24

Phips, William, 124n108, 209n19
Plimpton, John, 41n22, 47n40
Pocumtuck, village of, 1–2
 See also Deerfield (Massachusetts)
Pocumtucks, 1–2
Pocumtuck Valley Memorial Association, xiii,
 55, 256, 278
 Sadoques's address to, 255–61, 276–77
Pomroy, Esther, 102, 102n44, 281
Pomroy, Joshua, 281
Pomroy, Lydia, 281
Pontchartrain, Comte de. *See* Phélypeaux,
 Jérôme, Comte de Pontchartrain et de
 Maurepas
Portneuf, René Robinau de, 209, 209n17
Potter's American Monthly, 213
*The Present State of His Majesties Isles and
 Territories in America* (Blome), 37
Price, Samuel, 281
Proceedings (Pocumtuck Valley Memorial
 Association), 256
Protestantism, 182n3
Prouville de Tracy, Alexandre de, 207, 207n5
Puritanism, 138n135, 185n11
 captivity narratives and, xiv–xv, 11–15
Puritans among the Indians (Vaughan and
 Clark), 38
Pynchon, John, 50n3, 63

Quebec, 122–26, *123*, 131, 151–53, 169–70

Ramezay, Claude de, 19, 83, *84*, 122n105, 237
 Deerfield raid, account of, 83, 85, 86
Raudot, Antoine-Denis, 154n149
Raudot, Jacques, 154n149
real presence, doctrine of, 184, 184n10
"The Redeemed Captive Returning to Zion"
 (Williams), xiii, 4, *12*, 89–157
 as anti-Catholic tract, 15, 91, 141–49
 Catholicism, debate against, 125–28,
 129–30, 131–32, 132–35, 150–51, 151–53,
 155–56
 at Chambly, 107, 109
 at Chateau Richer, 126–30, 131–32
 dedication, 92–93
 Deerfield raid, 94–96
 Detroit news, 157
 at Fort Saint Francis, 109, 111–14, 116
 as jeremiad, 14, 90
 at Montreal, 116, 118–22
 New England, return to, 153–56
 New France, journey to 97, 98–107
 as political tool, 90–91
 publication of, xiii, 11, 89–90, 91